The Scandal of Sovereignty

Defending God's Crown in the Drama of Election

By

Ronald H. Gann

Aventine Press

Published by Aventine Press
55 East Emerson St.
Chula Vista CA, 91911
www.aventinepress.com

ISBN: 1-59330-773-X

Acknowledgments

It is with the deepest gratitude that I extend my appreciation to Robin Gann, Don Gann, Peter Anderson, Jeffrey Anderson, R. Bancroft McKittrick, Verlin Balsiger, and David Boutchia for their generous contribution to this work. Without their collective eye, the Doctrines of Grace would have suffered at my own hand.

Reviews

I enthusiastically recommend *The Scandal of Sovereignty* to those interested in the longstanding debate between Calvinism and Arminianism. Very rarely, in the arena of theological writing, will one find a book that successfully combines scholarly sophistication (for the thinking person) with an engaging writing style (for the casual reader). The author has accomplished this unique feat in the following pages. He honestly, accurately, and articulately frames the debate for the reader and demonstrates from Scripture, Church history, and logic the overwhelming evidence for Calvinism. My prayer for all who read this work is that their thinking will be stretched and that God will be glorified. May we all rejoice and celebrate in the scandal of the cross and, indeed, the scandal of God's sovereignty. Two thumbs up!

Donald R. Gann
Chaplain
Exec. Dir. Seasoned Saints Ministries
www.seasonedsaintsministries.org

Two years ago, I began for the first time to study seriously my faith, my religion, and the Bible. In large part this renewed interest was cultivated by Ron Gann on Sunday mornings. He challenged me to look deeper. So it is with this book. Pastor Gann leads the reader into a more complete understanding of the biblical basis for Calvinism. This book is for the layman who wants to know more about the Doctrines of Grace. The author does not pretend to be the final word on this the age-old debate; he merely documents the biblical support for Calvinism, and he does so thoroughly. This is not light reading, but the reader's effort will be rewarded.

Peter Anderson
Educator & Principal (Ret.)
North Carolina, Illinois, & Massachusetts

One of the things that I loved about *The Scandal of Sovereignty* was the use of Scripture to back up the points being made, and the calling upon those who have come before us to give us a peek into the minds of great theologians of recent history. I was amazed at how our God is TOTALLY sovereign and free to do whatever He wills. We truly are His subjects, and if we will understand that, there can be a greater measure of "shalom" in our lives. We can rest in the knowledge that, because He is in control of everything, things are now as they should be. In examining the doctrine of predestination, it seems to have lit a fire in my soul that has directed my prayers for the lost; that we have an ultimate responsibility to spread the seed of the gospel, even water it, but are to leave the results to God. For those whose minds crave this type of material, I highly recommend it in order that God might reveal more of Himself in ways you may not have thought possible before.

Verlin Balsiger III
Worship Pastor
BridgeWay Christian Church

The Scandal of Sovereignty by Pastor Ron Gann is an exacting read and appropriately so. Pastor Gann makes a strong biblical case for the Calvinistic position on the predestined selection of believers. You may not agree with Pastor Gann, but you will be impressed and challenged by his thesis and more clearly understand the significance of this theological position for the believer. After reading this compelling work that is biblically and historically referenced, I doubt the reader will remain neutral about Calvinism or Arminianism.

R. Bancroft McKittrick
Col., USMC (Ret.)
Elder, BridgeWay Christian Church

Foreword

Between 1999 and 2009 I was an adjunct professor for Puget Sound Christian College, just north of Seattle. During those years I met a number of wonderful people, and a few truly great students. Ron Gann was one of those "truly great students." As you read this book, particularly the Epilogue which recounts the genesis of our friendship, you may get the impression that Ron was initially bull-headed as a student, sometimes overbearing, and occasionally unwilling to listen to reason. Similarly, you may also get the feeling that, although I appeared to have an answer for everything as his professor, I too was bull-headed, and I was not always ready to listen to reason either. The truth is, Ron really was not as stubborn as he describes himself, and I was not nearly as quick with the answers as he depicts. His portrayal of me is overly generous (Thank you, Ron!). Nevertheless, Ron is correct in what he has to say in this work, and I am genuinely thankful that we agree on so many things within our "common salvation" (Jude 3).

There are a number of popular errors that Christians should be wary of as we approach the longstanding puzzle of God's sovereignty and its relationship to human responsibility in salvation (the central topic of this work). For example, we dare not approach it with the kind of reductionist thinking that says, *"Well, Calvinists have their set of verses, and Arminians have their pet verses, so what's the point anyway?"*—as if each party holds equal-parts truth and equal-parts error, so that complete truth is indiscernible. Such an attitude is, I realize, very much in vogue today, but it is also strikingly out-of-step with the Bible.

There is a problem with approaching the topic of God's sovereignty with an attitude of reticence. Simply put, the biblical writers themselves did not adopt such an attitude. Although the New Testament writers displayed genuine humility in their writing, they also showed that they were quite comfortable making strong assertions. For example, Jesus asked a group of Pharisees, "Why is my language not clear to you?" He then proceeded to answer his own question by saying, "It is because you belong to your father, the devil" (John 8:43-44). By anyone's assessment, that's pretty strong language! Another example is in Peter's comment to the Sanhedrin: "Salvation is found in no one else, for there is no other name under heaven given to men by which we must be saved" (Acts 4:12). Again, such a claim would be the very embodiment of arrogance, unless, of course, the assertion was true. Similarly, Peter left his readers scratching their heads in bewilderment when he wrote: "They stumble because they disobey the message—*which is also what they were destined for*" (1 Pet 2:8, emphasis added). As is evident, the biblical writers did not shy away from difficult statements or difficult subjects. Neither then should we. And for better or for worse, the subject of God's absolute sovereignty is a difficult one that demands difficult assertions.

There is another topic we should consider before embarking on the journey which Ron has prepared for us. Stated briefly, Jesus makes it clear that there is a direct correlation between the condition of our hearts and our ability or *in*ability to intellectually understand a given subject. An example may help clarify my point. In Mark 6:48-52 we read the account of Jesus walking on the lake.

> About the fourth watch of the night [Jesus] went out to them, walking on the lake. He was about to pass by them, but when [the disciples] saw him walking on the lake, they thought he was a ghost. They cried out, because they all saw him and were terrified. Immediately he spoke to them and said, *'Take courage! It is I. Don't be afraid.'* Then he climbed into the boat with them, and the wind died down. *They were completely amazed, for they had not understood about the loaves; [for] their hearts were hardened* (emphasis added).

When the disciples' saw Jesus walking on the water they obviously didn't know what to think. They had never seen or heard of anything quite like it, so they didn't have any intellectual categories by which to understand what they were experiencing. So, they used what categories they did have to conclude that they saw a ghost—a disembodied spirit. The (understandable) result was "terror." Jesus obviously took in the whole situation and sought to alleviate their fear. In attempt to comfort them, he explained to his disciples that it was really him (not a ghost), and then he attempted to demonstrate it by climbing into the boat. Yet—and this is the interesting point—in spite of his best efforts, their fears were not lessened, but rather magnified. The disciples were, in the words of the text, "completely amazed" (NIV), "utterly astonished" (NASB), "astounded" (ESV); they were "sore amazed in themselves beyond measure, and wondered" (AV). Every translation makes the same point: the disciples were not only still afraid after Jesus' explanation, but they were even *more afraid*! The question is *Why*? Why was their fear greater? The answer is found in verse 52. "For they [the disciples] had not understood about the loaves; [for] *their hearts were hardened.*"

Mark says the disciples' problem was not an insufficient amount of information—inadequate knowledge—rather, their problem was rooted in the hardness of their hearts. To be sure, what the disciples experienced was an emotional and intellectual disconnect, but the true cause of their dysfunction was spiritual; it was the result of their hard hearts. This is why Jesus draws a direct correlation between the condition of the heart and the ability or inability to intellectually understand a given subject or situation. Hardness of heart, even when we are unaware of it, can blind us to the reason—the real reason—behind certain fears, or why we resist certain people or ideas, or why we persist in certain actions. The condition of the heart affects the brain's ability to properly process information. In the case of the disciples, they could not correctly interpret the events directly in front of them because of their preexisting heart-condition.

You may be asking yourself, "But what does all of this have to do with the sovereignty of God and the Doctrines of Grace?" The answer is *everything*! Just as the disciples could not properly understand many of Jesus' warnings, teachings, and miracles due to the hardness of their hearts, so also we will never be able to genuinely see and understand the teaching of God's sovereignty if our hearts remain hard.

Virtually no one comes to the subject of divine sovereignty without bias. And these biases influence us constantly, including our theology, and in ways we don't recognize. My comments are not directed toward any particular group of people. Rather, my goal is to invite everyone—Arminians and Calvinists, as well as the undecided and indifferent—to earnestly pray, "O righteous God, who searches minds and hearts ... Search me, O God, and know my heart; test me and know my anxious thoughts. See if there is any offensive way in me, and lead me in the way everlasting" (Ps. 7:9; 139:23-24).

It is because our hearts can so easily influence and lead us astray that we so desperately need the eye-opening work of the Holy Spirit as we embark upon an important study such as the one you now hold in your hands. Will it be challenging? Of course. Will it be rewarding? Without measure. Will it be exhaustive? Not remotely (although some readers may understandably find it to be exhaust*ing*). Yet my greatest hope is that as you read *The Scandal of Sovereignty* you will find your own heart crying out with the apostle Paul: "Oh, I want to know Christ and the power of his resurrection and the fellowship of sharing in his sufferings, becoming like him in his death, and so, somehow, to attain to the resurrection from the dead" (Php. 3:10-11).

Rev., Dr., Jeffrey Anderson
D.Min., Ph.D., (A.B.D.)
March 30, 2012

Table of Contents

PART 3: Post Review

SECTION 6: Scandalized by Sovereignty

To Dr. Jeffrey Anderson

Your influence on me will last into eternity.

"There is no soul living who holds more firmly to the doctrines of grace than I do, and if any man asks me whether I am ashamed to be called a Calvinist, I answer—I wish to be called nothing but a Christian; but if you ask me, do I hold the doctrinal views which were held by John Calvin, I reply, I do in the main hold them, and rejoice to avow it."

Charles Haddon Spurgeon
1834-1892

The Doctrines of Grace

Within the broad scope of Church history it seems that there is no issue more hotly contested among evangelicals than Calvinism and Arminianism.[1] The debate continues to be as contentious in attitude as it is pedantic in words. Because both theological systems share the same history and many of the same doctrines, they are not far removed from one another. Nonetheless, they are rivals within evangelicalism owing to their profound differences concerning predestination, election, sovereignty, free-will, and the sequence of salvation (cf. Rom. 8:28-30). Although mostly peripheral, the differences between Calvinism and Arminianism are pronounced.

Because of Original Sin, Calvinists believe that fallen man is unable in and of himself to savingly believe the gospel. He is dead, blind, and deaf to the things of God; his heart is deceitful and desperately corrupt. Enslaved to his evil nature, a sinner will not—indeed he *cannot*—choose to do good, spiritually speaking. His will is effectively catatonic. Accordingly, Calvinism teaches that from among the vast sea of fallen humanity God has unconditionally elected certain depraved sinners to make alive in Christ, solely on the basis of His sovereign will. Those elected and predestinated are, over the course of time, irresistibly called to Christ by the Holy Spirit, spiritually regenerated, granted repentance and the gift of faith, and subsequently kept eternally secure by the Godhead. Thus, it is God's decision, not man's, Calvinists say, that determines who will ultimately be saved. From election to glorification, Calvinism regards the process of salvation as *monergistic*; that is, God saves certain men *by Himself*, absent of their cooperation.

Arminianism, on the other hand, takes the polar opposite position. It maintains that divine election is conditioned upon man's self-ability to exercise faith and God's foreknowledge of that applied ability. More specifically, Arminians believe that God elects beforehand for salvation those whom He foresees will respond positively and freely to the gospel in their lifetime. Moreover, the reprobation of natural man, they say, is only *partial*, not total, and does not retard his ability to make godly choices. An unregenerate sinner enjoys unhindered freedom to accept (or reject) the gospel. Assuming he musters the necessary faith within himself, Arminianism teaches that the sinner is then saved, which leads to his regeneration afterward, followed by his election (thus fulfilling what God already foresaw in eternity past). Saved by combined forces (God's grace and man's faith), the Arminian regards the entire salvation process as *synergistic*; that is, man saves himself by partnering with the grace of God.

Sound pedestrian? Hardly. As one young believer said to me recently, "Understanding the Calvinism-Arminianism debate is not unlike a three-year old trying to understand calculus." I couldn't agree more. Because the debate deals with concepts that go far beyond human comprehension, it continues to confound many evangelicals. No doubt the flames of disagreement between Calvinists and Arminians will continue to burn so long as finite sinners attempt to grapple with an infinite God.

Interwoven in this contest of theology are multifaceted doctrines which can cause the average layperson to convulse from confusion. What usually begins as an elementary inquiry into the biblical doctrine of salvation inevitably turns into a referendum on either the moral freedom of man or God's sovereign freedom, to say nothing about which is to blame for sin's introduction into the world.

Mystery, tension, and antimony are all inherent to the debate before us. So the reader must be forewarned: The journey ahead can be as theologically frustrating as it is rewarding, for many of our presuppositions and tightly-held traditions hang in the balance.

As a primer to help better explain the major points contained in this book and the vocabulary used throughout, I borrow from the published work of Dr. Michael Horton the below definitions.[2] The reader is encouraged to familiarize himself with the T.U.L.I.P. acronym, as it is a fitting summation of the Doctrines of Grace (also referred to throughout this book as either Calvinism or Reformed Theology).

- **T = Total Depravity:** Our bondage to sin in Adam is complete in its extensiveness, though not in its intensity. In other words, we're not as bad as we can possibly be, but original sin has thoroughly corrupted every aspect of our existence—including the will.

- **U = Unconditional Election:** Out of His lavish grace, the Father chose out of the fallen race a people from every race to be redeemed through His Son and united to His Son by His Spirit. This determination was made in eternity, apart from anything foreseen in the believer.

- **L = Limited Atonement:** Christ's death is sufficient for the whole world, but secured the redemption of the Elect.

- **I = Irresistible Grace:** The Holy Spirit unites a sinner to Christ through the gospel and faith is the effect, not the cause, of the new birth.

- **P = Perseverance of the Saints:** All of those chosen, redeemed, and regenerated will be given the gift of persevering faith, so that not one will be lost.

For the sake of readability, I have divided this book into three parts. Each part is dedicated to various aspects of the Doctrines of Grace which are central to our cause and therefore necessary for our examination. By no means exhaustive, Part 1 is both historical and philosophical in content, while Part 2 is theological and biblical. The content in Part 3 is mostly autobiographical.

Part 1—titled *Preliminary Review*—lays the groundwork for our journey by providing an overview of Reformed Theology.

It calls to mind the hostility Calvinism imbibes in the Western church, particularly in the United States, and unmasks the false assumptions imposed upon it by critics. I deal briefly with the language barrier that exists between its exponents and opponents while also devoting considerable space to the philosophical complexities inherent to divine sovereignty and human freedom. Because the nature of God's sovereignty is the perennial point of disputation between Calvinists and Arminians, historically speaking, I thought it best to address this scandalous doctrine at the onset.

Part 2—titled *Doctrinal Review*—is dedicated to the merits and demerits of Calvinistic theology and, no doubt, is the meat of this book. Comprised of fifteen chapters, I put the T.U.L.I.P acronym—Total Depravity, Unconditional Election, Limited Atonement, Irresistible Grace, and Perseverance of the Saints—to the acid test of Scripture. I scrutinize each petal within the purview of both biblical and historical theology. More than just offering a defense of Calvinism, Part 2 also mounts a major offensive against the errors of free-will theology.

Lastly, Part 3—titled *Post Review*—focuses primarily on the wonderful impact that Calvinism has had on my life and the footprints it has left in the Church. By way of epilogue, Part 3 contains a brief testimonial that recalls my conversion to Calvinism, followed by a lengthy Appendix that highlights the creeds and confessions of the Church which have illuminated her steps throughout antiquity. If for no other reason, my intent is to demonstrate to the reader that not only did I vigorously oppose Calvinism at one time but it has been the catechetical view of the *Church Militant* for the past fifteen hundred years.

The danger in writing a book that juxtaposes two theologies that are of the same religion (i.e. Calvinism and Arminianism) is self-evident: it can breed religious divorce. Against such familial acrimony, however, we must be on guard. We would therefore do well to remember the words of Rupertus Meldenius (1582-1651), as made famous by Richard Baxter (1615-1691): "In essentials, unity; in non-essentials, liberty; in all things, charity."[3]

But achieving unity for the sake of peace, or peace for the sake of unity, is easier said than done. Some who take the opposing position from the one I put forth in this study will find it difficult to get past the first chapter. Others who agree with my views and interpretation of Scripture might label me a sell-out for being too soft on the opposition. Still others, fearing motion sickness from the voyage ahead, may abandon ship before she ever sets sail. I would simply ask the reader to let the Scriptures be the final determinate (cf. Acts 17:11).

The conversation before us is an enriching one. I encourage the reader to carry on to the last page of this book no matter how herculean the content. It is true that much of the theological vocabulary found herein can be intimidating. The philosophical arguments are, at times, daunting. The religious concepts are, to some extent, abstract and perplexing. And the assertive voice in which this book is written is perhaps stronger than some would prefer. But I promise that the final destination will be well worth the journey. Stitched together by paradox and mystery, Calvinism weaves the power and providence of God into a marvelous tapestry that will leave the reader warm with excitement and prostrate in wonder.

Behold! The scandalous sovereignty of God!

Part 1:
Preliminary Review

Section 1:

The Gathering Storm of Calvinism

"The sovereignty of God is the stumbling block on which thousands fall and perish; and if we go contending with God about His sovereignty it will be our eternal ruin. It is absolutely necessary that we should submit to God as an absolute sovereign, and the sovereign of our souls; as one who may have mercy on whom He will have mercy and harden whom He will."

Jonathan Edwards
1703-1758

Introduction

Debating the Debatable

Al Pacino's words in the 1974 blockbuster *The Godfather Part II* are etched in movie history: "My father taught me many things," said his character Michael Corleone. "He taught me: keep your friends close but your enemies closer." This famous phrase suggests that maintaining a cordial relationship with an opponent and familiarizing oneself with his tactics increases the odds of success and for protecting what is important. This same sentiment, I suppose, can be said about the long-standing debate over sovereignty—particularly between Calvinists and Arminians. The more we know our rival's theology the better prepared we are to defend our own.

Although I am a Calvinist, by no means do I wish to imply that non-Calvinists are my "enemies." To the contrary, evangelicals of all stripes share a mutual love for Jesus Christ and for the deep-seated truths of the Word of God. Calvinists and Arminians are kinsmen in the faith. We stand shoulder-to-shoulder on the fundamentals of the faith and, together, we preach the gospel of Christ to a world that is hell-bent. With that being said, it is an unfortunate reality that we differ so profoundly over certain aspects of soteriology (the study of salvation) and Theology Proper (the study of God). It is therefore imperative that Christians on both sides of the isle first understand the weighty issues that separate them.

It is not uncommon for many evangelicals to dismiss as irrelevant the controversy between Calvinism and Arminianism. Some view this theological divide as nothing more than hairsplitting over semantics while others demote it to an intramural contest between ivory-tower academics. Some refuse to consider the debate altogether because they deplore the disunity it sometimes engenders. Still others are outright intimidated and thrust aside all theological disputes as too complex for their pay grade. They are content with "the elementary teachings about Christ" but discontented, so it seems, at the thought of having to "go on to maturity" in their faith (Heb. 6:1).

Debating Calvinism and Arminianism demands that we "Love the Lord [our] God ... with all [our] mind" (Matt. 22:37; Mark 12:30; Luke 10:27). It requires intellectualism that goes beyond the elementary and into the realm of academia and philosophy. Yet the sad reality is that the average Christian has little desire to do so, much less the aptitude to grapple over biblical truth. The church in America has developed a bubonic fever of sorts; we've become sickened by charismatic esotericism, social tolerance, moral relativism, pseudo-scholarship, and postmodernism to such a degree that we are too weak-minded to confront error, too spiritualistic to crack a book, and apparently too weak-hearted to discuss politically-incorrect doctrines.

The Church has become doctrinally lethargic. If today's headlines tell us anything it's that many liturgical and mainline evangelicals have exchanged historical orthodoxy for a charade of ceremony and ritual; they are adverse to defending issues of morality they once championed, unwilling to take a stand on cumbersome doctrinal matters, and disinclined to defrost the meat of Scripture. And this denominational apostasy is only compounded by a growing number of independent churches that, while socially conservative, are bent on staying theologically innocuous. We live in an era where the seeker-sensitive megachurch shines brightly with its sophomoric preaching while substantive teaching is tucked quietly away in the back pews of our seminaries. The Western church is arguably driving full throttle toward an entertainment-oriented and anti-intellectual destination. Left in its wake is a high-minded approach to Christianity that dares to unpack the theological complexities of Scripture, such as God's sovereignty in salvation.

A quick review of Church history reveals that virtually all of the Patristic Fathers, the Reformers, and the Puritan Divines regarded the relationship between man's free-will and the sovereignty of God as worthy of our attention. They didn't shy away from the puzzle. Leading the charge was Martin Luther who, contrary to popular notion, wrote more on predestination, sovereign election, and Total Depravity than did his predecessor Aurelius Augustine or his successor John Calvin. To Luther's way of thinking, abandoning the pursuit of intellectualism or bowing out of the sovereignty debate with the lame excuse that it is ultimately incomprehensible and pointless was "to think wickedly."[4]

Martin Luther was a German priest and theologian whose spirited revolt against certain practices of the Roman Catholic Church led to the Protestant Reformation. He is regarded as the primary founder of the Protestant branch of Christianity and a pivotal architect of Western culture. Luther himself regarded his work on the subject of human freedom—aptly titled *The Bondage of the Will*—as his most important piece of theological writing; one that lay at the heart of the gospel as he understood it. Luther's deductions regarding man's spiritual inability, as lifted from the initial work of Augustine, scandalized the world of his day and paved the way for Calvin, Jonathan Edwards, George Whitefield, and Charles Spurgeon to fan the flames of Reformational theology.

These grandmasters of Protestantism and the Puritan movement were able and willing apologists who built their legacies on the bedrock of formal debate. Their boldness echoed back to Acts 15 where the apostolic church convened a council in Jerusalem to debate the inclusion of Gentiles in the Church. It was a quorum that was undoubtedly heated and argumentative, and where explosive tempers held court. There the apostolic leaders—Peter, Paul, and James in particular—intellectually *duked it out* with Jewish loyalists over doctrine (cf. v. 6). My point is that if our apostolic forefathers, including our Patristic Fathers, the Protestant Reformers, and the Puritan Divines after them, were not reluctant to debate hot-button issues in the spirit of Acts 15, neither then should we. We must confront temperamental subject matter together—doctrinal and otherwise—and depose error decisively in light of revealed truth. The Calvinism-Arminianism debate welcomes such discourse.

When we return our focus to the historical conflicts in the Church that centered on God's sovereignty and man's free-will—

particularly the dispute between Augustine and Pelagius over Total Depravity; Luther's diatribe against Desiderius Erasmus on free-will; Calvin's debate with Arminius over Unconditional Election; or George Whitefield's rocky relationship with John Wesley concerning the Doctrines of Grace—we learn that the Church has been all the more enriched by the scandal of sovereignty. And the reason is obvious: Arm-wrestling over sovereignty, or any other divine attribute for that matter, is tantamount to theological boot camp. It gives juice to the proverb: "As iron sharpens iron, so one man sharpens another" (Prov. 27:17).

One of the apostle Paul's many prayers for the developing churches of his day was that Christians would grow in wisdom and understanding of God (cf. Eph. 1:17). While there is no shortage of Christians today who seek God's material blessings, it's my opinion that there is indeed a scarcity of those who seek to *know* Him better through theological study. Yet the Bible makes clear that growing in relationship with God—that is, maturing in theological knowledge—is the ultimate means for attaining His blessings, not the least of which is our sanctification. To the point, the apostle Peter wrote, "[God's] divine power has given us everything we need for life and *godliness through our knowledge of him*" (2 Pet. 1:3, emphasis added). To paraphrase the captain of the disciples, our advancement in theology serves as the primer for our advancement in godliness. To avoid theological study, therefore, is to not only short-circuit blessing but to be less godly, or even godless.

Studying theology (such as Calvinism and Arminianism) and debating its merits is centered upon unmasking error and exalting truth. In many respects, it is the lifeblood of the Church. It defines the boundaries of our thoughts concerning God and it takes into consideration all of the scriptural facts on a given subject, such as the attributes of God, the cross-work of Christ, and the ramifications of sin. It attempts to give an account for how God has revealed Himself to His people throughout redemptive history. In short, theological study is an exercise of discovery that uncovers who God truly is. This is why I contend that Bible study is ultimately the most *practical* and *important* part of a

Christian's life, save for confession and prayer. It reveals God to us in ways that merely accepting Scripture on assumption does not. And debating our conclusions with likeminded believers only fine-tunes what we believe.

As Christians, we should *welcome* difficult controversies and not stifle formal disputation. Indeed, it has been by means of the debate forum that the Church has discovered its doctrines, crafted its confessions, and rallied around its articles of faith. We agree to disagree agreeably on non-essential issues but rally to each other's side when the core issues of the gospel are under attack. As Rupertus Meldenius (1582-1651) once said, and Richard Baxter (1615-1691) later made famous: "In essentials, unity; in non-essentials, liberty; in all things, charity."[5] In other words, we are to debate the debatable with grace. And if done appropriately and with humility, such theological conflict should steer us toward Scripture for "wisdom and understanding" rather than repel us.

But, as I've already suggested, the reality in the Church today is that many Christians are in fact "turned off" by doctrinal debate. They see no need to be "approved" by God as "a workman who does not need to be ashamed and who correctly handles the word of truth" (2 Tim. 2:15). They exhibit little desire to "contend for the faith that was once for all entrusted to the saints" (Jude 1:3). They have no regard for the biblical directive: "Always be prepared to give an answer to everyone who asks you to give the reason for the hope that you have" (1 Pet. 3:15). Because today's postmodern culture deems it politically-incorrect to be dogmatic and narrow-minded, especially on matters pertaining to religion, many evangelicals fall victim to apathy. The pursuit of doctrinal integrity is lost on them. Thus, by abandoning yesterday's emphasis on apologetics and "head-knowledge" in exchange for today's quest for acceptance and "heart-knowledge," the Church has become desensitized to error and unmoved by heresy.

One of the disheartening realities of our anti-intellectual culture is the ease with which too many Christians surrender to "faith by proxy." By this turn of phrase I mean that the Church is filled with pew-sitters who sport "substitute beliefs" that are not their own but are inter-reliant upon the beliefs of someone else. This is especially true among our young people, many of whom confess Christ as Savior merely because their parents do. This is proxy faith in its most popular and dangerous form. The average evangelical, I fear, is more prone to rely on the sweat-equity of their spiritual mentor or favorite preacher (who has done the heavy intellectual lifting for them) than they are to investigate biblical truth for themselves.

The debate over Calvinism and Arminianism is not immune to "faith by proxy." It's not uncommon, in fact, for some Christians to confess: "I am a Calvinist because my pastor is" or "Arminianism must be the true teaching of Scripture because that is the position of my local church." Even worse, "I let my pastor decide my theology for me because he went to seminary. I just love Jesus." At best, this "faith by proxy" attitude suggests a lackadaisical faith; at worst, it champions an artificial one. But far from lazy or borrowed, the type of faith that God commends is a *growing* faith, likened to a small mustard seed that blossoms into a formidable oak (Matt. 17:20; Luke 17:6 cf. Heb. 6:12). And Peter reminds us that such blossoming faith takes place only when our hearts are fertilized by study and the increase of "our *knowledge* of [God]" (2 Pet. 1:3, emphasis added).

I've often it heard it said by well-meaning Christians, albeit somewhat snidely, that Christianity isn't about the pursuit of knowledge insomuch as it's about "experiencing" a dynamic relationship with God. Stated differently, "It's not about *what* you know," they say. "Rather it's about *who* you know!" While there is certainly some truth to this motto, it nevertheless misses the mark. The pursuit for knowledge through theological study is something that God highly esteems. Through the prophet Hosea, God laid down His expectations for His people in no uncertain terms: "For I desired ... the knowledge of God more than burnt offerings" (Hos. 6:6, KJV). What is more, God said through the prophet Jeremiah:

> "Let not the wise man boast of his wisdom or the
> strong man boast of his strength or the rich man
> boast of his riches, but let him who boasts boast

about this: *that he understands and knows me*"
(Jer. 9:23-24, emphasis added).

By pursuing a better grasp of what we believe and debating
why we believe it—and not just acquiescing to what our favorite
preachers say or what our traditions dictate—we will develop
a faith of our own and the confidence to defend it. More
importantly, as studious Christians grappling over the scandal
of sovereignty, we will be applauded by our Lord as one who
"correctly handles the word of truth" (2 Tim. 2:15), and who
"contend[s] for the faith" (Jude 1:3), and who is "prepared to
give an answer" (1 Pet. 3:15).

To politely bow out of the debate over Calvinism and
Arminianism does not make one less a Christian. But intellectual
apathy is risky. C.S. Lewis wrote, "[If] you do not listen to
Theology, that will not mean that you have no ideas about God. It
will mean that you have a lot of wrong ones—bad, muddled, out-
of-date ideas."[6] Likewise, Dr. J.I. Packer concluded, "Disregard
the study of God, and you sentence yourself to stumble and
blunder through life blindfolded, as it were, with no sense of
direction and no understanding of what surrounds you. This
way you can waste your life and lose your soul."[7]

Calvinists and Arminians alike must concede that there
is indeed a healthy tension that exists in the Bible between
man's freedom and God's sovereignty. And any Christian who
pretends otherwise is probably posturing. Prayer and humility
are critical in helping us to keep our egos in check and our
relationship with others in perspective. We will never—in this
life, at least—understand God fully; Isaiah reminds us that His
ways are higher than ours (Isa. 55:9). And Paul tells us that His
judgments and character are unsearchable, unfathomable, "and
his paths beyond tracing out!" (Rom. 11:33). Therefore we must
concede that some theological truths belong to the counsel of
God alone and are hidden from our understanding (Deut. 29:29).
However, instead of running away from the enigmatic fight or
writing it off as something untenable, the tension that exists
in the Bible between human freedom and divine sovereignty
invites us to dig deeper into its recesses to mine these truths

for ourselves (cf. Prov. 25:2). It requires meekness, teachable spirits, and personal discipline, not obstinacy or indifference.

We do not debate Calvinism with the mindset of fostering further division in a Church already divided by countless denominations and sects. Rather, we study to unite believers around sacred Scripture and to search out its teachings on the matter. We do not debate Calvinism with a view to win intellectual arguments above and beyond winning lost souls. We study in appreciation for the majesty of the Holy Bible and to win over God's heart by pining for truth and wisdom. Lastly, because "[s]in causes man to constantly seek to insert himself into the work of God in salvation," as one Reformed theologian wrote, we study Calvinism because "every generation has to be reminded of their complete dependence upon Him and of His perfect freedom [to save those whom He wills]."[8]

As a Calvinistic pastor, homegrown theologian, and long-time Christian in the Reformed tradition, I can state categorically that Arminianism is *not* heresy. Rather, I view it as serious error. There is a difference. And even if the preponderance of Church councils and synods were correct in labeling free-will theology heretical (see Appendix), it's important to remember that not all heresy is damnable. Indeed, I'm Calvinistic enough to accept that God has ordained (at least for the time being) that some of my brethren should hold Arminian opinions. We therefore must tread very carefully with our denunciations.

The quarrel between Calvinism and Arminianism is an in-house debate. Thus, let me be emphatically clear: In spite of their many differences over important issues, these two theological systems share more in common than they actually divide over. Both sides exhibit a mutual fever for God's Word and a high view of the nature of God. To that end, the Calvinist and the Arminian stand united over the proclamation and defense of fundamental doctrines; not the least of which are the inspiration of Scripture, the virgin birth of Christ, the deity of Christ, the bodily resurrection of Christ, the exclusivity of Christ in salvation, the Holy Trinity, justification by faith alone, heaven and hell, and the second coming of Christ. Because we champion these doctrines together, and much more, it can be rightly said that both camps fall within the pale of orthodoxy and celebrate the true gospel of Jesus Christ.

The debate between Calvinism and Arminianism will survive for as long as independent-thinking men continue to bend the knee to the primacy of Scripture. It's a lifelong devotional study that consists of elementary men making elementary inquiries into the nature of a highly sophisticated God. And any theological differences that come about as a result—and there certainly will be and historically have been significant differences—so long as they remain within the boundaries of convention, they are to be received with charity. We would also do well to remember that the contest before us is an intramural one, where the family of Christ comes together and elbows and jabs its way through the Doctrines of Grace in search of truth just as quibbling brothers wrestle over bragging rights after a pickup game. And, I might add, it is a contest of theology staged in the arena of Christendom to which all the beloved are invited—indeed are expected—to participate.

Reflection Questions:

1. Whether formal or informal, is there biblical precedent for debating theology and doctrine?

2. Does God expect all Christians to be theologians (cf. 2 Tim. 2:15; Jude 1:3; 1 Pet. 3:15)?

3. By emphasizing an academic approach to theology, does intellectualism contribute to a Christian's sanctification or hinder it (2 Pet. 1:3 cf. Matt. 22:37; Mark 12:30; Luke 10:27)?

4. While defending Protestant doctrine against the attacks of Rome, Martin Luther cautioned, "Peace if possible, truth at all costs." What do you suppose he meant?

Chapter 1

The Controversy of Calvinism in Contemporary Times

The English writer Aldous Huxley (1894-1963) once said, "The charm of history and its enigmatic lesson consist in the fact that, from age to age, nothing changes and yet everything is completely different." Similarly, French novelist Alphonse Karr (1808-1890) made famous the saying, "The more things change, the more they stay the same." Whatever else is meant by these words one thing is certain: They aptly describe the contentious history of the Christian Church. Despite two thousand years of numerical growth, theological reform, and cultural acceptance, the Body of Christ still suffers from the same internal strife it did while in her toddler years.

We're told by Church historians that there are no new heresies in Christianity, only new heretics or recycled echoes of old ones. This adage is as true today as it was during the Patristic era of the Church. Pitted against one another in today's coliseum of evangelicalism are the gladiators of post-modernism versus the celebrated confessions of the Church. It's the title bout of the third millennium. Representing the new vanguard is the seeker-sensitive or Emergent pastor who stands assertively in his corner armed with marketing gimmicks, pop-worship, and relativistic ideology. Standing opposite him, beleaguered and battle-worn, is the suited preacher who fights for absolute truth, tradition, and the supremacy of the Bible. It's a contest not unlike others in Church history. It's the new against the old; the ultramodern versus the supposedly outmoded.

The Lord taught his disciples that the "kingdom of heaven is like the owner of a house who brings out of his storeroom new treasures as well as old" (Matt. 13:52). This is a fitting description that speaks to the importance of tradition. Essentially, the Lord instructed his disciples not to spurn the old customs for the sake of the new. Rather, the new insights they gleaned from Jesus were to be understood in the light of the old truths found in Judaism. But questions still remain: Is it acceptable for the Church to embrace these "new treasures" at the expense of her historical creeds? Can the Church still be innovative and cutting edge without laying waste to her antique theology?

If the answers are to be gauged by the current track record of the evangelical church in America, England, and South Korea, then the answers are not very promising. It seems that with the renaissance of the seeker-sensitive movement in these countries, together with the health-and-wealth prosperity gospel, the charismatic movement, and the Emergent church revolution, the Christian Church has stepped further away from her confessions, creeds, and doctrines than at any other time in history.

Certainly civil unrest over tradition is hardly new in the Church. Whenever modern Christians are confronted by their creedal history a new posse of youthful crusaders tend to crop up who are quick to raise their javelins in protest rather than "quick to listen, slow to speak and slow to become angry" (James 1:19). Reacting on gut instinct rather than biblical exegesis, they pawn Church history off to the bookworm and dismiss its confessions as overstated. In a word, today's generation of young evangelicals *scowl* at classical theology and *hiss* at historical tradition. One contemporary pastor and prolific author went so far as to decry the Church's overemphasis on creeds by stating, "We need a reformation *not of creeds* but deeds." These champions of pop-Christianity seem to care more about social change in America and personal success than they do the biblical doctrines that have historically set men's hearts afire.

Nowhere is this gloomy truth more apparent than in today's megachurch where the revival of Reformed Theology is seen as a clear and present danger. Amid a Western church held hostage by capitalism, the return of John Calvin and Reformational teaching is, for some, an unwelcome homecoming. To preach about an omniscient God who sovereignly determines the end before the beginning (Isa. 46:10); who decides the outcome of cast lots (Prov. 16:33); and who determines the destiny of tribes and nations (Dan. 2:21) as well as the eternal fate of individuals (Eph. 1:4-5), is viewed by some as medieval hyperbole. What is more, the very fact that "a man plans his course, but the Lord determines his steps" (Prov. 16:9; 20:24 cf. Jer. 10:23) is an assault on the libertarian, democratic, and progressive sensibilities of many religious consumers in the West. Such biblical teaching, we are told, is scandalous to the curious seeker; it is neither user-friendly nor theologically-appealing.

In today's market-driven and program-oriented Church it is not uncommon for small-mindedness to prevail when faced with tradition. As recently as only ten years ago, for example, some evangelical leaders took it upon themselves to mount a campaign to rid the Church of her old-fashioned black sheep. Those who refused to surrender to the fad of the day were seen as nonconformists. Woe to the traditionalist who shunned *The Prayer of Jabez* on Sunday morning in exchange for gospel preaching! Woe to the church that snubbed *The Purpose Driven Life* and declined to participate in *The Forty Days of Purpose*! Woe to the pastor who thought it disingenuous to preach prepackaged sermons on *The Da Vinci Code* or *Fireproof Your Marriage*, but opted instead to exposit the Scriptures! Any preacher or church that stood outside the mainstream of pop-Christianity was not safe from the proverbial jabs of seeker-friendly critics.

Sadly, it wasn't long before these same watchdogs turned their sights to theology. And first on their chopping block, so it seemed, was Reformed Theology. Dave Hunt, an evangelical author, speaker, radio commentator, and cofounder of the apologetics ministry *The Berean Call*, took Calvinism to task in his book called *What Love is This? Calvinism's Misrepresentation of God*. Published in 2002, it became his most notorious work in an otherwise illustrious career.

In spite of his commendable work confronting abhorrent forms of Christianity, particularly Roman Catholicism, Hunt's take on Calvinism was grossly misguided and stunned the evangelical community. His book was subsequently panned for its lack of decorum, historical inaccuracies, divisive attitude, character assassinations, and misrepresentation of fact. Owing to the author's unwillingness to acknowledge these scholastic and theological blunders, his publisher, Multnomah Publishing, chose *not* to print a second edition, despite all the media hype surrounding it.

I lament the misconduct of evangelicals like Hunt. They mischaracterize as error certain Reformed doctrines that, once upon a time, were saluted by most as Christian orthodoxy. These self-appointed heresy-hunters are quick to publish poorly researched books with little to no historical veracity and use reckless jargon that alienates a significant segment of the evangelical church. Their multimillion dollar ministries provide a lavish platform to rail against what they perceive as a profanation of the gospel. Like a witch-hunt, they launch internet, radio, and television crusades to smoke out Calvinistic "heretics" while inexplicably ignoring the historical confessions of the Church which, much to their chagrin, actually endorse that which they protest. While no doubt sincere in their beliefs, some of these anti-Calvinist activists zealously cry *"heresy!"* without themselves having "examined the Scriptures every day to see if what Paul said was true" (Acts 17:11).

As it was just a century after the Protestant Reformation so it is today. Plastered on the backside of Calvinism is a proverbial bull's-eye with no shortage of cynics eager to take aim. They want only to strike a death blow to its heart and to rid the Church of it once and for all. The hostility it imbibes from certain "scholars," not to mention the acrimony shown toward those who champion it, echoes back to the Salem witch trials and the Crusades. Calvinism is regarded as a pariah to be expunged rather than a majestic truth to be celebrated.

The attitude among the laity is not much different. Simply mention the word "Calvinism" and watch how quickly a layperson's eyebrows point in confusion. Moreover, visit a local Christian bookstore and take notice of the small section tucked away in the back for Reformed writers in contrast to the vast amount of space reserved up front for self-help books, charismatic interests, and Arminian authors.

Calvinism seldom receives a fair hearing, particularly among the unacquainted. On more than one occasion, when discussing the Doctrines of Grace, I have heard lifelong Christians respond coldly: "I may not have gone to seminary or know the Bible as well as I should, but I refuse to believe that God would arbitrarily predestine people to heaven or hell—no matter what Calvinists say the Bible teaches. That's a different god and therefore a different gospel!" Yet when challenged to cite the chapter and verse which supposedly supports their provocative statements, many laypeople simply cry foul and abandon the discussion. In most cases, they walk away perturbed, having surrendered to their free-will traditions and presuppositions rather than to biblical scholarship.

It has been my pastoral experience that many laypersons pride themselves on being neophyte scholars who, regrettably, invest more stock in their own intuition than they do the science of hermeneutics or the rules of New Testament Greek grammar. They are homegrown and self-appointed "theologians" who think it is commendable to kick against the goads of organized thought—Reformed or otherwise. They are mavericks. Their own interpretation of God (and who they think He *should* be like) sits shotgun to who God has actually revealed Himself to be in Scripture.

Whether studied or clumsy, it seems everyone is a critic with a renegade interpretation. Hardly a Sunday goes by, in fact, where I am not approached by a layperson after service who, under the pretense of pleasantries, takes it upon himself to correct so-called Calvinistic errors in my teaching. But tossed to the wayside in much of their criticism are the ancient confessions of the Church, the blood-spilt creeds of Christendom, and the expository analysis of Scripture that informs what I teach from the pulpit. Historical *scholasticism*,[9] so it seems, doesn't figure much into their critical evaluation of my sermons.

Reformed Theology is no stranger to vitriol, especially within today's hodgepodge of commercial Christianity. For example, the founder of the Calvary Chapel denomination, Chuck Smith, along with his ministry cohort Brian Brodersen, once remarked on the radio: "Calvinism is Christianity *without Jesus* ... [it] is a heartless view of God." Brodersen alleged further: "The heart of Jesus is not existent in Calvinism."[10] Evidently, to these evangelical spokesmen, Calvinism is not only doctrinally cold-blooded but Jesus-less in spirit.

Roger Olson, author of *Arminian Theology: Myths and Realities*, wrote: "[M]y biggest problem with Calvinism ... is that it makes it difficult for me to tell the difference between God and the devil."[11] Similarly, John H. Boyd, in his book *Christianity Versus the God of Calvin*, mockingly wrote: "The god of Calvin is ... a truly needy individual. He needs a backbone. He is so insecure that he dares not give his created order even the slightest ability to choose."[12] Shockingly, both writers believe (and teach) that Calvinism promotes a devilish god who suffers from an inferiority complex.

Beloved preacher Adrian Rogers (1931-2005), the three-time president of the Southern Baptist Convention, once attacked Reformed teachers as "smug, satisfied, the elite, the wine and cheese theologian[s]" who supposedly look down upon non-Calvinists. He went so far as to conclude that the Doctrines of Grace "make infidels out of them."[13] To his way of thinking, or so it seems, those who champion Calvinism stand in line with rank and file unbelievers (infidels).

In his notorious book *Chosen But Free*, evangelical scholar Norman Geisler stated that Calvinism is "theologically inconsistent, philosophically insufficient, and morally repugnant." Likewise, the venerable Bible commentator John Phillips (1927-2010) decried the God of Calvinism as "monstrous ... a tyrant worse than any in the history of the human race."[14] Coming from theologians as respectable as Geisler and Phillips, such criticism is troublesome. But to imply, as Phillips does, that the God of Calvinism is worse than Adolf Hitler or Pol Pot is outright inexcusable.

Even more stupefying, a platoon of Southern Baptist churches recently conducted a series of seminars in Tennessee under the heading *"Reformed Red Flags."* In some of their pamphlets they went so far as to include a checklist of sixteen suspicious "behaviors" to be on the lookout for when "smoking out" Calvinistic pastors from their registry. Incredibly, one behavioral trademark said to be a dead giveaway was the Calvinist's "Tendency toward a highly logical Systematic Theology where all the questions about life and God have answers and fit neatly and nicely in a theological box." Absurd as it is, we are left to believe that the more intellectual, cogent, systematic, and logical one's theology is among Southern Baptists in Tennessee the more likely one is to be ousted as a heretic.

In 2007, only months before his death, Jerry Falwell (1933-2007) preached a chapel message to nearly two thousand prospective students at Liberty University. Under the title *Our Message, Mission and Vision,* Falwell, who "loathe[d] the very system" of Calvinism, described the Reformed doctrine of Limited Atonement as rank "heresy." Moreover, less than a year earlier, in February of 2006, then-president of Liberty Seminary, Ergun Caner, dared to claim that "Calvinists are worse than Muslims." He clarified his remarks later with the quip: "I call [the Reformed movement] a 'Calvinist Jihad.'"[15]

Did Jerry Falwell, Ergun Caner, and the aforementioned evangelical preachers and scholars really deem John Calvin—arguably the greatest biblical expositor in Church history—a heretic who worshipped a "heartless," "devil[ish]," "insecure," "morally repugnant," and "monstrous" God? If we take the remarks of these religious bomb-throwers seriously, as surely as we ought, then it stands to reason that they believe Albert Mohler, John Piper, R.C. Sproul, Alistair Begg, D.A. Carson, John MacArthur, J. Ligon Duncan, Mark Dever, Tom Nettles, Wayne Grudem, Sinclair Ferguson, James White, J.I. Packer, Michael Horton, Mark Driscoll, the late D. James Kennedy, James Montgomery Boice, John Stott, F.F. Bruce, and Francis Schaeffer are also supposedly heretics.

But the list of Bible teachers condemned indirectly by the statements of these anti-Calvinists does not end with the moderns. The roll call of historical Calvinists include Augustine, John Wycliffe, Martin Luther, Ulrich Zwingli, John Knox, George Whitefield, William Carey, John Newton, William Wilberforce, John Bunyan, John Owen, Jonathan Edwards, Matthew Henry, Augustus Toplady, George Mueller, John Gill,

Charles Hodge, B.B. Warfield, and Charles Haddon Spurgeon. It is on the shoulders of each of these men that we gratefully stand today. These heavyweights are only a fraction of the faithful heroes in Church history who, in the eloquent words of Spurgeon, proudly "hold in the main ... the doctrinal views which were held by John Calvin ... and rejoice to avow it."[16] Were all these epic statesmen—past and present—epically heretical because they were Calvinists?

Whether it is the ridiculous allegation that Reformed Theology is "warmed-over Roman Catholicism,"[17] as Dave Hunt suggests, or it is the more serious accusation that Calvinists worship a god of their own making and preach a distorted gospel of their own devising, the attacks on Reformed Theology are hardnosed. (In the interest of full disclosure, Calvinists also have dirty hands in this war of words).

As a Calvinist pastor, it should come as no surprise to learn that such inflammatory rhetoric (on both sides of the debate) undermines my task to preach the gospel. It instills in some of my Arminian congregants—particularly those uninitiated to Reformed Theology—the idea that my theology runs counter to historical norms. Consequently, I am suspected on occasion of interpreting the Bible through too skewed a lens; a scope so narrowly biased and bordering on the brink of heresy that it threatens to repel many "would-be seekers." And such a mischaracterization is unfortunate and does a disservice to Reformed ministers like myself who proudly wave the banner of evangelical Christianity.

That Reformed Theology colors my entire approach to pastoral ministry is an allegation to which I eagerly confess my guilt, and without apology. Once metastasized in the heart of a regenerated person, it most assuredly will broaden his perception of Jehovah, expand his sense of comfort and security, and arrest his innate narcissism and pride. Far from heresy, I see the Doctrines of Grace as the clearest representation of biblical Christianity.

I stand with Charles Spurgeon (1834-1892) who concluded, "Calvinism is the gospel and nothing else."[18] I echo the words of Princeton theologian B.B. Warfield (1851-1921) who said,

"Calvinism ... is the very breath of the nostrils of Christianity; without it Christianity cannot exist."[19] I align unequivocally with Kenneth Talbot, who remarked, "The doctrine of Calvinism ... is the true exposition of Scripture."[20] And I lock arms with John MacArthur who said, "The truths of Calvinism so much permeate the heart of the gospel message ... if you truly affirm the gospel you have already conceded the principle points of Calvinism."[21] In a nutshell, I endorse the foregoing statements made by these gladiators because I am convinced from Scripture that they are correct in their summations. When our presuppositions are deposed at the onset and we allow Scripture to speak for itself, the truth of Calvinism is inescapable. For this reason, I proudly tout the Doctrines of Grace.

Reformed Theology, for all intents and purposes, is a "game changer." It engenders controversy, fear, and rabid obsession by exponents and opponents alike whenever its truths are proclaimed in accord with Scripture. But if not properly handled with humility and scholastic honesty, as Falwell, Caner, and Hunt sadly illustrate, such rabid passion threatens to divide even the most agreeable Christians.

As I have grown in my faith over the years and labored to perfect my gifting as a Bible teacher, I have come to see Calvinism as native to Scripture. Indeed, it seems that wherever I turn in the Holy Writings, whether in my devotional reading or in my expository studies, I see the Doctrines of Grace plastered virtually everywhere. God's discriminate choices, His sovereign election, His initial and sustained grace in the salvation process, His absolute sovereignty over His creatures, and His thwarting of free agency (whereby He hardens those whom He wills) tend to jump from the page in alarming detail.

We witness God's Calvinistic sovereignty in the historical narratives of the Old Testament. We're taught about His Calvinistic sovereignty in the doctrinal teaching of the New Testament epistles. We're overcome by His Calvinistic sovereignty in the poetry of the Psalter, to include Proverbs, Ecclesiastes, and Job. We feel the tremendous weight of Calvinistic sovereignty in the Major and Minor Prophets. And we see Calvinistic sovereignty made manifest in Revelation. To the Reformed student of Scripture, the scandal of sovereignty is unavoidable. B.B. Warfield noted:

> The Calvinist, in a word, is the man who sees God [everywhere]. He has caught sight of the ineffable Vision, and he will not let it fade for a moment from his eyes—God in nature, God in history, God in grace. *Everywhere he sees God in His mighty stepping, everywhere he feels the working of His mighty arm, the throbbing of His mighty heart* ... Calvinism is just Christianity ... Calvinism thus emerges to our sight as nothing more or less than the hope of the world (emphasis added).[22]

Using various word pictures, the Scriptures are a canvas awash with the colors of Reformed Theology. For example, we see Calvinism in the story of the disloyal lame man at the Bethesda pool who alone was healed by our Lord out of a multitude of sick people presumably more deserving and faithful than he (John 5:1-15). It is brought to bear in the election of the Hebrew nation, chosen by the Creator to be His special people in spite of their wickedness (Deut. 9:4-7; 10:14-16). We see it in the account of Adam and Eve who, after their fall into sin and trespass, hid as fugitives among the garden trees to avoid the summons of God (Gen. 3:8-9).

What is more, Calvinism is unmistakable in the accounts of Egypt's Pharaoh Ramses II and King Sihon of Heshbon; two pagan rulers whose hearts were deliberately hardened by God so as to *prevent*[23] their repentance (Exod. 4:21; Deut. 2:30 cf. Rom. 9:17ff). The story of Jonah, whose rebellion against God was exercised voluntarily yet still mysteriously fit within God's sovereign paradigm, is ripe with Calvinism. Whether it is the story of God loving Jacob over Esau absent of foreseen faith (Mal.1:2-3 cf. Rom. 9:11-13) or the sovereign conversion of the apostle Paul on the road to Damascus (Acts 9:1-17), the fingerprints of Reformed Theology are found on virtually every page of sacred Scripture.

So exactly how do these biblical accounts buttress the Doctrines of Grace? To the unacquainted, it is understandable that it may not be readily apparent at first glance. But to those well-informed, Calvinism leaps loudly from the page, for in these narratives we see a God who chooses and overcomes those who otherwise had no inclination whatsoever to choose Him (i.e. Israel and Paul). We witness a God who seeks out those who do not seek Him nor possess any inherit righteousness or foreseen faith that warrants His grace (i.e. the Bethesda lame man and Jacob). We are privy to a God who deliberately hardens the hearts of certain sinners in order to bring His judgment to bear against them (i.e. Pharaoh and King Sihon). We are confronted with a God who trumps man's self-will in favor of His own divine purposes (i.e. Jonah). And lastly, we are eyewitness to a God who seeks out those who intentionally hide from Him and refuse to answer His outward call (i.e. Adam and Eve). All things being equal, the Bible is markedly Calvinistic.

But I must confess that this has not always been my viewpoint. George Whitefield (1714-1770), perhaps the best-known preacher in Britain and America in the eighteenth century, once said, "We are all born Arminians. It is grace that turns us into Calvinists."[24] In a similar vein, Baptist theologian Dr. Roger Nicole (1915-2010) remarked: "We are all by nature Pelagians"[25] (see Chapter 2). And I couldn't agree more with these men.

Indeed, I was not born a Calvinist; I was made one by grace (see Epilogue). And lest the reader think otherwise, I continue to be a student of this complex belief system, for it is not without its paradoxes. So with that confession duly noted, a multitude of questions remain to which we must attempt to give honest answers: What are the Doctrines of Grace that make up Calvinism? Why do I believe and teach them unflinchingly? What is Calvinism's history? What has been the historical position of the Church in its ecclesiastical confessions? How does the Bible support Calvinism? And how, if at all, does the Bible contradict Calvinism? But most importantly, what exactly is so scandalous about God's sovereignty? We will address each of these questions on the journey ahead.

Reflection Questions:

1. Christians can disagree agreeably over secondary doctrine. Is the Calvinism-Arminianism debate peripheral to orthodox Christianity or is it essential and worth dividing over?

2. In your view, does Calvinism and Arminianism fall within the pale of orthodoxy or is one (or both) entirely heretical?

3. As defenders of orthodoxy (cf. Jude 1:3), are Christians called to attack the heretic or the heresy?

Chapter 2

The Birth of Calvinism & Arminianism

Arminianism, which takes its name from its chief architect Jacobus Arminius (1560-1609), is an extreme revision of Reformed Theology that attempts to balance man's responsibility in salvation with the predetermined decrees of God. It is arguably the most widely *assumed* theological system in modern times. Systematized by the followers of Arminius in the early seventeenth century, it continues to be a growing force in evangelicalism. Yet despite its broad acceptance (particularly in America), many theologians view it as antithetical to the gospel and a mere reincarnation of old heresies. Arminianism, they say, limits the sovereignty of God, marginalizes the beauty of predestination, and glorifies the autonomy of man. Poles apart in their fundamental constructs, the debate between Calvinism and Arminianism reached a fever pitch in the medieval Church.

The Reformation brought freedom of religion to the West and with it the freedom of individual interpretation of the Bible. Although opponents to Calvinism saluted the Reformed stance on justification by faith and therefore shared in the Reformation cause, they also feared that the magisterial Reformers had theologically drifted too far from Rome's cooperative (synergistic) take on salvation. Consequently, by 1610 activists for free-will theology hoped to reform the Reformation, as it were. They rallied around the teachings of Arminius, a professor of theology at Leiden in the Netherlands, who taught that human dignity demands freedom of the will. Arminius and his followers took the Dutch Reformed Church to task over Calvinism.

But this familiar fight began long before 1610. Contrary to the opinions of many evangelicals today, Arminianism did not originate with Jacobus Arminius in the seventeenth century just as Calvinism did not originate with John Calvin in the century before it. In point of fact, both theological systems predate the two theologians by nearly a millennium. Calvinism and Arminianism are movements whose origins date back to the fifth century; to a time when free-will theology was known as *semi-Pelagianism* and Reformed Theology was labeled *Augustinianism*. (For this reason, Calvinism and Augustinianism are often used synonymously in theological discourse today in the same way that their counterparts—semi-Pelagianism and Arminianism—are also interchanged).

Credited mostly to John Cassian (360-435), semi-Pelagianism was a system of thought that attempted to reach a theological compromise between the British heretic Pelagius (354-420/440) and the Latin Church father Aurelius Augustine (354-430). The debate between these titanic theologians in the toddler years of the church set the stage for what would eventually become the free-will controversy of the Reformation a thousand years later.

Pelagius denied the inherent effects of Original Sin. He believed that all human beings were born *tabula rasa* (as a "blank sheet of paper"); sinless and pristine, and therefore perfectly capable of obeying and pleasing God. Adam's posterity possessed a natural free-will, he contended, which remained untainted by the scourge of the Fall. Thus, to Pelagius, divine grace was doled out to a person according to merit, and was not necessary in the salvation process. Man was capable of saving himself. This system of thought became known as *Pelagianism*.

In opposition to Pelagius stood the Bishop of Hippo, Aurelius Augustine. He viewed Pelagianism as a direct assault on the gospel. Owing to Adam's sin in the Garden, Augustine argued that Adam's posterity, far from *tabula rasa,* is unable *not to sin.* Due to the corruption of human nature, one's will is *not* free but rather is enslaved to sin, and therefore incapable of pleasing God. According to Augustine, every person is born spiritually dead and justly under the condemnation of God. In order for a person to be delivered from this dreadful state and receive eternal life, God must supernaturally intervene. This became known as *Augustinianism.*

At issue between Pelagius and Augustine was the true heart of the gospel. One side argued vehemently that salvation was entirely the work of man (Pelagius) and the other countered that it was entirely the work of God (Augustine). The early Church was therefore at an impasse and the stakes were huge. Dr. Adolf von Harnack (1851-1930), a German theologian and prominent Church historian, noted:

> There has never, perhaps, been another crisis of equal importance in Church history in which the opponents have expressed the principles at issue so clearly and abstractly ... The Arian dispute [concerning the deity of Christ] before the Council of Nicaea can alone compare with [the Pelagian Controversy].[26]

The town of Carthage on the north coast of Africa served as the hub for an ecumenical council to convene on May 1, 418 to determine once and for all which theological system was in line with Scripture. Not surprisingly, owing to his high view of man and his low view of sin, Pelagius was deposed as a heretic and Augustine's views on human nature, Original Sin, divine grace, and human imperfectability were hailed as true orthodoxy. But notwithstanding the formal ruling of two hundred bishops in favor of Augustinianism, the impact of Pelagianism survived beyond the grave and, only a decade later, bred a successor in John Cassian.

Cassian is largely credited as the theologian responsible for giving the much-maligned Pelagianism a facelift. In the eyes of many, his views successfully reconciled the theological fracture caused by Pelagius and Augustine. Distancing himself from Pelagianism, Cassian sided with Augustine over Original Sin but still agreed with Pelagius that God's grace is *not necessary* for a person to begin the conversion process.

Grasping for "the middle way," as he called it, Cassian denied that man was born sinless (as Pelagius argued) but neither did he believe that man was born spiritually dead in sin (as Augustine argued). Instead, Cassian suggested that, as a consequence of

Adamic sin, man was born spiritually sick. But being spiritually ill, he insisted, did not preclude the sons of Adam from exercising their free-will in salvation. In effect, semi-Pelagianism, as it was soon named, prided itself on being a hybrid theology, placing one foot in the camp of Pelagianism and the other in the camp of Augustinianism. While Pelagianism argued that salvation was entirely the work of man and Augustinianism insisted that it was entirely the work of God, semi-Pelagianism taught that it was the work of *both*. By doing so, Cassian introduced the concept of *synergism*—the belief that salvation is a cooperative process between man's free-will and God's sovereign grace.

This modified version of Pelagianism, although closer to orthodoxy than its predecessor, still landed outside the mainstream of prevailing thought in the Church (which upheld that salvation is *monergistic*—that is, the work of God *alone* absent of man's will, desire, effort, or cooperation). Because it was seen to miscast the grace of God in the drama of redemption from top billing to merely a supporting role alongside free-will, the teaching of Cassian, or semi-Pelagianism, was deemed heretical by the Patristic Fathers at the Third Ecumenical Council of Ephesus in 431 and again at the Second Council of Orange a century later in 529. Both councils were decisive and overwhelming in their verdicts. Nevertheless, in spite of the Church's clear *anathemas* against it, semi-Pelagianism refused to go away quietly. It resurged a thousand years later during the Protestant Reformation with one minor alteration.

Pelagianism Pelagius (354-420/440)	Original Sin did not infect human nature. Therefore the mortal will is still capable of choosing good or evil. In his natural state, man is born innocent and does not require divine grace to be saved.

Semi-Pelagianism John Cassian (360-435)	Original Sin injured mankind but the mortal will is still capable of choosing good or evil. While not denying the necessity of grace, the first step towards salvation is dependent upon man's will. Only afterward will God supervene with His grace.
Augustinianism Aurelius Augustine (354-430)	Owing to Original Sin, man is born spiritually dead. The mortal will is therefore not free but enslaved to sin. As such, every person is born sinful and justly under the condemnation of God. In order for a person to be saved, God's must graciously intervene and spark the dead sinner to life.

As the Roman Catholic Church continued into the Middle Ages and the bishop of Rome became the so-called "visible head of the church," the rank error of semi-Pelagianism resurfaced under a new moniker—*Arminianism*. By the dawn of the Reformation, apostate Rome had all but abandoned its allegiance to Augustinianism and was teaching that man saved himself by cooperating with the grace of God. This controversial way of thinking eventually metastasized and, like a cancer, began to spread throughout Protestantism. Named after its morningstar, Jacobus Arminius, the theology of Arminianism was unleashed on the Church.

Arminianism is not far removed from semi-Pelagianism; in fact, the two are virtually twin systems of thought. While it rightly concedes that God's grace is necessary to *start* the salvation process (the only point on which it disagrees with semi-Pelagianism), Arminianism insists that man is free to cooperate with or rebel against the *inward* call of the Holy Spirit.[27] And whether a person ultimately responds to God's salvific summons is the basis for one's election status. Stated more clearly, Arminianism argues, in contradiction to Calvinism, that election is based on faith. When a sinner believes in Christ of his own free-will it is only then that he *becomes* elect. In counter distinction, the Reformers taught that faith is borne from election. A person is only drawn to believe in Christ *because* he has been elected in eternity past to do so, and thereby granted the necessary faith and ability to repent in time and space (Acts 5:31; 11:18; 18:27; Eph. 1:1-4; 2:8-9 cf. 6:23; Php. 1:29; 2 Tim. 2:25; 2 Pet. 1:1).

What is more, consistent Arminianism argues that salvation cannot be assured. Just as a person is free to accept or reject the gospel so he is also free to renege on his salvific "decision" afterward. Authentically regenerated believers, says the Arminian, have the *freedom* to backslide irreparably, painful though it may be to God. Although some Arminians are quick to argue that their namesake neither affirmed nor denied that salvation could be lost, Arminius did concede the following:

> As regards the opinions of the Fathers, you doubtless know that almost all antiquity is of that judgment, that believers may fall away and perish[28] ... [That it is] possible for believers to fall away from the faith, has always had more supporters in the church of Christ, than that which denies its possibility or its actually occurring.[29]

In short, there are no guarantees in Arminianism. The atonement of Christ offers no promises as to its eternal effectiveness nor does man's so-called freedom guarantee the eternal security of his soul. These are but mere *teases* in Arminianism, contingent upon man's responsibility and perseverance, and the exercise of his reprobate will. And whether or not a sinner willingly complies with God's desire to save him (and perseveres to the end) is the difference between an atonement that is effectual and one that is hypothetical.

Free-will theology starts with God in its theological construct but ends with a disturbing emphasis on the self-will of man. It recognizes that God must initiate the conversion process in the life of a sinner in order to save him yet it maintains that same sinner still has a responsibility to join forces with Him to complete it. In this way, we are told, salvation is a joint-mission between a loving God and a cooperative sinner rather than a monolithic act of divine totalitarianism imposed upon a rebel will. In the final analysis, man's self-will—and whether or not it indulges God's desire to save him—is the key to eternal life in Arminianism.

As is evident already, free-will theology marginalizes sovereign election and nullifies eternal security by removing them both from God's domain and putting them into the realm of fickle men. Complete and final election (ergo salvation) remains only a *possibility* in Arminianism, contingent upon a believer's endurance; not a divine guarantee foreordained in eternity past by God's decretive will.

The Reformers saw this type of thinking as a giant step away from the Reformation and a leap backwards toward Catholicism. Therefore, fearing that semi-Pelagianism was making a comeback in the form of Arminianism, the Church took decisive action. Arminius was summoned by the Dutch Calvinists, particularly Franciscus Gomarus (1563-1641), to give a formal account of his teaching. But Arminius died before he could stand tall before a national synod.

Arminius' followers, not wanting to adopt their leader's name for fear of being stigmatized, called themselves the *Remonstrants* and continued to carry the free-will baton. Because their leader had died before he could satisfy Holland's State General's request for a 14-page paper outlining his views, the Remonstrants replied in Arminius' stead by crafting the *Five Articles of Remonstrance*. These five Arminian articles, or statements of protest, took direct aim at Reformed Theology. They were as follows: (1) Partial Depravity; (2) Conditional Election; (3) Universal (or General) Atonement; (4) Resistible Grace; and (5) Conditional Salvation.

First, the Remonstrants (Arminians) rejected outright Augustine's idea of Total Depravity. That the Reformed church taught that unregenerate man is deformed in *totality*, spiritually dead, and incapable of responding to the gospel was believed by the Remonstrants to be a theological fiction. They countered that, while humanity is indeed tainted by sin, man's depravity is only partial—*not total*—and does not retard his spiritual freedom. Fallen man still possesses libertarian will, they said, whereby he is able to accept or reject the gospel freely.

Second, the Remonstrants balked at the Reformed view that God must unconditionally elect for salvation those too depraved to ever want it. The Calvinist doctrine of Unconditional Election—whereby God sovereignly determines in eternity past who will be saved absent of foreseen faith—was viewed as celestial bigotry. As an alternative, the Arminians suggested that God's election is conditional; that is, He chose those who would be saved on the basis of knowing beforehand who would freely and willingly believe in Christ on their own.

Third, the Remonstrants believed that Christ atoned for the sins of the *whole world*. This contradicted the Reformed doctrine of Limited Atonement which teaches that Christ died only for the Elect. To that end, they argued that not only does God arbitrarily apply the benefits of the atonement to *all mankind* but, fourthly, He also woos *all persons* without prejudice to embrace the gospel. This wooing or enticement can be thwarted, however, since the final outcome depends on man's volitional will. By maintaining that God's grace is resistible, Arminianism stood in stark contrast to the Reformed teaching of Irresistible Grace, which teaches that those elected are incapable of defying the inward call of the Holy Spirit.

And fifth, the Remonstrants upheld that just as a believer *freely* came to God by grace through faith in Christ that same sinner can *freely* renounce his salvation and forfeit his eternal inheritance. They insisted that a Christian's heavenly destiny cannot be assured so long as man's free-will remains inviolate; a point that conflicted with the Reformed doctrine of Perseverance, which teaches that the truly regenerated are preserved eternally at conversion.

Beyond mere semantics, the crux of the debate boiled down to this: The Calvinists saw sinners as totally and wholly depraved (spiritually dead) and therefore unwilling and unable to come to Christ on their own. Arminians, on the other hand, viewed sinners as only partially depraved (spiritually wounded) who possessed enough moral freedom to accept or reject Christ at will. The Calvinists believed that God sovereignly determined in eternity past those who will be saved and those who will perish, irrespective of man's actions (whether good or bad). Conversely, the Arminians argued that salvation was ultimately determined by the sinner's free choice, and that God elects only those whom He foresees will choose to believe in Him. The Calvinists insisted that Jesus Christ died a substitutionary death on behalf of the Elect only, fully paying for their sins on the cross and securing their eternal redemption. The Arminians, however, maintained that Christ died for all men—believer and unbeliever alike— making salvation possible for all but guaranteed to none. The Calvinists argued that an elect sinner cannot resist the inward call of the Holy Spirit but will unfailingly come to faith in Christ. The Arminians argued contrarily, insisting that sinners can, and often do by way of their moral freedom, resist the Holy Spirit's leading. Lastly, the Calvinists argued that once an elect sinner is saved, he is eternally kept by God with no possible chance of losing his salvation. The Arminians countered that a saved sinner can in fact forfeit his salvation by an act of free will.

Arminianism Jacobus Arminius (1560-1609)	1. Partial Depravity 2. Conditional Election 3. Universal Atonement 4. Resistible Grace 5. Conditional Salvation
Calvinism John Calvin (1509-1564)	1. Total Depravity 2. Unconditional Election 3. Limited Atonement 4. Irresistible Grace 5. Perseverance of the Saints

The debate finally came to a head in 1618. Essentially, Jacobus Arminius and John Calvin were put on trial in effigy as their teachings vied against each other at the Synod of Dort, an international body representing Christian churches throughout Europe. Voting representatives from the Reformed churches in eight foreign countries were in attendance. The first meeting was convened on November 13, 1618, and ended 154 days later on May 9, 1619.

After prayerful deliberation, intense biblical scrutiny, and philosophical wrangling, the Synod rendered its verdict. The scholars of Dort accused the Arminian Remonstrants of rejecting the God of Scripture and, in His place, substituting one they had fashioned in their own image and to their own liking—one that was ultimately subservient to the will of man and to random chance. Dr. Rousas J. Rushdoony (1916-2001) noted:

> [The debate was] not between some law intermingled with a doctrine of chance, miscalled freedom, on the one hand, and the doctrines of "rigid Calvinism" on the other, but simply between God and chance. If an iota of chance is allowed into the universe, then God's sovereignty is denied, and God is not God.[30]

The Dort theologians recognized that, although there were minor differences between them, seventeenth-century Arminianism was inextricably linked to fifth-century semi-Pelagianism. Thus, they resoundingly rejected the teachings of Jacobus Arminius and the Remonstrants just as the Third Ecumenical Council of Ephesus in 431 and the Second Council of Orange in 529 had done with John Cassian's semi-Pelagianism. Regarded as anthropocentric (man-centered), scholastically dishonest, and without biblical merit, the Dort Synod unequivocally warned that, if brought to bear on the Christian Church, Arminian theology threatened to once again unleash "out of hell the Pelagian error."[31]

In the final analysis, the Reformed churches throughout Europe concluded that Arminianism, at best, was really semi-Pelagianism dressed up in evening clothes. At worst, they saw it as theological humanism. It was not lost on the Dort theologians that semi-Pelagianism and Arminianism were theological bedfellows, daisy-chained by their shared belief in synergism, and wholly at odds with Augustinianism and Calvinism.

The Reformed church spoke with a united voice against the Remonstrants. It is God's grace that determines who will be saved, apart from foreseen faith (contrary to Arminianism). It is God's grace that instigates salvation, apart from human will (contrary to semi-Pelagianism). And it is God's grace that completes the salvation process, apart from human merit (contrary to Pelagianism). Recognizing the grace of God in all aspects of the salvation process and disqualifying any contribution from man, to include conjuring up the faith to believe or the will to repent, the Reformed church rallied around *sola gratia*—the Latin term for *grace alone*.

Sanctioned at the Council of Carthage (418), ratified at the Third Ecumenical Council in Ephesus (431), confirmed at the Second Council of Orange (529), and canonized at the Synod of Dort (1619), the Doctrines of Grace have been tested, tried, and weighed by the Church's greatest legislative bodies and deemed scriptural (and free-will theology, in all its various incarnations, found wanting).

Not to be discounted either are the great confessions of faith that have also guided and illuminated the Church for centuries, each decisively Calvinistic: The Waldensian Creed (1120); The Belgic Confession (1561); The Heidelberg Catechism (1563); The Thirty-nine Articles of the Church of England (1563); The Westminster Confession of Faith (1646); and The Baptist Confession of 1689. And the list goes on (see Appendix for a more thorough listing). Indeed, in Article II of The Book of Concord (1577), which is the statement of faith for the Lutheran church, the monergistic position on salvation is affirmed:

> ... man of himself, or from his natural powers, cannot contribute anything or help to his conversion, and that conversion is not only in part, but altogether an operation, gift and

present and work of the Holy Ghost alone, who
accomplishes and effects it, by his virtue and
power, through the Word, in the understanding,
[of the] heart and will of man.

Each of the aforementioned councils and confessions
recognized the five points of Calvinism as being the clearest
representation of biblical Christianity. Codified in the acronym
T.U.L.I.P. (which we will explore in more detail in Part 2), these
five points were issued in response to the seventeenth century
revolt waged by the Remonstrants. They are as follows:

1. **T**otal Depravity (in response to Arminianism's Partial
   Depravity)
2. **U**nconditional Election (in response to Arminianism's
   Conditional Election)
3. **L**imited Atonement (in response to Arminianism's
   Universal Atonement)
4. **I**rresistible Grace (in response to Arminianism's
   Resistible Grace)
5. **P**erseverance of the Saints (in response to Arminianism's
   Conditional Salvation)

T.U.L.I.P.—also known as the *Five Points of Calvinism*—
stands in counter distinction to the *Five Articles of
Remonstrance* put forth by the Arminians at Dort. There is no
commonality between them, either small or large, on the points
in which they differ. Each petal in Calvinism cancels out the
corresponding point in Arminianism, and vice versa. They are
distinct theological systems which, try as we might, cannot be
reconciled (see Chapter 14).

Whatever agreement Calvinism and Arminianism may
share outside their five-point systems, and there are many, they
remain bitterly divided over the scandal of sovereignty. And this
division shows no sign of letting up. The mudslinging, in fact,
has only increased. Despite being declared the victor time and
time again by Church councils, synods, and various religious
bodies throughout history, the Doctrines of Grace are under

attack as much today as they were in Augustine's day, and in Luther's and Calvin's as well. The debate, therefore, is hardly settled.

Reflection Questions:

1. Is it relevant or irrelevant that four Church councils— each of which were comprised of the greatest theologians of the day—overwhelmingly deposed free-will theology as false teaching?

2. Why do you suppose free-will theology refuses to go away despite its repeated rejection throughout history by the evangelical Church?

3. What constitutes heresy? Is there a difference between theological heresy and doctrinal error?

Chapter 3

Scaling the Language Barrier

"So tell me Rick," I began casually, soaking in the beauty of the evening sky above us, "since there is a smorgasbord of various Jesus' in the world from which a person can choose these days, I'm curious to know: which Jesus do *you* choose to believe in?"

Rick met my question with a vacant stare. He took a deep drag from his cigarette and, like a dragon, slowly exhaled the smoke through his nostrils. He didn't say a word. His pointed eyebrows suggested that he was confused by my question. Normally an outspoken man who was seldom at a loss for words, Rick's uncharacteristic silence left me curious. Our late-night conversations on the graveyard shift usually proved exhilarating and moved the evening along faster. But on this particular nightfall my coworker was deliberately reserved.

Although I didn't share his vice, it was not out of the ordinary for me to accompany Rick on break to the outdoor smoking lounge where we would engage in our customary debates. He had dogmatic opinions about virtually every hot-button topic and exhibited an obnoxious compulsion to share them whether invited or not. And no topic was off-limits to his acerbic wit, including organized religion. We often chatted the night away unencumbered by subject matters considered taboo in the workplace. And we infrequently, if at all, agreed. Owing to our diverse worldviews, social backgrounds, and the twenty-year age gap that separated us, our ideological wrangling became a staple ingredient that defined our working friendship.

We were strange bedfellows indeed. Rick was a forty-five year-old intellectual and technical wiz; a two-pack-a-day cigarette smoker, a recreational drug user, a weekend alcoholic, and an egotist who prided himself on his lack of religiosity. He was, by a considerable margin, the most functional *underachiever* I had ever met in the corporate world. I, on the other hand, was a Bible-carrying Christian; a teetotaler, fitness enthusiast, and newcomer to technology whose days of lascivious living were mostly behind me at the age of twenty-five. Given our philosophical and social differences, it was not uncommon for us to lock horns on occasion.

By virtue of his position as nightshift supervisor and lead trainer, Rick regarded me as his understudy. But to my way of thinking, he was more my personal ministry than mentor. Notwithstanding my distaste for his personal habits and political affiliations—to say nothing about his caustic personality— our time together was compelling. If for no other reason we tolerated each other because it was there among the moonlit den of ashtrays and the odor of soot that both of us spun into homegrown philosophers, political pundits, and aspiring theologians.

On this particular occasion, however, Rick found it suitable to be strangely quiet. On the debate table before us was the tumultuous subject of Jesus Christ and his divine nature. Typically a lightning rod for invigorating discussion, the concept of a *different* Jesus seemed to puzzle him.

I had confessed to Rick earlier that I was planning to write a research paper on comparative religions. The topic that fueled my particular interest was the growing popularity of neo-orthodoxy in America which, as I saw it, bastardized the biblical portrait of Jesus. I made no secret of my agenda. The specific target in my crosshairs was The Church of Jesus Christ of Latter-day Saints—the Mormons. I explained to Rick that the main thrust behind my paper was to compare and contrast the Mormon Jesus with the Jesus of historical orthodoxy and to unleash on the doctrines of LDS theology the pen of higher criticism.

Rick showed little tolerance for my academic motives. Rather than accept my essay as a defense of historic Christianity, he accused me of writing a hit-piece on the Mormon faith. And to his way of thinking, while it was permissible for an irreligious person like himself to call into question the tenets of organized religion, it was the height of hypocrisy for an evangelical

Christian to do the same. My ambitious project therefore provoked a terse response from him: "Why don't you just let people believe what they want to believe, Ron? Who are you to judge someone's belief system?" I suspected that Rick's latest mission for championing freedom of religion—rather than his usual mantra of freedom *from* all religions—was due in large part to his disdain for my religious conservatism.

It was a fair question, to be sure; the moral of which Rick did not always adhere to himself. But before I could defend myself, he continued with his customary flair: "You seem to have a problem with people who don't believe in your religion the way you do." He then paused, took another drag from his cigarette, and concluded, "People possess the inalienable right to believe what they want to believe. I believe in Jesus in the same way a lot of other people do. *Many of us, however, just don't believe in him the way you do.* And God forbid anyone should believe in Jesus—like the Mormons—and not live up to your imposed standards."

I was flabbergasted. Certainly Rick's high view of sinful man, not to mention his loose living and perilous disregard for structured doctrine, did little to instill in me the confidence that his belief in Christ was genuine. Moreover, his own blasphemous ideas on religion, which he routinely vocalized, betrayed his double standard. At best, his newfound respect for religious tolerance was self-deceiving. At worst, he was a charlatan. With a smidgeon of ridicule in my voice, I responded: "So you're a Christ-follower, huh? You believe in Jesus? I wouldn't have guessed that in a million years given our many conversations on the topic."

His countenance turned sober. "Well, I believe in Jesus," he said. "Whether I follow him or not is a matter of subjective reasoning. In my view, I try to live my life by the set of guidelines that Jesus endorsed—loving my fellow man and being good to others. I guess you guys call it 'The Golden Rule' or something to that effect. In that regard I follow Christ, as we all should. But I'm not a zealot like you."

Rick was a walking contradiction to me. He was both a humanist and a spiritualist rolled into one who believed it acceptable, if not commendable, to redefine Jesus Christ to suit whatever standard he found agreeable with his tastes. In other words, God had created the original man in Eden, and Rick now returned the favor. He created a *personal* Jesus in his own image; a nonjudgmental guru who advocated ethics and morality but did not live beyond the grave. Kicked to the wayside in Rick's train of thought were the Lord's absolutist claims, his miraculous origin and activity, his call to obedience and holiness, his bodily resurrection, and the exclusivity of his work in salvation. When it came to the supernatural Jesus of Scripture, Rick dismissed him as hyperbolic; the stuff of which fairy tales are made. However, when portrayed as a pacifist hippy who taught peace, love, empowerment, enlightenment, and unity, Rick seemed quick to jump on the Jesus-train.

"I am positively amazed, Rick. How can two grown men like you and I accept the legacy of Jesus Christ yet live our lives so radically different? How can two people have such diametrically opposite definitions of what it means to follow Christ?"

Rick was fast to answer. "That's simple to understand. You live by wishful thinking. I live by intellectual reason."

"You think so?" I asked in response. "You believe that my passion for Christ is rooted in nothing more than wishful thinking?"

Never one for tact, Rick tried his best to be polite. "I suppose some people are born to be religious fanatics who fail to understand the danger that their extremism poses. Anything, whether it is religion, personal hobbies, or love, when taken to an extreme, is quite unhealthy. But when these enjoyments are practiced in moderation they can be good for the soul. We arrive at different understandings about Jesus because of our different upbringings, education levels, life experiences, personal needs, and, in your case, a strong desire for him to be as he is on the written page."

I wanted to be sure I understood his point. "So the reason you believe that we both claim allegiance to Jesus Christ but practice our allegiance in contrasting ways is because one of us is moderate and well-balanced in our beliefs whereas the other is fanatical and off kilter? One of us is more sensible whereas the other is merely a gullible optimist?"

"You'll see what I'm getting at one of these days when you get older, Ron," he said rather condescendingly. "You're young. And with age comes wisdom that you can't fully appreciate at this stage in your life. Right now you see Jesus through a narrow prism of dogma. In time you will come to understand that genuine spiritual enlightenment is borne *not* from indoctrination or propaganda but from inside the human heart and with the increase of wisdom. True spirituality has little to do with religion. And my fear, Ron, is that you are letting the best years of your life pass you by because of your infatuation with religion."

Whatever Rick may have meant by his patronizing statement one thing was certain: I wasn't buying it. I continued, "You know what I think, Rick? I think the reason you and I practice our faith so differently has nothing to do with being fanatical or tempered, young or old, much less our education levels. The reason we stand in opposite corners is because we don't believe in the same Jesus. We have two totally different Jesus' in mind. The Jesus I bow to is the one I worship as Creator and Redeemer. The Jesus you believe in is simply a man that you salute as a role model but who wouldn't dare call anyone to account for their sins. The Jesus you believe in is certainly convenient for you, that much is certain."

Rick's eyebrows raised in surprise, almost as though he were conceding my point.

"So tell me Rick," I continued, not letting him get a word in edgewise, "since there is a smorgasbord of Jesus' in the world from which a person can choose these days, I'm curious to know: which Jesus do you choose to believe in? Tell me more about him and on what basis you believe in him."

It was at this point in our conversation that Rick's uncanny silence set in. It was evident that he had no authority for his beliefs other than his own personal whims. He seemed to get lost in his cigarette, gingerly flicking its ashes with his index finger and watching the residue float away in the night breeze. Perhaps he was silent because he feared that I might be entrapping him with a loaded question and he therefore wanted to choose his words circumspectly. Even more, perhaps he wasn't prepared to be challenged on the merits of his confession of faith. Regardless, I wasn't about to let him off the hook. I stood motionless waiting for a response.

He finally mustered a reply. "There's only one Jesus. I just don't believe in him the way you do nor do I choose to put labels on him."

"Really?"

"Yes, really."

I baited him more: "You might be surprised to learn that the New Testament actually warns its readers to beware *another* gospel that is pervasive in the world; one that teaches *another* Jesus and *another* spirit. The apostle Paul stated this twice—once in Galatians and once in his second epistle to the Corinthians. So the question, really, is which one do you embrace, Rick? I only ask because I'm not convinced we're speaking the same language right now. We seem to be working from a different dictionary of terms in our explanations of Christ."

"And this is what you do best when you come under fire," he fought back. "You play word games."

Word games? I certainly expected a loftier answer from him. But I nevertheless considered his words. Did we *really* believe in the same Jesus—the one and only Christ of Scripture—and I simply cluttered the issue with semantics?

I think not.

The Christ of Scripture is certainly the best-known Jesus in the world. For Christians, he is utterly unique—the only Son of God and, as 1 Timothy 2:5 puts it, the "one mediator between God and men." But alongside this Jesus are many others. There is the Jesus whom Muslims have regarded as a prophet and messenger of Allah. There is the Jesus whom the Jews once deemed a blasphemer but now, centuries removed from the crucifixion, is recognized as a reputable rabbi and moral reformer. Then there is the Jesus of the humanists who claim his life was embellished by overeager and superstitious followers looking to start their own movement. Among many contemporary Hindus, Jesus has come to be revered as a self-realized saint who reached the highest level of spiritual illumination. In recent years, Buddhists like the Dalai Lama have recognized in Jesus a figure of great compassion much like the Buddha.

Alas, there is also the Jesus of modern times. For long stretches of Western history, Jesus was pictured as a Greek, a Roman, and a Dutchman. In Nazi Germany in the 1930s he was portrayed as a burly Aryan who ultimately served as the mascot for Nazi anti-Semitism. It is this peculiar European Jesus with his piercing blue eyes and dirty blonde hair that has supplanted the Mediterranean Jesus of the New Testament in the minds of many Westerners today. Moreover, in seeker-sensitive and market-driven churches, Jesus has been melded into a "big buddy" and "life coach" who wants his followers happy, wealthy, and successful; to be the best that they can be and to show loving-kindness to all—to include loving the environment and animals. In the last two hundred years in the West, the idea of Jesus has undergone a radical makeover altogether removed from the Semitic and divine Jesus of Scripture.

"Listen Rick," I said matter-of-factly, "if you think there is only one Jesus to contend with, you're sadly mistaken. In Mormonism, Jesus Christ is the spirit-brother of Lucifer; one god among a pantheon of gods in the universe. To the Jehovah Witness, he's the archangel Michael. In Christian Science, Jesus Christ was a good man who was merely emboldened by a 'Christ-consciousness.' In Scientology, he's a lesser god who attained legendary status. In the Baha'i Faith, he is one of nine manifestations of the divine Being. In Taoism, he's a guiding principle or life-force. To the Hare Krishna, he was an enlightened vegetarian teacher who taught meditation. And in the New Age movement, Jesus Christ is an advanced medium."

I paused, stole a breath, and then continued, "But in historic Christianity, Jesus Christ is the Son of God and God the Son; the second Person of the Triune God; immaculately conceived in the womb of a virgin by the Holy Spirit. He lived a sinless life and made a vicarious atonement for the sins of his Church through his substitionary death on a Roman cross. And, as the very being who spoke and all things leapt into existence, he was raised from the grave in bodily form and ascended to the right hand of the Father where he intercedes on behalf of his beloved. That's the historical and theological Jesus of Scripture."

Not surprisingly, Rick didn't seem impressed with my harangue. Ever since the dawn of modern rationalism, skeptics like Rick have sought to use textual criticism, archeology, human philosophy, and historical reconstructions to distinguish the "Jesus of history"—a wise teacher who said many wonderful things, but fulfilled no prophecies, performed no miracles, and certainly did not rise from the dead in triumph over sin—from the "Jesus of faith." And it was apparent to me that, despite his profession of belief, it was this secular Jesus that my coworker believed in—not the Christ of Christianity.

I continued without missing a beat: "Now Rick, I just listed for you a half dozen or so different Jesus' according to the world system. Which one do you choose to believe in? To say that there is only one Jesus from which to choose and that you believe in the same one I do is disingenuous. Between the two of us we have two totally different definitions of who Christ is and therefore two totally different Jesus'. This is not a matter of theological hair-splitting or 'word games.' Jesus said, *'If you do not believe that I am the one I claim to be, you will indeed die in your sins.'* Rick, this is a matter of life and death—heaven or hell. Who did Jesus claim to be?"

My friend dropped his cigarette into the ashtray beside him, stretched his arms out wide to ease the tension, and released a big yawn. The evening was coming to a close and the morning sunrise fast approaching. To my disappointment, he pulled out his cardkey, swiped it through the electronic reader to unlock the building door, and offered me only a careless smirk in return. "We better get inside and get back to work," he said. "I don't want to partake in your semantic gymnastics anymore. You believe in your Jesus and I'll believe in mine—whoever he might be."

Tricky Terminology

At the heart of my issue with Rick was our colossal discrepancy over language. Although we both invoked the name of Jesus to legitimize our personal ideology, we each poured different meanings into his name. To Rick, Jesus was a countercultural beatnik who balked at organized thought and institutionalized creeds. Rick's contention was that *his* Jesus was a free-loving peace-activist who denounced pious legalism and subverted pop-religion; he certainly did not intend to start his own. "He was all about love, just like the hippies," Rick once said to me. "He dressed like a hippy, with unkept hair and a long beard. He lived a communal lifestyle, lived off the land, and probably hardly ever bathed. He urged others not to judge. He traveled the dusty roads of his world in nothing but a robe and sandals. He was a hippy, not a Rhodes Scholar!"

In the end, Rick's tie-dyed version of Jesus clashed violently with my own. I approached the Savior from a theological perspective borne from Scripture; namely, that he is the divine Son of God and Messiah of Israel whose biography, teaching, conduct, atonement, and resurrection are rooted in biblical history. To put it simply, I interpreted Jesus through the lens of historic orthodoxy. Rick, on the other hand, approached Jesus merely as an abstract *idea* created in his own subjective imagination—no doubt influenced by the 1973 hippy musical *Jesus Christ Superstar*—by which he could conveniently redefine the Jesus of faith out of existence. Thus, it was apparent that between Rick and I stood a massive bulwark known as a *language barrier*.

The term language barrier is a figurative phrase used generally to indicate the difficulties faced when people who have no language in common attempt to communicate with each other. But in theological circles, the term carries with it a stricter classification. It usually means, in the words of Dr. Walter Martin (1928-1989), that certain religionists are faithful to the meanings of universally recognized words whereas others exercise "absolute freedom, having already redesigned these terms in a theological framework of his own making and to his own liking, but almost always at direct variance with the historically accepted meanings of the terms."[32] Stated differently, it is common—and quite popular in neo-orthodox circles—for some theologians to take license with the Bible and to use its terminology in an entirely different sense from that intended by the writers. This, in fact, was the charge that I laid at Rick's footstool. His definition of Jesus did not jive with the Jesus revealed in Scripture.

Rick and I used the same language but our words contained different subtext. What little we did agree on was at best a surface agreement based upon double meanings of words which, in Rick's case, could not stand the test of biblical context, grammar, or exegetical scrutiny. Unless our terms were properly defined at the onset by a mutually recognized authority, a successful dialogue with him was virtually impossible. Owing to our language barrier, mainly around the identity of Christ, we stood at an impasse.

Misappropriated language is a saboteur of theological truth. We must therefore guard the historic meaning of expressions that are crucial to Christianity and not skirt evangelical scholasticism. When etymologies (the study and history of word meanings) are ignored or liberally cast aside in dialogue there remains little at our disposal by which to ascertain divine truth or to recognize error. At the end of the day, either words mean what they say or, as Martin further noted, "we must be prepared to surrender all the accomplishments of grammar and scholastic progress, and return to writing on cave walls with charcoal sticks in the tradition of our alleged stone-age ancestors."[33]

Nowhere is this language barrier more apparent than with the *pseudo*-Christian cults. The Mormons, for example, appear as orthodox in their statement of faith as evangelical Christians who hold advanced degrees in theology. But a closer look at Latter-day doctrine reveals a vocabulary similar to historic Christianity but rooted in an entirely different dictionary.

In their attempt to appear orthodox, Mormon missionaries are well-rehearsed in declaring their allegiance to historic Christian doctrines, not the least of which are the virgin birth of Christ, the deity of Christ, the atonement of Christ, the Holy Trinity, and salvation by grace. To the casual Christian sitting idly unaware, the Mormon doctrinal statement seems orthodox and agreeable. Yet when these distinctives are unpacked at a deeper level and the Mormon missionary cross-examined more extensively, the well-informed Christian quickly realizes that there is a significant difference in language. When ultimately translated, it becomes apparent that the Mormon understanding of these essential doctrines differs fundamentally from the historical and universally-accepted interpretations. The point is that Mormons use the same lexicon, language, vocabulary, clichés, colloquialisms, terminology, and framework that ordinary Christians use but *redefine their meanings.*

The doctrine of the virgin birth, for instance, showcases this language divide like no other. To the Mormon, the virgin birth is man-centric. It stresses that God the Father—who once lived as a man before His deification to godhood—possesses His own corporeal body by which to procreate other gods. It was while in His so-called manifested flesh, says the Mormon, that God condescended to earth to impregnate Mary, who just happened to be a virgin at the time. Acting in the capacity of an exalted man, God the Father is said to have seduced Mary, which resulted in their *physical* tryst. In blunt terms, it was through *literal* sex with a teenager that God the Father *physically* begat Jesus Christ, according to various Mormon prophets.[34]

Any sober-minded Christian clearly recognizes that this abhorrent Mormon view of Christ's conception is sacrilegious and flies directly in the face of orthodoxy. Their idea of the virgin birth is not our idea of the virgin birth. However if a Christian were to ask a Mormon if he believes in Christ's supernatural conception, the Mormon is usually quick to offer his assent. Their response, if left undefined and unchallenged, is beguiling and leads the nominal Christian to wrongly assume that Mormonism is a legitimate contender for orthodoxy. Thus, the language barrier raises its ugly head.

Sadly, the evangelical Church is not immune to this verbal disconnect either. Simply ask the average Christian today to provide a definition of what it means to be "baptized in the Holy Spirit" or "Spirit-filled" and one is bound to receive a plethora of contradictions in return. Some charismatic teachers, for example, believe that the baptism of the Holy Spirit is an occurrence altogether removed from the initial act of salvation. They see it as a supplemental *experience*—a manifestation of God—whereby the Holy Spirit overcomes a Christian and injects into them an extra dose of spiritual power and boldness which equips them to live more victoriously. They typically argue that this spiritual baptism, or being Spirit-filled, is accompanied by such signs as speaking in tongues, words of prophecy or knowledge, and miraculous healings.

On the other hand, along more traditional lines, the baptism of the Holy Spirit is interpreted in a less fantastical manner. It is considered to be a *private* phenomenon that occurs inwardly and only at the moment of salvation. It is a supernatural work of the Spirit that places a believer into everlasting union with Christ (soteric union) and alongside other believers within the Body of Christ (somatic union). Symbolized by the outward act of water baptism, this inward dwelling of God's Spirit washes a person in the redeeming blood of the Savior. It is a permanent event that occurs only once at conversion and is imperceptible to the naked eye.

The final verdict, therefore, is mixed. One segment of the Christian population understands the Spirit's baptism, or being filled with the Holy Spirit, to be an outward manifestation of phenomena whereas another segment interprets it as an invisible and inward rite of incorporation. Well-meaning and intelligent Christians continue to disagree over this issue.

Although I am a pastor who subscribes to the latter definition, occasionally I am asked by charismatics if my church is a "Spirit-filled" church. My default response is to reply, "Oh, of course! The Spirit of God indwells all true believers in our congregation and, in the same way, guides the ministry of the church as a whole." But forced to grapple with the obvious language barrier, I inevitably surrender to the more trendy definition and interpret the question to really mean "Is your church *charismatic*?" This language barrier is loud and pronounced and has muddied the dialogue in virtually every area of Christian theology and ecclesiology.

So what does this spin on language have to do with the merits of Calvinism and free-will theology? In a word, *everything*! Calvinism rightly represents God's action in salvation while Arminianism, for the most part, represents man's response to God's action. It would seem, in that case, that these two sides have little to quibble over. The problem, however, lies in how both sides attempt to reconcile their views by using a different glossary of terms. When a Calvinist speaks of "atonement," for example, he does not have in mind what the Arminian does. Likewise, when the Arminian speaks of "the world" or "regeneration" he means something different than what the Calvinist understands. And these are but a few examples.

It's no secret that the honest Christian, in his longing for unity, would prefer to believe that Christians agree on everything. Certainly no Christian wants to learn that our Lord's *High Priestly Prayer* was offered in vain when he prayed "may [they] be one as we are one" (John 17:11). But this oneness in the Church is hardly the case thus far in our current age, as our numerous denominational distinctives sadly remind us. Notwithstanding our petty disagreements over the color of the sanctuary carpet, our disunity is rooted mostly in maverick opinions that stand unbridled by Scripture. Dubious scriptural interpretations based on presuppositions or political bias, lazy hermeneutical disciplines, a flagrant disregard for the Word of God in favor of our own ideas, or the stubborn unwillingness to acknowledge scholastic fact has historically yielded much discord. What is more, our growing ignorance of the Bible's original languages and our refusal to defer to lexicons when confronted with semantic differences has, in recent times, only compounded our doctrinal disparities.

Relative to the Bible's original languages, Shakespeare's *Hamlet* said it best: "Therein lies the rub." In other words, many free-will pundits face a difficult challenge, or "rub," when forced to defend their Arminian views in light of the Hebrew, Aramaic, and Greek languages of Scripture. And their frequent failure to contend with the original languages is irresponsible at best and disingenuous at worst. In many respects it is within the environs of the Koiné Greek, coupled with English grammatical context, that Reformed Theology discovers its best friend.

Familiarity with biblical Greek often demolishes the language barrier and provides insight that might otherwise go overlooked by the layperson. Furthermore, it opens up for us the Bible of the early Christians. The Greek text of the Hebrew Law, the prophets, and the writings (the Septuagint), was in fact, the Scriptures of the apostles; the foundation upon which the theology, the historical faith, the prophetic understanding, and the eschatological view of the New Testament was built.

It is to the Greek language of Scripture that the Calvinist and the Arminian must turn in order to scale the language barrier that has blockaded fruitful conversation. To a fervent mind in hot pursuit of some important biblical truth, a word used—or a word *not* used—in the Greek text usually opens up new vistas of thought not readily emphasized in modern English translations.

New Testament phrases such as "born again" and "atoning sacrifice" have theological nuances in Calvinism that are missing in Arminianism. Likewise, buzzwords such as "dead," "seek," "world," "all," "many," "predestination," "foreknowledge," "elect," "chosen," and "draw"—just to name a handful—all hold debatable connotations that directly impact the Doctrines of Grace. But because neither side can agree on their meanings within the context they occur in our English Bibles, it is to the original languages we must turn for clarification.

In the chapters that follow, we will not only mount a formidable defense of the Doctrines of Grace—namely, the T.U.L.I.P. acronym—but we will also launch a major offensive against its rival by first scaling the language barrier. We will examine some of these words in their original language, within the context they are used in Scripture, and within the Reformed doctrines they are found. And our reason for doing so is because the debate between Calvinism and Arminianism stops short of its effectiveness if both sides cannot agree on the language involved. We must come to terms with word definitions if we hope to effectively communicate with one another.

Understanding the language of Scripture and comprehending the aforementioned word meanings are indispensable to our task at hand. But as important as it is that we understand each of these buzzwords, they all take a backseat to the most controversial term in Calvinistic theology. If ever there was a term that has engendered blowback from sinners, caused division between Christian brothers, wreaked havoc among scholarly friends, split philosophers and theologians alike, and troubled religious liberals and Jewish rabbis for eons, it is the word "*sovereignty.*"

God's sovereignty, in general terms, is His exercise of rule (as "sovereign" or "king") over His creation. This definition is seemingly benign, no doubt, and hardly worth fighting over. Nevertheless, its application in Scripture tells another story. The tension between God's sovereign control and man's self-will is the perennial puzzle that penetrates to the very core of the dispute between Calvinism and Arminianism; both theological systems rise and fall over the proper understanding of this divine attribute.

The enigma that is God's sovereignty, especially as it relates to His ordaining all things, has been captured historically in the form of two familiar but complex questions. To an Arminian, the Calvinist asks: *If man supposedly has the freedom to do as he wishes, as Arminianism teaches, how then can God truly be in control over all that transpires throughout the course of human history?* Conversely, to that same Calvinist the Arminian rebuts: *If God sovereignly ordains all things that come to pass, as Calvinism maintains, how then is He not responsible for causing the fall of Adam and the proliferation of sin?*

These are tough questions, indeed.

It is the sovereignty of God and its relationship to human freedom that is, without question, the pivot on which Reformed Theology turns. Dismantle Calvinism's high view of divine sovereignty and Reformed Theology will go the way of the dinosaur. In the same way, dismantle Arminianism's moderate view of divine sovereignty and it, too, will quickly fossilize. Therefore, when considering the scandal of God's sovereignty, particularly through the Greek lens of Scripture, it is imperative that we first have a shared understanding of the language involved.

Reflection Questions:

1. Is the Calvinism-Arminianism debate simply a war of semantics between likeminded believers or are there more substantive issues at risk?

2. Are hermeneutics and the study of the original languages of Scripture (Hebrew, Aramaic, and Greek) essential to determining truth, or merely an overstated exercise by intellectuals in pursuit of academic standing?

Chapter 4

How Sovereign is Sovereign?

History tells us that absolute power, when left unchecked, tends to corrupt absolutely. For this reason, most Americans are squeamish when it comes to the concept of sovereignty. Ever since the colonial revolt against King George III in 1776 and our secession from Great Britain, monarchial rule is seen as a threat to democracy. It is literally a *foreign* concept to Americans.

The paranoia of absolute power has infected almost every area of our Constitutional Republic—from the Bill of Rights to the Declaration of Independence—and is the underlying reason behind our separation of powers. If the history of our nation tells us anything it's that Americans will go to great lengths, to include establishing three branches of government, to protect the rights of its citizens against the infringement of a sovereign. We cherish our freedom. It is no wonder, then, that in the "land of the *free*" the doctrines of free-will theology have found a happy home among the body politic. Arminianism and Americanism is a match made in heaven, as it were, for a people and a theology that share the same battle cry: "*Liberty for all!*"

In what seems to be a theological overreaction to imperialism, the American church has effectively imposed its democratic ideals onto the theocratic rule of God. That is to say, the concept of God's sovereignty has, in the minds of many Western evangelicals, become increasingly *Americanized*. With an earnest smile on their face and open Bible in hand, many well-intentioned believers admit unequivocally that God is sovereign; that He is "in total control" over all things and that nothing comes to pass under His watch without His ordination or permission. Yet when God's sovereignty is said to reach as far and wide as determining the eternal destinies of men and is no respecter of free agency, these same believers suddenly choke. They insist that such a caricature of sovereignty is totalitarian—anti-American, really—and is beneath the benevolent and impartial character of God.

When the veneer of American evangelicalism is pulled back, a suspicious Theology Proper emerges. A quick survey finds that there is widespread affirmation among evangelicals which states that God rules sovereignly over His creation. This is fine and well enough. But it's not long before we realize that what many Christians attest to on paper they deny in actual practice. When examined at length over their view of divine sovereignty, it becomes apparent that a vast majority hold to an oxymoronic point of view rather than an orthodox one. God is utterly sovereign, they tell us, but when it comes to how His sovereignty interplays with the affairs of men and their free-will, we are then told that "God is sovereign, *with limitations*." In other words, God rules supremely, but *only insofar as mankind has a vote in the matter*. We are then expected to believe that, relative to salvation, there is no greater atrocity imaginable that God should enforce His will on man or, in the words of Puritan historian Perry Miller (1905-1963), commit "holy rape of the soul."

By demanding that man still holds the freedom to command his own destiny, whether temporal or eternal, these believers unwittingly align themselves with Arminianism. Jacobus Arminius, the godfather of free-will theology, said: "The providence of God is *subordinate to creation*; ... it should not impinge against creation, which it would do, were it to inhibit or hinder the use of [man's] free will" (emphasis added).[35]

Was Arminius right? Are we really expected to believe that the providence and sovereignty of God take a backseat to the whims and will of man? Can God truly be God if, as Arminius contended, some of His attributes are "subordinate" to those of His creatures? Is the Potter really subservient to the will of His clay (Rom. 9:20-21 cf. Isa. 64:8)?

This role reversal (whereby man is said to be the ultimate sovereign in salvation) led the prophet Isaiah to lament: "You turn things upside down, as if the potter were thought to be like the clay" (Isa. 29:16). In other words, in his pursuit of freedom, man's sinful pride turns the decree of salvation on its head by assuming for himself the autonomy and sovereignty that belong to God alone. By way of illustration of the potter and the clay, Isaiah anticipates Jeremiah (cf. 45:9; 64:8 cf. Jer. 18:1-6). Each writer made somewhat different points, yet each argued from this analogy the indisputable sovereignty of God over against the freedom of man.

The words of Isaiah and Jeremiah appear to have fallen on deaf ears today. It is only when the dust settles that we begin to see that God's sovereignty, in the thinking of many American Christians, plays second fiddle to man's free-will. Apparently God is not so sovereign after all. Charles Spurgeon saw glimpses of this type of thinking in his own day. He bemoaned:

> Men will allow God to be everywhere except upon His throne. They will allow Him to be in His workshop to fashion worlds and make stars ... but when God ascends His throne, His creatures then gnash their teeth ... for God on His throne is not the God they love. They love Him anywhere better than they do when He sits with His scepter in His hand and His crown upon His head.[36]

Many mainline Christians might be surprised to learn that American evangelicalism has drifted far afield from the Protestant ground on which she was staked. Too many have been lured astray by liberal politics, junk-food theology, or a steady diet of self-help Arminianism. Today the vast majority deem as biblical a form of religion that has been widely condemned as unbiblical by our greatest theologians in the past—namely, the teaching that man has the freedom to save or condemn himself. They convince themselves that free-will theology is the historical norm of the Church. But only the opposite is true. One needs to look only at the birthplace of the Reformation and its proliferation throughout Europe to see that Calvinism has always been the mainstay of historic Christianity, notwithstanding its fall from grace in America.

To most Europeans today who live under monarchial rule—particularly in the United Kingdom, Belgium, Denmark, Norway, the Netherlands, Sweden, and Spain—the scandal of sovereignty is not so scandalous. In fact, because imperial sovereignty is, by and large, a celebrated form of government, there is an innate susceptibility among European Christians to embrace Calvinism on a wider scale than exists with their American cousins across the pond. Their rich history of monarchial supremacy has deadened their spiritual nerve endings whereby it is relatively painless to bend to the idea that a lone Ruler in the universe ordains all things and actually orchestrates the outcome of events.

Among evangelicals in Europe, where monarchial rule has a stronghold, Calvinism is the majority view by a considerable margin. In democratic America, however, it goes without saying that Arminianism holds the title belt. Dr. John MacArthur observed:

> Whenever I travel around in Europe ... wherever you find evangelicalism, you almost always find Reformed Theology. You come to America and wherever you find evangelicalism, you find Arminianism in one form or another, with few exceptions. And it has to do with [our democratic culture]; we just really have a hard time understanding that somebody is the king, and the king does whatever the king wants to do [regardless of the will of his subjects].[37]

MacArthur does not stand alone in his observation. In his *magnum opus* on Reformed Theology entitled *The Potter's Freedom*, Dr. James White comments:

> I believe one of the reasons modern men struggle with some of the plain biblical truths of old is because so few of us any longer have a "king." Royal power and authority was fundamental when the Scriptures were written, and often

the power of God to properly rule over His own creation is likened to the power of a king to rule over his realm. Since most of us do not bow to a king, we see little reason why we should have to bow to God.[38]

The sovereignty of God has historically been a hotbed for controversy. While both the Calvinist and the Arminian declare their allegiance to this divine attribute, at issue in the debate is its scope and to what extent God exercises it. As already noted, many Christians are quick to concede, "Oh yes, I believe in the sovereignty of God." Yet when pressed on the matter, that is, when forced to determine whether or not God can truly do as He pleases without getting permission from man, we discover that many who in fact confess such a belief in practice deny it. God is not so sovereign, they conclude, that He would predetermine the destinies and choices of His creatures without their say-so. Therefore we must ask the following: Exactly *what* is God's sovereignty and *how* does He exercise it? Depending on how one answers this question is the difference between whether one is a Calvinist or an Arminian.

Most Arminians define God's sovereignty in imperial terms, or in reference to His kingship. He is a Ruler, they insist, who governs majestically but always with respect for the freedom of His subjects. The strength of their argument is derived from their strict reading of the Greek word *dunastes*—translated "sovereign"—which means "a prince, a potentate; a courtier, high officer, [or] royal minister who rules with great authority."[39]

In keeping within the strictest sense of the Greek definition, these evangelicals further contend that God has absolute power and holds the right to rule supremely as the Monarch of the universe. He has the authority to do whatever He wishes; to decree what is lawful and what is not, to impose His will on others while demanding conformance to that will, and to reward obedience and to punish disobedience. But as it relates to His rule over men, at no time does divine sovereignty go beyond the kingly office and enter the murky grounds of *determinism* (the philosophical doctrine that says all events, including human actions and choices, are fully predetermined by God so that freedom of choice is illusory). Arminianism maintains that God's *permissive* will allows for human independence and natural events to run their course even if such events are contrary to His wishes and result in evil or spiritual damnation.

Arminians prefer the concept of imperial sovereignty over against the exhaustive sovereignty taught in Calvinism. Their rationale is simple enough: At no time does the imperial view clash with human freedom. Arminian commentator John Phillips often references in his writings the imperial view this way: "Whatever may or may not be said about the sovereignty of God in human salvation, one thing is sure ... Divine omnipotence never violates the sanctity of the [human] will. God does not ravish; he woos. The Lord will neither heal nor save people against their will[40] ... He will invite, but He will not invade[41] ... Nor does he violate our moral accountability by ravishing anyone's human will."[42]

Greg Laurie, the influential senior pastor of Harvest Christian Fellowship in Riverside, California, apparently agrees with Phillips. "You have a free-will," he once said, addressing the topic of salvation, "and God will not violate it."[43] Norman Geisler, a much revered professor, theologian, and evangelical scholar, concurs: "God will achieve the greatest number in heaven that He possibly can ... that is actually achievable without violating their free choice."[44] Finally, Rob Bell, the controversial pastor, writer, and purveyor of post-modernistic theology, wrote: "Although God is powerful and mighty, when it comes to the human heart God has to play by the same rules we do. God has to respect our freedom to choose to the very end, even at the risk of the relationship itself."[45]

It is a curious oddity that none of these respected Bible teachers can produce a single proof-text from Scripture which supports their assertions. Their theology, presuppositions, and traditions simply *assume* it. To suggest that a sinner's will is inviolate—so hallowed and untouchable that God would dare not violate it—is to aggrandize the autonomy of fallen man at the expense of God's sovereign freedom. Moreover, it contradicts Scripture, as we will soon see.

Reformed Theology rejects any view that eclipses God's ability to act in whatever way that He so chooses—even if it means overturning the self-will of man, violating human cognition, or circumventing man-made plans. God's right to act is not submissive to the will of man. The world order, political achievement, and human destiny fall under the umbrella of God's sovereign will. He controls the happenings of nature, He decrees the rise and fall of governments, and He grants the increase or decrease of man's abilities according to His purpose:

> Praise be to the name of God for ever and ever;
> wisdom and power are his. He changes times
> and seasons; he sets up kings and deposes them.
> He gives wisdom to the wise and knowledge to
> the discerning (Dan. 2:20-21).

The Calvinist maintains that God's sovereignty is exhaustive—not merely imperial. *All things* are under God's rule and control and *nothing happens* without His direction or permission. His purposes are all-inclusive and never thwarted; nothing takes Him by surprise. He is not merely sovereign *de jure* (in principle), but sovereign *de facto* (in practice). In terms of salvation, the sovereignty of God does not bend the knee to the free agency of His creatures or to random chance of fate. God is the ultimate determinate of *all things*—including a person's eternal destiny.

To the Calvinist, the sovereignty of God is not restricted to just governance. The Lord can, and indeed does on occasion, invade the farthest recesses of the human heart whereby He sovereignly overcomes a person's self-will in accord with His divine purposes. Should God so desire, the Calvinist says, He can invoke His right to induce godly motives in an evil person (in order to bring about good) or to veto the evil intentions of a godly person (so as to prevent a willful act of transgression [cf. Gen. 20:6]). While God does not approve of a person's sinful choices, He does sovereignly grant that they be made (cf. Gen. 50:20). And by granting sin to exist in His creation and accomplishing His divine legislation through it, and in spite of it, He is ultimately glorified as the Holy King who sovereignly controls all things under His footstool.

The Calvinistic definition of sovereignty is utterly comprehensive and goes well beyond the Arminian concept of imperialism—and for good reason. The Bible says so. "For from him and through him and to him are all things," wrote the apostle Paul. "For in him we live and move and have our being" (Rom. 11:36; Acts 17:28). In other words, all things find their purpose and sustenance in and from God's sovereignty. Certainly no earthly king can claim such right. More than just a prefect, God decrees "the end from the beginning" (Isa. 46:10 cf. Acts 15:18) and ordains the steps of man "before one of them came to be" (Psa. 139:16). He ordains everything in conformance with His good pleasure, including the evil acts of men and the calamities of nature (Isa. 45:7; Amos 3:6; Lam. 3:38). Nobody in the universe falls outside His reach and nothing occurs without His sovereign consent. The Westminster Confession of Faith summarizes the Reformed view this way:

> God, from all eternity, did, by the most wise and holy counsel of his own will, freely, and unchangeably ordain whatsoever comes to pass: yet so, as thereby neither is God the author of sin, nor is violence offered to the will of the creatures; nor is the liberty or contingency of second causes taken away, but rather established.[46]

Most evangelicals, regardless of their theological bent, agree in large part with The Westminster Confession of Faith. Yet the preponderance of them rejects uniformly the notion that God "freely, and unchangeably ordain[s] whatsoever comes to pass." They take issue with this sentence on the grounds that inherent to its meaning is the idea that every event, including human cognition, behavior, decision, and action, is causally determined by God. This is unthinkable to them. To suggest such a thing, says the Arminian, is to recklessly dismiss human autonomy and to miscast God as a despot. One evangelical expressed his Arminian outrage this way:

> The belief that God controls everything that
> happens to us is one of the devil's biggest
> inroads into our lives. If this belief is true, then
> our actions are irrelevant, and our efforts are
> meaningless. What will be will be.[47]

One cannot help but notice the sacrilege in this statement. To this particular Arminian's way of thinking, God apparently *doesn't* control all things—that is, He's not *that* sovereign— and to suggest otherwise, we're told, is to dance with the devil. But to the Calvinist, such an assertion is absurd; a theological profanity at its ugliest.

Arminians maintain that Calvinists mischaracterize the rule of God by their liberal manipulation of the Koiné Greek. They insist that the Reformed definition of sovereignty is *extra-biblical*, even perverse, and goes beyond the meaning of *dunastes* (i.e. "a prince, a potentate; a courtier, high officer, [or] royal minister").

Furthermore, when logically fleshed out, Arminians insist that Calvinism's view of exhaustive sovereignty (as opposed to their concept of imperial sovereignty) puts God on the hook for the fall of Adam and for the perpetual existence of evil. *If God ordains everything,* so begins their customary argument, *He would then be responsible for not only all loving-kindness, good will, sunshine, rainfall, and bountiful crop in due season but also for all hatred, ill-intentions, murder, rape, tyranny, and natural disasters that come to pass.*

To suggest, as Calvinists do, that God's sovereignty is so extensive that He ordains the sinful actions of men, including the temper tantrums of Mother Nature, is *anathema* in the canon of Arminianism. God forbid that He should be *that* sovereign! To save God from the bad press found in Calvinistic thought, therefore, most anti-Calvinists have no alternative but to conclude that mankind, by necessity, must possess some provisional sovereignty. In this way the blame for all things unseemly can be conveniently shifted from God to man and, thus, eliminate a theological headache. Andrew Womack, a prominent evangelical and unabashed Arminian, unwittingly highlights the elements of humanism hiding in this type of logic:

> [Reformed] teaching on the sovereignty of God puts Jesus in the driver's seat ... On the surface that looks good ... However, the Scriptures paint a picture of *each of us being behind the wheel of our own lives. We are the one doing the driving. ... He doesn't do the driving for us* ... God is sovereign in the sense that He is paramount and supreme. There is no one higher in authority or power, *but that does not mean He exercises His power by controlling everything in our lives* (emphasis added).[48]

Again, we see another Arminian example where God apparently *doesn't* control all things—that is, He's not *that* sovereign. Notice Womack's repeated emphasis on man's self-will as the driving force "behind the wheel of our *own* lives." He adds, "*We* are the one doing the driving [not God]!" If we read between the lines in Womack's statement we can clearly see the glorification of man and his abilities. This is *humanism* in its rankest form. In place of God's sovereignty and providence, Womack says, is the reprobate will of man who is supposedly in charge.

The Reformed Christian is quick to object to Womack's man-centered thinking. His version of God's sovereignty, which is emblematic of the Arminian view, is not only limiting but is dangerously close to blasphemy. It displaces the right of sovereign determination, which is reserved for God alone, and puts it into the hands of spiritually dead sinners. Man becomes the chief determinate of his life and God becomes a bystander. Loosely paraphrasing Womack's remarks, God is demoted in rank to a hitchhiker in the vehicle of salvation whereas man sits sovereignly in the pilot's seat, mapping the course and steering as he wills.

While such a view appeals to carnal man, Womack's conclusion outright ignores Jeremiah 10:23: "I know, O Lord, that a man's life is not his own; it is not for man to direct his steps" (Jer. 10:23). He also ignores Proverb 16:9: "a man plans his course, but the Lord determines his steps" (cf. 20:24). Unlike Womack, it seems Jeremiah and Solomon understood clearly who is actually in the driver's seat.

So how does the Calvinist respond to this rival teaching? At the footstool of the Arminian we lay the charge of *theological humanism*—the erroneous belief that holds the human condition in much higher regard than does the Bible. Not only this, but the Arminian is also charged with a second count of a deficient Theology Proper (the study of God's attributes). God is to some extent an impotent Sovereign in Arminianism, or a puppet rather than the Puppet-Master, whose rule is hogtied by the free-will of His subjects. Countless Arminian writers, to include A.W. Tozer (1897-1963) concede as much. In fact, Tozer's words are especially alarming on this point and should give us pause:

> God is good toward all who accept His goodness. And for those who reject His goodness, *there's nothing that even the Almighty God can do if He's going to allow man his free will* ... He's given us a little provisional sovereignty out of His absolute sovereignty. He has said, "I'll allow you, within a little framework, to be your own boss and to choose to go to heaven or to hell" ... *There is nothing God can do* ... (emphasis added).[49]

Again, here we see another Arminian example where God apparently *doesn't* control all things—that is, He's not *that* sovereign. But is Tozer correct in his analysis? Are we really supposed to believe that an omnipotent God *can do nothing* in opposition to man's free-will in salvation? Moreover, is God still wholly sovereign if in actual fact He affords His creatures some "provisional sovereignty" by which they become the ultimate determinate of their own salvation? Stated differently: Can God still be all-controlling if, as Tozer suggests, He grants provisional control to His creatures?

By very definition, to relinquish *some* control (to the will of man) does violence to the phrase *all*-controlling. Similar to a woman who is pregnant (and not just *mostly* pregnant), one is either utterly sovereign or not sovereign at all. God either has full control or none whatsoever.

The impotency that these Arminian teachers ascribe to God would be forgettable were it not so heretical. As noted earlier, to Geisler's way of thinking, God will save those whom "He possibly can" (as if anything is *impossible* with God). To Bell, "God has to play by the same rules we do" (as if God *has* to do anything He doesn't want to, much less bend to our rulebook). To Phillips and Laurie, "The Lord will neither heal nor save people against their will ... God will not violate it" (as if man's freedom is more sacred than God's freedom to act). To Womack, God "doesn't do the driving for us" (as if God's sovereignty takes a backseat to anyone or anything). And to Tozer, "there's nothing that even the Almighty God can do if He's going to allow man his free will ... there's nothing God can do" (as if God is incapable of saving those whom He wills). The statements of these men, the majority of whom I respect and read often, leave me breathless with disappointment.

To be fair, Calvinism does not go unscathed either. The Calvinist is often accused by the Arminian of being an unsympathetic fatalist who has embellished God's sovereignty to such an unhealthy degree that inevitably God stands guilty as the primary source behind sin. Their logic is reasonable: *If Calvinism is correct and God ordains all things, He must therefore ordain that which He hates, such as sin and evil.* (We will address this argument in the following chapter).

Calvinism is also indicted on the grounds that it allegedly takes excessive liberties with the biblical texts. This is no small accusation. We are charged with inventing word definitions or alien tenses and applying them to select phrases in the Bible which suit our theology. Arminians bite hard on this point. "Nowhere in Scripture," says Dave Hunt, "do we find Calvinism's extreme [exhaustive] sovereignty, which allows man no freedom of choice."[50] To that end, Brian Broderson, the associate pastor to Chuck Smith at Calvary Chapel Costa Mesa, California and the featured speaker on the Bible teaching program *Back to Basics*, frames the allegation accordingly:

> [Calvinists] have redefined certain words, and so they've taken the word sovereignty and they've given it sort of their own definition— their definition meaning that nothing can possibly happen that isn't caused by God. And if God doesn't cause everything to happen then somehow He's not sovereign. That's a wrong definition of sovereignty ... So I think the whole debate between free-will and sovereignty is a misguided debate in the first place because it's based on the wrong definition of sovereignty.[51]

In one respect, I agree with Broderson' diagnosis but, at the same time, I vehemently object to his conclusions. To be sure, the language barrier is evident between Calvinists and Arminians, as we've already noted. And Broderson is correct when he states that a "wrong definition of sovereignty" has muddied the debate. But he is incorrect on whom he places the blame. He offers no biblical evidence to refute Calvinistic sovereignty; only philosophical suppositions in support of his Arminian agenda. In the end, he stops short of letting the totality of Scripture inform his remarks.

For example, as an evangelical, I trust that Broderson believes that God is above all things and before all things; that God knows all things past, present, and future; that God can do all things and accomplish all things in accord with His holy nature; and that God is in control of all things and rules over all things. Yet, strangely, Broderson can't bring himself to believe that God also *ordains* all things. Somehow this facet of divine sovereignty escapes his theology. To him, God is sovereign over rulers; He is sovereign over nations; He is sovereign over nature; and He is sovereign over suffering. But it's unimaginable to Broderson that God is also sovereign over salvation. Such thinking is not only inconsistent but grossly short-changes the power of God (cf. Gen. 4:25; Exod. 4:11; 21:12; Deut. 10:22;

32:39; Prov. 16:33; Psa. 33:9-11; 115:3; 135:3; 139:16; Isa. 45:5-7; 46:10; Eccl. 7:13-17; Lam. 3:37-38; 1 Sam. 2:6-7; Amos 3:6-7; Ruth 4:13; Matt. 5:45; 6:26, 30; 10:29-30; Acts 15:18; 17:26-28; Rom. 11:36; Eph. 1:4; James 4:13-15).

It therefore bears repeating one more time: To the Arminian, God is a heavenly governor whose sovereignty is more or less a kingly kind of sovereignty. Like an earthly monarch, God is a legislator who governs righteously and enforces His edicts as the Chief Law Enforcement Officer of His realm. Yet to the Calvinist, the sovereignty of God transcends mere magisterial governance. While it includes all of the kingly elements germane to imperial sovereignty, Calvinistic (exhaustive) sovereignty also involves the foreordination of all events and actions that transpire in His kingdom and in the lives of His subjects. *All things* are under God's rule and control and *nothing happens* without His direction or permission, including the godly acts of saints and angels or the wicked doings of sinners and demons. In short, God ordains *everything*.

Despite their differences there is in fact common ground between the two sides. Both Calvinism and Arminianism agree that God is the King of the universe and is answerable only to His triune Self. Both theological systems assent to the omnipotence and immutability of the Lord in the affairs of His creation. And both sides take solace in the fact that God commands His realm with supreme authority and benevolence. The main difference, however, is that the consistent Arminian cannot accept that God will act in violation of man's free agency, at least in terms of his salvation, whereas the Calvinist argues that such salvific free-will is illusory; a man-centered falsehood imposed upon Scripture.

But when we turn our searchlight onto Calvinism we do not behold in our line of sight a pristine theology either, at least not at first glance. Arminians have credible arguments against Calvinism that must be dealt with, such as: How does Reformed Theology reconcile a God who ordains all things yet is not responsible for sin? How do Calvinists justify going beyond the Greek definition for the word *sovereignty* in their application of the word? And if Calvinism is true, how then can men be held responsible for their sins if indeed God has foreordained that they should commit them?

These are complex questions, indeed; some of which have already been addressed or, at the very least, touched upon. We have hinted that Calvinism's view of exhaustive sovereignty does indeed go beyond the parameters of the Greek word from which it is translated—*dunastes*—but for good reason: The Bible clearly demands it (Gen. 4:25; Exod. 4:11; 21:12; Deut. 10:22; 32:39; Prov. 16:33; Psa. 33:9-11; 115:3; 135:3; 139:16; Isa. 45:5-7; Eccl. 7:13-17; Lam. 3:37-38; Isa. 46:10; 1 Sam. 2:6-7; Amos 3:6-7; Ruth 4:13; Matt. 5:45; 6:26, 30; 10:29-30; Acts 15:18; 17:26-28; Rom. 11:36; Eph. 1:4; James 4:13-15).

In fact, it's worth noting that many scriptorians are on record arguing that the English words *sovereign* and *sovereignty* do an injustice to what the Bible is really trying to convey concerning God's all-encompassing, all-controlling, and comprehensive power. The word *sovereign* (or *sovereignty*), they say, is inadequate in description *not* because it goes beyond its Greek equivalent (*dunastes*) but rather because it doesn't go *further* beyond, or express *more*, just how powerful and controlling God truly is! In other words, human language—whether it is Hebrew, Aramaic, Greek, or English—fails to capture sufficiently God's omnipotence, control, strength, and providence in a manner that is in keeping with full disclosure. The full weight of this divine attribute escapes our vocabulary. Nevertheless, Bible translators from all eras recognize that, because we are bound by the limitations of language, *sovereign* is the closest English word available to us that even remotely touches upon this inestimable characteristic of God.

As we continue on in our examination of God's exhaustive sovereignty and attempt to address some of the Arminian objections—particularly *How can God ordain all things and yet not be responsible for sin?*—one principle must remain paramount in our assessment: Scripture is our final authority, not human reason. This isn't to say that the scriptural thesis on divine sovereignty is necessarily against reason. It's merely an affirmation that human reason is not always up to snuff in fully grasping the unsearchable ways and means of God. Therefore, in order to jump the final hurdle before us, we will consider God's sovereignty in light of the vast revelation of Scripture. It is to its authority that we must submit our rationalizations—not vice versa.

Reflection Questions:

1. Is God limited by man's moral freedom in what He can or cannot do? Is man limited by God's divine sovereignty in what he can or cannot do?

2. How does your view of God's sovereignty differ from the Calvinist or the Arminian view?

3. How can God be sovereign over human history if He does not control and oversee the actions and decisions of human beings who affect it?

Chapter 5

Sovereignty & Sin: The Blame Game

Virtually all Christians give at least verbal assent to the doctrine of God's sovereignty. There are simply too many biblical passages which teach this truth to say nothing about the hundreds of scriptural references where the title "O Sovereign Lord" is ascribed to God. The Lord is utterly self-ruling and in control of all things (Prov. 16:4 cf. Rom. 8:28). Everything that exists in the universe exists because God sovereignly ordained it, decreed it, and called it into existence according to His good pleasure. The psalmist declared, "Our God is in heaven, he does whatever pleases him" (Psa. 115:3), and "The Lord does whatever pleases him in the heavens and on the earth, in the seas and all their depths" (Psa. 135:6). The Psalter summarizes God's exhaustive power as follows:

> For he spoke, and [all creation] came to be; he commanded, and it stood firm. The Lord foils the plans of the nations; he thwarts the purposes of the peoples. But the plans of the Lord stand forever, the purposes of his heart through all generations (Psa. 33:9-11).

As is evident in the first chapter in Genesis, the God to whom we are introduced is showcased as a patently sovereign God. He speaks, and so it becomes. He decrees, "Let there be light," and there is light (Gen. 1:3). His Word does not fail to have its intended effect (cf. Isa. 55:11). He commands according to His will, and all creation leaps to do His bidding. His infinite power invades time and space in order that the finite world, His chosen people in particular, might revel in who He is.

Far more than simply a King who exercises His supremacy, God's controlling power is boundless, immeasurable, and inestimable. Nothing exists outside the ordination of God's will, including sheer happenstance (Prov. 16:33), human plans or mishaps (Exod. 21:12; James 4:13-15), the birth of children (Gen. 4:25; Deut. 10:22; Ruth 4:13), health, prosperity, and calamity (Exod. 4:11; Deut. 32:39; 1 Sam. 2:6-7; Eccl. 7:13-17; Isa. 45:5-7; Lam. 3:37-38; Amos 3:6-7), and the workings of nature (Matt. 5:45; 6:26, 30; 10:29-30). That God is in complete control over history and the affairs of mankind is the collective voice of both the Old and New Testament:

> Yours, O Lord, is the greatness and the power and the glory and the majesty and the splendor, for everything in heaven and earth is yours. Yours, O Lord, is the kingdom; you are exalted as head over all. Wealth and honor come from you; you are the ruler of all things. In your hands are strength and power to exalt and give strength to all (1 Chron. 29:11-12 cf. Acts 17:26; Psa. 33:10; 47:1-4).

The various scriptures that support God's exhaustive sovereignty, particularly His foreordination of events, are legion. To the point, we learn that the Lamb was slain *before* the foundation of the world (Rev. 13:8), the Elect were chosen *before* the foundation of the world (Eph. 1:4), and all of God's works were in fact known *before* the foundation of the world (Acts 15:17-18).[52] Another way of expressing this truth is to say that long before creation ever came to be, God's plan of redemption was already sovereignly accomplished in principle under His foreordained decree.

God not only orchestrates but fulfills all of redemptive history by way of predetermined ordination. "Long ago I ordained it," He declared. "In days of old I planned it; now I have brought it to pass" (2 Kings 19:25 cf. Isa. 37:26). He said elsewhere, "Surely, as I have planned, so it will be, and as I have purposed, so it will stand" (Isa. 14:24). In Isaiah 46:11 we read, "What I have said, that will I bring about; what I have planned that will I do." Moreover, Jeremiah wrote, "The Lord your God decreed this ... And now the Lord has brought it about" (Jer. 40:2-3). The prophet later lamented, "The Lord has done what he planned; ... which he decreed long ago ... Who can speak and have it happen if the Lord has not decreed it" (Lam. 2:17; 3:37). From the earliest pages of the Bible to its final doxology in Revelation, the truth is everywhere proclaimed that what God accomplishes He also foreordained; that whatsoever comes to pass in the world He "planned it long ago" (Isa. 22:11).

But acceptance of this particular element to God's exhaustive sovereignty is not widely shared among free-will Christians. Notwithstanding the clear testimony of Scripture, the Reformed assertion that God foreordains everything that comes to pass, to include the evil rebellion of the wicked and the eternal destinies of the godly, is often met with contempt. The Arminian usually concludes: *If the Calvinist doctrine of God's sovereignty is correct then God is the ultimate cause behind Adam's sin.* What is more, *If God is the direct cause of all things, which He has supposedly foreordained, then He is not only responsible for Adam's sin but also for the sins of Adam's posterity.* To the Arminian way of thinking, the Calvinistic view of foreordination makes God out to be the architect of evil by virtue of the fact that it insists that God ordains *all things.*

The objections raised by these Christians concerning exhaustive sovereignty are honest and reasonable. How can Reformed Theology insist that God ordains everything that comes to pass, including the *existence* of sin, yet still agree with The Westminster Confession of Faith that clearly affirms, "neither is God the author of sin ... nor is the liberty or contingency of second causes taken away"? Also, why wouldn't a holy and sovereign God eradicate sin and evil if it is in His power to do so? These questions, ostensibly, are conundrums. But like the facet of an exquisite diamond, every angle of this profound puzzle adds new dimension and insight into the nature of God.

First, any effort to debunk exhaustive sovereignty on the grounds that God is made liable for sin is simply a red herring. Such a charge fails to take into consideration word meanings. The Calvinist does not teach that God *causes* all things to happen but instead argues that God *ordains* all things as they are and will be. The nuances behind these two words—*cause* and *ordain*—are different in definition and essential for fully grasping exhaustive sovereignty. Secondly, while many skeptics question why a holy God would permit evil to exist in the first place, the biblical evidence seems to suggest that the very existence of evil is a concession that God allows by ordination for the purpose of His glory.

Regarding the accusation that Calvinism makes God the author of sin, the framers of the Westminster Confession rejected this charge outright. They clearly expressed the idea that the majority of what happens in the world, particularly with people, comes through *secondary causes*. While God is always the primary causation by virtue of his ordination of all things, the secondary causes are the natural actions of men—both sinful and honorable—which are willfully committed under His decree. It is at the feet of these secondary causes (i.e. the natural acts of men) where responsibility for sin is laid. The primary cause (God) only grants that they should occur (with a view to a greater good).

Jonathan Edwards (1703-1758), arguably the most revered philosophical theologian in American history, stated: "If by 'the author of sin,' be meant the sinner, the agent, or the actor of sin, or the doer of a wicked thing ... it would be a reproach and blasphemy, to suppose God to be the author of sin. In this sense, I utterly deny God to be the author of sin."[53] John Calvin (1509-1564) put it this way: "For the proper and genuine cause of sin is not God's hidden counsel but the evident will of man," although the fall of Adam was "not without God's knowledge and ordination."[54]

So what did Edwards and Calvin mean? Similar to temptation, God does not *cause* the sin of sinners. Rather, "by [a sinner's] *own evil desire*, he is dragged away and enticed. Then, after desire has conceived, it gives birth to sin" (James 1:14-15, emphasis added). Sin, in other words, originates in the evil desires of men and is made manifest in the deeds of the flesh (cf. Gal. 5:19-21). The very fact that God *foreordains* the existence of sin and temptation, and even uses them to His own benefit, is not to be misconstrued as God *causing* them to happen (cf. Prov. 6:16-19; Psa. 5:4-6; Zec. 8:17; James 1:13). There is a line of demarcation between the two verbs that must be acknowledged. The act of ordaining in certain biblical contexts means "to put in place" or "to point in advance" whereas the act of causation means "to produce an effect." While God appoints sin by sovereign ordination, He neither produces it nor induces it.

For example, the Bible teaches that God *ordained* the existence of Lucifer—"for so I ordained you," (Ezek. 28:14, NIV)—but at no time did God *cause* His greatest cherub to sin. Instead the context of Ezekiel 28 clearly indicates that by "ordain" God simply *installed*—or "put in place"—Lucifer as His guardian cherub in the same way that God *ordained* the Aaronic priests in the Levitical order. (Thus, the NASB renders Lucifer's appointment in Ezekiel 28:14 as "And I placed you there"). Furthermore, the Bible clearly teaches that Lucifer conjured up from within his own heart the ambition to sin (vv. 15b, 18 cf. Isa. 14:12-15). His cosmic treason originated, or was caused, within himself.

God is not a provocateur of evil. He has established a world, says Edwards, where He permits iniquity but does not induce it by "positive agency." Stated more clearly, God made evil *possible*, but it is men who make evil *actual*. God ordained the *fact* of evil, but it is men who willfully perform the *acts* of evil.

This truth begs more questions: Why would a holy and sovereign God permit evil and ungodliness to exist in His creation at all? Why would God plant in Eden a tree of knowledge adorned with forbidden fruit to begin with? One possible answer is that God allowed Lucifer's sin to come to pass, as well as the proliferation of human iniquity in the Garden, if for no other reason than the existence of unrighteousness reflects God's righteousness by way of contrast. Mankind cannot sing of God's holiness, moral rectitude, and perfection if they do not first understand what ungodliness, immorality, and imperfection look like. By decreeing sin and evil to exist, God shows Himself to be holy and righteous in contrast. His grace, love, perfection, mercy, and justice are magnified in juxtaposition.

Arminians struggle a great deal with Romans 11:32. In that passage Paul reveals that "God has bound everyone over to disobedience so that he may have mercy on them all." If we understand Paul's words correctly, the inspired apostle seems to be placing the blame for man's disobedience on the shoulders of God's sovereign will. But isn't such a notion sacrilegious? Why would a holy God who hates the sin of disobedience bind *all men* to it? Paul does not leave us without an answer. Behind every act that God ordains—whether righteous or apparently unseemly—there is a greater good that He has in mind; namely, that it might glorify Him in return (either at the present time or in eternity to come). On this point Dr. J. Ligon Duncan III does us a great service. He writes:

> Paul is saying that our sovereign God forced even the entrance of sin into the world and the preterition of the lost to serve the interests of the display of his glory in the display of his mercy and grace. Paul is saying that original sin, and all the actual sin that flows from it, and God's just condemnation of the wicked have been made (in the inscrutable wisdom of God) to show, demonstrate, display, evidence, and magnify his grace to the objects of his mercy. In other words, God has used spectacular sins and relentless judgment to display the glory of his grace.[55]

It's no doubt difficult for Christians to fathom that a holy God, who is allergic to sin, in point of fact "forced ... the entrance of sin into the world." Yet it's nevertheless the brutal truth of Scripture, as Paul clearly implies in Romans 11:32 and Dr. Duncan accurately elucidates. Thus, in one sense God wills that which He hates to come to pass (to contrast His glory), as well as that which He loves (to showcase His glory). By foreordaining Lucifer's existence and appointing him as guardian cherub, including removing him from office on account of his willful sin, God is ultimately glorified as sovereign, holy, and just.

Moreover, by decreeing the very existence of sin and evil, to include the disobedience of our federal parents in Eden, the glory of God is more clearly seen in contrast.

Lastly, according to Edwards, God is "the permitter ... of sin [not the committer]; and at the same time, a disposer of the state of events, in such a manner, *for wise, holy and most excellent ends and purposes*, that sin, if it be permitted ... will most certainly and infallibly follow" (emphasis added). To paraphrase Edwards, God routinely ordains that which He hates to accomplish that which He loves.

Nowhere is this paradoxical reality more clearly seen than in the accounts of Jesus' crucifixion (Matt. 27:33-44; Mark 15:22-32; Luke 23:33-43; John 19:17-30), the betrayal of Joseph by his brothers (Gen. 37:19-22 cf. 50:20), and the rise and fall of the Assyrian Empire (Isa. 7:1-10:5). In each of these stories we witness a holy God who reverses the sinful acts of men and Satan, which the Lord Himself ordained, "for [His] wise, holy and most excellent ends." This is an unsettling truth that confounded many prophets, particularly Habakkuk (cf. Hab. ch. 1).

There is no question that in His exhaustive sovereignty God foreordained the atonement of Christ for the *propitiation* of human sin (i.e. the satisfaction of God's wrath). Moreover, evangelical scholarship stands with Scripture when it states that God ordained the sordid events which led Joseph to Egypt as well as the demise of Israel at the hands of Assyria. But the larger questions in view here are: Did God cause the Romans and Jews to murder Jesus? Did God provoke Joseph's brothers to throw him into a pit and to leave him there to die? And did God punish Assyria for the very wrongdoing that He allegedly purposed them to do?

Without question, at the root of each of these events were unspeakable atrocities committed by evil men. If God preordained that these events should come to pass then it stands to reason that, contrary to Edwards, Calvin, and The Westminster Confession of Faith, God is indeed a purveyor of iniquity and the author of sin. But a closer look at each of these

accounts reveals, rather than conceals, how God's exhaustive
sovereignty works in harmony with man's self-will. It is to each
of these paradoxical examples that we now turn.

In eternity past God foreordained that Jesus would die an
atoning death as part of His predetermined plan in the drama
of redemption. To the Jews, Peter made this point clear:
"This man was handed over to you by *God's set purpose and
foreknowledge*; and you, with the help of wicked men, put
him to death by nailing him to the cross" (Acts 2:23, emphasis
added). Peter testified later: "Indeed Herod and Pontius Pilate
... [conspired] against your holy servant Jesus, whom you
anointed. *They did what your power and will had decided
beforehand should happen*" (Acts 4:27-28, emphasis added).

In these passages Peter reveals that the execution of the
Savior was due not only to the wicked intentions of men but
also to the sovereign will of God, each of which worked in
cooperation to bring about God's ultimate "set purpose." In
their determination to punish Jesus for what they perceived as
blasphemy and treason, the Messiah was sentenced to death
by the Jews and eventually executed by the Romans (Mark
3:6; Luke 13:31). Yet the prophet Isaiah confirms that the true
Puppeteer pulling the strings was God, for "it was the Lord's will
to crush him and cause him to suffer" in order "to make his life
a guilt offering" (Isa. 53:10).

The Lord's executioners conducted themselves in a manner
that was in keeping with their own sinful depravity and at
no time were they tempted, induced, prompted, baited, or
hypnotized by God to sin against their wills (cf. James 1:13).
They acted from their own voluntary choice. Sinners stand
guilty as charged for doing only that which they are naturally
enslaved to do (cf. Rom. 6:20). We can therefore agree with the
apostle Peter that the Jews and Romans, like all mankind, stand
culpable for the homicide of the Holy of Holies. Indeed, each
and every one of us, as Paul put it differently in another context,
"are without excuse" (Rom. 1:20; 9:19-20).

Mysteriously, God ordains the means as well as the ends
without violating human freedom or promoting evil. This is an
inexplicable tension in Scripture that fallen men are incapable

of fully understanding. While never authorizing sin, God uses the sinful acts committed freely by wicked men to accomplish His ordained purposes, to include turning the greatest sin in history into the greatest victory ever to premiere in the theater of redemption.

Thus, in the atonement of Christ we witness the fusion of independent wills working in tandem to fulfill God's eternal decree. God's motivation to send "his Son as an atoning sacrifice" was the primary cause (1 John. 4:10 cf. John 3:16; Isa. 53:10) and man's impulse to "put him to death by nailing him to the cross" served as the secondary cause (Acts 2:23b cf. Matt. 27:22-23). In one sweeping statement in Acts 2:23 Peter presents the total sovereignty of God alongside the complete responsibility of man.

This same startling truth is evident in the Genesis account of Joseph and his rise to prominence. As a seventeen year-old, Joseph's brothers were jealous of him (Gen. 37:11), hated him (vv. 4-5, 8) and then sold him into slavery to Midianite merchants on route to Egypt (v. 28). And if that wasn't egregious enough, Joseph was then wrongfully imprisoned for two years, having been falsely accused of attempted rape (ch. 39). Yet a little over a decade later, when a severe famine reunited him with his brothers in Egypt, a reinstated Joseph could say to them with theological sincerity, "God sent me before you to preserve life" (45:5, ESV), and "you meant evil against me, *but God meant it for good*" (50:20, emphasis added).

Here we once again see the evil deeds perpetrated by sinful men stage-managed by God's providential control. God used the sinful behavior of Joseph's brothers—who were rightly held accountable for their betrayal of their brother—to accomplish His foreordained purposes. God oversaw the actions of Joseph's brothers in accord with His overarching plan to save Israel from starvation, but at no time did He induce the brothers to attempt premeditated murder. They acted freely and in accord with their own sinful natures.

God ruled against the immoral motivations of Joseph's brothers and turned the unfortunate events of Joseph's life— the very events which God Himself had predetermined—into the very means by which He would fulfill His greater purpose—namely, "the saving of many lives" (Gen. 50:20b)! Had Joseph *not* been betrayed by his brothers, Israel would have never entered Egypt and escaped the fatal effects of the famine. Joseph's famous words "but God meant it for good" form the theological heart of divine providence in the Old Testament. A person's heart may be filled with evil intent, as was the case with Joseph's siblings, yet God will often use such evil to accomplish His good purposes. Thus, both Paul and Solomon could mysteriously conclude, "[W]e know that *in all things* God works *for the good* of those who love him ... *according to his purpose*" (Rom. 8:28 cf. Prov. 16:4; emphasis added).

This same principle is found in 1 Chronicles 5:25-26 and Isaiah 10:5-12 where God used Assyria as an instrument of judgment against the rebellious house of Israel. Ultimately it was God who had commissioned the barbarian Assyrians to rise up in opposition to Israel. God gave Assyria marching orders to "to seize loot and snatch plunder," and, in general, to do what the Assyrian army naturally did best—to pillage and to trample their enemies underfoot (Isa. 10:6). Even the king of Assyria recognized God's providence in his conquests and admitted "The Lord himself told me to march against this country and destroy it" (2 Kings 8:25; Isa. 36:10). The drama unfolds in 1 Chronicles 5:25-26:

> But [the Israelites] were unfaithful to the God of their fathers and prostituted themselves to the gods of the peoples of the land, whom God had destroyed before them. *So the God of Israel stirred up the spirit of Pul king of Assyria* (that is, Tiglath-Pileser king of Assyria), who took the Reubenites, the Gadites and the half-tribe of Manasseh into exile (emphasis added).

God sovereignly used to His advantage the intrinsic wickedness of the Assyrians. He didn't cause them to be more evil than they actually were nor did He force them to behave in a manner that was not already in keeping with their sinful depravity. He merely used for His sovereign purposes their existing sinfulness to mete out His retribution against an apostate Israel.

Later, however, God held Assyria accountable. While the Lord had ordained their rise in military might and sanctioned their victory over the Northern Kingdom of Israel, He did not approve of Assyria's arrogance. By the time the pagan nation had encroached upon the Southern Kingdom of Judah, Assyria had forgotten the exhaustive sovereignty of God that had been surreptitiously at work behind the scenes. They became proud conquerors rather than humble servants. Therefore, owing to their failure to give credit to God for their amassed victories, God brought into account the Assyrian Empire for defeating His people; an act which He originally ordained them to do. In the words of Ezekiel, "because [Assyria] was proud ... I cast it aside" (Ezek. 31:10-11). Isaiah said elsewhere:

> "Woe to the Assyrian, the rod of my anger, in whose hand is the club of my wrath! I send him against a godless nation, I dispatch him against a people who anger me ...
>
> When the Lord has finished all his work against Mount Zion and Jerusalem, he will say, "I will punish the king of Assyria for the *willful* pride of his heart and the haughty look in his eyes" (Isa. 10:5-6a, 12, emphasis added).

In addition to her pride, God judged Assyria on the basis of her *intentions*, as Scripture teaches, *not* her God-ordained actions. "But this is not what [Tiglath Pileser III, the King of Assyria] intends, this is not what he has in mind;" said the Lord in Isaiah 10:7, "his purpose is to destroy, to put an end to many nations." In other words, since Assyria came against Israel with a haughty attitude, malice aforethought, and an insatiable lust to lay waste to the nations—all the while refusing to recognize God's providence in her victories—Assyria too was judged. God held the Gentile army responsible for its sin—which Isaiah depicts as willful rather than divinely induced (Isa. 10:13)—regardless of the fact that God used it for His divine purposes. What Assyria did obediently God had sovereignly predetermined, and what she did sinfully God sovereignly judged.

As limited human beings, when attempting to reconcile the relationship between the willful actions of sinful men and the sovereign actions of a sinless God, we must admit to a lack of full disclosure in Scripture. We plead ignorance with Solomon who said: "A person's steps are directed by the Lord. How then can anyone understand their own way?" (Prov. 20:24). But our human limitations remind us that, rather than take an existential approach to doctrine, we dare not go beyond the written page of Scripture and into the valley of presupposition simply to make God more pliable to our personal theology.

That the Romans and Jews stood guilty before God for willfully crucifying Christ (but whose actions were in accord with His predetermined plan) is a biblical fact. That Joseph's brothers were guilty of wickedly betraying him (yet behaved in a manner in keeping with God's will to preserve His people in Egypt) is irrefutable. And that King Tiglath-Pileser was guilty of arrogantly raging against the nations (but whose actions were in accord with God's decree to judge those pagan societies through him) is ironclad. In all three instances, we see sinful men perpetrate heinous crimes of their own free-will and for which they bore responsibility and were rightly judged, while fulfilling God's sovereign will. These truths go beyond the scope of our comprehension. Nevertheless, as Christians, we must prostrate ourselves before Scripture and submit to Proverbs 19:21 as the final verdict: "Many are the plans in a person's heart, but it is the Lord's purpose that prevails" (Prov. 19:21).[56]

God is most glorified when He overturns sin for His holy and righteous purposes. It was God's *permissive will* (i.e. He permits things that are otherwise contrary to His liking, etc.) which tolerated the willful sin of Joseph's brothers. However, His *decretive will* (i.e. His eternal, foreordained decrees, which will not change and cannot be thwarted, etc.), was to overturn their transgression and use it as the very means by which to preserve His elect people from famine. Similarly, it was God's *permissive will* which allowed for the Roman government and the Jewish religious establishment to willfully crucify Christ. While certainly the most horrific atrocity ever committed by men, God allowed the murder of His Son because it was ultimately His *decretive will* to ransom the Elect from the penalty of sin through blood atonement. It was God's *permissive will* that ordained the defeat of the Northern Kingdom of Israel at the hands of the Assyrians, while at the same time it was his *decretive will* to judge Assyria for her superfluous barbarism and arrogance. And lastly, it was God's *permissive will* that allowed Adam and Eve to willfully sin in the Garden of Eden and tolerated the rebellion of Lucifer in heaven. But behind God's *permissive will* in both catastrophes was His *decretive will* to put on display the glory of His majesty by restoring His creation from evil and redeeming His creatures from sin.

Calvinism's case for exhaustive sovereignty is biblical. It exonerates God, rather than indicts Him, of any wrongdoing. Although human sin is allowed by God (His permissive will), it is not His desire that we sin. God is keenly aware that sinners will always live up to their reputations by living down to their base natures. Thus, there is no need for God to persuade, trick, coerce, force, manipulate, induce, or cause a sinner to do what comes naturally to him. Sin begins and ends in the heart of fallen man. Accordingly, the guilt of transgression is rightly credited to the perpetrator of the sin—the secondary cause—not to the One who ordained that it should come to pass (with a view to a greater good). For this reason, Reformed Theology can stand with the Westminster Confession and say in good conscience that God is neither "the author of sin ... nor is the liberty ... of second causes taken away."

Furthermore, exhaustive sovereignty is in no way antithetical to the imperialistic definition contained in the Greek word *dunastes*. It simply goes beyond the Arminian view by taking into account the compendium of Scripture on the subject. It reveals to us a God who sovereignly determines the destiny of cast lots, ordains the very steps of men, manipulates the hearts of kings, presets the boundaries of nations, and decrees the number of days a person will live (cf. Prov. 16:33; 19:21; 20:24;

21:1; Job 14:5). In short, "My purpose will stand," says the Lord, "and I will do all that I please" (Isa. 46:10). More than just a governing King, the Lord foreordained all that is, including those who would make up His Church. And He did so "before the creation of the world" (Eph. 1:4).

In summary, God's sovereignty is unquestionably comprehensive. His confluent involvement in all that occurs does not violate the natural order, ongoing causal processes, or the free, responsible agency of human beings. God's sovereign control does not take away the responsibility and power of secondary causes; on the contrary, they are created willfully by man and have their roles by appointment. God does not cause the sinful acts of His creatures insomuch as He *ordains* that their sin should exist in order that He is glorified when He accomplishes His holy legislation through it and redeems sinners from it. And lastly, God inexplicably upends the evil actions committed by wicked men—actions that He Himself ordained or "put in place"—for the express purpose of accomplishing good and showcasing His grace, mercy, power, and glory.

The doctrine of exhaustive sovereignty, notwithstanding its perplexities, teaches Christians that they are never in the grip of blind fortune, chance, luck, or fate. All that happens to them is divinely planned, and each event comes as a new summons to trust, obey, and rejoice, knowing that "The Lord works out everything to its proper end" (Prov. 16:4a) and "in all things God works for the good ... according to his purpose" (Rom. 8:28). This truth is captured most superbly by Isaac Watts (1674-1748) in his poetical hymn *Let the Whole Race of Creatures Lie*:

> *Ten thousand ages ere the skies,*
> *Were into motion brought,*
> *All the long years and worlds to come,*
> *Stood present to His thought;*
> *There's not a sparrow or a worm,*
> *But's found in His decrees,*
> *He raises monarchs to their throne,*
> *and sinks them as He pleases*

Reflection Questions:

1. In your estimation, how sovereign is God?

2. Is man's hard-heartedness toward spiritual things outside of God's control or is it indicative of it (cf. Rom. 11:32)?

3. Does God "ordain" or "cause" the sinful actions of sinners? What is the difference?

4. How exactly is God exonerated from wrongdoing in the death of Christ, the betrayal of Joseph by his brothers, and the rise and fall of Assyria when in fact it was He who ordained each of these atrocities?

Part 2:
Doctrinal Review

Section 2:

The Scandal of Total Depravity

"Whoever is soft on depravity should go see 'Schindler's List' ... How could such hatred, such extreme, vicious hatred, fill the minds of those wearing swastikas? How could they walk back into their barracks or offices or homes and smile or carry on their duties or forget what they had just done? I believe I know. Really, the answer is simple. One word will do. Depravity. It's not a sickness. It's death. Living death. It's the filthy cesspool of the unregenerate heart."

Chuck Swindoll
1934-Present

Chapter 6

The Order of Salvation (Ordo Salutis)

In January, 2010, *Time Magazine* published an interview with Dr. Jeffrey Long, a radiation oncologist in Tacoma, Washington, under the provocative headline *"Is There Life After Death?"* Drawing upon twelve years of research on near-death experiences—some 1,300 cases in fact—Dr. Long claimed that the evidence indicates that human beings live beyond the grave. Not surprisingly, when he published his findings in his book *Evidence of the Afterlife,* the reputable doctor became a media sensation overnight. A nationally recognized expert, his work was featured on ABC News, FOX News, and NBC's *The Today Show,* as well as in national periodicals such as *Newsweek* and *The Wall Street Journal.* Dr. Long's research represents the largest concentration of scientific study on near-death experiences ever reported.

Dr. Long contends in his book that a large majority of near-death experiences are remarkably similar. Irrespective of age, race, gender, religious affiliation, geographical location, or cultural boundaries, the accounts studied of those who have apparently died offer several lines of evidence that, says Long, send a "consistent message of an afterlife." Among them are crystal-clear recollections, heightened senses, reunions with deceased family members, and long-lasting positive effects after the person is brought back to life.

Needless to say, *Evidence of the Afterlife* has become a hot commodity among religious and skeptical readers alike. Belief in life after death is quite common—recent polls indicate that 82% of Americans believe in some form of an afterlife—but until now, scientific support was scant. While his critics remain unconvinced, Dr. Long's extensive research (which boasts the largest database of its kind) has been hailed as groundbreaking by many in the scientific and religious communities.

But investigating the existence of an afterlife is nothing new. Eons before *Evidence of the Afterlife* was published, inquisitive minds have contemplated life after death. Indeed, one of the godliest men in all of recorded history, Job, was the first to ask the question, "If a man dies, will he live again?" (Job 14:14). Thousands of years removed from Job's era, Dr. Long's clinical deductions appear to have affirmatively answered this age-old question—at least in the minds of the faithful.

As Christians, what are we to make of these fantastic claims about people returning from the *almost*-dead? Do these accounts jive with God's revealed revelation? The answer is not easy to ascertain since some of these near-death experiences appear at odds with the Bible while others are more agreeable. But where there is incongruity we must ask the question: *Are we to believe people's experiences over against the Word of God?* Although these reports are fascinating, to be sure, we must narrow our scope to only those experiences that are in keeping with Scripture, maintaining an ever watchful eye on what is being postulated in order to "test the spirits" (1 John 4:1-3).

The Bible offers a few insights into near-death phenomena. In Jesus' story of the rich man and Lazarus, for example, we are told that the beggar Lazarus died and "the angels carried him to Abraham's side" (Luke 16:22). Although Lazarus did not return to physical consciousness in the parable, the angelic chaperone that accompanied his spirit in the hereafter is a common thread interwoven in many near-death stories.

Moreover, just before being stoned to death, Stephen, a righteous leader in the early Church and the first martyr in Christendom, caught a glimpse of "the glory of God." Some eccentric interpreters equate Stephen's vision with the "bright light" that is all-too-familiar in near-death accounts. Stephen's dying words bear witness: "I see heaven open and the Son of Man standing at the right hand of God" (Acts 7:55-56).

Paul records an apparent out-of body experience as well, which some scholars believe to have happened after he was stoned and left for dead in Lystra on his first missionary journey (Acts 14:19-20). It seems that he actually teleported in some way to "the third heaven" where he heard "inexpressible things, things that man is not permitted to tell" (2 Cor. 12:1-5).

There is certainly no reason for discerning Christians to discount as unbiblical *all* near-death experiences but neither should we accept them *carte blanche*. Since most, if not all, of the patients in Dr. Long's study were not biologically or irreversibly dead, *but were near death*, we can hardly ascertain their eternal state of existence and therefore the biblical validity of their claims. What is more, while we are to assess all things by the Word of God (1 John 4:1-3), we must also admit that what little we do know about the hereafter remains mostly a mystery to even the most studied theologian.

The real point at issue here, as it relates to Calvinism and free-will theology, is the cohesion that exists between the Bible's depiction of resurrections and Dr. Long's near-death studies. What is particularly true in Dr. Long's case studies is also comparable to the accounts contained in Scripture—namely, that whenever and wherever resuscitations occur, a *resuscitator* is present!

Science is unaware of any documented near-death experience where a person miraculously returned to life by exercising the power of his deceased will. A second party is *always* responsible. Whether it is a physician, hospital orderlies, nurses, paramedics, firemen, policemen, lifeguards, or the heroics of nearby bystanders, the vast majority of near-death experiences tell the story of someone or something responsible for resuscitating a person back to life. On this point there is little disparity. To resuscitate someone from the brink of death dictates that someone is first willing to come to their rescue.

Consider each of the resuscitations[57] recorded in the Bible. Notwithstanding the resurrection of Christ, the Bible records nine such cases where men, women, and children were brought back to life by a prophet, an apostle, Jesus Christ, or God Himself. Those who were raised to life were not merely *near death,* or clinically dead for just a few minutes, but were dead for days, and in one case, even years (cf. Matt. 27:51-53).

We are first introduced to the concept of regeneration in the historical narratives of the Old Testament. The prophet Elijah raised from the dead the son of a single mother in the town of Zarephath—an act of divine mercy meant to relieve a widow's grief (1 Kings 17:19-24). Likewise, the prophet Elisha—Elijah's successor—raised the son of a Shunammite woman from the grave (2 Kings 4:32-35). In 2 Kings 13:21 we read of a man who inexplicably came to life when his corpse came into contact with the bones of Elisha. This miracle was a sign that God's power continued to work in relationship to Elisha even after the prophet's death. In each of these Old Testament examples the dead were restored to life through the agency of a prophet of God, with God being the ultimate power source behind each miracle.

The New Testament is also ripe with resuscitations, not the least of which is the resurrection of Jesus Christ. After being dead for three days, the Bible teaches that the triune God—the Father, the Son, and the Holy Spirit—each respectively participated in the Lord's resurrection (Rom. 6:4; 8:11; Gal. 1:1; Eph. 1:15-20; John 2:19-22; 10:17-18). What is more, we learn that an untold number of people were raised from the dead at the very moment of Jesus' own death on the cross (Matt. 27:51-53). On three separate occasions during his earthly ministry Jesus himself raised the dead, substantiating his messianic claims (cf. Matt.11:5). Among those raised by Jesus were Lazarus, who had been dead for four days (John 11:43-44), Jairus' twelve-year-old daughter (Mark 5:34-43), and a widow's son in Nain (Luke 7:11-17).

Just as the prophets Elijah and Elisha raised the dead in the Old Testament so too did the apostles in the New Testament. Eutychus was raised back to life by the apostle Paul after falling from a third-floor window and apparently breaking his neck (Acts 20:9-10). The apostle Peter also raised Tabitha from the dead, a Christian caregiver who had succumbed to a fatal illness (Acts 9:36-43). And it is implied in Jesus' marching orders in Matthew 10:7-9 that the other apostles also performed ad hoc resuscitations from time to time as they preached throughout Galilee and Judea. In each of these New Testament examples the dead were restored to life through the agency of an apostle, with God being the ultimate power source behind each miracle.

Both in Scripture and in the accounts of Dr. Long's case studies, the restoration of life is *monergistic*. It is a single-handed operation whereby an external force acts directly to bring about regenerated life, and always *without* any assistance or cooperation from the dead.

Nowhere is this truth better illustrated than in John 11:43-44 and the resuscitation of Lazarus. On word of Lazarus's severe illness, Jesus set out for Bethany in Judea at the behest of Lazarus's sisters, Mary and Martha. The Lord was at Bethabara beyond the Jordan in Perea at the time, about twenty-five miles from Jerusalem; only a day's journey from Bethany.

The situation, we are told, was desperate and the two sisters were in anguish, hoping that the Lord would return in time to heal their bed-ridden brother. But one day eventually turned into four before Jesus finally arrived. *But he was too late*; Lazarus had died in the interim. The two sisters, heartbroken and to some extent pessimistic, were confounded as to why the Lord delayed his coming.

All human hope was gone. Lazarus was laid to rest. Friends and neighbors could only offer tender condolences to Mary and Martha. Jesus, himself, offered his tears. The Lord wept for Lazarus out of sorrow, but he also wept for the sisters, their relatives, and their friends (vv. 33, 35). He wept because his heart was broken at the sadness of death and by sorrows that knew no solace. He wept because he was God and he could see what they could not—Lazarus in paradise surrounded by the saints of God.

Lazarus was dead, not critically ill or on his death bed. He was a lifeless corpse. Nevertheless, having arrived at Lazarus's tomb, a cave located on a nearby hillside, Jesus ordered that the stone in front of the entrance be rolled away. What happened next is nothing short of breathtaking. With a quiet prayer followed by a loud shout Jesus instantly reversed Lazarus's rigamortis and summoned his friend back to life: "Lazarus, come out!" he exclaimed (v. 43). (It has often been observed that the Lord's power was so great that had he not addressed Lazarus by name, all the dead in all the graves in the entire world would have come forth).

Suddenly, to everyone's amazement, a strange figure—bound hand and foot in grave wrappings—appeared out of the shadows of the tomb. The eyes of the watching crowd squinted for focus. It was Lazarus, and he was alive! Doubtless hysteria ensued as word quickly spread throughout Judea (cf. John 12:9-10).

By all accounts Lazarus was clinically dead—and for four days no less! Accordingly, he was unresponsive and incapable of raising himself to life. But the power of Christ overcame his lifeless remains. As he had done with Adam in the Garden so Jesus did with Lazarus in Bethany and "breathed into his nostrils the breath of life, and the man became a living being" (Gen. 2:7). The Lord sovereignly uttered a single command, not a request or an invitation beseeching Lazarus to cooperate with the miracle. He made no attempt to woo him from the tomb. The resuscitation was strictly monergistic—the act of God *alone*. Lazarus was first raised to newness of life and only afterward did he have the ability to respond. In short, his supernatural regeneration *preceded* his natural response of obedience.

The *physical* resuscitation of Lazarus serves as a picture for the Reformed understanding of *spiritual* regeneration. Only after the Holy Spirit has miraculously imparted life to a dead sinner is he then able to obey Christ and repent of his sin and believe on him as Savior. Until then, a sinner remains confined in a spiritually depraved tomb; he is an unregenerate cadaver incapable of responding to or seeking after the Savior. Charles Spurgeon commented:

> The raising of Lazarus stands at the head of the wonderful series of miracles with which our Lord astonished and instructed the people. Yet I am not in error when I assert that it is a type of what the Lord Jesus is constantly doing at this hour in the realm of mind and spirit. Did he raise the naturally dead? So does he still deliver men from loathsome sins![58]

Not unlike physical regeneration, spiritual regeneration reverses the sinner's natural blindness, enabling him to understand his need for a Savior and endowing him with spiritual sight and determination. Scripture sings the unmistakable refrain that, just as it was with an entombed Lazarus and a formless Adam, it is the work of God alone that "[breathes] into [their] nostrils the breath of life; and [elect people become] ... living being[s]" (Gen. 2:17). Brian Schwertley, a Reformed pastor serving in Waupaca County, Wisconsin and author of numerous books on Presbyterian doctrine, sums it up well:

> A biblical understanding of man's state after the fall ought to cure us of the sinful and somewhat blasphemous notion that a thrice holy God has associated Himself with sinful depraved man as only a minor partial cause of a sinner's salvation. The fact that the natural man is a spiritual corpse without any ability to seek God or take even one step toward Jesus means: [1] that regeneration must precede and not follow saving faith; [2] that God works directly upon the human soul in salvation; [and 3] that Christ is not passively waiting, but is actively saving His people.
>
> An understanding of the fall leads to the doctrine of salvation by the grace of God alone. Salvation is totally a work of God. Man does not have the ability to contribute anything to his own salvation; even faith and repentance are gifts from above (Eph. 2:8; Phil. 2:13; Ac. 5:31, 11:18).[59]

Regeneration & the *Ordo Salutis*

The *Ordo Salutis* is a Latin phrase which means "the order of salvation." It draws from Scripture a sequence, or a series of building blocks, that defines the salvation process of a believer.

Also known as *The Golden Chain of Salvation*, it is derived primarily from the writing of the apostle Paul in his epistle to the church in Rome. The *Ordo Salutis* is as follows:

> For those God *foreknew* he also *predestined* to be conformed to the likeness of his Son, that he might be the firstborn among many brothers. And those he *predestined*, he also *called*; those he called, he also *justified*; those he justified, he also *glorified* (Rom. 8:29-30, emphasis added).

The salvific progression in this passage is instantly recognizable. Beginning with God's foreknowledge, we learn that believers are predestined in eternity past to believe in Christ, called and justified in time and space, and eventually glorified in eternity future. To the casual reader, this chain of succession seems fairly benign. For partisan theologians with an axe to grind, however, Paul's words are a cobweb of mystery. Convinced that there is more to this passage than what initially meets the eye, theologians have wrestled for centuries over the finer points of the *Ordo Salutis*; the final consensus being that there is no consensus. Using the totality of Scripture as their compass, Calvinists and Arminians go beyond Paul's expansive overview in Romans 8:29-30 and add their own particulars to their respective chains.

In more granular terms, Calvinists see the order of salvation as follows: Those whom God *fore-loved* in eternity past He also *elected* for salvation and *predestined* to believe savingly in Christ. These same fore-loved, elected, and predestinated sinners are then, in the fullness of time, effectually *called* to Christ by way of the outward call (the preached Word) and the inward call (the Holy Spirit's leading). At the same time, the Holy Spirit—who works in tandem with the Father's electing purposes and the Son's redemptive work—*regenerates* the elect sinner so as to enable him to respond positively to both summonses. Upon conversion, the saved sinner is placed in a state of *justification* where he is declared legally right before God. Afterward, the cleansing waters of *sanctification* flow naturally whereby routine acts of godliness are made manifest in the convert's life. Finally, upon his death and entrance into heaven, the fore-loved, elected, predestined, called, regenerated, saved, justified, and progressively sanctified sinner is *glorified*. Sequentially, the Reformed chain of salvation is as follows:

Calvinism Order of Salvation (*Ordo Salutis*)	1. Fore-love 2. Election 3. Predestination 4. The outward call (the preached Word) 5. The inward call (the Spirit's leading) 6. **Regeneration** 7. Conversion (faith and repentance) 8. Justification 9. Sanctification 10. Glorification

Within the Calvinist *Ordo Salutis* is the strategic placement of the new birth (in bold above). The reader will note that, according to Reformed scholarship, the act of spiritual regeneration occurs *after* the Holy Spirit's irresistible calling but *prior* to the sinner's conversion. In other words, the chain-reaction of salvation ultimately pivots on this all-too-crucial work of the Spirit of God. Calvinists insist, therefore, that in order for a person to be saved, justified, sanctified, and glorified, a sinner must *first* be born again. Were it not so, the Calvinist reasons, a sinner is ill-equipped to recognize his need for a Savior. Everything pertaining to salvation, says the Calvinist, hinges upon the preliminary and monergistic miracle of spiritual regeneration.

The English word *regeneration* is the translation of *paliggenesia*, from *palin* (again) and *genesis* (birth).[60] It simply means "a new birth," corresponding to reproduction, renewal, renovation, and re-creation. In biblical language, it is "the production of a new life consecrated to God, a radical change of mind for the better."[61]

Regeneration, then, as it relates to a sinner's spiritual condition, is best understood as an act of God whereby He bestows new life upon a sinner that enables him to look upon Christ with new eyes (Acts 26:18), to respond to Christ with new ears (cf. Deut. 29:4), and to believe in Christ with a new heart of flesh (Ezek. 11:19; 36:26–27). Those who have undergone this internal transformation are described in Scripture as "partakers of the divine nature" (2 Pet. 1:4, ESV), "created in Christ Jesus" (Eph. 2:10), "made ... alive in Christ' (Eph. 2:5; Col. 2:13), "born ... of God" (John 1:13), "born again" (John 3:3, 7), and "a new creation" (2 Cor. 5:17). Thus, regeneration is not something that man does but is something that God does. It is a change wrought in a man, not an act performed by man. In a word, it is monergistic.

When the term monergism is linked with the word regeneration, the phrase describes an action wherein the Holy Spirit transforms a human being *without* that person's collaboration. The Spirit of God quickens the spiritually dead sinner through the irresistible call cast forth by the Holy Spirit and the preached Word, disarms his innate hostility, removes his blindness, illumines his mind, creates understanding, and transforms his heart in order that the sinner will—with renewed affections—freely and gladly embrace Christ. In brief, it is God alone who proactively makes alive in Christ those whom He so chooses, without any contribution, cooperation, or consent from the passive sinner.

The echo of monergism can be heard throughout the Doctrines of Grace. With symphonic expression, the apostle John refers to the children of God as those "which were born [spiritually regenerated], not of blood, nor of the will of the flesh, nor of the will of man, but of God" (John 1:13). The beloved disciple declared in unequivocal terms that the new birth occurs irrespective of man's desire or cooperation but on account of God's independent work and sovereign will.

Moreover, in his conversation with Nicodemus, Jesus credited the Holy Spirit as the *only* agent involved in the renewal of spiritual life. To the puzzled Pharisee, our Lord said: "The wind blows wherever it pleases. You hear its sound, but you cannot tell where it comes from or where it is going. So it is with everyone born of the Spirit" (John 3:8). This profound statement, while seemingly harmless on the written page, is pregnant with toxicity. It left the leading Pharisee in Israel mystified. Just as the wind cannot be controlled or manipulated but blows "wherever it pleases" so the sovereign work of regeneration in the human heart can neither be controlled nor predicted. It is entirely the work of God, according to His pleasure, and unaided by human effort. Not surprisingly, this truth did not land well for the sanctimonious Pharisee.

Calvinism regards monergism as crucial to biblical Christianity. Without it, dead men cannot live. And if dead men cannot live, they cannot make a saving commitment to Christ. Charles Spurgeon put it this way:

> Do not think Christians are made by education; they are made by creation. You may wash a corpse as long as you please, and that corpse could be clean, but you cannot wash life into it! You may deck it in flowers, and robe it in scarlet and fine linen, but you cannot make it live! The vital spark must come from above! Regeneration is not of the will of man, nor of blood, nor of the will of the flesh, but by the power and energy of the Spirit of God, and the Spirit of God alone![62]

Needless to say, Arminians take issue with Reformed Theology's stance on monergism. It implies to them that unconverted man bears no responsibility in the new birth; that God regenerates and saves men robotically without respect for their autonomy.[63] They therefore counteroffer Calvinism with an *Ordo Salutis* that is in marked contrast. They maintain that sinners are expected to come to Christ by their *own* faith, through their *own* choice, and on their *own* effort. While God initially sparks the flame of regeneration, they readily admit, it is only on the basis of a sinner's autonomous cooperation that it catches fire. In other words, the act of being born-again is a synergistic operation in Arminianism, not a monergistic one.

The doctrine of synergism is front and center in Arminianism. It is the flawed teaching that suggests that there are *two* capable agents in regeneration, namely the human will and the divine Spirit, which, in the strict sense of the term, *combine forces* to achieve a mutual end. This theory holds to Cassian's semi-Pelagian supposition that the human soul has *not* lost in the Fall of Adam all inclination toward holiness or the power to seek God under the influence of ordinary motives (see Chapter 2). To put it simply, synergism teaches that unregenerate men produce saving faith on their own and, in turn, knowingly and willingly participate with the Holy Spirit to perfect the new birth.

As an example of this line of reasoning, Billy Graham, the famous Arminian evangelist, once remarked: "... the new birth is something that God does for man *when man is willing to yield to God*," and "He gives the Holy Spirit to draw you to the cross, but even after all this, *it is your decision whether to accept God's free pardon or to continue in your lost condition*" (emphasis added).[64] In the same vein, Lewis Sperry Chafer (1871-1952), the founder of Dallas Theological Seminary and former Professor of Systematic Theology, wrote: "... *all* who have believed were, *at the moment of believing*, made alive with Christ" (emphasis added).[65] To the thinking of both men, not only is spiritual regeneration a byproduct of belief (rather than the means of it) but it's a cooperative effort.

Synergism infects and affects Arminianism to such degree that it produces an *Ordo Salutis* that bears no resemblance whatsoever to the Golden Chain found in Calvinism. The two are hardly on the same playing field. In point of fact, Arminians see the order of salvation as follows: Those whom God foresaw would exercise their free choice by receiving Christ as Lord and Savior were predestined to hear the preached Word during their lifetime. Upon a positive confession of *faith*, the foreseen and confessing believer then becomes *officially* elected. Following this, he is called to *repent* so as to receive temporary forgiveness and salvation. Only when contrition is made does the believer then undergo spiritual *regeneration*. He is next placed in a transitory state of *justification* where, for the time being, he is declared legally right before God. The process of *sanctification* follows afterward whereby godly fruit is made manifest in his life. Upon his death, assuming the sinner did not backslide or disavow his confession of faith, his temporal forgiveness, justification, and salvation are ratified and made permanent. The saved sinner then receives his *glorification* in heaven. Sequentially, the Arminian chain of salvation is as follows:

Arminianism Order of Salvation (*Ordo Salutis*)	1. 2. 3. 4. 5. 6. 7. 8. 9.	Foreknowledge (divine foresight) The outward call (the preached Word) Faith/conversion Election Repentance Regeneration Justification Perseverance Glorification

The two chains of salvation proposed by Calvinists and Arminians are ripe with dissimilarities, especially with regards to spiritual regeneration. While the Calvinist *Ordo Salutis* maintains that spiritual life, or regeneration, is the work of God alone and is a prerequisite that triggers the domino effect of conversion, the Arminian *Ordo Salutis* insists that fallen man retains the moral capacity within himself to cooperate with God to be saved *before* regeneration takes place. Stated differently, Calvinism insists that regeneration is *monergistic* and *precedes* faith (that is, it is necessary for salvation to occur), whereas Arminianism contends that it is *synergistic* and *follows* faith (that is, it is the result of salvation). This is no minor disagreement. Thus, whatever else may be said about the *Ordo Salutis* one thing is certain: Calvinists and Arminians see the cycle of salvation from two totally different angles.

So we must address the following questions: Does a sinner exercise self-generated faith *before* he is born again and *then* synergistically cooperate with the Holy Spirit to make it so (Arminianism)? Or is a sinner *first* born again by the Spirit monergistically and *then* granted the faith to believe unto salvation (Calvinism)? Also, if Arminianism is correct, and regeneration is the result of salvation but not a precondition for it, then how do spiritually dead God-haters, who instinctively want nothing to do with Christ, muster the ability within their dead selves to believe savingly on Jesus in the first place?

Reflection Questions:

1. In your view, noting the distinct Chains/Orders of Salvation in Calvinism and Arminianism, which *Ordo Salutis* glorifies God more, and why?

2. How does the fact that God fore-loved believers from eternity past, predestined and called them in time and space, and regenerated and saved them for future glorification affect the way you view the Doctrines of Grace? Does it change your perception of God and your understanding of how He perceives you?

3. What is the importance of spiritual regeneration (being born-again) in salvation? Is it something that man does for himself, in tandem with the Holy Spirit, *after* salvation is received? Or is it the work of God alone that occurs in an elect sinner *before* salvation is received?

Chapter 7

Monergistic Regeneration

As documented in the previous chapter, the regeneration of physical life is a trademark of Scripture. Certainly no well-meaning Arminian would deny the singlehanded handiwork of God in the various resuscitations depicted in Scripture (cf. Acts 3:15; 13:36-38; 26:8). Only those who espouse ludicrous theology would dare to suggest that Lazarus, Eutychus, Tabitha, and Jairus' daughter, together with the widow's son in Nain, the Shummanite's son, and the son of the Zarephath widow, were raised to physical life because their corpses first willingly believed and then cooperated with the miracles. The science of biology, the laws of hermeneutics, and the *Analogy of Faith*—the rule which stipulates that Scripture interprets Scripture—militate against such nonsense. The dead are not physically capable of believing in or cooperating with anything, nor do they possess the functioning ability to self-regenerate to newness of life. They lack the mental, emotional, and physical stimuli to feel, ponder, or to rationalize; they are powerless to will, want, or desire anything. The dead are *lifeless*. To suggest otherwise is to invite charges of madness.

Calvinism teaches that reprobate man is as much spiritually dead as he is alive biologically. More than just spiritually deaf, dumb, and blind, man's fallen condition is such that he is effectively stillborn. He enters the world handcuffed to corruption and imprisoned to his sin nature, from which there is no escape. In his natural affections, man is unresponsive to the things of God, unable to ascertain any spiritual happenings around him, and completely powerless to turn to God (cf. 1 Cor. 2:14). In short, he is without a spiritual heartbeat.

Man's incurable state of depravity, or terminal diagnosis, is not Calvinistic conjecture or a Reformed rumination, as is so often the charge. It's *Pauline* theology in its bare form. To

113

the Colossians, Paul wrote candidly: *"you were dead in your sins* and in the uncircumcision of your sinful nature" (Col. 2:13, emphasis added). Likewise, he declared to the Ephesians:

> As for you, you were *dead in your transgressions and sins*, in which you used to live ... we were *dead in transgressions*—it is by grace you have been saved (Eph. 2:1-5, emphasis added).

The wages of sin, we're told by the apostle, is death (Rom. 6:23), and because man is born in sin he is born to death. Man does not become spiritually dead because he sins on occasion, he is spiritually dead because by nature he is sinful. Except for Jesus Christ, that is the condition of every human being since the Fall, including every believer before he is saved. It is the past condition of believers and the present condition of everyone else.

A person who is spiritually dead has no life by which he can respond to spiritual things, much less live a spiritual life. No amount of pleading, begging, or demanding from God can spark the spiritually dead to newness of life. They are alienated from God and therefore alienated from His life-giving power. Notwithstanding their blasphemies, unregenerate sinners have neither the capacity to engage in, nor the interest to dwell on, spiritual matters. To the point, they are spiritual zombies—the walking dead—who do not know they are dead. They go through the daily motions of life, but they do not possess it. Apart from the monergistic work of the Holy Spirit, a sinner is nothing more than a lifeless corpse—no more capable and no less willing to respond to the gospel than a cadaver. This is the brutal truth of Total Depravity (as will be explained further in the following chapter).

While virtually all evangelicals admit that man comes into this world dead on arrival, spiritually speaking, there remains a massive disconnect as to the extent of his deadness and what it means in terms of his salvation. The confusion stems from the fact that, in their respective treatments of Ephesians 2:1-5 and Colossians 2:13, Calvinists and Arminians apply different meanings to the word *dead*. This scholastic difference of opinion has survived the better part of five hundred years.

As we have seen, Calvinists understand Paul's use of the term *dead* to be literal in connotation. Man is spiritually incapacitated and unresponsive. He is without a spiritual pulse. The natural man cannot awaken himself to spiritual consciousness any more than Lazarus could awaken himself to physical awareness (cf. John 11:43-44). When Paul writes that sinners are "dead in transgressions" Calvinists take the apostle at his literal word.

Arminians, on the other hand, take a metaphorical approach in their analysis of man's deadness. They do not look upon man as being *really* dead, at least as we understand the term, insomuch as he is simply separated from God, alienated from righteousness, and sick from sin. As it relates to the severity of Paul's language, Arminians suppose that the apostle used some license with his language; that is, he wrote in poetical, if not hyperbolical, prose to convey the degree of separation that exists between a holy God and rebellious sinners. Man is indeed dead in sin, they admit, but only in the sense of *alienation*, not in the Calvinist sense of lifelessness. Arminians conclude, therefore, that while unregenerate man is sick and alienated, he is not so flat-lined that he is incapable of contributing on his own to the *Ordo Salutis*, and by a faith that is his own. One anonymous blogger, in his attempt to refute Calvinism, put forth the free-will perspective on man's deadness in no uncertain terms:

> To be dead in sins means that we are cut off from the relationship with God that is necessary for spiritual life. Our sin separates us from a holy God and causes spiritual death. This is both actual and potential. The sinner is presently "dead" because, in the absence of faith, he is not enjoying life giving union with Christ. The sinner is potentially dead because if he continues in this state he will be forever cut off from the presence of the Lord in Hell (2 Thess. 1:9) ...

The Bible plainly teaches that those who are dead in sin resist the Holy Spirit. Now have you ever seen a corpse resist something? Of course not. So if we adopt the implications of the Calvinistic definition of "dead in sin" then we must deny that anyone who is dead in sin can resist the Holy Spirit or reject the gospel (Acts 7:51; 2 Thess. 2:10; 1 John 4:10; Rom. 10:21). Corpses can't resist or reject anything any more than they can see or hear anything. This, of course, should tell us something about the Calvinistic understanding of dead in sin. It is not biblical.

Now it is important to remember that Arminians do not deny the need for God's gracious enabling before a sinner can believe and embrace the gospel. Without divine initiative and enabling no one would ever come to God in faith. We are confident, however, that God is powerful enough to overcome our depravity and there is no need for the [Calvinist] priority of regeneration since there is no strict parallel between the inability of a physical corpse and the inability of those dead in sin. We can therefore accept the biblical teaching of depravity and God's Prevenient Grace without needing to turn the Bible on its ear in an effort to put spiritual life [regeneration] before faith.[66]

As noted by the blogger, Arminians contend that Calvinists go astray in their interpretation of Ephesians 2:1-5 and Colossians 2:13 when they equate spiritual death with biological death. We are told that they are not the same thing and should not be misconstrued as such. That is to say, natural man, while spiritually dead, can still think, talk, reason, laugh, cry, and make decisions in his life that the physically dead cannot. Therefore Arminians infer that the apostle Paul must have had something else in mind (other than literal deadness) when he referred to the unregenerate as "dead in transgressions." Thus, by interpreting

Paul's words euphemistically rather than literally, Arminians soften the blow of Scripture. Another Arminian writer frames the argument this way:

> We cannot assume that the effects of death are uniform for all the forms of death ... Unresponsiveness is really an effect that is unique to physical death and does not occur with spiritual death. ... Calvinists confuse the effects that death has on the body with the very definition of death in general ... [and] assume that part of what it means to die is to lose functionality.
>
> A dead spirit is only "dead" in the sense that God has departed from it, but that does not mean it is unable to make decisions freely including the decision to accept God if such an option were made available by God (such as through the atoning work of Christ Jesus).[67]

Here we see a spin on words that proves to be a classic case of Arminian doubletalk. "Calvinists confuse the effects that death has on the body," the writer alleges, "with the very definition of death in general." Astoundingly, this Arminian writer asks non-Arminians to suspend all common sense by blindly accepting that physical death differs in definition somehow from general death. To his way of thinking, and in Arminianism by extension, the idea of being dead in sin doesn't really mean dead in function. In physical death a corpse cannot respond or cooperate. It has no power to do either because it is dead. But there is a difference, Arminians tell us, between physical death and spiritual death. A spiritually dead person is still alive organically and, as such, possesses various abilities of function. It stands to reason: If a spiritually dead person can still function biologically he must therefore still have the functional ability in spirit to affirm or deny God's grace in regeneration. This is the standard Arminian refutation to Paul's use of the word *dead* in Ephesians 2:1-5 and Colossians 2:13.

While it true that spiritual death is demarcated from physical death in Scripture (since one is immaterial whereas the other is material), the end result for both is the same. Whether taken literally or figuratively, or when understood materially or immaterially, the word *dead* in the Bible always means dead. The Greek term from which it is translated, in fact, appears 132 times in the *Authorized Version* and 128 times in the *New American Standard Version*. In each instance, and without exception, the term has only one connotation: *lifelessness*. The idea of alienation and separation, on which Arminian tradition rests, never presents itself in any of the scriptural contexts in which the word is found.

So what exactly is the nature of man's deadness? According to *Strong's Concordance*, the Greek word *nekros* (dead), which Paul used in Ephesians 2:1-5 and Colossians 2:13, has both proper and metaphorical meanings—neither of which support the Arminian allusion to separation or alienation. Literally defined, *nekros* means "one that has breathed his last; lifeless; deceased; departed" and "one whose soul is ... without life; inanimate."[68] It is to be in a state of "declension," says *Vine's Expository Dictionary*, "inasmuch as in that state it is inactive and barren."[69] This is the proper or literal use of the word "dead" (*nekros*).

Even more concrete is Strong's metaphorical definition for *nekros*. It carries with it the symbolism of being "spiritually dead; destitute of a life that recognizes and is devoted to God, because [one is] given up to trespasses and sins; inactive as respects [to] doing right; destitute of force or power; inactive; inoperative."[70] In other words, while Arminians sidestep the literal meaning of man's spiritual deadness, the metaphorical definition for *nekros* undermines their argument. To be dead in sin, metaphorically, is to be "destitute of force or power;" it is to be spiritually "inoperative." Likewise, to be dead in sin, literally or properly, is to be "inanimate" and "without life." In either case, we learn that fallen man's *functional* abilities are dormant!

The Greek verdict is unambiguous. Paul's deliberate use of the word *nekros* teaches that natural man, in his unregenerate state, is a spiritual cadaver whose will is "inanimate," "inactive," and "inoperative." No matter how we cut the linguistic pie—whether taken literally or metaphorically—the word *nekros* likens man's ability to that of a corpse. More than just spiritually alienated or sick, a sinner is *lifeless*. His only hope for salvation rests in the grace of God to first raise him to newness of life and to infuse into him a new will and a renewed mind so that he may receive the salvation that is offered freely in Jesus Christ.

It should be pointed out, however, that Reformed Christians do not deny that alienation from God is a byproduct of Total Depravity. On this point we agree with our Arminian friends. Indeed, every human being is born into a fractured relationship with their Creator where they are estranged from His merciful love. In fact, Paul said as much in three of his epistles (cf. Gal. 5:4; Eph. 4:18; Col. 1:21). Furthermore, the Old Testament makes clear: "But your iniquities have *separated* you from your God" (Isa. 59:2, emphasis added).

Just as physical death separates the soul from the body so spiritual death, which is of greater significance, separates the soul from God. Like Adam hiding in the Garden (cf. Gen. 3:8), natural man is isolated from God. To conclude, however, that Total Depravity boils down to nothing more than mere separation from God (and to ignore Ephesians 2:1 and Colossians 2:13 concerning man's deadness) is to stop short of the Bible's full teaching on the extent of man's fallen condition (see Chapter 8).

Calvinism maintains that alienation *and* lifelessness are both derivative of being spiritually dead. The Bible describes spiritual death as a state of being that is separated from its source of life. If something or someone has been separated from its source of life, it dies a pitiful death. Take a fish out of water and it suffocates. Uproot a plant from its bed of soil and it will eventually wither and die. In the same way, separate a sinner from God, from whom the source of all life flows, and the sinner will die, both spiritually and biologically. While the separated parts still exist, the source of its life has departed and he therefore lives a dead existence.

Where Arminian tradition breaks down is its refusal to go beyond the surface teaching of Scripture and to dig deeper into *why* man is separated and alienated from God. Instead of applying the *Analogy of Faith*—which is the rule that stipulates that Scripture interprets Scripture—they go no further than the boundaries of their presuppositions and traditions. While it is certainly true in the broader context of Scripture that man is alienated from God because of his sins, upon closer examination we learn that sinful man is alienated from God ultimately because he is spiritually *dead* in his sins ("inanimate," "inactive," and "inoperative").

My father, for example, passed away in 2009 at the age of 75. His body was eventually cremated and his ashes ensconced in an ornate urn that resides in my mother's home. It goes without saying that I am now alienated from my father. We no longer enjoy the relationship we once had when he was alive. When I visit my mother's home and pay my respects to my father's memory sitting polished on the shelf, he is incapable of dialoging with me. When I whisper a term of endearment in his memory, my father does not answer. When a childhood recollection comes to mind and moves me to mutter, "I miss you dad," he does not return my call. No matter what I say or do, my dad no longer interacts with me. Why? Are we separated from one another simply because of our individual wills or conduct and behavior? The answer is obviously no. My father is alienated from me, and I from him, because of his *disposition*. In his current state he is nothing more than a pile of ash. He is lifeless. He is estranged from me ultimately because he is not alive.

So it is with the unredeemed and their relationship with God. While sin certainly receives the ultimate blame in Scripture for man's spiritual separation, the Calvinist understands such a statement to be much more comprehensive than what initially meets the eye. It is the *consequence* of Original Sin—spiritual death—that actually alienates a sinner from God, not just the fact that he practices sin. For this very reason, unless he is first regenerated, the prayers of a spiritually dead man go largely unanswered by the living God (Prov. 28:9 cf. 15:29; Ps. 66:18; Isa. 59:2; John 9:31).

Preliminary, Preparatory, & Preconditioned Regeneration

While monergism and synergism continue to be a source of contention between Calvinists and Arminians, the debate reaches new plateaus when the particulars of the Reformed *Ordo Salutis* are discussed in greater detail. At issue for many Arminians is *where* and *why* Calvinists place the work of regeneration in the salvation chain. And the same thing can be said in reverse. Calvinists balk at *where* and *why* Arminian's place regeneration in their sequence.

As already noted, Reformed Theology claims that spiritual regeneration is the monergistic work of the Holy Spirit which occurs in the heart of an elect sinner *prior* to his conversion. And this is because unregenerate man, in his bondage, desires sin more than he desires God. He is infatuated with darkness, enslaved to the world, and captivated by wickedness. Consequently, when left to his natural devices, he is incapable of believing the gospel or bending his knee to Christ. He is void of the means (1 Cor. 2:14). The Holy Spirit—in light of Christ's work of redemption—must act independently of the human will in His merciful work of regeneration, or none would be saved. A sinner cannot see the things of God, let alone appreciate God's provision of salvation, unless he is first granted a renewed constitution.

The Lord clearly taught that spiritual regeneration precedes the act of salvation. "I tell you the truth," Jesus said to Nicodemus, "no one can *see* the kingdom of God *unless* he is born again" (John 3:3, emphasis added). We can paraphrase our Lord's words this way: "Unless a sinner is first spiritually regenerated, he or she cannot even begin to *see* the kingdom of God, much less believe in it or enter it." Sinners must be raised from spiritual death to new life before salvation is even visible. Only then are they in the irresistible position to believe in Jesus Christ and "see the kingdom of God."

Spiritual regeneration is *not* tantamount to salvation—as many evangelists like Graham and Chafer erroneously preach (see Chapter 6)—but lays the groundwork for it. The apostle Paul implied as much when he said: "no one can say, 'Jesus is Lord,' except by the Holy Spirit" (1 Cor. 12:3). Reformed Christians understand this verse to say that it is only through the preliminary, preparatory, and preconditioned work of the Holy Spirit that a sinner's darkened mind is illuminated and he is able to profess Christ as the Lord of lords, and *sincerely* mean it (cf. Rev. 17:4; 19:6).

The rationale behind preliminary regeneration is not only commonsensical but is native to orthodoxy and informs much of our historical theology. Various confessions, catechisms, and articles of the faith say so. The 1833 New Hampshire Baptist Confession, for example, reads as follows:

> We believe that, in order to be saved, sinners must [first] be regenerated, or born again; that regeneration consists in giving a holy disposition to the mind; that it is effected in a manner above our comprehension by the power of the Holy Spirit, in connection with divine truth, so as to secure our voluntary obedience to the gospel; and that its proper evidence appears in the holy fruits of repentance, and faith, and newness of life.

Most Arminians balk at this point and reject outright any teaching which dares to suggest that spiritual regeneration is preliminary, preparatory, or a precondition to salvation, to say nothing about being monergistic and devoid of human decision. They flat-out ignore our Lord's teaching to Nicodemus in John 3:3, which we already took care to note, and bypass Paul's words in 1 Corinthians 12:3. As proof of their denial, Dave Hunt and Norman Geisler state the Arminian view succinctly: "Those dead in sin," says Hunt, "can and must believe [first] to be regenerated"[71] and "Faith is logically prior to regeneration," adds Geisler.[72] Both men see saving faith as a precondition for regeneration rather than regeneration as a precondition for saving faith. And they are not alone in their analysis. In his commentary on Romans 7, Jacobus Arminius proved to be the trailblazer for this teaching: "Besides," he wrote, "even true and living faith in Christ precedes regeneration strictly taken."[73]

Putting aside the clear teaching of John 3:3 and 1 Corinthians 12:3 for a moment, we must take Hunt, Geisler, and Arminius to task. The Bible teaches emphatically, as we will see in the following two chapters, that natural man is besotted with iniquity and comfortably entrenched in darkness; he hates the light and will not come into it (John 3:19-20). And since man's hardened resistance to God is seated in his affections—the inner core of his being—only God, by His grace, can lovingly change, overcome, and disarm man's rebellious disposition. The natural man, apart from the quickening work of the Holy Spirit, will not come to Christ on his own since he is at enmity with God and cannot understand spiritual things. Like Lydia whom "the Lord opened her heart to respond to the things spoken by Paul" (Acts 16:14), God must give His elect people spiritual life and understanding whereby their hearts are opened to "respond to the things" of Christ in faith (see Chapter 18). Only then can and will salvation follow.

To suggest, as Arminians like Hunt and Geisler do, that saving faith comes before regeneration, rather than regeneration before faith, is to put the cart before the horse, so to speak. It is to credit dead men with spiritual abilities that the Bible does not ascribe to them outside the new birth. In the end, Jacobus Arminius, the Remonstrants, classical Arminians, Hunt, Geisler, and today's crop of libertarian believers champion a higher view of fallen man's abilities than do the Scriptures.

While I am grateful for the lasting friendships I enjoy with a number of good-hearted Arminians, many of whom sit under my teaching week after week and whose passion for Scripture I respect, it's difficult for me to remain silent concerning much of what they believe. I have no desire to fracture relationships beyond the strain already evident between Calvinists and Arminians. But it is my earnest passion (as a Christian) and my responsibility (as a clergyman) to confront inaccuracy with truth whenever as I see it, and no matter where it lies or with whom it originates. While we can agree to disagree agreeably

over peripheral minutia, we must not shy away from promoting
the whole truth of Scripture, especially as it relates to the
character and work of God. Thus, it is in the spirit of truth
that I ask my Arminian friends: How, exactly, are dead sinners
supposed to respond savingly to the gospel—so as to enter into
union with Christ—if they are not first regenerated? Where does
the spiritual cognizance come from that enables the dead to
respond in faith if regeneration has not first occurred?

The answers that are given by a preponderance of Arminians
to the foregoing questions, unfortunately, are as theologically
muddled as they are philosophically inconsistent. In the end,
they leave us with an unsatisfactory view of regeneration that
elevates the autonomy of man to unwarranted levels while
demoting the freedom of God to unacceptable lows. They leave
us with a theological system that wreaks havoc on Scripture
and subverts the historical theology of the Church. They
leave us with teaching that robs many Christians of the joy of
their salvation (since they can never be sure it's secure) while
belittling the majestic omnipotence and sovereignty of God. And
lastly, Arminians leave us with a belief system that jeopardizes
the marvelous work of regeneration by putting it into the hands
of reprobate men to finalize. I have no choice, therefore, but to
concur with the rather hard words of Presbyterian author Brian
Schwertley:

> A proper understanding of the new birth is
> crucial to the Christian faith. An unbiblical view
> of the new birth will compromise and pervert
> many other important doctrines (e.g., the
> doctrines about God, original sin, human ability,
> predestination, perseverance of the saints, etc.).
> It is remarkable that most fundamentalists and
> evangelicals who champion the new birth have
> completely perverted the doctrine. They have
> made it dependent on man's choice rather than
> God's choice. There is no excuse for anyone to
> misunderstand this doctrine; the Bible is very
> clear in this area, as we have seen. If you do not

believe what the Bible teaches regarding the new birth, then you must repent and submit to Christ's teaching. If you have changed your view of the new birth and yet find yourself in a church that rejects the Bible's teaching in this area, it's time for you to find a new church. Jesus Christ clearly implied that men who did not understand this doctrine were not fit to be teachers of His people (cf. John. 3:10).[74]

At long last, the rickety train of Arminianism can be mapped as follows: (1) dead men must *want* to be saved; (2) dead men must *seek* out salvation; (3) dead men must *self-generate* the faith to believe; (4) dead men must *repent*; and lastly, (5) dead men must *cooperate* with the Holy Spirit by making a free-will "decision" to accept Christ. Only when the foregoing is achieved, so we are told, is the dead sinner *then* made alive in Christ.

The door remains wide open in Arminian theology for unregenerate men to frustrate the sovereign intentions of a thrice-holy God in saving him. The Father may decree a person's salvation, the Son may die to obtain his redemption, and the Spirit may exercise His divine power in bringing conviction and enlightenment. But all of this, Arminian tradition tells us, is not enough to bring about salvation unless the will of the *dead* creature cooperates and perseveres. This is what I refer to as the *anti-evangelion*, or the bad news, of the synergistic gospel. God's predetermined decrees, theoretically speaking, rise and fall under the supposed cooperation of unregenerate sinners.

The differences between the two sides could not be more pronounced. If the Calvinist's take on Original Sin is correct, then the sons of Adam are spiritually dead in *totality*; morally incapable, unable, and unwilling to reconcile with God. Owing to their deadness, sinners are not free to choose Christ but are enslaved to sin (John 8:34; Rom. 6:6, 16-18). God must therefore do the reconciling on their behalf. And this He has done in eternity past, the Calvinist teaches, by electing unconditionally certain souls to make alive in Christ in order that they may believe in Him (1 Cor. 15:22; Eph. 2:1-5; Col. 2:13). This newness of life includes the spiritual ears to hear and the ability to obey the command of Christ so that, once awakened from the coffin of depravity, the sinner will irresistibly respond like Lazarus and "come out!"

Conversely, if the Arminian's take on Original Sin is correct, then the sons of Adam are only *partially* dead. They still possess the wherewithal to respond to the gospel invitation by an act of their unregenerate will. They are not only morally capable of igniting the quest for salvation on their own via common grace[75] but are also the final determinate as to whether or not God's hope of saving them will be realized. And only when sinners respond positively from their self-will and accept Jesus Christ as their Savior are they subsequently regenerated and inducted into the fold of the Elect.

Thus, one side of the camp sees salvation as the work of God alone (monergism), whereas the other views it as an initial work of God that is completed by man (synergism). One side sees regeneration as a precondition for salvation (Calvinism) while the other views it as the result (Arminianism).

The all-too-important issue on the table before us, therefore, is the first petal in the T.U.L.I.P. acrostic—*Total Depravity.* To what degree are men depraved? A proper understanding of the answer is indispensable, for the validity of monergistic regeneration and the biblical view of God's sovereignty in salvation hang in the balance.

Reflection Questions:

1. Why do you suppose unregenerate men insist upon contributing to their salvation?

2. What kind of spiritual abilities does the unregenerate person have?

   a. Does unregenerate man have the ability to spiritually see on his own?
   b. Does unregenerate man have the ability to spiritually discern on his own?

   c.   Does unregenerate man have the ability to seek after God on his own?

3. Taken either literally or metaphorically, what does the Bible mean when it says that unregenerate man is "dead in sin"?

4. If a chosen, predestined, and called sinner is "dead in sin" and therefore void of spiritual ability, what is the most reasonable explanation for his conversion? In other words, what best explains the fact the some spiritually dead people eventually do come to faith in Christ, repent of their sin, and surrender to the lordship of Christ?

Chapter 8

The Walking Dead

Filmgoers are no strangers to a good ghost story. With the advent of motion pictures and television a century ago, screen depictions of ghouls and goblins have scared up profitable returns for Hollywood. Even the classical works of Shakespeare, Dickens, and Wilde—each of whom published tall tales about ghosts—have been made into cinematic masterpieces. From poetical yarns such as *Hamlet, Macbeth,* and *The Canterville Ghost,* to more populist and contemporary blockbusters such as *A Christmas Carol* and *Poltergeist,* Hollywood's take on the *undead* has haunted audiences for decades. The notion of wandering spirits portrayed on celluloid never fails to capture our notice at the box office.

But not all ghost stories are spooky; many span a variety of film genres. There are those rare gems that thrive as comedies, such as *Ghostbusters,* starring Bill Murray and Dan Aykroyd, while others succeed as suspenseful thrillers like Harrison Ford's *What Lies Beneath.* But seldom does a movie about ghosts arouse our collective romanticism or make a cultural splash like one such film did in 1990. Nominated for five Academy Awards, including Best Picture, the romantic thriller *Ghost,* starring Patrick Swayze, Demi Moore, and Whoopi Goldberg, took the North American box office by storm.

An unapologetic crowd pleaser, *Ghost* follows the spirit of a mild-mannered New Yorker as he attempts to both solve his own murder and say goodbye to his devoted girlfriend. Patrick Swayze stars as Sam Wheat, an investment financier who discovers financial irregularities at work and is promptly murdered in what is disguised as a random mugging. Devastated, his live-in girlfriend Molly (Moore) is incapable of being consoled. As Sam gathers himself in the non-corporeal afterlife, his spirit begins to learn how to reach out to the living, primarily through a seemingly bogus psychic named Oda Mae Brown (Goldberg). After a lifetime of swindling suckers, Oda Mae is as surprised as anyone to learn that her clairvoyant skills are apparently legitimate. Through a series of ethereal encounters with Sam's spirit, she becomes determined to help him on his dual-quest to solve his murder and save Molly from imminent danger.

With its sentimental and sexually charged love story sautéed in the lore of the supernatural, *Ghost* struck a chord with audiences. And after earning a quarter billion dollars at the domestic box office, it went on to become a worldwide juggernaut. The rest, as they say, is cinematic history.

But the success of *Ghost* did not come without theological headaches for the Church. Spawned by the film's popularity, an albatross of hucksters, spinsters, and cultists—most of whom claimed to have the power to channel the dead—set up shop on television hocking their medium abilities for a price. And no shortage of customers—especially among women—greeted them! Hoping to capture for themselves the mystical romance portrayed by Swayze and Moore on the silver-screen were countless grieving widows eager to make contact with their dead husbands.

Even stranger, séances were suddenly *en vogue* again, as they once were in Houdini's day nearly a century before. And still other thrill seekers started dubious careers as "ghost hunters." Alas, more and more Westerners began to take seriously Eastern mysticism and occultism and, in so doing, legitimized a brand of paganism frowned upon in Scripture (Deut. 18:9-13; Lev. 20:6, 27; Isa. 8:19 cf. 1 Chron. 10:13-14). Proving to be more than just popcorn-fare entertainment, *Ghost* sparked a quasi-religious revival that sent shockwaves throughout evangelical circles for years to come.

At the center of the wreckage left in the wake of *Ghost's* success was the mystery surrounding the human soul. Irreligious people from all walks of life started asking questions once thought taboo by the sophisticated elite: *Do the dead really have the ability to reach out to the living? Is the spirit of man on a quest for good?* Moreover, *Does man's spirit have the ability to make contact with God?* Predictably, the motion picture industry offered little in terms of sound theological advice. Instead, through films like *Ghost*, they pointed people to eccentric and charismatic mystics who show-boated a gift for gab. It seems virtually everything and everyone was consulted about the condition of the human spirit, except, of course, for the Bible and the God it reveals.

When probing the anonymity of the human spirit, Christians can give confident answers to a skeptical world. The Bible is not silent on the topic. Nevertheless, many Christians stake their ground on opposite ends of the theological spectrum and offer conflicting answers that often confuse sincere inquirers. For example, while both Calvinists and Arminians agree that the art of pagan spiritism is demonic—despite its glamorization in *Ghost*—both sides disagree over the nature of a person's spirit.

Reformed Theology teaches that human beings enter this world spiritually stillborn. They possess neither the ambition nor the cognizance to pursue spiritual matters of a godly sort. In counter distinction, Christians who subscribe to free-will theology maintain that sinners are born spiritually alive, albeit handicapped, and indeed possess the wherewithal to seek reconciliation with God. So which side is theologically accurate? Does reprobate man possess enough life and the necessary resolve to reach out to the living God?

The Bible reveals an apparent conundrum when it comes to the condition of the human spirit. On one hand, it teaches that man's soul was created *immortal* by God (Gen. 2:7 cf. Psa. 49:7-9; Eccl. 12:7; Dan. 12:2-3; Matt. 25:46; 1 Cor. 15-12-19) while on the other hand it teaches that man is born spiritually *lifeless* on account of Original Sin (Eph. 2:1-5; Col. 2:13). To put it simply, man is born spiritually eternal while simultaneously spiritually dead. Herein lies the mystery. We conclude, therefore, that the only sufficient answer is that man's spirit is everlasting in terms of its existence but dead in sin as it relates to its operability. All men, says the apostle Paul, are "dead even while [they] lived" (1 Tim. 5:6). That is to say, in the words of Dr. R.C. Sproul, "To be spiritually dead is to be diabolically alive."[76]

If fallen man is spiritually dead, the Calvinist reasons, then it logically follows that he is incapable on his own to seek after, respond to, or believe in his Creator. On balance, because the biologically dead can do neither of these things, it stands to reason that neither can the spiritually dead. Thus, the view one takes concerning salvation will be determined, to a large extent, by the view one takes concerning Original Sin and its effects on the human condition.

The Calvinistic view of man's spiritual state of being is bleak. The Bible teaches that man's heart is "deceitful and desperately wicked" (Jer. 17:9) and his thoughts "continually evil" (Gen. 6:5). Man is born "dead in transgressions and sins" (Eph. 2:1-5 cf. Psa. 51:5; 58:3; Col. 2:13) and held captive by his love for iniquity (John 3:19; 8:34). Owing to his spiritual deadness, a sinner will not—and cannot—seek the living God (Rom. 3:10-11). He loves the "darkness instead of light" (John 3:19) and "does not accept the things that come from the Spirit of God, for they are foolishness to him" (1 Cor. 2:14 cf. 1:18). Blinded by Satan (2 Cor. 4:4), sinners naturally "suppress the truth by their wickedness" (Rom. 1:18) and "their thinking [becomes] futile and their foolish hearts [are] darkened" (v. 21b). They willfully live in disobedience and rebellion while convincing themselves they are in the right (Prov. 14:12).

The post-Fall condition of mankind is referred to in Reformed circles as *Total Depravity*. And it is on this point that the merits of Reformed Theology ultimately rest.

When Calvinists speak of man as being totally depraved, they mean that man's nature is corrupt, perverse, and sinful throughout. The adjective "total" does not mean that each sinner is as totally or completely corrupt in his actions and thoughts as he possibly can be. When judged by human standards, for example, we can see an obvious degree of separation that existed between the depravity of Adolf Hitler and that of Mother Theresa. Instead, the word "total" is used to indicate the *whole* of man's being, the sum total of all his faculties—to include his body, soul, mind, will, and heart. The entire essence of man is polluted by iniquity.

But the doctrine of Total Depravity cannot be whittled down to just mean inherent wickedness. It also encompasses disturbing elements such as man's bondage to sin, his oppression by Satan, his spiritual blindness, his spiritual deadness, and his moral inability to accept the gospel. When combined, these six sobering truths—wickedness, enslavement, blindness, oppression, deadness, and inability—define the depravity of man in totality.

The first factor of Total Depravity is *wickedness*: man is innately and pervasively sinful. Contrary to the teaching of Pelagius, who taught that human beings are born spiritually innocent or as a blank slate (see Chapter 2), the Bible teaches that man is steeped in sin from the womb. This is known in schools of theology as Original Sin or Adamic Sin. The scriptural basis for Original Sin is found in Romans 5:12-21 and 1 Corinthians 15:22, in which Paul identifies Adam as our federal parent whose transgression in the Garden brought physical and spiritual death to his posterity. Owing to Original Sin, mankind's wickedness is therefore intrinsic.

Scripture teaches that mankind enters the world in a fallen condition. We are sinful "from the womb;" "from birth;" and "from childhood." To the point, Moses tells us that "every inclination of [a man's] heart is evil *from childhood*," (Gen. 8:21 cf. 6:5, emphasis added). Moreover, "Even *from birth* the wicked go astray," writes David, "*from the womb* they are wayward and speak lies" (Psa. 58:3, emphasis added). David implies elsewhere that, like himself, all men are "brought forth in iniquity" and "in sin ... conceived" (Psa. 51:5, NKJV). Human beings, as Paul puts it another way, are "by nature the children of wrath;" born at "enmity with God" (Rom. 5:10; Col. 1:21; James 4:4). We are "by nature objects of wrath" bent on "gratifying the cravings of our sinful nature and following its desires and thoughts" (Eph. 2:3).

Like apostate Israel, with whom universal depravity can be easily compared, mankind is a "rebel from birth" (Isa. 48:8) where "everyone is ungodly and wicked, every mouth speaks vileness" (Isa. 9:17b) and among whom "not one upright man remains ... The best of them is like a brier, the most upright worse than a thorn hedge" (Mic. 7:1). Analogous to wayward Judah, sinful men are "eager to act corruptly in all they [do]" (Zeph. 3:7); they "are vile and corrupt, who drink up evil like water" (Job 15:16). "They go from one sin to another," adds Jeremiah, "they weary themselves from sinning" (Jer. 9:3, 5).

This innate wickedness, which ensconces all men from conception, pollutes a person to the core. In other words, man's corruption is *total*, infecting every part of him. The penmen of Scripture catalog this truth repeatedly in stark detail, listing the human heart, mind, conscience, mouth, throat, lips, tongue, eyes, feet, and body as collateral damage. Nothing inside or outside a human being remains unmarred by sin.

Solomon lamented, "The hearts of men ... are full of evil and there is madness in their hearts" (Eccl. 9:3). Paul bemoaned that "their minds and consciences are corrupted" (Tit. 1:15), including their "throats," "tongues," "lips," "mouths," "feet," and "eyes" (Rom. 3:13-18, 23). He also likened man's flesh to a "body of sin" and a "wretched ... body of death" (Rom. 6:6; 7:24). Jeremiah added that "The heart is deceitful above all things, and desperately wicked" (Jer. 17:9, KJV). And David lamented that man's mouth is "full of curses and lies and threats; trouble and evil are under his tongue" (Psa. 10:7). In short, "All men are liars" (Psa. 116:11). These are but a handful of verses that capture the profound impact of Adamic sin on the human race. Again, man's entire faculty system—his heart, mind, conscience, mouth, throat, lips, tongue, eyes, feet, and flesh—has been perilously flawed by the effects of the Fall.

Given Scripture's testimony concerning human reprobation, it is no wonder that the psalmist Asaph rendered the following verdict: "From their callous hearts comes iniquity; *the evil conceit of their minds knows no limits*" (Psa. 73:7, emphasis added). Man's love for sin, in other words, is boundless. And because this is tragically the case, Jesus took a dim view of those he came to save. In fact, he denounced his disciples—and all of humanity be extension—as transparently "evil" (Matt. 7:11; 12:34; Luke 11:13); comprised of "men [who] loved darkness instead of light because their deeds were evil" (John 3:19). We conclude, therefore, in light of the biblical evidences cited, that what was written of stubborn Israel can be rightly applied to the entire human family: "Your whole head is injured, your whole heart afflicted. From the sole of your foot to the top of your head there is no soundness" (Isa. 1:5b-6).

In the final analysis, Job, Moses, David, Solomon, Isaiah, Jeremiah, Asaph, Paul, and Jesus all bear witness to man's inborn wickedness and total corruption. It encompasses all that man is, both inside and out. For this reason the Bible concludes, "There is not a righteous man on earth who does what is right and never sins" (Eccl. 7:20); "for all have sinned and fall short of the glory of God" (Rom. 3:23 cf. 5:12); and "All of us have become like one who is unclean ... and like the wind our sins sweep us away" (Isa. 64:6).

The second factor that makes up Total Depravity is *spiritual enslavement*: mankind is in bondage to sin. The Savior revealed this sober truth to a group of self-righteous Jews who saw themselves as "Abraham's descendants [who] have never been slaves of anyone" (John 8:33). In arguably the most heated exchange recorded in Scripture, Christ pronounced his ruling against them: "I tell you the truth, everyone who sins is a *slave to sin*" (John 8:34, emphasis added). His indictment is all-inclusive and couldn't have been clearer. Every single human being is born genetically enslaved to sin; the strongest evidence for which is that all human beings sin habitually and without regret.

From his own life in particular and from his observations of the world in general, a contemplative Solomon could see clearly the evidence for mankind's spiritual imprisonment. Enslaved, in bondage, and held captive to their flesh, he wrote of the wicked: "the cords of his sin hold him fast" (Prov. 5:22). To that end, he lamented that the reprobate cannot free themselves from their captivity. "As no one has power over the wind to contain it," he concluded, "so wickedness will not release those who practice it" (Eccl. 8:8). In other words, there is no parole program available to those imprisoned by sin.

Likewise, the apostle Paul had much to say about man's bondage. He writes that sinners are "unspiritual, sold as a slave to sin," whose "sinful nature [is] a slave to the law of sin" (Rom. 7:14b, 25b). A person's evil nature is his taskmaster, he prefaced earlier, to which "both Jews and Greeks" inevitably submit (Rom. 3:9-12). Men are "foolish, disobedient, deceived and *enslaved* by all kinds of passions and pleasures." They conduct their lives "in malice and envy, being hated and hating one another" (Tit. 3:3, emphasis added). He reminded the Galatians that "the whole world is a prisoner of sin" (Gal. 3:9) and that, prior to their conversion, they "were in slavery under the basic principles of the world ... slaves to those who by nature are not gods" (Gal. 4:3, 8). The apostle was unflinching when he twice concluded that all men are "*slaves to sin*, which leads to death" and "*slaves to sin* ... free from the control of righteousness" (Rom. 6:16, 20, emphasis added).

On this issue, the apostle Paul had a compatriot in the apostle Peter. Speaking of unregenerate man, Peter wrote, "they themselves are *slaves of depravity*—for a man is a slave to whatever has mastered him" (2 Pet. 2:19, emphasis added). Like Simon the Sorcerer who was disgraced by Peter, the final conclusion from Scripture is that all men are naturally "full of bitterness and *captive to sin*" (Act 8:23, emphasis added).

Dr. James Montgomery Boice (1938-2000), a Reformed theologian, radio host, and evangelical speaker, was straightforward in his treatment on man's enslaved condition. He wrote:

> There is no such thing as absolute freedom for anyone. No human is free to do everything he or she may want to do. There is one being in the universe who is *totally* free, of course. That is God. But all others are limited by or enslaved by someone or something ... Since you and I are human beings and not God, we can never be autonomous. We must either be slaves to sin or slaves of Jesus Christ.[77]

The third factor that makes up Total Depravity is *spiritual blindness*: mankind walks in darkness. God created man to have fellowship with him and to live in light. As such, Adam enjoyed full and free communion with his Creator while tending to his garden. But when Adam and Eve sinned, their freedom was retarded and their spiritual growth arrested. Since then, Adam's posterity has only been able to hear the voice of God and see biblical truth as God has enabled them. In their natural state, the sons of Adam (all unregenerate sinners) are deaf and dumb to spiritual truth, and "are darkened in their understanding" (Eph. 4:18). They walk in abject sightlessness.

Even more shocking, we learn from Scripture that this burden of blindness under which man labors is attributed to both God and Satan, who apparently work in tandem but toward different ends. The god of this age, Satan, blinds the minds of unbelievers so they cannot understand the gospel, whereas God makes them spiritually blind and spiritually deaf so they cannot turn and believe. This joint-operation is indicative of God's judgment against *Adamic* depravity. Concerning Satan's role, Paul declared:

> And even if our gospel is veiled, it is veiled to those who are perishing. The god of this age has blinded the minds of unbelievers, so that they cannot see the light of the gospel of the glory of Christ, who is the image of God (2 Cor. 4:3-4).

The sad reality concerning man's intrinsic blindness goes beyond the words of Paul in 2 Corinthians 4 and is borne out in Isaiah 6, John 9, and John 12. Even after Jesus had performed countless signs and wonders in their presence, to include healing the blind and raising the dead, the Jewish leadership refused to believe in him. As incontestable as his miracles were, the Jews *would not* nor *could not* accept what they saw. God had yet to shed their chains of degeneracy and grant them eyes to see or ears to hear. This was something the prophet Isaiah had foreseen seven hundred years earlier, which the apostle John took care to recite: "Lord, who has believed our message and to whom has the arm of the Lord been revealed?" (John 12:37-

38 cf. Isa. 53:1). Their spiritual blindness was compounded by
God's divine blindness. John continues:

> For this reason they could not believe, because,
> as Isaiah says elsewhere: "[God] has blinded
> their eyes and deadened their hearts, so they can
> neither see with their eyes, nor understand with
> their hearts" (John 12:39–40).

The Jewish leadership *would not* believe in Jesus because
they *could not* believe in him. "Israel's watchmen are blind, they
all lack knowledge; they are all mute dogs, they cannot bark;
they lie around and dream, they love to sleep" (Isa. 56:10). Like
all men shackled by unbelief, they were totally depraved. And
in keeping with their depravity, God compounded their innate,
satanic blindness with divine blindness. "As it is written," Paul
said of the Jews, "'God gave them a spirit of stupor, eyes that
could not see and ears that could not hear, to this very day'"
(Rom. 11:8 cf. Deut. 29:4). But, as already noted in 2 Corinthians
4:3-4 and Ephesians 4:18, this spiritual blindness does not
belong to the Jews alone. It is universal in scope.

Spiritual blindness reveals the lost man in his fallen state.
He cannot see that which is spiritual any more than a blind man
can see that which is natural. No person apart from Jesus has
been born without this fatal handicap. And only God, through
the miracle of the new birth, can open blind eyes (cf. John 9:32).
The will of man is irrelevant. "Ears that hear and eyes that see,"
said King Solomon, "the Lord has made them both" (Prov.
20:12).

The fourth factor that makes up Total Depravity is *spiritual
oppression*: mankind is under the spell of Satan. As we've
already noted, "The god of this age [Satan] has blinded the minds
of unbelievers so that they cannot see the light of the gospel of
the glory of Christ" (2 Cor. 4:4). In their state of reprobation,
sinners are subject to the prince of darkness; they are shackled
under his thumb, as it were. They follow "the ways of this world
and of the ruler of the kingdom of the air, the spirit who is now
at work in those who are disobedient" (Eph. 2:2).

The apostle John wrote that "the whole world is under the control of the evil one" (1 John 5:19). Peter said to Cornelius that "all ... were under the power of the devil" (Acts 10:38). Likewise, Jesus made clear to Paul that sinners, at their base level, are fettered under "the power of Satan" (Acts 26:18). Like the Pharisees who were scolded by our Lord on the Mount of Olives, an unregenerate person "belong[s] to [his] father, the devil, and [he] want[s] to carry out [his] father's desire" (John 8:44). The entire human race, we read in Scripture, is captured in "the trap of the devil, who has taken them captive to do his will" (2 Tim. 2:26).

The fifth factor that makes up Total Depravity is *spiritual deadness*. If intrinsic wickedness, spiritual enslavement, spiritual blindness, and demonic subjugation aren't bad enough, we are told in Scripture that mankind also suffers from spiritual lifelessness. Bringing to mind their former way of life prior to regeneration, Paul reminded the Christians in Colosse: "you were dead in your sins and in the uncircumcision of your sinful nature" (Col. 2:13). To his protégé Timothy he spoke of unbelievers as "dead even while [they] lived" (1 Tim. 5:6). Speaking of the false teachers of his day, Jude cursed them as "twice dead" (Jude 1:12). And to the Ephesians, Paul said:

> As for you, you were *dead in your transgressions and sins,* in which you used to live ... *All of us* also lived among them at one time, gratifying the cravings of our sinful nature and following its desires and thoughts. Like the rest, we were by nature objects of wrath. But because of his great love for us, God, who is rich in mercy, made us alive with Christ even when we were *dead in transgressions*—it is by grace you have been saved (Eph. 2:1-5, emphasis added).

The unregenerate, according to the New Testament, are in a state of lifelessness and subjection. They live in a continual state of condemnation. No person is excluded. "All of us" says Paul, prior to our regeneration, lived a life devoted to "gratifying the cravings of our sinful nature and following its desires and thoughts" (Eph. 2:3). This deadness is the universal state of all men apart from Christ. The spiritually dead can no more see spiritual truth or choose Christ than a rotting corpse can play tennis or debate philosophy. Paul sums it up candidly in Romans 5:12: "Therefore, just as sin entered the world through one man, *and death through sin,* and in this way *death came to all men,* because all sinned" (emphasis added).

On this point it should be noted that Arminians put forth a couple of reasonable questions to which Calvinist must give answers. If Total Depravity is true and mankind is innately wicked, enslaved to sin, in bondage to Satan, spiritually blind, and spiritually dead, why does the Bible then teach (no less than fifteen times) that God occasionally hardens the hearts of certain sinners? Isn't it pointless at best and redundant at worst for God to do so if sinners are already spiritually depraved?

The answer, as I see it, is as much philosophical as it is theological. Total Depravity is God's *universal* judgment on *all* mankind in consequence for the federal sin of Adam. Men everywhere incur this all-pervasive sentence at conception. With that being said, while mankind is totally depraved and dead in Adam, it is true that God still providentially hardens *particular* hearts beyond their original depravity. He mindfully does so not because He needs to or because a sinner's natural depravity and spiritual subjugation are insufficient for the task. Rather, in this way God compounds His *universal* judgment with His *personal* wrath. Another way of saying this is that God hands certain sinners over to the full extent of their depravity in personal judgment against them. In the words of Paul, "Therefore God gave them over ... to a depraved mind" whereby they "received in themselves the due penalty for their perversion" (Rom. 1:24-28). Ezekiel prophesied: "I also gave them over to statutes that were not good and laws they could not live by; I let them become defiled ... that I might fill them with horror so they would know that I am the Lord" (Ezek. 20:25-26).

Gary Ridgeway, for example, the notorious Green River serial killer who was apprehended in 2001 and is currently serving a life-sentence in prison without parole, was recently indicted for the 1982 slaying of a 20-year-old woman. Ridgeway received a second life-sentence for the crime. Why? What's the point? Why indict, arraign, and put on trial a convicted criminal who is already serving a life-sentence in prison for other homicides? Why issue a second life-sentence when the first one is more than sufficient for meting out justice?

It boils down to moral principle. While another life-sentence will not change Ridgeway's state of being in any way—he is already behind bars for the rest of his life—his additional sentencing has more to do with morality than legality. As redundant as it very well is, a second life-sentence is, at best, a legal formality. The true intent behind it, however, is to demonstrate society's ethical indignation for the killer *himself*. In other words, beyond the illegalities of his crimes, there is the *personal* indignation society has for the killer. And it is this moral outrage against Ridgeway that instigates further judgment against him, even if such judgment is ultimately superfluous.

And so it is with God hardening the hearts of certain people. Although the human race is collectively and legally imprisoned unto spiritual death because of Adamic sin, God hardens the hearts of certain individuals beyond their depravity out of *personal* indignation. That is to say, whereas Total Depravity is God's *universal* judgment on the human family so the hardening of certain hearts is His *personal* judgment against those who knowingly "suppress the truth by their wickedness, since what may be known about God is plain to them, because God has made it plain to them" (Rom. 1:18-19). Like issuing a second life-sentence to a convicted felon, God "hardens whom he wants to harden" (Rom. 9:18) with the intent "that he might destroy them totally, exterminating them without mercy" (Josh. 11:20).

That God goes beyond man's universal depravity and hardens hearts—though seemingly gratuitous—is simply a matter of prerogative rooted in His judgment against *that* individual. It is no wonder, then, that Isaiah lamented: "Why, O Lord, *do you make us wander from your ways and harden our hearts* so we do not revere you?" (Isa. 63:17, emphasis added). Notice how Isaiah not only laid the blame for Israel's hardening at the footsteps of a sovereign God but also credited their backsliding to His divine providence. God judged Israel *personally*, in anger against them, by hardening their hearts further.

The testimony of Scripture reveals that man's spiritual condition is tragically desperate. The human race is instinctively wicked, enslaved to sin, spiritually blind, under the dominion of Satan, and spiritually dead. Man is totally, wholly, and universally depraved. As a result, human beings are actuated by wrong principles. The thoughts of unregenerate man, including his words and deeds, are corrupt because they all flow from a corrupt source that is beyond human repair. Apart from God's enablement, a sinner *cannot* choose, much less desire, to perform spiritual acts of goodness. He *cannot* generate the love of God in his own heart. And he *cannot* do anything meriting salvation. In short, he is spiritually, emotionally, and mentally powerless.

It is not surprising, then, to learn that King David and the apostle Paul each admitted that not one human being in the history of the fallen world ever voluntarily and willingly "seeks God" (Rom. 3:11 cf. Psa. 14:1-3; 53:1-3). Far from demonstrating any godly inclination, the unregenerate "suppress the truth [of God] by their wickedness" (Rom. 1:18). So while Scripture famously says in John 3:16 that "whosoever" comes to Christ will be saved (a favorite verse for Arminians [see Chapter 17]), David and Paul remind us that "whosoever" ends up really being *no one* at all. Isaiah adds, "No one calls on your name or strives to lay hold of you" (Isa. 64:7) and "We all, like sheep, have gone astray, each of us has turned to his own way" (53:6). Man's inability and unwillingness to "seek God," we learn, is not only universal in scope but woefully evident in practice.

I belabor this point for good reason. What we understand about the human condition, prior to regeneration, ultimately determines what we understand about theology. When left in their natural state, men are unable to repent of their sin, ill-equipped to believe the gospel, and powerless to come to Christ. They have neither the ability of will nor the moral inclination to facilitate their redemption. Like Lazarus—who was four days dead in a tomb in Bethany—sinners are spiritually incognizant.

They are blinded by Satan, deaf to spiritual truth, and enslaved to the flesh; their minds are darkened by sin and their hearts imprisoned by their satanic taskmaster. This ugly truth behind Total Depravity led Charles Spurgeon to conclude: "As the salt flavors every drop in the Atlantic, so does sin affect every atom of our nature. It is so sadly there, so abundantly there, that if you cannot detect it, you are deceived."[78]

Despite the plethora of biblical evidence already noted, it seems Arminians, semi-Pelagians, Pelagians, and anti-Calvinists everywhere protest with extreme prejudice such Calvinistic coloring of Scripture. Each group argues in their own way but to the same end. They reject Total Depravity in favor of *Partial* Depravity.

Here we reach the ultimate point of separation between semi-Pelagianism and Augustinianism; between Calvinism and Arminianism; and between Rome and the Reformation. Arminianism softens the blow of Scripture and purports that an unregenerate sinner, who is dead in sin and in bondage to wickedness and Satan, has the ability to shed his chains on his own, revive his spiritual vitality, and muster the required faith so that he may be regenerated afterward. In a very real sense salvation is not so much a gift in this schema as it is a reward for overcoming all of the obstacles inherent to Total Depravity. God takes the initiative, Arminians admit, but men must cooperate and meet God in the middle. Spiritually dead men must work with God somehow to *pre*-regenerate themselves in order to take a mediatory step toward full regeneration. They must willingly respond to common grace by overcoming their inherent wickedness, enslavement to sin, satanic oppression, and their blindness and oblige God in His redemptive purposes. If the sinner refuses to cooperate with the initial pricking of the Holy Spirit, then grace is to no avail.

Why do free-will evangelicals, who have such a high view of Scripture, err so badly on such an important aspect of Christian doctrine? The answer, sadly, is because they subscribe to a defective view of Original Sin and reject God's absolute sovereignty over man in salvation. If man is spiritually dead, helpless, enslaved, and a hater of God who is blind and deaf to spiritual truth (as the Bible clearly teaches) then man cannot cooperate with God at all in regeneration.

How can a spiritually dead person (Eph. 2:1-5)—who hates the way of holiness (John 3:19-21; 8:44), who hates Jesus Christ (John 15:18, 24-25), who dwells in darkness (John 1:4-5), who has a heart of stone (Ezek. 11:19), who is helpless (Ezek. 16:4-6), who cannot repent (Jer. 13:23), who is enslaved to Satan (Acts 26:17-18), and who cannot see or comprehend divine truth (1 Cor. 2:14)—transform into someone who not only understands the truth, but is drawn to it and embraces it? Such a radical, all-pervasive change in a sinner's heart is something that only God the Holy Spirit can accomplish. And this He indeed does through "the living and enduring word of God" (1 Pet. 1:23) and "through the word about Christ" (Rom. 10:7).

Reflection Questions:

1. According to the Bible, is unregenerate man depraved in totality or only partially?

2. How does (or should) the doctrine of Total Depravity affect the Church's approach to evangelism and missions?

3. Between Total Depravity and Partial Depravity, which viewpoint is theocentric (God-centered) and which one tends to be anthropocentric (man-centered)?

4. What *source*—or tool—does the Holy Spirit use to make alive an unregenerate person (Rom. 10:7 cf. 1 Pet. 1:23)?

Chapter 9

The Moral Inability of the Reprobate Will

The space race of the 1960s helped to define a generation. What started out in the 1940s as theoretical war games between the East and the West eventually evolved into an international contest to land the first human being on the moon. But the race to the moon proved to be more than just a matter of national defense. Also at stake were bragging rights for the winner.

As the 1960s got underway, the cultural, technological, and ideological rivalry between the United States and the Soviet Union intensified. The two world powers volleyed for space superiority and military clout. Particularly disconcerting to the West were the pioneering efforts of the Soviet space program. Their advanced satellite technology, manned spaceflight, and heavy lift capability (essential for astral rocketry) dwarfed U.S. ingenuity by comparison. This grand display of Russian achievement openly embarrassed the United States government. It not only called into question the dominance and creativity of the American people but threatened the self-confidence of the country. Moved by passion and political savvy, then-presidential candidate John F. Kennedy made space exploration a staple issue of his campaign.

With the Cold War reaching a fever pitch by 1961, the newly-elected president took decisive action. On May 25, before a special joint-session of Congress, Kennedy expressed his growing concern over the United States failure to compete in aeronautics. As he had on the campaign stump, the President asserted that landing an American on the moon by the close of the decade was the only surefire way the United States could "catch up to and overtake" its Eastern nemesis. President Kennedy's challenge extended beyond the halls of Congress and into the home of every American. It was a test of national resolve. He said:

> First, I believe that this nation should commit itself to achieving the goal, before this decade is out, of landing a man on the moon and returning him safely to the earth. No single space project in this period will be more impressive to mankind, or more important for the long-range exploration of space; and none will be so difficult or expensive to accomplish ... But in a very real sense, it will not be one man going to the moon—if we make this judgment affirmatively, it will be an entire nation. For all of us must work to put him there.[79]

Tragically, President Kennedy did not live long enough to see his dream realized. He was assassinated only two years later on November 22, 1963, in Dallas, Texas while riding in a presidential motorcade. Despite his premature death, the president's vision set in motion a chain of events that would guide mankind to his greatest technological achievement.

Six years later, on July 16, 1969, with President Richard M. Nixon in the White House, Apollo 11 launched from the Kennedy Space Center in Florida. It took only twelve minutes for the American spacecraft to enter orbit. Aboard Apollo 11 were cosmonauts Neil Armstrong, Command Module Pilot Michael Collins, and Lunar Module Pilot Edwin "Buzz" Aldrin.

Four days following the launch, July 20, 1969, the Apollo 11 crew landed safely on the moon. Their first act was to commemorate the historic landing by observing an even greater triumph in mankind's history—the atonement of Jesus Christ.[80] Aldrin writes in his memoirs:

> In the radio blackout, I opened the little plastic packages which contained the bread and the wine. I poured the wine into the chalice our church had given me. In the one-sixth gravity of

the moon, the wine slowly curled and gracefully came up the side of the cup. Then I read the Scripture, *'I am the vine, you are the branches. Whosoever abides in me will bring forth much fruit.'*... I ate the tiny Host and swallowed the wine. I gave thanks for the intelligence and spirit that had brought two young pilots to the Sea of Tranquility [on the moon]. It was interesting for me to think: the very first liquid ever poured on the moon, and the very first food eaten there, were the communion elements.[81]

Four days after liftoff, six hours after touchdown, and only minutes following an intergalactic Communion service, Aldrin and Armstrong disembarked the spacecraft for the first time. As Armstrong descended the ladder of the Lunar Module Eagle and touched ground on the moon's surface, he greeted a televised audience watching from earth with the soliloquy: "That's one small step for man, one giant leap for mankind."

Not surprisingly, the mission was extensively covered by the global media. Over 53 million households in America, or over 93% of the population, tuned in to watch the launch of Apollo 11 on television, and over 125 million viewers watched the moon landing. Conservative estimates indicate that half a billion people worldwide saw Armstrong take his first lunar step. This easily broke all previous television viewing records at the time. While the citizens of earth watched from 235,000 miles away as two human beings explored the New Frontier, mankind collectively turned a page in human history.

Praising the astronauts by way of satellite telephone was President Nixon who spoke personally to Aldrin and Armstrong. In addition to a silicon disc containing goodwill messages from 73 world leaders, together with medals honoring American and Soviet spacemen who lost their lives in earlier space tests, an American flag was hoisted on the moon and left behind by the astronauts. Today, the plaque on the Lunar Module reads: "Here men from the planet Earth first set foot upon the Moon, July 1969 A.D. We came in peace for all mankind."

So momentous were the events that transpired on July 21, 1969 that the United States acknowledged the occasion with a national day of celebration. All but emergency and essential employees were allowed a paid day off from work, in both the government and in the private sector. A decade later a replica of the footprint left by Neil Armstrong on the moon's surface was placed in Tranquility Park in Houston, Texas as tribute to the American space program and in memorial to John F. Kennedy.

For most, the idea of spaceships moving at the speed of light and humans living and traveling through space is incomprehensible. Throughout six millennia of recorded history, the idea of putting a man on the moon was thought impossible and a figment of overeager imaginations. But when the scientific ingenuity of America proved otherwise in 1969, critics became believers and a new dawn of self-reliance was born.

The successful mission of Neil Armstrong, Buzz Aldrin, and Michael Collins, coupled with the growing science of the National Aeronautics and Space Administration (NASA), showed the world that man is capable of accomplishing virtually anything he sets his mind to. Far from a Neanderthal, man's impressive aptitude has defied its known limitations. If the mission of Apollo 11 proved anything it was that human beings can make even the seemingly impossible quite probable and the unimaginable a reality. The events of July 21, 1969 saw man at his finest hour. But with its achievement also came the rebirth of the age-old heresy known as *humanism.*

Humanism is a progressive philosophy that, without theism and other supernatural beliefs, affirms the ability and responsibility of men to lead ethical lives of personal fulfillment that aspires to the greater good of humanity. In elementary terms, humanism asks the question: *Who needs God if human beings possess the wherewithal to be happy and the skill to accomplish the improbable?* It is a philosophy that exchanges the biblical credo, "with God all things are possible" (Matt. 19:6 cf. Mark 10:27; Luke 18:27) with the blasphemous notion that "all things are possible with *men.*" The triumph of the 1969 moon landing, in conjunction with the rise of liberal sciences, coagulated and spread this error like never before. Man had become his own god. He appeared capable of accomplishing *anything*.

While certainly an awe-inspiring achievement, the Apollo 11 mission brings to mind a form of humanism rivaled in the early pages of the Old Testament. According to the account in Genesis, the Tower of Babel was erected by the citizens of ancient Babylon as an attempt to build a structure so immense that its top could reach the netherworld. Similar in scope to the moon landing, such a grand accomplishment was thought impossible for primitive man.

Humanism is front and center in the Tower of Babel story. The early Babylonians were convinced that by building a man-made structure that reached the heavens their self-promotion was justified. Motivated by pride, they no longer chose to glorify and honor their Creator who endowed them with the resourcefulness to survive, build, and thrive. Instead, they sinfully heaped up recognition for themselves in effort to gain independence from God. Rather than bring their ingenuity and creativity under God's authority, the ancient Babylonians sought to "make a name for [themselves]" (Gen. 11:3). Moreover, by working as a cohesive unit in a centralized location, they defied God's command to "Be fruitful and increase in number and fill the earth" (Gen. 9:1).

The self-reliance and overconfidence of the citizens of Babylon, both technologically and entrepreneurially, usurped God's command and challenged His leadership. As each rung or step was completed in their impressive edifice, a new height of egotistical satisfaction was attained.

Not surprisingly, God took a dim view of the Tower of Babel. Displeased with their prideful rebellion and their failure to replenish the earth, He took decisive action against the Babylonians. God confused their language and scattered them throughout the earth, bringing an abrupt halt to the building project. Regrettably, despite God's intervention, the early seeds of humanism had been effectively planted.

So what is the common denominator linking the success of Apollo 11 with the failure of the Tower of Babel? In brief, both events suggest that man can do virtually anything with a little sweat and determination. "If as one people speaking the same language they have begun to do this," God observed, "then nothing they plan to do will be impossible for them" (Gen. 11:6). To that end, ironically, NASA achieved what the citizens of Babel could not. After countless centuries of fanciful speculation, the ingenuity of man finally reached the heavens with the Lunar Module.

It is certainly not my aim to bring into disrepute the sacredness of the 1969 moon landing, or even to suggest that the motivation behind it was rooted in sinful pride, as with the Tower of Babel. The mission of Apollo 11 stands forever as a hallmark of man's strength of mind. My intent, rather, is to demonstrate that the sin of humanism seems to have an uncanny way of creeping back into the stream of human consciousness with each new success that man attains. Sinful man prides himself on his abilities.

This self-righteousness, which comes naturally to egotistical sinners, has infected almost every area of our way of life, to include our theology, religion, and spirituality. Not surprisingly, to suggest (as Calvinism does) that unregenerate man is too depraved to spiritually heal himself and morally incapable to seek after, respond to, or desire his Creator is an assault on his haughty self-image. If we can find a way to put a man on the moon, we reason, surely we have the ability to find God on our own.

The doctrine of Total Depravity rules this out altogether. Not only is man innately wicked, enslaved to sin, subjected to Satan, spiritually blind, and spiritually dead but he is helpless in and of himself to seek a remedy. To be clear, it is not as though the remedy eludes his grasp. Instead, he is simply incapable of conjuring up the will or the fortitude to put forth the reach. He is enslaved by his terminal disease. Since the corruption of sin extends to every part of man's nature (whereby his heart is hostile to God and he recoils from spiritual truth), the unregenerate person does not have the spiritual prowess or discernment to savingly embrace Christ or believe the gospel. Men are void of the means. Our lack of desire for the things of God in our fallen state renders our natural will effectively comatose.

Sin is a cruel tyrant. It corrupts the entire person— infecting the soul, polluting the mind, defiling the conscience, contaminating the affections, and poisoning the will. "It is the life-destroying, soul-condemning cancer," wrote one theologian, "that festers and grows in every unredeemed human heart like an incurable gangrene."[82]

While Arminians are quick to acknowledge the stain of sin on the human *spirit*, they tend to retreat concerning its effect on the human *will*. They would have us believe that a sinner's free agency basically retains its pre-Fall impeccability. In flowery terms, Arminian tradition seems to imply that the unregenerate will is an island of righteousness amid a tsunami of fallen flesh. The Calvinistic doctrine of moral inability, for that reason, undermines the very fabric of Arminian DNA. It removes man's freedom of will in the salvation equation altogether and pronounces a death sentence on his body, mind, and soul. Thus, the dogma of inability, biblical though it may be, has caused much dissention throughout Church history and fractured many a relationship.

The bondage of the human will, as Luther later coined it during the Protestant Reformation, first gained considerable thrust in the fifth century. Augustine's counterassault on the free-will views of Pelagius at the Council of Carthage in 418 led to the Council of Ephesus in 431 and the Council of Orange in 529. Each council decisively declared Augustine's doctrine of *inability* the victor (see Chapter 2). It also fueled the historic debates to follow between Luther and Erasmus in the sixteenth century; the followers of Calvin and the Arminian Remonstrants in the early seventeenth century; and George Whitefield and John Wesley in the eighteenth century.

Augustine of Hippo was the first Church father to unmask man's overall depravity and his moral inability. He saw man's capacity to exercise his freedom as a burden of Original Sin, and was therefore forced to conclude it had been lost through the Fall. For him, as well as for the Reformers who followed in his train of thought, a sinner is both free and in bondage at the same time, *but not in the same sense.* A sinner is free to act according to his own inclinations, to be sure, yet "every inclination of the thoughts of his heart [is] only evil all the time" (Gen. 6:5). In other words, a sinner is free only insofar as his slavery to sin permits him. Since the Fall, our natural hearts are not captured to the will of God but are held captive to our taskmaster, Satan. Augustine wrote:

> But whence comes this liberty to do right to the man who is in bondage and sold under sin, except he be redeemed by Him who has said, "If the Son shall make you free, ye shall be free indeed" [John 8:36 KJV]? And before this redemption is wrought in a man, when he is not yet free to do what is right, how can he talk of the freedom of his will and his good works, except he be inflated by that foolish pride of boasting which the apostle restrains when he says, "By grace are ye saved, through faith" [Eph. 2:8, KJV].[83]

In effect, Augustine argued that when man committed spiritual suicide in Eden he became powerless to restore himself to life. He forfeited any ability to pursue his Creator. "It was by the evil use of his free-will," he wrote, "that man destroyed both it and himself."[84] Dr. J.I. Packer, one of the most influential evangelicals in North America and Western Europe, does us a favor on this point by offering a fitting analogy:

> A prisoner has the freedom to pace up and down in his cell, but he is constrained by the walls of that cell and can go no further, no matter how much his will might desire it. So it is with man. Because of sin, man is imprisoned within a cell of corruption and wickedness which permeates to the very core of our being. Every part of man is in bondage to sin—our bodies, our minds, and our wills.[85]

Dr. Loraine Boettner (1901-1990), a dominant voice in Reformed circles in the early twentieth century, offered a pithy comparison. He wrote, "As the 'bird' with a broken wing is 'free' to fly but not able, so the natural man is free to come to God but not able." He concluded:

> Man is a free agent but he cannot originate the love of God in his heart. His will is free in the sense that it is not controlled by any force outside of himself ... How can he repent of his sin when he loves it? How can he come to God when he hates Him? This is the inability of the will under which man labors.[86]

So how do Calvinists respond to well-meaning Christians who insist that an unregenerate sinner can indeed seek God? The answer boils down to etymology and the properties found in a single word. To better understand the Bible's teaching concerning man's moral inability it is imperative that we first have a proper understanding of the word "can." This word plays an all-too-important role in the debate. As any language lexicon plainly states, the word "can" connotes *ability*. The translated verb *dunamai* in the Greek means "to be able, [to] have power whether by virtue of one's own ability and resources, or of a state of mind."[87] English synonyms for the word "can" include: (1) "be able to;" (2) "know how to;" and (3) "be capable of." (On this point the Greek definition and English synonyms for "can" are crucial and must be kept in mind by the reader).

With the original language serving as our guidepost, Reformed Theology assumes that unregenerate sinners are neither "capable of" nor do they "know how to" seek after the living God. Man's moral ability is naturally and severely retarded; he lacks any capacity to subject himself to God's Law. Crystallizing Augustine's thoughts, The Westminster Confession of Faith postulates the Reformed view as follows:

> Man, by his fall into a state of sin, hath wholly lost all ability of will to any spiritual good

accompanying salvation; so as a natural man, being altogether averse from good, and dead in sin, is not able, by his own strength, to convert himself, or to prepare himself thereunto.[88]

So how did Augustine, the Patristic Fathers, the Reformers, the Puritan Divines, and a myriad of Church confessions and creeds throughout the ages derive such an unpopular doctrine? The answer is found in sacred Scripture. The Bible expands upon man's depravity to include his moral inability in no uncertain terms. Under the inspiration of the Holy Spirit, for example, the prophet Jeremiah said:

> "**Can** the Ethiopian change his skin or the leopard its spots? *Neither* **can** *you do good who are accustomed to doing evil*" (Jer. 13:23, emphasis added).

Notice the negative sense in which the word "can" is used in the prophet's statement. This vivid analogy assumes that sinners do not have the ability to change their sinful natures or do good, just as people of color are incapable of changing their skin pigmentation or an animal the composition of its fur. By asking and answering his own rhetorical question, Jeremiah asserts that sinners—particularly those in Judah to whom he writes—are unable to repent and obey the Lord. At issue here in Jeremiah's scathing statement is man's lack of ability.

The fundamental incapacity of natural man to know God is also brought to bear in the New Testament. The apostle Paul tells us that unregenerate sinners are adverse to the things of God. But man's rejection of spiritual things, Paul says, is more than just willful rejection. Man does not have the *capacity* to accept them. In the words of the prophet Amos: "They do not know how to do right" (Amos 3:10). Unless he is spiritually regenerated, a sinner is both unwilling and unable to believe the gospel. The apostle's words are biting:

The man without the Spirit does not accept the
things that come from the Spirit of God, for
they are foolishness to him, *and he* **cannot**
understand them, because they are spiritually
discerned ... no one **can** say, 'Jesus is Lord,'
except by the Holy Spirit" (1 Cor. 2:14, 12:3b
emphasis added).

A sinner may very well understand the proclamation of the
gospel itself, but until spiritual life is given to him, the words
remain void of any real meaning. He lacks the spiritual ability
to appraise spiritual truths. The same apostle who wrote 1
Corinthians 2:14 echoes his own point in his epistle to the
church in Rome. Paul explains further:

Those who live according to the sinful nature
have their minds set on what that nature desires;
but those who live in accordance with the Spirit
have their minds set on what the Spirit desires.
The mind of sinful man is death, but the mind
controlled by the Spirit is life and peace; the
sinful mind is hostile to God. It does not submit
to God's law, *nor* **can** *it do so*. Those controlled
by the sinful nature **cannot** please God (Rom.
8:5-8, emphasis added).

In 1 Corinthians 2:14 and Romans 8:5-8 Paul insists that
unregenerate sinners "cannot understand" the gospel nor can
they submit to the Word of God. Paul does not merely say that
sinners *will not* understand or submit, although that is clearly
inferred, but emphasizes the fact that sinners *cannot* do these
things. An unsaved person *cannot* live a godly and righteous
life because he has no godly and righteous motives or internal
resources that propel him in that direction. He therefore *cannot*
have genuine love for God nor can he fathom the things of God.
Unbelievers are *incapable* of doing anything good, spiritually
speaking, because they are not motivated or empowered by the

Holy Spirit (cf. Isa. 64:6). It clearly follows, then, that if the fleshly mind does not and *cannot* subject itself to the Law of God, those who operate in the sinful flesh *cannot* please Him. Spiritual regeneration is required before a sinner can acquire the compulsory enablement.

Probably the most forceful words on this issue were submitted by the Lord Jesus. In John 6:25-70, Jesus preached a sermon that forever altered the course of his ministry and ultimately put him on the cross. In the *Bread of Life* discourse, the Lord stunned the crowd by implying that his origins were from old, and that he had come down from heaven to provide spiritual food to the Israelites that not even Moses was able to provide during their wilderness wanderings (vv. 32-37). Moved to indignation by the Lord's seemingly sacrilegious statement, the crowd became fierce and grumbled against him. But their fickleness was not lost on Jesus:

> "Stop grumbling among yourselves," Jesus answered. "No one **can** come to me unless the Father who sent me draws him, and I will raise him up at the last day ... no one **can** come to me unless the Father has enabled him" (John 6:43-44, 65).

The Lord's words concerning man's inability could not be more potent. Jesus made it clear that unbelievers *cannot* come to the Savior on their own initiative. If God did not irresistibly draw sinners to Christ pursuant to their regeneration, no one would ever come to him. (Likewise, no one can come to the Father except "those to whom the Son *chooses* to reveal him" [Matt. 11:27, emphasis added]). Not surprisingly, by emphasizing man's helplessness and utter inability to respond to God apart from His sovereign enablement, the Lord's prideful disciples responded in a way that is eerily similar to modern-day Arminians: "This is a hard teaching," they balked. "Who can accept it?" (v. 60). To reject the doctrine of man's spiritual and moral inability, therefore, is to ultimately sympathize with those whom our Lord chided in John 6.

Not long afterward, when this squabble reached a crescendo in John 8:42-47, the Lord delivered the final death knell on free-will and human ability. To the teachers of the Law and the Pharisees, he declared, "Why is my language not clear to you? Because you are **unable** to hear what I say … The reason you do not hear is that you do not belong to God" (vv. 43, 48).

Again man's inability leaps from the page and cuts the heart out of Arminian theology. The unregenerate Jews, to whom our Lord admonished, were "unable" to hear Christ's words because their hearts were spiritually dead. They *wanted* only to do the desires of their father, the devil (v. 44). It is certainly true that our Lord's enemies chose not to hear his words. But Jesus is more to the point: they *could not* hear his words because they "[did] not belong to God." The point is that outside of the grace of God no one would ever respond to Christ and his teachings. One must first be regenerated by God's Spirit and brought into His fold in order to hear His words and thereby believe.

So how do Arminians respond to this Calvinistic assertion of inability? When faced with the weight of biblical argumentation stacked against them, most tend to retreat to logic rather than Scripture: *God wouldn't give us a command that we are unable to fulfill,* they argue vehemently. *If He commands us to seek after Him, then it only stands to reason that sinners have the ability to do so! God does not set us up for failure by telling us to do that which He knows we cannot!*

Although this is an honest response that deserves a respectful answer, this type of logic is the identical trap that ensnared Pelagius fifteen hundred years ago. His pretentious motto was plain enough: "If I ought, then I can." In other words, if God commands it, then it's only commonsensical that human beings must be capable of doing it. To suggest otherwise, Pelagius claimed, is to paint God as unrighteous and cruel. The British monk elaborated:

> We ascribe to the God of knowledge the guilt of twofold ignorance; ignorance of his own creation and of his commands. As if, forgetting the weakness of men, his own creation, he had

laid upon men commands which they were
unable to bear. [...] we ascribe to the Just One
unrighteousness and cruelty to the Holy One; the
first, by complaining that he has commanded the
impossible, the second, by imagining that a man
will be condemned by him for what he could not
help ...[89]

For Pelagius, the command to obey implied the ability to
comply. And many Arminians, it seems, would agree. But
overlooked in such logic is the judgment of Scripture. From
Genesis to Revelation, the Bible is replete with divine commands
that human beings are expected to keep but are instinctively
incapable of obeying. Therefore, it doesn't necessarily follow
logically that unregenerate sinners have the ability to seek
after salvation simply because God puts forth the command in
Scripture.

For example, all men are commanded to "Love the Lord
your God *with all your heart* and *with all your soul* and *with
all your strength*" (Deut. 6:5 cf. Matt. 22:37; Mark 12:30; Luke
10:27, emphasis added). This is a nonnegotiable imperative. Yet
there is not a human being on record, apart from Christ, who has
been, or ever will be, capable of loving God with such absolute
commitment. In the end, we all fall short of the mandate because
we all fall short on ability.

Moreover, as Christ-followers we are commanded to "Be
holy because I, the Lord your God, am holy" (Lev. 10:3 cf. 1
Pet. 1:15-16). In New Testament jargon, we are to "Be perfect,
therefore, as your heavenly Father is perfect" (Matt. 5:48). These
commands are fundamentally one in the same and are binding
on every believer. Yet once again, despite his best efforts, it
is painfully obvious that no sinner can meet such impossible
standards.

While God commands all sinners to love and to emulate
Him, and to be holy and perfect like Him, it is a biblical verity
that man can do neither to God's satisfaction. In the same
way, relative to salvation, it does not prove that a sinner can

seek after God on his own simply because the Bible contains marching orders to that effect. We stand with the Patristic Fathers, therefore, who unanimously deposed Pelagius as a heretic, and we reject as felonious his motto "If I ought, then I can." It is theological humanism in its slickest form, the likes of which we must be on guard against.

Here, then, stands the final verdict: Total Depravity, we read in Holy Writ, ravages like a deadly cancer the nature, heart, intellect, and the self-will of man from conception to death. No faculty of man is left unmarred by Original Sin. As a consequence, King David lamented its debilitating effects on the unredeemed will:

> The Lord looks down from heaven on the sons of men *to see if there are any who understand, any who seek God.* All have turned aside, they have together become corrupt; there is no one who does good, not even one (Psa. 14:2-3, emphasis added).

The apostle Paul echoes, and then expands upon, the Davidic psalm in Romans 3:11-12 and concludes outright: "no one ... seeks God" but "All have turned away." What is more, owing to mankind's wickedness, the author of Psalm 10:4 chimes in: "In his pride the wicked does not seek him; in all his thoughts there is no room for God." It appears that David, Paul, and the psalmist understood clearly the bondage of the human will and its unwillingness to seek after the things of God.

If, then, as we have seen throughout Scripture, every inclination in the heart of man is wicked whereby no person can or will seek God, it stands to reason that Arminianism is built upon a faulty premise. If there truly exists in this fallen world enemies of God who seek after Him on their own accord—in contradiction to their spiritual blindness and deadness, enslaved wills, innate wickedness, moral inability, and bondage to Satan—then neither David, Jeremiah, the psalmist, Jesus, nor Paul knew anything about them. To suggest that unredeemed man has the means, let alone the interest, to seek a holy God is simply a theological fiction that flies in the face of Scripture's clear exposé on universal depravity.

So what are unbelievers and so-called seekers searching for when they go to church? Are they not fulfilling the commands of Scripture that Calvinism maintains are undoable? What they are seeking, the Calvinist responds, is happiness and contentment, not holiness and conversion. They seek the benefits and blessings of God rather than the Benefactor of those blessings. They covet material gifts reminiscent of children on Christmas morning but are uninterested in the Gift-giver. They seek to fulfill their quest for eternity that God has purposely placed in their hearts "yet they cannot fathom what God has done from beginning to end" (Eccl. 3:11). They long for the emotional comfort and security that often comes from participating in religious ceremonies but flee from God whenever the word "surrender" is mentioned.

The notion that fallen men have the ability to facilitate or thwart God's sovereign work of salvation by exercising free-will does not find its origin in the exegesis of inspired Scripture. It is quite simply a tradition of men (cf. Matt. 15:1-6). But there is good news. Despite the fact that the prize of redemption is beyond man's reach, there is a God in heaven who has the power to save. He overcomes the impossible with His impossible grace. And how exactly does He do this? I close this section on Total Depravity with the words of Charles Spurgeon:

> Christ is not only *'mighty to save'* those who repent, but He is able to make men repent. He will carry those to heaven who believe; but He is, moreover, mighty to give men new hearts and to work faith in them. He is mighty to make the man who hates holiness love it, and to constrain the despiser of His name to bend the knee before Him ... Believer, here is encouragement. Art thou praying for some beloved one? Oh, give not up thy prayers, for Christ is *'mighty to save.'* You are powerless to reclaim the rebel, but your Lord is Almighty. Lay hold on that mighty arm and

rouse it to put forth its strength ... Whether to
begin with others, or to carry on the work in you,
Jesus is *'mighty to save;'* the best proof of which
lies in the fact that He has saved *you.*[90]

Reflection Questions:

1. How has unregenerate man's greatest achievements
    in life affected his self-perception and his capacity to
    pursue spiritual matters?

2. The belief in unregenerate man's moral ability, as
    crystallized by Pelagius in his motto *"If I ought, then I
    can,"* is thoroughly refuted in Scripture, specifically by
    Jeremiah, Paul and Christ himself. In light of this, why
    do you suppose God refuses to lower His holy standards
    or "grade on a curve" to accommodate man's inability to
    obey and repent?

3. Why do you suppose the doctrine of Moral Inability is so
    offensive to many inside and outside the Church?

4. In light of unregenerate man's spiritual inability, why
    does God still command all men—regardless of their
    incapacities—to repent of their sin, believe in Christ,
    and seek after Him in faith?

Section 3:

The Scandal of Unconditional Election

"We say, then, that Scripture clearly proves this much, that God by his eternal and immutable counsel determined once for all those whom it was his pleasure one day to admit to salvation, and those whom, on the other hand, it was his pleasure to doom to destruction. We maintain that this counsel, as regards the elect, is founded on his free mercy, without any respect to human worth, while those whom he dooms to destruction are excluded from access to life by a just and blameless, but at the same time incomprehensible judgment."

John Calvin
1509-1564

Chapter 10

Unconditional Election in the Old Testament

At the time of Jesus' birth, Israel was a hotbed of spiritual and civil unrest. The Jews had been a conquered people for over five centuries and Jerusalem, their capital city, a sewer of political squalor. Considered by many Gentiles to be the backwater of the Mediterranean world, Israel's glory days were behind her. Were it not for the Torahic writings, particularly the historical narratives of Kings and Chronicles, the conception that Israel was once a national powerhouse was laughable. Jewish life in the first century bore no resemblance to the stories of grandeur passed down in the oral traditions of the scribes. What once was a model theocracy under King David and King Solomon was now—by way of Roman occupation—the punch line of jokes.

Foreign occupation in Israel was a mainstay, despite a routine changing of the guard. Whoever ruled Mesopotamia, by default, ruled Israel. First came the Assyrians (2 Kings 15:29; 18:11-12; 1 Chron. 5:26), then the Babylonians (2 Kings 24:12-16; Jer. 39-43; Dan. 1-6), followed by the Persians and Greeks (2 Chron. 36:22-23, Ezra 1:1-4), and eventually the Roman Empire (Luke 2:1 cf. Matt. 22:15-21). Control over Israel's territory passed from one Gentile army to the next. That the Jews were treated like commodities and their land up for grabs to the highest bidder only infuriated Jewish hardliners. Hence, with every Gentile flag that unfurled in Israel the seeds of sedition were firmly planted alongside it.

After General Pompey's conquest of Jerusalem in 63 BC, the Roman Empire's ruthless occupation policy fueled, rather than squelched, Jewish nationalism. Rome's Hellenistic customs and pagan garrisons—adorned with idolatrous emblems no less—drew the ire of patriotic Jews, not the least of which was the zealot party. These anti-Roman freedom-fighters plotted retribution against their foreign taskmasters, and fanned the flames of insurrection among their countrymen. As the Caesars grew more maniacal and tyrannical with each passing administration, so the Jewish zealots grew more ferocious in their terrorist plots.

Tension between Jew and Roman reached a boiling point in 66 AD—a full century after Pompey's conquest and only a few decades after the ascension of Christ. Rome's excessive taxation and extortion, to include her rabid polytheism, promiscuity, priestly appointments, and Emperor Caligula's earlier attempt to defile the Temple with a self-aggrandizing statue, was provocation for revolt. Spearheaded by the zealots, the Jews took up the sword against their Roman invaders. Sadly, it was a bid toward independence that, while not without initial promise, ultimately became the nation's undoing. Rome answered the uprising with an impressive, excessive, and overwhelming show of force.

To quell the various pockets of Jewish resistance, Roman battalions were dispatched to Jerusalem under the command of General Vespasian (9-79 AD), and later his son, General Titus (39-81 AD). Overpowered and outmanned, approximately 1.1 million Jews sought refuge behind the city walls while others fled to the foothills. As the Roman legions blockaded Jerusalem, thereby preventing escape and the admittance of food, they choked the life out of the Jewish stronghold.

Many Jews trapped inside the city died of starvation and pestilence. Others managed to survive on cannibalism. Those caught trying to escape in desperation were whipped and tortured, and eventually crucified. During the three-year siege, crosses sprang up as far as the naked eye could see, filling the Judean landscape with a forest of impaled bodies. The Jewish death tally was so astronomical, according to ancient eyewitnesses, that the region was laid waste of all its vital trees and metals (key resources for crossbeams and nails used in the mass crucifixions).

In 70 AD the Romans finally penetrated Jerusalem's outer wall. In due time the city and most of its population was brought to ruin by sword, spear, and fire. The assault culminated in the demolition of the Temple—the exclamation point on Israel's collapse. Doubtless the haunting prophecy of the Savior just a few decades earlier rang in the ears of many survivors: "As for what you see here," Jesus had warned, "the time will come when not one stone [of the Temple] will be left on another; every one of them will be thrown down" (Luke 21:6).

And so it was.

In victory, the Romans slaughtered upwards of one million Jews indiscriminately. What few survivors remained—some 97,000, according to Josephus—were sentenced to a life of forced labor in Egyptian mines or sent to Roman arenas where they eventually fell to the lions and gladiators. The Temple's sacred relics were impounded to Rome and put on public display in celebration of the conquest.

With the Temple in rubble and the Jews dispossessed, Israel ceased to be a nation. The *Diaspora*, as historians call it, saw fugitive Jews disperse to alien lands throughout Europe, bringing a sudden end to a Semitic presence in the land of Canaan. Geo-political Israel was erased from the world map. It would be nearly two millennia before the Star of David would once again shine brightly in the Middle East.

How Israel became an independent state in the twentieth century, after 1,878 years of persecution and exile, is nothing short of miraculous. Against the backdrop of World War II, and while in the despotic grip of a German madman—Adolf Hitler—the Jews experienced their darkest hour yet. However in the midst of their despair God remembered His covenant promises to Abraham.

Few biblical prophecies are as stupefying as that which came about in the wake of World War II. Hitler's firebrand hatred for European Jewry is well documented, ultimately realized in the Holocaust—the state-sponsored extermination of approximately six million Jews. All persons suspected to be of Semitic heritage were rounded up by Nazi stormtroopers in German-occupied countries throughout Europe, dislocated from their families and homes, imprisoned, tortured, and put to death in Nazi concentration camps in the most grisly ways. For six years, 1939-1945, Nazi persecution of the Jews was unremitting. Finally, with the Allied victory over Germany, Italy, and Japan in 1945, World War II came to an end, and with it Hitler's anti-Semitic rampage.

When the American soldiers discovered the Jewish mass graves left by the Nazis—as well as the Jewish survivors left to die in the concentration camps—they were unprepared for what they saw and shocked by what they found. The Jews were a ravished people. Because their communities had been decimated by Hitler's regime, surviving Jews had no homes to return to, little or no family remaining, and were suffering in dire poverty. At best, the future of the Jewish people looked bleak.

When the Nuremberg Trials brought Hitler's war crimes to life before a watching world, sympathy for the Jews grew markedly. From 1945-1948, there was a groundswell of public support for the State of Israel by Jews worldwide, and in the United States in particular. But Palestinian Arabs, who inhabited much of Jerusalem while under British rule, refused to heed the universal call for a Jewish nation. They would not be displaced without a fight. Aware of the volatile situation, Great Britain keenly relinquished its rule over Palestine and handed over the thorny problem to the United Nations to negotiate.

No sooner had England evacuated Palestine did various Jews who had already immigrated to the area declare statehood. The Jewish People's Council gathered at the Tel Aviv Museum on May 14, 1948, and issued its formal declaration. It read in part: "This right is the natural right of the Jewish people to be masters of their own fate, like all other nations, in their own sovereign State ... it will be based on freedom, justice and peace as envisaged by the prophets of Israel."

With the support of the United Nations, America was the first country to officially recognize the new Israel—eleven minutes, in fact, after the declaration of independence was announced. U.S. President Harry Truman signed a letter of recognition, despite the objections of the State Department. The USSR followed Truman's lead three days later.

The rebirth of Israel as an independent nation in 1948 is one of the most significant events in world history. Never before has an entire race of people, especially one as persecuted as the Jews, ever been without a homeland for so long without assimilating into surrounding populations. That being said, no other conquered race could claim for themselves the ironclad promises of God, who had pledged to the patriarch Abraham: "The whole land of Canaan ... I will give as an everlasting possession to you and your descendants after you" (Gen. 17:8). Centuries later, through the prophet Jeremiah, God also promised the descendants of Abraham:

> "The days are coming," declares the Lord, "when I will bring my people Israel and Judah back from captivity and restore them to the land I gave their ancestors to possess," says the Lord ... "I will surely gather them from all the lands where I banish them in my furious anger and great wrath; I will bring them back to this place and let them live in safety" (Jer. 30:3; 32:37).

Some 2,800 years before the events of World War II, and three centuries before the abovementioned prophecy issued by Jeremiah, God hinted through Isaiah that Israel would be nationally restored. But even more breathtaking, God promised to accomplish this feat in *a single day*. Isaiah records God's words as follows:

> "Who has ever heard of such things? Who has ever seen things like this? Can a country be born in a day or a nation be brought forth in a moment? Yet no sooner is Zion in labor than she gives birth to her children. Do I bring to the moment of birth and not give delivery?" says the Lord. "Do I close up the womb when I bring to delivery?" says your God (Isa. 66:8-9).

On May 14, 1948 God set in motion the fulfillment of His prophetic promise to Israel. Having been brought to the brink of extinction by the horrors of the Holocaust, facing persecution around the world, and surrounded by their Arab enemies, the Jewish people gathered together in Israel and declared themselves a nation in *a single day*. Two thousand years in the making, God had brought the Jews to full delivery and gave birth to them a second time.

God sovereignly reversed the horrors perpetrated in World War II for His own glorious ends. For this reason (as well as many others) most Bible-believing Christians today are prone to love and support the State of Israel and Jews the world over. We are enamored by the remarkable story behind Israel's rise and fall in ancient history, and her tumultuous resurgence in modern times. The chronicles of Israel tell the story of a God who is faithful to His promises and who deliberately interferes in the affairs of human history to affect His sovereign purposes. The extraordinary renaissance of the Hebrew nation in 1948 reminds Christians of the veracity of Scripture and the irrevocability of the Lord's covenant commitments.

The election of Israel as God's chosen people, and her eventual restoration, has its origin with the patriarch Abraham. God promised that He would make Abraham's name great (Gen. 12:2); that his physical descendents would rival the stars in number and become a colony of nations on earth (Gen. 13:16; 17:4-5). Even more remarkable, from Abraham's vast posterity God promised to set apart a special race for Himself—the Hebrews/Jews—through whom a channel of blessing would come into the world (Gen. 12:3; 22:18). Included in this promise was the inheritance of a strategically-located land that flowed with milk and honey (Exod. 3:8); the boundaries of which are described in Genesis 15:18–21.

The contract God made with Abraham—known as the Abrahamic Covenant—was an unconditional contract. God's promise required nothing from the patriarch in return. In fact, its unconditional nature is described in Genesis 15 where Abraham, while subdued in a deep trance, envisioned God moving between the halves of slaughtered animals in the form of a smoking furnace and a flaming torch. This theophany was a sign of ratification that told Abraham that the stipulations attached to the divine contract fell upon, and were bound to, God alone. In effect, God was saying to Abraham through the furnace and torch: *"May it be to Me as one of these slaughtered animals if I do not fulfill My promise to you and make you into a great nation with an everlasting land for your possession"* (e.g. Jer. 34:18, 20b).

God's promise to Abraham was the sole basis for Israel becoming God's chosen people. The nation's divine election is emphasized elsewhere by Moses, who told the Hebrews: "Yet the Lord set his affection on your ancestors and loved them, and he chose you, their descendants, above all the nations—as it is today" (Deut. 10:15). Moreover, God vowed to Israel on Mount Sinai: "Out of all the nations you will be my own special possession" (Exod. 19:5). As a God of covenant blessing, He betrothed Himself to Israel as her Groom (Jer. 3:14; Hos. 2:2, 16, 19-20; Isa. 54:4-8).

The exclusive choice of Israel as God's chosen people, at its most basic meaning, speaks to unmerited grace. God did not choose the Hebrews because they were more commendable than their surrounding neighbors or because they possessed inherent goodness that earned them His favored-nation status. To the contrary, the Bible unmistakably declares that, in God's eyes, Israel was "a stiff-necked people" and the "fewest of all peoples" in whom righteousness was found wanting (Deut. 7:6-8; 9:5-7). In other words, they were far from impressive and arguably the least worthy. Yet God unconditionally chose them, in covenant relationship with Abraham, to be His elect people in accord with His good pleasure. Dr. Claude Mariottini, Professor of Old Testament at Northern Baptist Seminary, writes:

> God chose a people who were slaves in Egypt, redeemed them and established a special relationship with them. The point that [Moses] was trying to convey to the new generation of Israelites was that it was because of God's faithful love and because of the promise he had made to Abraham that he, in his sovereignty,

> elected Israel to be his special people and his
> special possession [not because of any inherent
> righteousness of their own].[91]

It is beyond doubt in Scripture that God gave preferential treatment to Israel. And He did so, we learn, at the expense of all other nations on earth (Exod. 19:5; Deut. 20:16-17; Mal. 1:2-3 cf. Rom. 9:12-14). Yet strangely enough, this divine *particularism*—that is, God's exclusive choice of, and unique affection for, the Hebrew people—is largely innocuous to most Christians today. Though we stand united against favoritism and racism, it's a curious thing that so few Christians—Arminians especially—object to the idea that God set apart for Himself an elect nation in whom were "entrusted ... the very words of God" (Rom. 3:2) while ordering the annihilation of others countries (Deut. 2:34; 3:6; 20:16-18, Josh. 11:20; Judges 2:1-3 cf. 1 Sam. 15:2-3). But why favor the Israelites? Why didn't God choose the Egyptians, the Ammonites, the Hittites, or the Moabites instead?

That Christians see God's fingerprints all over Israel's decimation in 70 AD and, more importantly, her extraordinary resurgence in 1948 is attested to widely throughout the Church. We also admit to the unique calling of Abraham as a man beloved of God and from whom the chosen people were born. Furthermore, we are quick to concede that Israel, when she least deserved it, was handpicked by God—elected and set apart—as His chosen people to be a channel of blessing to the world. In short, we agree, essentially, on God's unconditional election of Israel through Abraham.

However, when the subject at hand changes from God's election of *Israel* to God's election of *individuals*, the love-fest between Calvinists and Arminians grows cold. Unconditional Election suddenly becomes a bone of contention, even hostile divorce, rather than a shared fundamental truth. It seems that no other doctrine within the canon of Calvinism, with the possible exception of Limited Atonement, is more despised by Arminians than that which teaches God's unconditional election of *people*. "It's one thing to say God loves one particular nation at the expense of others," Arminians will protest, "but it's altogether another thing to suggest that He chose one person for salvation while arbitrarily passing over someone else."

Here Arminianism entangles itself with contradiction. It is a peculiar thing, if not theologically inconsistent, that many Christians have no problem with Israel's unconditional election in the Old Testament. Yet they wholeheartedly object to the election of *persons* unconditionally as taught in the New Testament. That God should show the same sovereign discretion in choosing a people for salvation as He did in choosing a nation for blessing is *anathema* to them. It is the height of unfairness, they contend. One Reformed writer captures the Arminian inconsistency this way:

> Nobody seems to have a problem that God called out Israel and set them apart and set his love upon them and distinguished them ... God didn't come in a bush to Pharaoh and say, "Hey Pharaoh, I'm going to be your God. I'm going to take care of you and all your people and I'm going to give you my law and I'm going to place you in a land and I'm going to give you grace galore and through you the nations will be blessed." But now in the New Testament, [according to the Arminian] supposedly God cannot set his affection upon this person as distinct from that person [as He did with Israel in distinction from the other nations].[92]

According to the Old Testament, God chose Israel out of all the nations of the world to be His special people on earth. In the same way, according to the New Testament, He has chosen specific saints from an international community to comprise His royal priesthood in heaven. But if the Reformed doctrine of Unconditional Election is true—that God elects unconditionally certain people for salvation in the same manner that He unconditionally elected Israel for blessing—we must be prepared to answer certain questions: On what basis does God elect people for salvation, if not on His own sovereign will? And, if God elected the Jews to be His people of blessing why then do Calvinists presuppose that individual election goes beyond blessing to include salvation? These questions, and more, will be answered in the following three chapters.

Reflection Questions:

1. Most Christians accept the fact that God sovereignly elected Israel out of all the nations on earth to be His chosen people. Yet some object to the idea that God elects *in the same way* certain individuals to be part of His Church (while passing over others). When God passed over the nations of old in His election of Israel, did He not pass over the people of those nations also?

2. What attributes does God put on display when He elects a person (for salvation) or a nation (for blessing)?

3. What attributes does God put on display when He passes over a person for salvation?

4. Suppose a rich man observed a line of vagabonds begging for bread at the local mission. How would you regard the rich man if, moved by compassion, he gave half of his riches to a vagrant of his choice? Would you consider the rich man gracious and generous for his benevolence or would you chide him as unfair and unloving because he did not divvy up his wealth equally to all?

5. Does God have the right to predestine unto salvation those whom He chooses and to pass over others at His discretion (cf. Rom. 9:16)?

Chapter 11

The Chosen of God

Jean Sibelius (1865-1957), the Finnish music composer, was no stranger to criticism. On more than one occasion, after being criticized by his detractors over the composition of his symphonies, he remarked, "Pay no attention to what critics say. No statue has ever been put up to a critic." Whether or not Sibelius was right in his historical assessment we cannot be sure. But about one thing I am certain: When reflecting on my early days in ministry, to include my collegiate career and a brief stint as a pastoral intern, no monument was ever erected in my honor. I was a critic of the worst sort.

A critic, by and large, is a person who expresses a value judgment about someone or something, particularly when that someone or something is perceived as a disappointment. But criticism itself often reveals much more about the critic than the subject matter under scrutiny. And my knack for criticizing, while nothing short of shameful, revealed much about my spirituality.

Camouflaged as "discernment," my judgmental attitude was an albatross of jealousy, envy, and insecurity rolled into one. Moreover, it was no respecter of persons. Its ugly reach extended beyond politicians, professionals, public personas, and pop-culture and included pastors in the pulpit. It was not uncommon for me to draw uninformed opinions about my fellow clergymen regardless of their reputations and in spite of their accomplishments. Whether it was their attire, oral presentation, command of Scripture, or differences in theology, many pastors often failed to meet my imposed standards. Judging a book by its cover, as it were, came natural to me. And nowhere was my unsettling attitude more apparent than when I spent an entire weekend under the training of Dr. Steve Viars. His life-story not only exposed my critical spirit for the sin that it was but it also illustrated the grace behind the

Reformed doctrine of Unconditional Election. It was a tutorial in theology and humility that I will never forget.

Hosted by a church near my hometown, Dr. Viars was the keynote speaker at a weekend symposium on Nouthetic[93] counseling. No sooner had he walked into the auditorium were all eyes fastened on him. Dr. Viars greeted the seminar crowd with a polite nod and a megawatt smile that seem to light up the room. As a pastor, I admit that I was a little green with envy at how effortlessly he commanded the attention of the conference hall. Tall and handsome, well-dressed, nicely tanned, and obviously at ease before a slew of unfamiliar faces, he appeared to be everything one might admire in a megachurch senior pastor. Still jetlagged from his red-eye flight the night before, he managed to captivate the audience on sheer charisma alone.

In addition to his flawless gift for gab, Dr. Viars had an imposing intellect and an even more imposing résumé. He had achieved by the age of fifty what most pastors only dream of in a lifetime. An ordained minister since 1987, he was the senior pastor of one of the largest Reformed churches in Lafayette, Indiana. In addition to his pastoral work, he was an instructor of biblical counseling, a fellow at the National Association of Nouthetic Counselors and board president, an adjunct faculty member at Word of Life Bible Institute and Baptist Bible Seminary, an instructor and counselor at Faith Biblical Counseling Ministries, a published author, and a highly sought-after conference speaker. He was one of only a few dozen pastors nationwide whose counseling expertise was in high demand on the speaking circuit. Married for over twenty-five years and the father of three, Dr. Viars was the quintessential image of success.

I suppose it was Dr. Viars' many achievements and accolades, in comparison to a glaring lack of my own, which triggered my critical spirit. I was still honing my craft as a novice pastor, desperately trying to earn the respect of my peers in the ministry, whereas he had obviously mastered both. That he was well-liked and the toast of the town, in a manner of speaking, was a source of contention for my covetous ego. I wanted for myself what he had dutifully accomplished on his own through hard work, self-determination, and God's blessing.

My focus drifted away from the conference curriculum and onto Dr. Viars' many successes. Curiosity and daydreaming got the best of me. I couldn't help but wonder what sort of pampered life he and his wife enjoyed. The square footage of his house, including the luxury vehicle he probably drove, was enough to rapture my imagination. Owing to his immense popularity, I could only guess the number of Christmas cards the Viars' received each year. How many invitations to black-tie ministry functions landed in their mailbox? What exotic location did they call their summer home? Their spin through the lap of luxury must be staggering, I thought to myself.

My delirium didn't end there. Publishing houses, I assumed, were probably knocking down Dr. Viars' door, eager to offer him an advance for the rights to his next book. I imagined long lines of radio producers greeting him at every turn, soliciting his talent for their airwaves. There was little doubt in my mind that those he ministered to as senior pastor at his megachurch serenaded him endlessly with appreciation, if not adoration. Furthermore, when I stopped to consider the various men of notoriety with whom Dr. Viars probably rubbed elbows in ministry, my imagination ran wild with the names of celebrity preachers. Dr. Viars had it all, so it seemed. Popularity. Prestige. Praise. What more could a man want? In all likelihood a minister of his caliber and reputation probably gave little thought to amateurish pastors like me. Surely I was beneath his notice.

Never before had I been more wrong about a person. As the familiar lyrics go to an old song, *"Things aren't always as they seem; we see with our eyes but look behind the dream."*[94] Regrettably, I had embellished this man and his character to such an unhealthy degree that I judged him to be something that he was not. My critical spirit was eventually arrested by the truth.

So what was it, specifically, that disarmed my guns of envy and changed my outlook about the man? As the conference wore on, Dr. Viars slowly but surely showed the audience his *true* character and allowed us access into his *real* life; the details of which were tear-jerking. Far from the enchanting fairytale I had concocted in my mind, and nowhere near smug or sanctimonious, Dr. Viars lived a modest life of burden, *not* convenience. While he was certainly successful, some aspects of his life were far from desirable. In fact, one might say they were woefully tragic.

Dr. Viars dropped the bombshell on the conference crowd midway through the course study. Illustrating some point he was making, he mentioned rather unceremoniously that one of his children was mentally disabled. But more than just behavioral slowness, his son suffered from profound developmental delays, to include extreme physical disabilities that rendered him immobile, heightened dementia, a complete absence of mental acuteness, and dysfunctional motor skills. Diagnosed with severe mental and physical retardation, his son was given a life-sentence in a wheelchair with little to no way of communicating with those who loved him most.

Such a candid admission brought silence to the room. The Viars would never see their teenage son outgrow his diapers or liberated from the prison of his chair. In all likelihood he would never marry or have a family of his own. He would never possess the intellectual acuity to vocalize a sentence, much less utter the words that every parent longs to hear: "*I love you, mom and dad.*" Dressing, bathing, even eating—common tasks taken for granted in normal life—were uncommonly difficult in the Viars' household. Their son could not be left alone in a room; he required unyielding care around the clock. Simple commutes to the local store or church on Sunday morning were anything but trouble-free; they were arduous and painstaking to facilitate. Costs for medications and treatments were never-ending. Hospital visits were routine. And the house was always in state of flux so as to make it handicap accessible and compliant. In short, Dr. Viars and his wife lived a life of burden.

Having a handicapped child is one of the most stressful experiences a family can endure. Dr. Viars and his wife knew this firsthand and in ways that I could not. The threat of communicable illnesses haunted their son and social awkwardness dogged their every step. Their son's circumstances informed their every decision—what to eat, when to go out, and how to go about the most menial of errands. Their family life was an emotional roller coaster, seesawing back and forth between frequent hospitalizations and fending off one life-threatening crisis after another. Entertaining friends and family or hosting ministry functions at their home was simply a wishful figment of their imaginations.

Then there was the financial strain to consider. Providing for the necessary medical expenses, special equipment, special schools, and licensed care takers to assist his wife with their son while he was away handling ministry affairs or preparing his next sermon put an enormous amount of pressure on Dr. Viars. Indeed, the thought of retirement was unthinkable, much less affordable.

My heart went out to the Viars family. The hardship that was theirs, particularly for Mrs. Viars who was the primary caregiver to their son, was unfathomable. But it quickly became evident that Dr. Viars was neither interested in my sympathy nor wanted my commiseration—or anyone else's for that matter. The irony of his situation was not lost on me: What many of us saw as his beast of burden, he chose to see as a *blessing*. What he cherished most about his life, we in the conference crowd pitied.

But the biggest bombshell from Dr. Viars was yet to come. And it was a revelation that would forever change the way I viewed the man, to say nothing about my personal theology and how I viewed the Doctrines of Grace.

Some parents perceive their handicapped child as an extension of themselves and often feel shame, social rejection, ridicule, or embarrassment. Many cannot cope beyond the emotional disintegration that occurs within a healthy family when an unhealthy child enters their fold. The reactions of parents to the realization that their child is "abnormal" usually include shock, depression, guilt, anger, sadness, and anxiety. Given over to despair—that is, their profound grief over the death of a dream—they cry out to God, *"Why us? Why did You let this happen to us?"* But self-pity was imperceptible in

Dr. Viars—in fact, only the opposite appeared true. The Viars'
response to their son's fate was anything but common.

One can imagine the collective gasp that came over the
conference hall when Dr. Viars revealed another secret to the
audience. Their son—a sheltered young man with impaired
cognitive functioning and neurodegenerative disease—was *not*
born to them. He was *not* their natural child. Rather, the Viars
had chosen to adopt him.

Adopted?

I could hardly believe my ears. My first thought, much to
my embarrassment, was *Why?* Why did Dr. Viars and his wife
choose to adopt a child that most rational minds, to include
many well-informed case workers, consider un-adoptable?
Moreover, what compelled an affluent couple like them, who
had the world by the tail, so to speak, to disrupt their life of
normalcy and ease by receiving into their family a person who
only placed heavy demands on them? What was it about their
son that was so worthwhile that it meant throwing their future
into a wastebasket of uncertainty? Essentially, their decision
to adopt a multi-impaired child meant that they were adopting
a life of hardship, financial strain, and social discomfort. Why
take on such an onerous task if they didn't have to?

The answers to all of these questions are not terribly
difficult to ascertain for a student of Scripture. In a word, it
was *grace* that moved the Viars' heart toward adoption. To
some, the climax of adoption is the sweet smell of a newborn
baby in their arms; to others, it is the rescue of a child from
the foster-care system. Still for others, it is the long-awaited
answer to infertility. To the Viars, however, adoption meant
demonstrating the unconditional love of Jesus Christ. Where
most people see only hardship and burden in connection to the
handicapped, they saw an opportunity for love and mercy.

Fraught with disabilities, there was nothing inherently
winsome about Dr. Viars' son that made him more desirable
than others like him. In fact, one could argue that, given the
extent of his condition, he was the least likely candidate
for adoption. Furthermore, Dr. Viars and his wife were all
too aware that their son, through no choice of his own, was

incapable of reciprocating the affection lathered upon him. Stunted in cognition, the closest he ever came to expressing any heartfelt feeling, apart from hunger pangs, was his excitement over oddities in nature, such as falling snowflakes. Intrinsically selfish and co-dependent, he had neither the motor faculties nor the mental awareness to express himself. He was an emotional and physical convalescent. He was powerless to fathom, much less appreciate, the lifetime of sacrifices that awaited his parents. But none of this mattered to Dr. Viars and his wife. They loved their adopted son unconditionally. And were it not for their unbending grace, he would have long ago been consigned to a state hospital, banished among a host of forgotten outcasts that society deemed convenient to throw away.

Dr. Viars' sacrificial love for his adopted son dropped my jaw. It sucker punched me, if you will. Indeed, my first impression of the man, which was stained by judgmental bias, exposed my foolishness. I had no choice but to repent of my critical spirit at once and seek God's forgiveness. If I were only half the man Dr. Viars was, I realized, I could count myself a spiritual success.

But more to the point, there was another important lesson gleaned from Dr. Viars' example. His decision to adopt a special-needs child is not unlike God's adoption of His elect children. With the same independence that Dr. Viars exercised his option to adopt, irrespective of anything meritorious in his son that influenced his decision, so God sovereignly did the same with His children. When sinners lacked any desire or acuity to know Him—that is, they had no mental, spiritual, emotional, or physical consciousness of God—He instead did the choosing on their behalf.

In John 6:44 Jesus said, "No one can come to me unless the Father who sent me draws him." Our Lord's statement is a serious blow to man's autonomy. Apart from the regenerative work of the Holy Spirit, man is spiritually inept and impotent. He is darkened in his understanding (Eph. 4:18), dead in sin (Eph. 2:1-3), enslaved to sin (Rom. 6:17), and overcome by demonic influence (Eph. 2:2). Like a severely challenged person who is plagued with retardation, unregenerate man is incapable of understanding the things of God (1 Cor. 2:14). His wisdom is demonic and earthly (James 3:15). He cannot comprehend the words of Christ (John 8:43, 47). He is not able to subject his flesh to the Law of God (Rom. 8:7-8). Just as people cannot change the color of their skin, sinners cannot do the necessary good to please a holy God (Jer. 13:23). From the womb, every intention of man's heart is only evil continually (Gen. 6:5; 8:21; Psa. 51:5). In a word, man is spiritually *disabled* apart from the grace of God. Were God to have decided *not* to adopt sinners for salvation in eternity past—or had He acquiesced to our natural protests of rebellion—all mankind would remain confined to spiritual wheelchairs and lost in their sin.

Unconditional Election is a phrase that is used to summarize what the Bible teaches about the predestination—or the election—of specific people for salvation. It represents the second letter in the acronym T.U.L.I.P. Referred to by some theologians as "Adopted by God," Unconditional Election is not only the very heart of Calvinism, but it is the heart of salvation as a whole. It is a divine act of the sovereign, eternal, immutable, and omnipotent Creator who effectively determined in eternity past those whom He would lavish His grace upon and those He would leave in their sins.

Like the story of Dr. Viars and his son, Unconditional Election is a doctrine that tells the story of a gracious God who saw fit to shower His love upon those who, by all accounts, were un-adoptable. What is more, in contrast to most adoption stories we read today, Unconditional Election places a heavy emphasis not on the adoptee under grace but on the Adopter who gives it. What we believe about God's sovereignty, therefore, will directly affect our view of spiritual adoption, and ultimately how we view salvation.

Predestination & Election

Because of Adam's transgression in the Garden, all human beings enter the world as fallen sinners, "darkened in their understanding and separated from the life of God" (Eph. 4:18). Conceived in spiritual rebellion, the unregenerate have no desire for fellowship with their Creator. They are born, in actual fact, blameworthy and at enmity with the One who created them. As noted already in our study, the effects of Total Depravity on the human condition are far-reaching and comprehensive. Mankind is inherently wicked, spiritually stillborn, enslaved to sin, blinded to God, captive to Satan, and incapable of responding to the things of God.

The disparity between God's holiness and man's ungodliness defies adequate description. The Lord is righteous, just, and perfect, whereas human beings are sinful, perverse, and corrupt. Owing to their spiritual bankruptcy, unregenerate men inevitably follow the god of this world, the devil, and live in subjugation to his rule. Consequently, the human race has cut itself off from the Lord of heaven and has forfeited all rights to His love and favor. With this gloomy reality in view, it would have been perfectly just for God to have left all men in their sin and misery and to have shown mercy to none. God was under no obligation whatsoever to offer salvation to anyone, much less to do so free-of-charge. Yet within this ominous context God revealed His graciousness by setting in motion His glorious plan of predestination and election.

The terms "predestination," "election," and "chosen" abound in Scripture and are inextricably linked with soteriology (the study of salvation). Because they are essentially three sides of the same coin (though theologians acknowledge slight variances between them) they are often used interchangeably in theological discourse. As a matter of record, *predestination* describes what God has decided in advance to accomplish. It implies that He has planned an outcome of events before the creation of the world, as indicated by the prefix *pre* before the word *destination* (cf. Acts 4:27-28; 15:8). Going beyond mere events, the words *chosen* and *election* are more pinpointed in meaning and refer to an act of choice whereby God chooses an individual or group according to His predetermined purpose. As it relates to the doctrine of salvation in Reformed Theology, to be chosen is also to be elect. To be elect is also to have been predestined. And to have been predestined is also to be among those chosen. These terms are fundamentally synonymous.

With the exception of perhaps Limited Atonement (see Section 4), no petal in the T.U.L.I.P. acrostic is more troublesome to the Arminian mind than Unconditional Election. The concept militates against our democratic sensibilities. To suggest—as Calvinism does—that our ancestral sin in Adam incapacitates our will and retards our ability to freely choose God—thereby requiring God to choose us instead—is the height of folly to many free-will evangelicals.

That the Bible teaches the concepts of predestination and election is nonnegotiable. Both Calvinists and Arminians agree on this fact (e.g. Matt. 22:14; 24:22; Luke 18:7; John 13:18; 15:16a; Eph. 1:4-5; 1 Pet. 1:1-2). Christians are described in the Bible as "those who have been chosen of God" (Col. 3:12 cf. 1 Pet. 1:1) and those whom "God from the beginning chose ... for salvation" (2 Thess. 2:13-14). In fact, the term *elect* is ascribed to *chosen believers* nearly a dozen times in the New Testament.

But mere agreement over the *fact* of election hardly settles the longstanding debate over its application. At issue is whether or not election is dependent upon man's foreseen response to the gospel or God's sovereign decree irrespective of man's actions. In other words, the questions we are tasked with answering are: *Who* or *what* is elect and on what basis is God's divine choice made?

To these questions we are given two opposing answers. Arminianism views election as *conditional*. It is the *Church Militant*, as a universal body, that is elect, comprised of a people God predestined for blessing on account of their foreseen faith. One expert in Arminian theology writes, "Arminians believe that election is corporate, that God has chosen to have a people *and that predestination is God's foreknowledge of who will freely choose to be among God's people*" (emphasis added).[95] Notice how this explanation emphasizes man's choice (as seen by God's foreknowledge) as the basis for predestination rather than God's sovereign decree. God, we are told, looked down the corridor of time to see who would willingly believe in Him and, on that basis alone, predestined them accordingly.

The Calvinist understanding of election, however, negates divine foresight and human will. It teaches that God, before the foundation of the world, chose certain individuals from among Adam's fallen race to be the objects of His underserved favor.

These, and these only, He purposed to save. His eternal choice to save some individuals was not based on any foreseen act or response on the part of those elected, but was based solely on His own good pleasure and sovereign will. Thus, election was *not* determined by, or conditioned upon, anything that men would do in their lifetime but resulted entirely from God's self-determined purpose in eternity past. In a word, it was *unconditional.*

Herein lies the difference between the two camps. Dr. J.I. Packer explains, "The Arminians say: 'I owe my election to my faith,' The Calvinist says: 'I owe my faith to my election.'"[96]

The prominent evangelical view in the West, regrettably, sides mostly with the Arminian position. By way of analogy, American Christians tend to view the universal Church as a train on route to heaven. It is the locomotive (the Church) that is elect, but *not* necessarily the passengers on board. Individual sinners are said to have free-will whereby they can hop on or off the heaven-bound train at their discretion. Those who purchase a train ticket, as it were, have been predestined only because the Great Conductor saw in advance that they would do so willingly. God's foresight into man's actions—or lack thereof—is therefore the heart behind election in Arminian theology.

Calvinists couldn't disagree more. Continuing with our analogy, the Reformed view teaches that it is the passengers who are elect, not merely the proverbial train. And their election is *unconditional* because God's choice is not hinged upon whether or not the passengers willingly purchased a ticket beforehand but is independent of it. It is based on God's sovereign decree irrespective of constraints or influence from anyone or anything. Calvinists purport that God reserved and purchased an individual seat for each passenger on the train, not because He saw in advance that they would do so on their own accord or because there existed in them something meritorious. Rather, it was His good pleasure to give first class seating to certain people too destitute to afford a boarding pass.

Calvinism's take on election lands sideways for many American evangelicals. To suggest that God sovereignly chose in eternity past all those whom He was pleased to bring to a saving knowledge of Himself, thereby granting them eternal life, while abandoning others to their sin, invites fits of hysteria. It quite simply blindsides the uninformed. Haunted by its shocking truth and staggered to learn of its abundant scriptural support, Unconditional Election elicits a kneejerk response from anti-Calvinists. They are quick to complain: *"How could God arbitrarily choose Tom and Debbie for salvation, absent of foreseen faith, but pass over Kenny and Sarah through no fault of their own?"* Told that God does so for His own good pleasure and in accordance with His will, they balk further: *"Such teaching makes God out to be unfair, capricious, and even a celestial chauvinist!"*

That the God of Reformed Theology challenges the flannel-board God and coloring-book Jesus taught in many Sunday schools today is apparent in the doctrine of Unconditional Election. The contempt people have for this doctrine is usually rooted in the fact that it leaves no room for man's prized accomplishments, meritorious works, religious rituals, sacraments, presuppositions, or the exercise of his supposedly autonomous will. Moreover, the doctrine reveals a God who is not only infinitely gracious and sovereign but is also mysteriously selective. This radical truth is no small hit to sinful man's pride or his fallen sense of equality and fairness. When litigated in the court of public opinion, it is hardly surprising that Unconditional Election engenders an allergic reaction from most.

Intoxicated by their belief in free-will, many Arminians have no choice but to philosophize, rather than exposit, their way out of the biblical texts stacked against them. Others sweep aside Unconditional Election with a nonchalant wave of the hand, apparently incapable of moving beyond their emotions and traditions. Still others treat the doctrine as invisible despite its ubiquitous presence throughout Scripture. When the subject is broached, they merely shrug their shoulders in apathy and change the topic of conversation. In many cases, at least so it seems, the doctrine seldom receives a fair hearing.

I remember one such occasion when I was driving with an Arminian friend on a lengthy road trip. It was not long into our journey before the conversation inevitably turned to Unconditional Election. I presented to him the biblical texts in support of the Calvinist position and the arguments behind them. I countered his Arminian responses concerning *conditional* election as articulately and as authoritatively as I could. When it was evident that he had exhausted all biblical ammunition at his disposal, but to no avail, I then asked him to give an account for the plethora of biblical texts which I had cited in support of Unconditional Election. To my reasonable arguments my friend, a longtime Christian, shrugged indifferently and said, "I just can't believe God would choose certain people to be saved and not others. He loves everyone the same." He then added, "*Even though the Bible appears to teach otherwise*, I choose to believe we have a choice in the matter. I just don't think we can be sure."

Regrettably, to my friend's way of thinking, his personal feelings about how he thought God *should* behave trumped the Bible's teaching on how God actually *does* behave. His presuppositions colored his theology. Not only had he mischaracterized the Calvinist position on personal choice, which Calvinists believe to be fundamental in salvation (see Chapter 12), but he deliberately turned a blind eye to the rational exposition of Scripture. He swapped hard truth for the comforts of a flannel-board God and a coloring-book Jesus who, equally and without prejudice, loves saint and sinner alike. For many evangelicals like him, who stubbornly refuse to allow God's Word to speak in any other way than how they have been accustomed to understand it, Unconditional Election is an affront to their senses. My friend's response only evidenced this. Arthur Wallis, in his book *The Chosen Fast*, observed:

> When our minds are conditioned by prejudice or paralyzed by traditional views, we may face a truth in Scripture again and again without its ever touching us. Our spiritual inhibition concerning that truth permits us to see, but not to perceive. The truth lies dormant within, mentally apprehended but not spiritually applied

> ... The outcome of the struggle reveals whether
> or not we are open to receive and obey fresh light
> about God, and so grow in the knowledge of the
> truth ...[97]

Unlike my friend, believers of all stripes must be prepared to submit our ideas about divine election and man's supposed free-will to the acid test of God's Word. Suppositional theology, no matter how darling to our hearts, must be tested and tried by an authority greater than our personal preferences and whims (cf. Acts 17:11).

The testimony in Scripture concerning divine election is overwhelming. The New Testament tells us that the names of those in eternity past whom "God ... destined ... to obtain salvation through our Lord Jesus Christ" (1 Thess. 5:9)—that is, the Elect—were "written in the Book of Life of the Lamb slain from the foundation of the world" (Rev. 13:8 cf. 17:8). That is to say, "He chose us in Him before the foundation of the world ... having predestined us to adoption as sons by Jesus Christ to Himself ... being predestined ... according to the counsel of His will" (Eph. 1:4, 11). Here the apostles John and Paul set forth the unmistakable teaching that, before the world was created, God preordained certain people "to obtain salvation" and for "adoption as sons," and recorded their names into the Lamb's divine ledger. In other words, the salvation of the Elect was decided upon and catalogued long before the creation account in Genesis 1:3-2:4! This truth is borne out in the clearest terms in 2 Timothy 1:9 where Paul writes that God "saved us and called us ... before the beginning of time" (cf. Tit. 1:2).

Neither John nor Paul was scandalized by God's sovereignty in election. In fact, writing with intent to destroy, both apostles took aim at so-called free-will election. John writes, "[We have] become children of God ... not of ... *human decision ... or will, but born of God*" (John 1:13, emphasis added). To John's words are added those of the apostle Paul in Romans 9:16: "[Salvation] does not, therefore, depend on *human desire or effort*, but on God's mercy" (emphasis added). Neither apostle could be clearer on the matter. To their way of thinking, a person's conversion to Christ falls squarely within the camp of God's predetermined will and providential mercy. To quote the apostles directly, "human decision," "human desire," and our "will" and "effort" are excluded from consideration. When all is said and done, "[God] saved us, not because of righteous things we had done, but because of his mercy" (Tit. 3:5). In biblical theology, it is God's free and merciful will, not man's, which determines who is elect and who is not (Rom. 9:16).

And Paul and John are not alone. The Savior himself was unflinching when he taught that man does not choose God in salvation, but God chooses man. "No one," Jesus stated plainly, "can come to Me unless it has been granted him from the Father" (John 6:65, NASB). Elsewhere he declared, "no one knows the Father except the Son and those to whom the Son *chooses* to reveal him" (Matt. 11:27, emphasis added). This latter statement clearly implies that God reveals Himself only to those He has chosen while the former teaches that man does not come to Christ at his own discretion, but only by God's will.

Unconditional Election is also seen in the election of the Twelve Disciples. "You did not choose me," Christ made clear to them, "but I chose you and appointed you to go and bear fruit— fruit that will last ... I have chosen you out of the world" (John 15:16, 19 cf. 6:70). This same calling in which the Twelve were chosen for ministry is the same calling by which all believers are chosen for salvation. "For we know, brothers loved by God," greeted Paul to the Thessalonians, "that he has chosen you" (1 Thess. 1:4). Elsewhere we learn that "many are invited [to the banquet of salvation], but few are chosen" (Matt. 22:14).

It is God who sovereignly chooses His elect. It is God who elects unconditionally His chosen. And it is God who calls to salvation those He has predestined. Unconditional Election is the decisional work of God for a select people too destitute to ever elect Him in return: "I was found by those who did not seek me," the Lord declared, "I revealed myself to those who did not ask for me" (Rom. 10:20, cf. Isa. 65:1). That God proactively supersedes in the eternal destinies of certain human beings for His own electing purposes is an indisputable fact.

Returning to predestination, Paul writes elsewhere, "And those he predestined, he also called; those he called, he also justified; those he justified, he also glorified" (Rom. 8:30). Known as *The Golden Chain of Salvation*, or the *Ordo Salutis* (see Chapter 6), this passage lays the grid for election. Certain people are chosen for salvation in eternity past by the Father and, in time and space, called to faith in Christ by the Holy Spirit. Without fail, this calling ends with the justification and glorification of those chosen, predestined, and elected (cf. Php. 1:6).

Luke, the writer of Acts, brings Paul's statement on the *Ordo Salutis* and its connection to Unconditional Election to full circle in Acts 13. While Paul and Barnabas ministered in Pisidian Antioch on their first missionary journey, he writes, "and as many as were ordained to eternal life believed" (v. 48). Notice the tense and order of Luke's words. Luke unmistakably uses the passive voice ("were ordained") indicating that God had *first* chosen these specific people in Pisidian Antioch beforehand, and now through the conviction of His Spirit, brought them to faith in Christ according to election. The structure of his inspired words teaches unequivocally that those in Pisidian Antioch who believed Paul's message did so only because they had *first* been ordained in eternity past to believe. As Dr. James White notes: "This divine appointment [of believers in Pisidian Antioch to eternal life] obviously precedes and brings about the act of faith. God has appointed them to eternal life, and [for that reason] they believe."[98]

So why, we may ask, does God save people at all, much less predestine the conversions of unregenerate sinners before they are ever born? The answer is given to us, albeit somewhat ambiguously, in Romans 9:11. The Lord discriminatively preordains select people unto salvation, according to the apostle Paul, "in order that God's purpose in election might stand." And this He does, the apostle says elsewhere, "because of his own purpose and grace" (2 Tim. 1:9) and "in accordance with his pleasure and will" (Eph. 1:5). Whatever else Paul may have meant by these statements, it is clear that God had a premeditated purpose behind His actions; the rhyme and reason for which remain shrouded to us (cf. Deut. 29:29; Prov. 25:2). Notwithstanding this ambiguity, one thing is certain: God could have chosen to save everyone (for He had the power and authority to do so) or He could have chosen to save none (for He was under no obligation to show mercy to any)—but He did neither. Instead, He chose to save *some* while leaving others to the consequences of their sin. By choosing to save some, when none warranted saving at all, God's superlative grace is put on full display.

It is the overwhelming scriptural evidence for Unconditional Election which rescues many open-minded Christians from the despair of Arminian theology. The proof-texts are too many to evade. C.S. Lewis (1898-1963), for example, a beloved thinker in Christian literature and a supposed champion of classical Arminianism,[99] had no choice but to surrender to the Reformed doctrine of Unconditional Election. Despite his own theological convictions to the contrary, Lewis conceded:

> I was in fact offered what now appears a moment of wholly free choice. *But I feel my decision was not so important. I was the object rather than the subject in this affair. I was decided upon.* I was glad afterwards at the way it came out, but at the moment what I heard was God saying, 'Put down your gun and we'll talk'. ... It is a paradox ... I chose, *yet it really did not seem possible to do the opposite* (emphasis added).[100]

Lewis rightly captured the sentiment behind Unconditional Election (not to mention Irresistible Grace [see Chapter 18]). God sovereignly decrees the salvation of those whom He elects; and those whom He elects He positively draws through the miracle of regeneration. In the words of Lewis, we have been "decided upon."

Reflection Questions:

1. Like C.S. Lewis, has there ever been an occasion, when confronted by Scripture, you were compelled to reconsider your personal doctrine or your traditional perception of God?

2. Knowing that God has specifically and especially elected, chosen, and predestined certain people for salvation, does this affect your attitude toward God and how you perceive His sovereignty or sense of justice? Moreover, does the doctrine of Unconditional Election affect how you perceive *yourself* and your role in salvation?

3. If the Arminian view of election is correct, and God predestines for salvation those He *foresees* will believe in Christ on their own, who then is the ultimate sovereign, or determinate, in a sinner's redemption?

Chapter 12

Faith & Repentance

I know from firsthand experience what it means to be part of an inseparable duo. I am an identical twin. And having a lookalike who shares my DNA is one of the greatest thrills in my life. My twin brother is my closest confidant. He is a likeminded friend with whom I have everything in common and in whom I share the deepest passions. Even though we are separated by three thousand miles, there is hardly a time when we are not conjoined at the proverbial hip in some way, either psychologically or spiritually.

As with all identical twins, I enjoy a genetic synthesis with my brother that defies explanation. There have been times when I have seen things with what I know are his eyes, spoken words I knew were really his, and heard things through his ears. To the point, there are moments when I feel we are essentially the same person. From a passing glance, I tend to know my twin's thoughts before he speaks them—and he mine.

Much to the chagrin of wives everywhere, the relationship between twins usually exceeds the bounds of matrimony. And I suppose my brother and I are no different in this regard. On more than one occasion, for example, my wife has bemoaned the fact that I am more inclined to seek out my brother's opinion on a matter rather than her own. And this is no small issue between us. Having to play second-fiddle to a husband's sibling is a difficult assignment for any wife to tolerate. That it comes natural for me to gravitate toward him instead of her, regardless of the circumstance at hand, is but one of many crosses my wife bears in our marriage. Notwithstanding the occasional protest, she has come to accept the undeniable truth that my twin and I enjoy a level of intimacy that no other relationship—including the institution of marriage—can rival.

Having an identical brother who looks, behaves, thinks, laughs, talks, and walks like me, although certainly uncanny, is not without its social advantages. Growing up in the public school system (where popularity and image are coveted idols), I inherited some semblance of celebrity that I otherwise didn't deserve. Everyone knew who I was, so it seemed, or at the very least they knew *of* me by name. To them, I was either "Ronny or Donny" or "one of the twins" or they identified me as simply "one-half of the Gann brothers." There is a strange brew of fame mixed with confusion that comes with having a body-double.

At the same time, being part of an inseparable duo has its disadvantages. Raised in a middle-class home, it was not uncommon for my brother and me to share birthday and Christmas gifts when the family budget was tight. This was always a harsh pill for us to swallow. *What kid in his right mind ever wants to go halves with his sibling?* Moreover, I recall our freshmen year in high school when we both tried out for the varsity baseball team. My skills were sorely lacking that year, which my countless fielding errors and strikeouts clearly showed, while my brother performed well-enough to earn a spot on the roster. Yet our coach, who evidently had no experience with coaching twins, was uncertain how to keep one twin around while letting go of the other. In the end, my brother paid the price for my poor exhibition of skills. We *both* were cut from the roster.

Discovering our individual value as young men—that is, our own identity—amid a community that refused to see us as anything other than joined at the hip proved challenging. Like a pair of familiar shoes, they would often say, what value is there in appreciating one without the matching other? In the minds of most everyone, my brother and I were, and in some respects still are, indivisible. Yet the reality is that we each have our own destiny in life, our own relationship with God, our own calling and gifting from the Spirit, our own personality quirks, our own families, and our own sins. We are individuals with similar but nevertheless distinct feelings, similar but unique likes and dislikes, and similar but separate hobbies and skills. We are two human beings, not one. I suppose our main complaint is that people tend to perceive us only as a package deal; a plight common to most sets of twins, perhaps even those in the Bible like Jacob and Esau (Gen. 25:24), Perez and Zerah (Gen. 38:27), and Thomas and his twin (John 11:16; 20:24; 21:2).[101] We are, and will always be, an inseparable duo.

It has been said that "two are better than one." There is certainly some truth to this adage, especially as it relates to solving problems and making history. All of human culture, the West in particular, has benefited in some degree from the talented teamwork or pedigree of inseparable duos, going as far back as Adam and Eve in the Old Testament. At the beginning of history, Adam and Eve brought life to humankind and, according to Genesis 3:16-19, the pollutant of sin shortly thereafter. They are arguably the most eminent duo known to man. Adam and Eve represent the male and female genders respectively just as their sons Cain and Abel—a famous duo in their own right—prefigure those who are righteous and those who are disobedient.

Beyond biblical history, the entertainment industry has been a cradle for famous twosomes. Abbott and Costello, two burlesque comics in the 1930s, joined together to make balderdash humor a serious art form. They continue to be worldwide sensations a half-century after their deaths. Another iconic duo from the classical era of American comedy is Laurel and Hardy. They entertained audiences for decades with their slapstick tomfoolery which spanned some 100 feature-length films and movie shorts. Both of these comedy teams paved the way for the vaudevillian stage acts of Martin and Lewis in the 1950s, the Smothers Brothers in the 1960s, and the comedic magicians Penn and Teller in the 1990s—famous duos each and every one of them. It's worth noting, however, that when pursuing their solo careers, hardly any of these comedians were able to replicate the success they enjoyed as a couple.

The comedy circuit does not stand alone in producing celebrated duets. Many chart-topping songs and high-quality stage productions are the result of creative collaborations among brilliant composers, skillful musicians, vocalists, and lyricists. Over the past century classical music has produced the award-winning duos of Gilbert and Sullivan, Rodgers and Hammerstein, and George and Ira Gershwin. Likewise, pop-music boasts impressive double-acts such as Simon and Garfunkel, The Everly Brothers, and Sonny and Cher, not to mention The Righteous Brothers, Jan and Dean, and Hall and Oates. Each of these acts experienced exceptional success performing as pairs, yet virtually all of them stumbled embarrassingly when venturing out on their own. Without their counterpart in tow, many of them found success as a soloist fleeting.

In the world of fiction, the creative writing of William Shakespeare and the animation of Walt Disney also introduced famous pairings. Owing to their commitment to each other, Romeo and Juliet are the quintessential Shakespearian couple who embody undying love. They are arguably the most tragic duo in all of romantic literature. On the opposite end of the spectrum, Disney's Mickey Mouse and Donald Duck have entertained children for decades with their cartoonish shenanigans. They are the face of Disneyland and Disneyworld today. But none of these characters are as gripping without their significant other beside them. The story of Romeo loses its appeal without his Juliet. And with no protagonist like Donald Duck to goad him, Mickey Mouse is just another animated rodent.

Whether it's Bonnie and Clyde, Batman and Robin, Barbie and Ken, Astaire and Rogers, or simply the wonder of identical twins, inseparable duos tickle our collective imagination. It takes a unique melding of personalities, talents, and skills to develop into a team that captures the attention of an entire generation, to say nothing about the generations that follow. Every walk of life, every field of interest, and every culture has certain pairs that rise to the top of their field. A select few, such as those already described, outshine all others by their chemistry.

The theology of Christianity knows something about dynamic duos. The doctrine of justification, for example, goes hand-in-hand with the doctrine of salvation. A sinner cannot be declared righteous before a holy God on account of his faith in Christ (justification) without also being eternally delivered from God's wrath (salvation). Conversely, the Bible knows nothing about a saved sinner who, at the same time, is not also legally righteous before God. To suggest otherwise is to entertain a theological fiction. Where there is a saved sinner there stands also a justified one. And where there stands a sinner who has been justified, there also stands a saved sinner. Although they are distinct components in the act of redemption, the doctrines of justification and salvation are an inseparable duo.

This same truth can be said about the relationship between God's grace and mercy. As it relates to salvation, the definition of God's mercy is best understood in simplistic terms. We may define mercy as "a sinner *not getting* what he in fact *does* deserve." The idea in view here is that God's mercy saves a guilty sinner from where he ought to go in death—hell. But only the opposite is true for the definition of God's grace. We define grace as "a sinner *getting* what he in fact *does not* deserve." The idea here is that God's grace awards a guilty sinner with what he ought not to have in death—heaven. Thus, while God's mercy and grace are independent of each other and have unique roles by decree, they are ultimately conjoined at the hip. In point of fact, whenever God saves a sinner from hell (by mercy), that same sinner is automatically and simultaneously given heaven instead (by grace). God's mercy and grace are an inseparable duo.

Each of these amazing duos—justification and salvation as well as mercy and grace—play pivotal roles in Christian theology. And each is inherently the work of God alone. However, within the scope of redemption, Calvinism sees another set of twins—albeit somewhat fraternal—crucial to the doctrine of Unconditional Election. And these twins are called faith and repentance. They are joined at the hip. Saving faith always leads to repentance. And authentic repentance always leads to emboldened faith. Where there is a repentant sinner there stands also a faithful one. And where there stands a sinner with faith, there also stands a penitent one. As Charles Spurgeon so eloquently put it:

> Repentance is the inseparable companion of faith; ... [they] are vitally joined together ...

> [and] are but two spokes in the same wheel, two handles of the same plow ... Repentance and faith are like Siamese twins. If one is sick the other cannot be well, for they live but one life. If ever you are asked which comes first, repentance or faith, you may answer by another question: Which spoke moves first when the wheel begins to move?[102]

These twins are not without controversy in Reformed Theology, for to suggest as Calvinists do that repentance and faith are divine *gifts* exclusively granted to the Elect, as opposed to human *rights* universally procured at will, makes many Arminians apoplectic. It removes man's autonomy in the act of salvation and places it in the court of God's sovereign benevolence. That is to say, just as justification and salvation are divine prerogatives, together with mercy and grace, so are the twins of faith and repentance. And it is to this fraternal relationship we now turn.

Gifts or Entitlements?

Without question, there is a healthy tension that exists in Scripture between the responsibility of men and the sovereignty of God in salvation. Calvinists openly acknowledge this fact, as do Arminians. And to suggest otherwise is simply disingenuous. Like the inscrutability of the Trinity, the paradox of a double-natured Christ, or the mysterious relationship between faith and works, apparent conundrums abound in Scripture. But when Calvinists admit that a sinner does in fact possess a moral will they are not conceding that he is free to exercise it in the pursuit of godliness. In other words, it is one thing to say that a fallen person can willfully choose which cereal to eat for breakfast, says the Calvinist, it is altogether a different thing to teach that unregenerate, sinful, and enslaved God-haters can freely choose to follow the path of holiness. With his tongue planted firmly in his cheek, even the notorious and formidable atheist Christopher Hitchens (1949-2011) saw the paradox of so-called free-will, albeit from a different set of eyes. He said the following:

> Yes, I think we have free will. And when asked why I think so, I would have to take refuge in philosophical irony and say, "because I don't think we have any choice but to have free will." But at least I know at this point that I'm being ironic and that some of the irony is at my own expense, and it's a risk I have to be willing to run. But the Christian answer is, "Of course you have free will; the Boss insists upon it!" This somewhat degrades the freedom and redefines the idea of [free] will.[103]

To Hitchens, the concept of free-will is ironical, even though he had no choice but to admit to its certainty. And to some extent Calvinists would agree. We do not deny that man has a will, as is so often mischaracterized by our opponents, insomuch as we deny its effectiveness in the act of salvation. Owing to man's total reprobation, the Calvinist insists that the will of man is rendered ineffective in terms of seeking after or yearning for salvation. "Not free-will but self-will," concluded Dr. Loraine Boettner, "would more appropriately describe man's condition since the fall."[104]

Reformed Theology not only acknowledges the reality of self-will but recognizes that the Scriptures speak volumes about how man exercises it. In fact, what many evangelicals prize as inviolate—that is, man's volitional freedom—the Bible laments. How man exercises his moral freedom in his natural depravity is a matter of biblical and historical record.

Human autonomy, for example, is directly responsible for the fall of the Adamic race into sin and trespass (Rom. 5:12); the first homicide (Gen. 4:2-25); the universal wickedness that led to the Great Flood (Gen. 7); the rebellion of the Tower of Babel (Gen. 11:1-9); the sexual debauchery and inhospitality of Sodom and Gomorrah (Ezek. 16:49; Jude 1:7); the golden calf of idolatry (Exod. 32); Israel's forty-year wilderness wanderings (Num. 14:33-34) and recurring backsliding (Judges 2:17-19); the illicit behavior of Samson and Delilah (Judges 16:1-22); the sin of David and Bathsheba, and the murder of Uriah (2 Sam. 11); familial intrigue, incest, rape, and bestiality (Lev. 18 cf. 2 Sam. 13:1-22); governmental corruption, oppression, and priestly sacrilege (Jer. 32:31-33; 44:8-10); the overthrow of Israel by Assyria (2 Kings 17:1-21); the fall of wayward Judah to Babylon (2 Kings 24:12-16); the assassination of godly prophets and apostles (Luke 13:34); and most disturbingly, the crucifixion of God incarnate (Matt. 27:33-44; Mark 15:22-32; Luke 23:33-43; John 19:17-30).

Sadly, the truth of Scripture reveals that the more fallen man exercises his reprobate will the more it leads him away from God, *not toward Him*. Is it any wonder, then, that God chose to sovereignly act beforehand by proactively choosing, predestinating, and electing for Himself a special people too depraved to choose Him? That God chose to do so, rather than relegating our salvation to the court of human autonomy, is the beauty of Unconditional Election.

Once again, Calvinists do not deny the existence of self-will. We affirm that people are free to choose whatever they so desire. But when given the freedom to choose good or evil, unregenerate man will instinctively choose evil because "every inclination of the thoughts of his heart [are] only evil all the time" (Gen. 6:5). As Jonathan Edwards reasoned, free and fallen sinners will choose evil, and only evil, because that is what the unregenerate heart desires most. Commenting further in an audio lecture, Dr. R.C. Sproul summarized the Reformed position this way:

> I don't know any Augustinian [Calvinist] who does not strongly affirm that we have free-will. We are volitional creatures. God has given us minds and hearts, and He has given us 'will.' And we exercise that will all the time. We make choices every minute of the day. And we choose what we want. And we choose freely ...

We choose only according to our desires, which are only wicked all the time, the Bible tells us. And we are, as it were, dead in sin and trespasses ... and we're walking according to the course of this world and according to the prince of the power of the earth, fulfilling the lusts of the flesh ... And so the Bible makes it clear that we are actively involved making choices, for which we are ultimately responsible and which exposes us to the judgment of God. [So while man is free] at the same time the Bible teaches us that we are enslaved. We're free from coercion, but we ... are not free from ourselves. We are not free from our own sinful inclinations, and our sinful appetites, and our sinful desires. We are slaves to our sinful impulses.[105]

Man's enslaved-freedom—an oxymoronic term if ever there was one—is self-evident. The Scriptures make clear that the fruit borne from man's so-called autonomous agency is "fruit for death" (Rom. 7:5) but not "fruit of righteousness" (Php. 1:11). Man's self-will *does not* and *cannot* produce a craving for godliness, a yearning for holiness, or a hunger and thirst for righteousness. Instead, it yields only "sexual immorality, impurity and debauchery; idolatry and witchcraft; hatred, discord, jealousy, fits of rage, selfish ambition, dissensions, factions and envy; drunkenness, orgies, and the like" (Gal. 5:19). These are the stocks and bonds in which sinful men invest and the only crop they produce from it.

In terms of man's moral independence, the Old Testament prophets were remarkably forthright. "Can the Ethiopian change his skin or the leopard its spots?" asked a rhetorical Jeremiah. "Neither can you do good who are accustomed to doing evil" (Jer. 13:23). Far from championing man's moral liberty, Jeremiah captures with one swipe of the quill the slavery inherent to all men. Furthermore, whatever "righteous acts" man may think he is capable of doing from within the confines of his enslaved-freedom, they are put in proper perspective by Isaiah who equated them with "filthy rags" (Isa. 64:6). In the end, we learn that man's free-agency, when carried out to its full potential, is limited only to his freedom to sin.

But if this is true, how do we then explain the myriad of Bible verses that suggest man can choose to do otherwise? How do we reconcile Calvinism's low view of man's abilities and inclinations with God's high expectations for sinners? The Calvinist's response is straightforward. While it is true that all men are commanded in Scripture to exercise their self-will and "choose for yourselves this day whom you will serve" (Josh. 24:15); and "choose to fear the Lord" (Prov. 1:29), "choose the right" (Isa. 7:15-16), and choose "to do God's will" (John 7:17), the Scriptures also make clear that man cannot oblige these commands on his own for he does not possess the wherewithal. Moreover, whereas all people are encouraged to "Look to the Lord and his strength; seek his face always" (1 Chron. 16:11) and to "seek [God] with all your heart" (Jer. 29:13), the Bible also reminds us that, when left to his own resources, no sinner actually does (Rom.3:11 cf. Ps. 14:1-3; 53:1-3; Eccl. 7:20).

Mankind *cannot* and *will not* pursue the things of God or seek His face any more than he can attain moral perfection and practical holiness in the flesh, although Christ commands the sinner just the same (Lev. 10:3 cf. Matt. 5:48; 1 Pet. 1:15-16). To suggest that fallen man has the natural ability to comply with righteousness solely on the grounds that God commands it is to fall into the trap set by Pelagius, who famously said, "If I ought, then I can." Because the Bible does not bear his statement out, this brand of theological humanism was deposed resoundingly by the Patristic Fathers (see Chapter 2). They understood that the command to obey does not prove man's ability to comply. In other words, just because God commands His creatures to love and emulate Him, to seek after Him with absolute abandonment, and to choose the path of godliness over wickedness does not logically follow that sinners, by default, have the innate capacity to do so. (We have already seen in Section 2 the degree to which unregenerate man is spiritually impotent and unable to obey the salvific imperatives of Scripture).

So if the unregenerate are in bondage to sin and lack the liberty to choose Christ for salvation, then how exactly do elect sinners ever come to saving faith and repent? The answer is as humbling as it is wonderful. God graciously grants to those whom He has chosen, through the miracle of spiritual regeneration, the ability to appropriate that which is alien to them (faith and repentance) in order that they might become "as aliens and strangers in the world" (1 Pet. 2:11 cf. Heb. 11:13b). Stated differently, God grants *as gifts* to His beloved people both the required faith and the necessary repentance for salvation whereby they are "no longer foreigners and aliens, but fellow citizens with God's people and members of God's household" (Eph. 2:19 cf. Php. 3:20). These gifts are not afforded to all the sons of Adam uniformly but are reserved only for the sons of the "last Adam"—Jesus Christ (1 Cor. 15:45)—who have been elected for salvation unconditionally.

That faith and repentance are said to be gifts from God undercuts Arminian theology at its core. It removes man's so-called moral freedom to do either in exchange for God's sovereign freedom to grant both according to His will. And try as it might, to suggest that God denies these gifts to some while granting them to others does not wash well in an anthropocentric (man-centered) theology like Arminianism. Thus, for Pelagians, semi-Pelagians, and Arminians, the only alternative is to object as loudly as possible to any teaching that dares to rob boastful man of his own ability to repent and believe. Dave Hunt sounds the Arminian alarm accordingly:

> ... never do we read of saving faith as God's gift to a sinner. The Bible speaks continually of faith as something for which the individual is responsible. ... There is not one verse that says faith comes by regeneration ... Clearly there is [free-will] responsibility on the part of the person exercising faith.[106]

Like Hunt, those who subscribe to free-will theology counter the Reformed view with a library of assumptions which seek to make faith and repentance universal entitlements open to all rather than exclusive gifts allocated only to some. While God graciously equips *every* sinner *everywhere* with the ability to repent and believe, they say, He does not interfere with man's freedom to do either. Faith and repentance are part and parcel of man's free-will responsibility, they continue, which precedes the new birth (but does not result from it). A sinner's faith is his gift to God rather than God's gift to the sinner; it is man's contribution to the salvation formula. Most Arminians conclude, therefore, that faith and repentance are universal rights available to all men simply for the choosing.

Arminianism is correct when it states that the gospel calls everyone to repentance and exhorts all men to believe. And Calvinists agree that it is man's duty and privilege to do just that. Yet what Arminians refuse to accept, lest their entire theological system crumble, is that all men, being sinners by nature, would rather wallow in their sin and spurn the gracious promises of God than repent and be reconciled to Him. "Of them the proverbs are true," Peter declared. "'A dog returns to its vomit,' and, 'A sow that is washed goes back to her wallowing in the mud'" (2 Pet. 2:22). In other words, the unregenerate prefer their sinful filth to the cleansing waters of spiritual purification. And why is this so? "This is the verdict," Jesus declared, "Light has come into the world, but men loved darkness instead of light because their deeds were evil" (John 3:18).

While all men are certainly entreated, beseeched, commanded, and pleaded with in Scripture to turn to God in faith and repentance, the sad reality is that they simply *will not* nor *cannot* because of their infatuation with darkness. A sinner's only possible escape from the shadows of sin is the hope that God will sovereignly grant him faith and repentance whereby he is given new eyes to behold the "light of the world" (John 8:12; 9:5).

While Dave Hunt's personal theology and tradition retards his lucidity on this point, the Bible is emphatically lucid: Faith and repentance are gifts from the Holy Spirit who works in the hearts of those unconditionally elected. This is evident in the words of Paul to the Corinthians: "What do you have that

God hasn't given you? And if everything you have is from God, why boast as though it were not a gift? (1 Cor. 4:7, NLT). To paraphrase Paul, all that a sinner exercises in terms of coming to Christ—whether it is his freedom of the will, the ability to repent, or the faith to believe—comes ultimately "from God." Moreover, Jesus said, "No one can come to me unless the Father who sent me draws him," and again, "no one can come to me unless the Father has enabled him" (John 6:44, 65). Another way of stating this truth is to say that no one can repent and believe in Christ unless the Father enables him to do so. This is in keeping with the Bible's teaching that the ability to believe in Christ and the willingness to turn away from sin—far from being universal entitlements doled out to all men—are special gifts uniquely given to those whom the Father draws to the Son and those whom the Son chooses to reveal the Father (Matt. 11:27; Luke 10:22).

Concerning the act of repentance (i.e. to undergo "a change of mind [about sin]"),[107] the apostle Paul said that the Lord's servant should gently instruct unbelievers "in the hope that *God will grant them repentance* leading them to a knowledge of the truth" (2 Tim. 2:25, emphasis added). Here repentance is clearly seen as a gift that is *granted* by God. Similarly, the apostle Peter declared that God exalted Jesus to his own right hand as Prince and Savior "that he might *give repentance and forgiveness* of sins to Israel" (Acts 5:31, emphasis added). In this passage we see that repentance is *given* by God as a gift. On another occasion, when the Jewish believers heard about the conversion of the Gentiles, they "praised God, saying, 'So then, *God has granted even the Gentiles repentance unto life*'" (Acts 11:18, emphasis added). Here again, we see repentance in the form of a divine grant. Thus, the picture that is painted by the inspired artists of Scripture depicts an elect people, comprised of both Jewish and Gentile believers, who inevitably turn to the Lord in repentance because God mercifully *grants* that they should.

Repentance of sin, however, is not a stand-alone gift from God. It is always accompanied by the gift of saving faith. They are an inseparable duo. As with penitence, the ability to believe in Christ is not doled out indiscriminately to all people, much less in equal allotments. Instead, some individuals are given great measures of faith (cf. Rom. 12:3; 1 Cor. 13:2) whereas others apparently weaker faith (cf. Rom. 14:1), and still others none at all (cf. Heb. 3:18-20).

The apostle Paul reminded the Ephesians—and all Christians by extension—that they had been saved "by grace through faith—and this is not from yourselves, it is the gift of God" (Eph. 2:8-9). We learn from this statement that the faith we exercise as believers is not of ourselves. Rather, "it is the gift of God." That the apostle saw saving faith as a gift, alongside salvation, is evident by his later comment that "faith comes from God the Father and the Lord Jesus Christ" (Eph. 6:23, CEB). Paul clearly saw that saving faith does not originate in the heart of man but comes as a love gift from the heart of God. As he expressed to the Galatians: "But the fruit of the Spirit is ... faithfulness" (Gal. 5:22), which can also be translated "faith."

Continuing, the apostle Peter wrote that those chosen in Christ "have received a faith as precious as ours" (2 Pet. 1:1). What is of paramount importance here is the significance of the Greek verb *lagchano* that is translated "have received" (NASB) or "have obtained" (ESV). This verb carries with it the idea of an endowment. It specifically means "to obtain by lot" or "to receive by divine allotment"[108] (see Luke 1:9; John 19:24; Acts 1:17). A person cannot receive something without it first being given. In this case, the faith to which Peter refers is removed from the realm of human free-will and placed in its proper perspective as having originated in the sovereign and altogether gracious will of God. The apostle maintains that it was not by random chance or luck of the draw that some came to saving faith. Rather, a "faith as precious as ours" was *allotted* to believers by virtue of "the righteousness of our God and Savior, Jesus Christ."

Elsewhere, the Elect of God are described as those "who by grace have believed" (Acts 18:27) and have been "granted" saving faith (Php. 1:29). Moreover, each believer has been spiritually gifted "in accordance with the measure of faith God has given [them]" (Rom. 12:3). We learn from these passages that, just as with repentance, saving faith is "granted," "given," and "measured" out to the people of God "by grace." These are not statements applied liberally to all men; they refer only to believers, as their contexts explain. God grants faith and repentance as gifts and distributes them to those whom He has unconditionally chosen. To suggest otherwise, as Arminians do, is to betray these texts.

So how do Arminians like Dave Hunt evade the clear testimony of Scripture that teaches faith and repentance are gifts from God? Regrettably, in his rebuttal, Hunt has no alternative but to turn the Bible into a pretzel. He wrote:

> [The Bible] does not say that faith to believe is a gift without responsibility on man's part, but that the privilege to believe on Christ has been granted. Yes, one of the fruits of the Spirit is faith, *but this is faith given to believers for living the Christian life, not faith given to the unsaved for believing the gospel.* ... Not one [verse in the Bible] clearly states that faith to believe unto salvation is a gift of God that causes sinners to believe the gospel (emphasis added).[109]

Astoundingly, when faced with over a half dozen verses that speak of saving faith as a divine grant, according to the will of God, Hunt has no choice but to create a straw-man argument. He actually fabricates two categories for faith to escape his quagmire. To him, as with many Arminians with whom he is in lockstep, the Bible supposedly sees a difference between the faith "to believe on Christ ... for living the Christian life" and the faith "to believe unto salvation." Are we seriously expected to believe that the Bible distinguishes between the two—that faith in Christ (which enables faithful Christian living) somehow differs from salvific faith? God grants the former, Hunt concedes, but not the latter. Yet in what passage and in what manner the Bible actually differentiates between these two types of faith—to say nothing as to why God would graciously grant one and not the other—Hunt does not say.

In the end, the breadth and scope of Scripture sides with Reformed Theology. Man cannot lay claim to any aspect of the salvation process, to include the ability to repent and believe. If a person humbles himself to submit to God it is only because the Holy Spirit has granted that person the capability to do so. While God requires faith and repentance of *all* men, to be sure, He only gives them to those whom He has predestined, chosen, and elected.

It bears summarizing: Unconditional Election is the sovereign act of God whereby He graciously chose for Himself in Christ Jesus—and on account of His good pleasure—certain sinful people to be the recipients of His saving grace. And this He has done before the foundations of the world. Furthermore, those chosen to receive His grace will invariably arrive at faith in Christ—not through human decision, will, effort or foreseen merit (John 1:13; Rom. 9:16 cf. 9:11)—but on account of His sovereign decree. This beautiful picture of sovereignty drove Kay Arthur—an international Bible teacher, a four-time ECPA Christian Book Award winning author, and co-founder of *Precept Ministries International* (and arguably the premiere female Bible teacher in the Church today)—to confess the following:

> God is the one that saves. I am not the Savior. I am the messenger. And God assures me [that] *"He that comes to me I will in no wise cast out—I will raise him up on the last day. You come to me because I have drawn you, because I have brought you"* and ... God doesn't lose any of his sheep ... I know that God is sovereign over salvation. I know that I cannot save my child. I know that I cannot turn him from darkness to light. I know that only God can; and I know that if that's God's intention that God will accomplish it and that I am to rest and be about my Father's business.[110]

Arthur is spot on. It is God who elects. It is God who predestines and chooses. It is God who draws. It is God who grants repentance. It is God who grants faith. And it is God who therefore grants salvation. For this reason the Scriptures can declare without apology, "It is because of him that you are in Christ Jesus" (1 Cor. 1:30). Like the believing remnant in Pisidian Antioch in Acts 13, the Elect in Christ inescapably repent and believe the preached gospel because God has ordained in eternity past that they should and gifted them in time and space with the capability to do so. Like Arthur, we rest in the comfort that God is in control of all things; meanwhile we go humbly about our Father's business.

Reflection Questions:

1. Judeo-Christianity is not short on fantastical tales. From a duplicitous snake (Gen. 3:1-4) and a talking donkey (Num. 22:21-31) to the story of a prophet surviving in the belly of a fish for three days (Jnh 1:17), the Bible demands belief in the outlandish. Can today's unregenerate man, who prides himself on his intellectual enlightenment and scientific ingenuity, accept such improbable claims without divine initiative?

2. How, if at all, does the gift of repentance differ in Scripture from the world's idea of "inner reform," "personal rehab," and "self-help"?

3. Is the gift of saving faith the same as intellectual belief (cf. James 2:19)?

4. If repentance and faith are divine gifts, how then can the non-elect be judged for lacking both if it is God who gives them to whomever He so chooses?

Chapter 13

Fore-Love or Foresight?

For the archaeologist of truth who mines the caverns of Scripture, the doctrine of Unconditional Election is an inescapable find. Yet, for many, the treasure-trove of New Testament teaching on the matter tends to raise more questions than it answers. To be sure, Calvinists and Arminians agree that, although somewhat vague in description, predestination is an undisputable *fact*. But where disagreements emerge is over the *manner* in which God predestinates, and to what extent.

Election, according to Calvinism, rests on the will of God. As already noted, the Calvinist argues that certain sinners are predestined *unto salvation* in eternity past on the basis of God's sovereign choice, in accordance with His grace, and irrespective of man's foreseen actions. Moreover, His decision to save some individuals, while overlooking others, is neither capricious nor arbitrary, but is determined "according to the good pleasure of his will" (Eph. 1:5) and "according to His own purpose and grace ... from all eternity" (2 Tim. 1:9). Dr. James White summarizes the Reformed view accordingly: "It is God's mercy, not man's will or effort, that determines the outcome of salvation ... God, and God alone, is the determining agent. His choice is not determined by human action. It is therefore unconditional."[111]

To the Calvinist way of thinking, election falls squarely in the camp of God's providence. The God-given faith exercised by a believer (in time and space) is the inevitable result, rather than the cause, of his election (in eternity past). The Westminster Confession of Faith bears this point out markedly:

> Those of mankind that are predestinated
> unto life, God, before the foundation of the

world was laid, according to His eternal and
immutable purpose, and the secret counsel and
good pleasure of His will, hath chosen in Christ
unto everlasting glory, out of His mere free grace
and love, *without any foresight of faith or good
works, or perseverance in either of them, or
any other thing in the creature, as conditions,
or causes moving Him thereunto*; and all to the
praise of His glorious grace.

As God hath appointed the elect unto glory, so
hath He, by the eternal and most free purpose of
His will, *foreordained all the means thereunto*.
Wherefore, they who are elected being fallen in
Adam, are redeemed by Christ; are effectually
called unto faith in Christ by His Spirit working in
due season; are justified, adopted, sanctified, and
kept by His power, through faith, unto salvation.
Neither are any other redeemed by Christ,
effectually called, justified, adopted, sanctified,
and saved, but the elect only (emphasis added).[112]

As it relates to predestination, or Unconditional Election,
Arminians object to this historical confession for a number of
reasons, but in particular its assertion that "mankind ... [is]
predestinated unto life ... *without any* [divine] *foresight of
faith or good works* [in man]." To them, such a statement is
unbiblical, if not absurd, because it seemingly exonerates man
of his responsibility. Furthermore, in outright negates divine
foreknowledge, which supposes that God sees in advance a
sinner's future response to the gospel and, on that basis, chooses
either to elect him or pass him over.

Not surprisingly, the Westminster Confession of Faith tends
to cause tremors among free-will evangelicals. If Calvinists
succeed in convincing others that the will of man is *not* the
ultimate determinate in his salvation, but rather God's sovereign
choice is to blame, Arminians then fear that humanity will be
robbed of its dignity and God will be perceived as totalitarian. To

allay their worries, they therefore insist that God's choice must be predicated on human choice. In this way, God is absolved of any potential injustice and man's autonomy remains intact.

Moreover, most Arminians argue that God predestines a sinner merely *unto blessing*, not necessarily or inevitably unto salvation, as Calvinists teach.[113] And this election is conditional, they further allege, since it is based on God's *foreknowledge* of a sinner's response to the gospel. In other words, God's choice in who He saves is in no way a dictatorial decision but rather is an informed one. Dave Hunt represents the vanguard of Arminian thought on this point. "Election" he writes, "is not unto salvation [as Calvinists believe] but unto blessings, and foreknowledge is the basis. God knew from eternity past who would believe the gospel, and it was for these that God predestined for blessings."[114]

To paraphrase Hunt, God is said to have looked down the passageway of time and foresaw who, of their own free-will, would believe in Him. Those who were seen to respond positively to the gospel, so the story goes, He therefore chose to shower His blessings upon. In the Arminian panorama, divine election is conveniently democratic; it falls squarely in the camp of man's foreseen freedom. A believer's election, as it therefore turns out, is the result, rather than the cause, of foreseen faith, we're told.

On this point the language barrier between Calvinists and Arminians rears its ugly head once again (see Chapter 3). In the same way that both groups differ over the meaning of *sovereignty* (imperial versus exhaustive) and the meaning of *dead* (separation versus lifelessness) so they also differ over the meaning of *foreknowledge*. It has been a source of debate and semantic wrangling for centuries.

Arminians define God's *foreknowledge* as His ability to read or predict the future actions of men, which effectively determines who He will and will not choose for salvation. And to be fair, their understanding of the term jives reasonably with today's English definition, which defines it as "knowledge or awareness of something before its existence or occurrence."[115] Most Arminians apply this modern definition to God's foreknowledge, as Hunt obviously does, and insist that it is on this basis alone that God predestinates. The entire skeleton of Arminian theology therefore hangs on the assertion that God's choice is predicated upon man's foreseen choice. Arminius wrote:

> From this follows the fourth decree to save certain particular persons and to damn others, which decree rests upon the foreknowledge of God, *but which he has known from eternity which persons should believe* according to such an administration ... *and also who should not believe and persevere* (emphasis added).[116]

Arminius was not alone in his position, as the Remonstrance of 1618 clearly demonstrated. Today entire denominations have been built on this view. Perhaps the most well-known and oft-quoted Arminian, second only to Arminius himself, is John Wesley (1703-1791), founder of Methodism. In his sermon entitled *On Predestination*, Wesley implied that predestination begins and ends with God's foreknowledge. He argued, "God foreknew those in every nation who would believe,"[117] and that, "In a word, God, looking on all ages, from the creation to the consummation, as a moment, and seeing at once whatever is in the hearts of all children of men, knows every one that does or does not believe, in every age or nation."[118]

Wesley saw no conflict between human freedom and divine sovereignty. Following Arminius' lead, he simply redefined the biblical concept of foreknowledge to alleviate a potential headache. He affirmed that although God knows an individual's future, He does not determine it. In league with Arminius, he believed that it is man—not God—who ultimately determines his spiritual destiny, and this he does by exercising his free-will. To that end, Wesley believed that we must not think that all things are, or come to pass, simply because God knows them (that is, decrees them). Rather, God simply knows *about* them because He foresees that they are natural happenstances committed voluntarily by men. Thus, because God has advanced awareness of man's future actions and decisions, He therefore can make an informed assessment in choosing those whom He will save.

Arminius and Wesley were in lockstep with one another. Both theologians saw God's divine foreknowledge—His ability to know in advance who would believe in Him—as the sole condition for His predetermination to elect individuals. God's sovereign decree, while important to His eternal majesty, is beside the point.

Armed with the bullhorn of Scripture, Reformed Theology objects to Arminius' and Wesley's interpolation of foreknowledge on the grounds that it overrules the sovereignty of God. To suggest, as these men did, that the basis for election rests on man's foreseen response to the gospel (in time and space) rather than on God's sovereign choice (in eternity past) is to idolize the self-will of reprobate man. It ascribes spiritual muscles to sinners that the Bible insists are atrophied from birth. What is more, by putting the "option" for election in the court of human autonomy, sinners are afforded a generous opportunity to boast, which the Bible strictly forbids (Eph. 2:9; 2 Cor. 10:17 cf. Jer. 9:24). A sinner can lay claim to the notion that, by virtue of his own free-will decision (not God's sovereign choice), he was *smart enough* on his own, or *lucky enough* through happenstance, or *favored enough* by God, to come to saving faith in Christ independently.

The train wreck of free-will theology is clearly identifiable. When God's sovereignty is dethroned from the pedestal of salvation we are left with the autonomy of man wearing the crown. Arminianism ultimately credits man with saving himself which, according to Scripture, entitles him to the praise that comes with it. In other words, it is *not* God who is glorified in the Arminian process of redemption but the sinner's volitional response to God's offer. God makes salvation possible, to be sure, but sinners make it actual. And just as unsettling, if we compromise with the Arminian on this point and concede that God's sovereignty works *in conjunction* with man's freedom to bring about his salvation, we are then forced to conclude that God is willing to *share* His glory with man, a concept that is also foreign in Scripture (Isa. 42:8).

As is already evident by now, Calvinists uphold that God is utterly sovereign. He will not share His glory with, nor surrender His sovereignty to, the reprobate. It is the will of God, not the decisions of men, that is the final determinate in the redemptive process. God elects and saves only those whom He has predetermined to save in the counsel of His will, independent of foreseen faith or perceived merit in the objects of His mercy. John 1:13 is clear: "[We have] become children of God ... not of ... *human decision ... or will, but born of God*" (emphasis added). Romans 9:16 adds: "[Salvation] does not, therefore, depend on *human desire or effort*, but on God's mercy" (emphasis added). Clearly, the element of human free-will is removed from the plan of salvation.

So how do Calvinists answer Arminius and Wesley concerning God's foreknowledge in salvation? The answer is that Scripture, not philosophy, is our final say. Calvinists contend that God's foreknowledge is best understood in Scripture as *fore-love* or *foreordination*; that is to say, Calvinists believe that when the Bible speaks of foreknowledge in relationship to salvation, it is speaking of God *fore-loving*, or loving in advance, His foreordained elect. Beyond mere awareness of what will happen in the future, it is the divine *predetermination* of what *will* happen. It speaks of planning, not simply observing (cf. Jer. 1:5; Acts 2:23). In this context, it indicates that God pre-thought and predetermined each relationship He enjoys with His elect people. Dr. R.C. Sproul explains:

> From all eternity God foreknew his elect. He had an idea of their identity in his mind before he created them. He foreknew them not only in the sense of having a prior idea of their personal identities, but also in a sense of foreloving them. When the Bible speaks of "knowing," it often distinguishes between a simple mental awareness of a person and a deep intimate love of a person. The Reformed view teaches that all whom God has foreknown, he has also predestined to be inwardly called, justified, and glorified. God

sovereignly brings to pass the salvation of his elect and only his elect.[119]

Taking a slight detour for just a moment, a word must also be interjected in refutation to the Arminian belief that predestination is unto blessings *only* and not salvation. Dave Hunt packages the Arminian argument this way:

> [Calvinism] assures us that Ephesians 1 and Romans 8 and 9 present God's "predestination of a particular people to salvation." Yet salvation isn't the subject ... Election is not unto salvation but unto blessings, and foreknowledge is the basis. God knew from eternity past who would believe the gospel, and it was for these that God predestined special blessings...[120]

Hunt's logic is myopic, to say the least. It is true that, according to the Bible, believers have been predestined to be "conformed to the image of his Son" (Rom. 8:29) and to be *adopted* as children of God (Eph. 1:5). These are breathtaking blessings, indeed. But to suggest that such things equate *only* to "blessings" is to stop short of what it really means to become like Christ or to be adopted as a child of God. Are not those who are made Christ-like those who have been redeemed? Are not those who have been adopted into God's family as sons and daughters the recipients of salvation? To be a child of God is to have been adopted through saving faith in Christ. Therefore, it logically follows that to be predestined to adoption and Christ-likeness is equivalent to being predestined to salvation. We do not receive one without the other. They are paired together in matrimony just as faith and repentance are inseparable. What Hunt fails to realize is that *salvation* is the ultimate *blessing* for which the Elect have been predestined.

It is a hermeneutical fallacy of Arminianism to dismiss salvation in the predestination process. The apostle Paul was unequivocally clear on this point: "God has chosen you from the beginning *for salvation*" (2 Thess. 2:13, emphasis added). We can safely conclude, therefore, that God predetermined both the blessings and benefits of salvation for a believer in Jesus Christ.

Returning to God's foreknowledge, it is evident that the gulf between Calvinism and Arminianism is vast. To recap, the Calvinist suggests that God's foreknowledge is tantamount to God "*loving* in advance" those whom He foreordained to believe in His Son. The Arminian, however, responds that God's foreknowledge merely means He "*knows* in advance" who will freely believe in His Son thereby affecting His decision who to predestinate. In the final analysis, one side holds to a view that puts the onus of election on the sovereign will of God (Calvinism), whereas the other places the onus on the foreseen actions of man (Arminianism). One side argues that predestination relates to salvation (Calvinism), whereas the other maintains it pertains only to blessings (Arminianism). So which side is correct?

It can be rightly said that finding a common bridge between the two positions hinges on a proper understanding of what God's foreknowledge is and does. This is the perennial point of contention in the doctrine of Unconditional Election. So we must ask: Do contemporary English definitions of foreknowledge ("to know in advance"), which Arminians liberally apply, mesh with the contextual analysis of Scripture?

Any linguist or scholar will attest that presupposing word meanings in ancient texts based upon modern-day lexicons is a clear and present danger to interpretation. Notwithstanding this warning, this is precisely the violation that Arminian theology makes concerning God's foreknowledge in election. We need look no further than the King James Bible (KJV) to see the danger this type of hermeneutic poses.

When the KJV refers to "amazement" in 1 Peter 3:6, for example, it does not mean "wonder" or "astonishment," as the word means today. Instead, the KJV has in mind the idea of being *frightened*. Furthermore, the KJV translators used the Elizabethan expression "by and by" four times in the gospels. While today this expression carries with it the idea that something will happen "eventually or occasionally," the contextual sense in the KJV actually means *immediacy* (cf. Matt 13:21; Mark 6:25; Luke 17:7; 21:9, NIV). In the same way, the word "careful" in the KJV does not denote "cautiousness" or "wariness" as we understand the term; rather, to the medieval translators it meant *anxious* (Luke 10:41; Phil 4:6).

The list of confused terminology is seemingly unending. The word "conversations" in the KJV refers to "way of life;"[121] the "bowels" actually has in view the "heart,"[122] and "accursed" really means "devoted."[123] Each of these terms—"conversations," "bowels," and "accursed"—defy our modern dictionary in their Elizabethan usage.

Arminians stand accused by Calvinists for winking at this variance in language. They apply the modern definition of *foreknowledge* to each and every verse in which the word is found in the New Testament while flagrantly ignoring both context and subtext. And by doing so, they unleash mayhem on a good chunk of Scripture.

As a final example, the KJV renders James 2:3 as follows: "And ye have respect to him that weareth the gay clothing." The problem becomes immediately apparent to the reader. If we default to modern definitions when interpreting the King's English, we have no choice but to conclude that James is exhorting his readers to beware showing partiality to those who dress like homosexuals. But any sober-minded Christian understands that this explanation is far from what James's had in mind. Obviously the word *gay* has a different connotation today than it did when the KJV was translated. We therefore should take caution not to impose upon classical words their contemporary meanings without first paying our respects to context.

If Arminians like Hunt persist in their argument that the Bible's use of the word *foreknowledge* only means how we define it today, then they betray their poor scholarship. They have no choice but to overturn the meaning of 1 Peter 1:20, which says: "[Christ] was foreordained before the foundation of the world, but was manifest in these last times for you" (KJV). More succinctly, the NIV renders it: "For [Christ] was *foreknown* before the foundation of the world, but has appeared in these last times for the sake of you" (emphasis added). Are we really supposed to default to the Arminian understanding that Peter is simply saying that God only had advanced information about Jesus before his incarnation and nothing more?

In speaking of Christ as foreknown to the Father, Peter has in mind the Calvinist concept of fore-love. More than just passing awareness, the Father *loved* his Son with deep affection that spanned the eons of eternity. Jesus attested to this special relationship when he prayed in his *High Priestly Prayer*: "Father, glorify me in your presence with the glory *I had with you before the world began*" (John 17:5, emphasis added). In other words, the two Persons in the triune Godhead enjoyed a mutual love with one another from all eternity; a love equally shared by the Holy Spirit. Therefore, we understand Peter to be saying in 1 Peter 1:20 that, as the second Person of the Trinity, Christ was fore-loved by the first Person of the Trinity. Yet, if we apply the Arminian definition of God's foreknowledge to this text—that is, "advanced knowledge"—the meaning is lost. In its place we are left with the unconvincing argument that God simply had preliminary awareness of His Son to be.

All things being equal, it is true that Arminians are not necessarily wrong in their limited explanation of the word *foreknowledge*. But my point is that they're not entirely right either. The word can, and sometimes does in a couple of passages, mean *foresight* (e.g. Acts 26:5; 2 Pet. 3:17). However, their overall conclusions prove shortsighted and irresponsible when they impose the modern English definition *uniformly* on Scripture. By ignoring context and Greek tenses, as noted in 1 Peter 1:20, they fall short of sensible interpretation in most of the passages in which the word *foreknowledge* is found. By dismissing the fact that it is always *persons* God is said to foreknow in Scripture, *not the actions of those persons*, Arminians frustrate the intent of the writers (cf. (Matt. 7:23; John 10:14; 1 Cor. 8:3; 2 Tim. 2:19).

The Greek words translated "foreknow" and "foreknowledge" are the verb *proginosko* and the noun *prognosis*. The verb has the basic meaning of "to know beforehand," or "to know in advance," but the noun, according to Strong, means "previous determination."[124] The verb *proginosko* is used five times in the New Testament (Rom. 8:29, 11:2; Acts 26:5; 1 Pet. 1:20; 2 Pet.

3:17), while the noun *prognosis* is attested twice (Acts 2:23; 1 Pet. 1:2). At first glance, Arminian theology seems to have a friend in the original language. But when performing contextual analysis on the Bible, many scholars insist otherwise. Additionally, we must keep in the forefront of our minds a cardinal rule of biblical interpretation: "If the plain sense makes sense, seek no other sense, otherwise it is nonsense."

Dr. Louis Berkhof (1873–1957), a systematic theologian who taught for nearly four decades at Calvin Theological Seminary and whose written works have been influential in colleges and seminaries throughout North America, deduced the following:

> *Proginoskein* and *prognosis* in the New Testament ... do not denote simple intellectual foresight or prescience, the mere taking knowledge of something beforehand, but rather *a selective knowledge which regards one with favor and makes one an object of love* ... these words [in the aforementioned passages where foreknowledge occurs] simply lose their meaning, if the words be taken in the sense of simply taking knowledge of one in advance, for God foreknows all men in that sense (emphasis added).[125]

According to Berkhof's scholarship, foreknowledge means far more than knowing beforehand what will happen (or who will exercise faith). It implies an intimate relationship with someone who is the object of God's redemptive love. Yet to the protesting Arminian, explanations like Berkhof's are dismissed as Calvinistic sleight of hand. Therefore, in order to determine which school of thought is correct, we must provide an overview of the hotly-contested Bible passages where the verb *proginosko* and the noun *prognosis* occur.

By way of example, if we apply the Arminian definition of foreknowledge to Acts 2:23 we are left with a diluted text. Luke cites the apostle Peter as saying, "...this Man [Jesus Christ], delivered over by the predetermined plan and foreknowledge [*prognosis*] of God, you nailed to a cross by the hands of godless men and put Him to death."

In effect, Arminians would have us believe that the apostle is telling his audience that God only "knew in advance" that Jesus would be delivered into godless hands. Certainly all Bible-believing Christians agree that God foresees all things, including the crucifixion, but to suggest that *only* His omniscience is in view here is to restrict the meaning of foreknowledge and to distill the text of its import.

Here, as in other passages, Arminians pay no attention to the importance of Greek syntax. Significantly, the word *foreknowledge* in Acts 2:23 is in the *instrumental dative case* (that is, it shows the "means" or the "instrument" by which something is accomplished). In other words, God's foreknowledge in Acts 2:23 is the very means, or instrument, by which Christ's atonement was made. It does not simply speak to God's passive awareness of what will transpire but to His foreordination of the actual event itself, a point which Peter plainly emphasizes. "This man was handed over to you by God's ... foreknowledge," the apostle said, "... to conspire against ... Jesus" (Acts 2:23; 4:27-28). Jesus did not die *in accord* with the foresight of God but rather *because* or by means of God's foreknowledge.

Calvinists understand this passage to mean far more than what initially meets the reader's eye. God foreordained, as satisfaction for His people's sins, the atoning sacrifice of Christ. This foreordination was based on God's fore-love for those whom Christ died, and in accord with His predetermined decree. It cannot be stressed enough: Foreknowledge, in this passage, is determinative (causative) and not merely predictive. Divine foreknowledge as it relates to any element of God's predetermined purpose must pertain to God's active involvement in bringing the event to come to pass. The *instrumental dative case* in the Greek demands this. Dr. Edgar C. James commented:

> Now the question is: Was it possible for Christ to be delivered over to His enemies "by the foreknowledge [prescience] of God?" Certainly

foreknowledge knows, but it does not perform an act like the delivering of Jesus to His enemies. Are not those who contend otherwise reading something more than the English meaning of foreknowledge into this passage? However, if we translate that Christ was delivered over by the determinate counsel and forethought of God, that is, by His decision reached in eternity, then we have a thought which is both intelligible and satisfying. Thus it is that "determinate counsel and forethought" are synonymous expressions, both describing one and the same act, one stressing the element of will, and the other of knowledge.[126]

If we were to paraphrase Acts 2:23 according to the Reformed view, and in conjunction with the original language, we understand Peter to be saying the following: "Jesus was the Son of God, and he proved it by many signs and miracles, but in spite of this wicked and sinful men nailed him to the cross. *This was no accident, for long ago God not only knew about it but foreordained that this should happen.* Sinful men did not know it but even in their wickedness they fulfilled *the predetermined purpose of God for His Son to die,* bearing the sins of men and women He long ago fore-loved."

The Greek word *gnosis* (and its cognates *prognosis* and *proginosko*, from which we get the term *foreknowledge*) finds its linguistic counterpart in the Hebrew word *yada*. Among several other meanings, depending on context, this Hebrew word often refers to knowing with experience or intimacy, not just foresight or awareness. For example, it is used of sexual union (Gen. 4:1, 19:8), personal acquaintance (Gen. 29:5; Exod. 1:8), knowing good from evil (Gen. 3:5, 22), and knowing the true God (1 Sam. 2:12-3:7; Jer. 3:22). The noun and verb *prognosis* and *proginosko* in the Greek are derivative of the Hebrew word *yada*. And it is this experiential intimacy that Calvinists apply to God's foreknowledge.

We see this concept of fore-loving in God's intimate "knowledge" of Moses. Exodus 33:17 reads, "And the Lord said to Moses, 'I will do the very thing you have asked, because I am pleased with you and I know [*yada*] you by name" (emphasis added). Here God's personal affection for Moses is captured in the Hebrew word *yada* ("to know, be acquainted with") which goes far beyond mere foresight or awareness of Moses as a person. That God "knew" Moses was to imply that he had found favor with the Lord and was specifically chosen to be a recipient of God's tender mercy. A unique and special relationship is in view in Exodus 33, not just head-knowledge. This truth is borne out six verses earlier: "The Lord would speak to Moses face to face, as one speaks to a friend" (Exod. 33:11).

Again, we see this same thought in view in Amos 3:2. In speaking of Israel, God declared, "You only have I known [*yada*] of all the families of the earth: therefore I will punish you for all your iniquities" (KJV, emphasis added). If we apply the Arminian argument for *prognosis* and *proginosko* ("to know in advance"), keeping in mind that both cognates are derived from the Hebrew *yada* ("to know, be acquainted with"), we must therefore ask the following: Are we really expected to believe that God was unaware of any other nations in existence besides Israel? If Amos' words are true, and Arminians are right that foreknowledge (*prognosis* and *proginosko*, as derived from *yada*) simply means advance awareness, then how do we interpret God's quotation, "You only have I *known*"?

It's obvious that God didn't merely know about Israel, and possessed no such knowledge of other nations, nor does this passage suggest that God merely knew the future actions of Israel, but didn't know the future actions of other nations. This "knowing" of Israel is deeply personal and intimate and speaks of God's grace in choosing Israel as the object of His loving concern.

The word *yada* is used also in Genesis 4:1 in relationship to Adam and Eve. In this passage we are told that Adam *knew* his wife, Eve. In what manner, we may ask, did Adam know Eve? Was he simply aware of her and have insight about her? The answer is evident. That "Adam knew [*yada*] Eve his wife" (Gen.

4:1, ESV) meant he had a conjugal relationship with her, which resulted in Eve's pregnancy. As with Exodus 33:17 and Amos 3:2, to "know" means more than perception or acuity. It entails a personal relationship.

We learn that God also had a predetermined relationship with the prophet Jeremiah. "Before I formed you in the womb I knew [*yada*] you, and before you were born I consecrated you; I have appointed you a prophet to the nations" (Jer. 1:5). More than just mere foresight of the prophet's ministry, God enjoyed an intimate relationship with Jeremiah before he ever came to be. He was fore-loved by God and therefore foreordained to prophetic ministry.

Finally, to the Galatians, the apostle Paul wrote in manner reminiscent of Jeremiah: "But now that you know God—*or rather are known* [proginosko] *by God*—how is it that you are turning back to those weak and miserable principles?" (Gal. 4:9, emphasis added). Even though the Galatians had come to know God, Paul hints at a much deeper meaning. The Galatians knew God only because God first knew them and set His affection upon them in eternity past! More than mere omniscience, a predetermined relationship is in view.

God "knew" Moses from all eternity and raised him up to be His mouthpiece to the house of Israel and before the seat of Pharaoh (Exod. 33:17). He "knew" Israel and chose them as His bride out of all the people groups on the earth (Amos 3:2). He "knew" Jeremiah before he was born and appointed him to be a prophet (Jer. 1:5). So too, the Galatians had come to know God because He first "knew" them, having loved them in advance.

Romans 8:29, which reads "For *those* God foreknew he also predestined to be conformed to the likeness of his Son," is often cited by Arminians as the basis for *conditional* election—that God knew in advance who would believe in Him and, on that basis, predestined them for blessing. But the Calvinist is quick to point out that Paul does not say "*that*" which God foreknew (namely, the actions of these men, such as their faith and belief). Rather, the apostle emphasizes "*those*" who God foreknew. In using the pronoun "those" instead of "that" it is clear that individual people are in view here not merely their future actions. The point of God's foreknowledge is not that He simply had future information *about something*, but that He had an intimate relationship *with someone*. Moreover, it's causative, and not merely predictive. It's instrumental not passive.

I take the time to hash over some of these Old Testament passages concerning *yada* ("to know, be acquainted with") because this Hebrew verb sets the stage for its Greek counterparts *prognosis* and *proginosko* in the New Testament. It elucidates for the student of Scripture what the words "foreknow," "foreknew," and "foreknowledge" actually mean in passages germane to salvation. Furthermore, for the Calvinist who stands in awe of the unbending grace of God, it offers new insight into the beautiful refrain, "God has not rejected His people whom He foreknew" (Rom. 11:2, NASB).

The foreknowledge of God carries with it a much broader meaning than mere omniscience. In the contexts which speak to God's electing or predestinating, the idea of instrumental causation is always present, borne out of God's personal affection for the object elected and predestined. Thus, in the various passages related to salvation where the word is found, we conclude that to foreknow on God's part means He *fore-loved*. And that God foreknew His elect is another way of saying that He set His gracious and merciful regard upon us; that He knew us from eternity past with a sovereign and distinguishing delight. Like the Galatians, we have come to know God only because He first knew us. In the words of John, "We love [Him] because he first loved us" (1 John 4:19).

Reflection Questions:

1. Some argue that Calvinism disrespects the will of man and robs him of his identity. How does the fact that God fore-loved certain sinners from eternity past glorify God but still honor man's dignity?

2. If God fore-loved the Elect, is it possible that He also "fore-hated" His enemies (Rom. 9:11-13 cf. Lev. 20:23;

Psa. 5:5, 11:5; Prov. 6:16-19; Hos. 9:15)? Why or why not?

3. On what basis does God fore-love certain sinners and forsake others (Eph. 1:5; 2 Tim. 1:9)?

4. What role do the ancient creeds, confessions, and doctrinal statements of the Christian Church play in the debate between Calvinism and Arminianism? Do such creeds inform your beliefs?

Section 4:

The Scandal of Limited Atonement

*"It will be seen at once that this doctrine necessarily follows
from the doctrine of election. If from eternity God has
planned to save one portion of the human race and not
another, it seems to be a contradiction to say that His work
has equal reference to both portions ... These two doctrines
must stand or fall together. We cannot logically accept one
and reject the other. If God has elected some and not others to
eternal life, then plainly the primary purpose of Christ's work
was to redeem the elect."*

Loraine Boettner
1901-1990

Chapter 14

The Rise of Frankenstein Theology

Many Americans find social profiling objectionable, and not without good reason. Like the Hindu caste system, our class structure in the West has a history of grouping people together based on income, race, religion, or gender irrespective of who they are, what they believe, or with whom they associate. Simply submerge a person into the eclectic stream of Western culture and, before long, they'll emerge from its waters with a proverbial watermark tattooed on them, courtesy of social stratification.

Among our young people, especially, is a growing outcry against labels. To arbitrarily stereotype a teenager as a jock, a brain, a skater, a rocker, or a gang-banger without firsthand knowledge of their back-story is prejudicial, we're told. And teens are not alone in their protests. Many adults, too, share this same acrimony. They lament that society pigeonholes them as a blue-collar laborer or a white-collar professional; a Republican or a Democrat; a conservative or a liberal; a Soccer-Mom or a Working Mother; or as lower-class, middle-class, and upper-class citizens. But if the recent rise of the Log Cabin Republicans, Blue-Dog Democrats, and political independents tell us anything, it's that an increasing number of people in America jockey against type.

But in the Christian Church only the opposite is true. We tend to thrive on labels. We have a tag, in fact, for just about every type of spiritual persuasion found under our cathedral ceilings. For example, the terms "Premillennialist," "Post-Millennialist," "Amillennialist," and "Dispensationalist" have been with us now for the better part of a century, each of which conveniently imparts a person's eschatological bent. Labels such as "Charismatic" and "Cessationist" are also widespread and speak to a person's views on the *charismata*, or spiritual phenomena. Moreover, titles such as "Baptist," "Episcopalian," "Lutheran," and "Methodist"—just to name a few—go back centuries and are ecclesiastical boundary markers. To wear any one of these labels is to essentially identify with a particular eschatology, theology, or ecclesiology. And many Christians wear them proudly.

That Christians are quick to pin labels on other Christians is, to some degree, a matter of expediency. After all, it's much easier to quantify someone's theology with *a single word* than it is to invest the time fleshing out the details. Rightly or wrongly, religious labels offer a high-level summary about a person and their viewpoints without requiring much homework. For this reason the use of labels, politically incorrect though they may be, are likely to be with us for a long time to come—both inside and outside the Church.

Without a doubt two of the more provocative labels to achieve notoriety in the Christian Church are *Calvinist* and *Arminian*. More than any other, these labels tend to spark a firestorm of controversy. Simply mention them by name, or espouse either position in debate, and watch how passionate, if not contentious, many evangelicals become. Like greased lightning, cordial conversations can turn electrifying and cool tempers overheated when these labels are brandished at large. And with the recent resurgence of Reformed Theology in the West,[127] these labels are once again *en vogue* and remind us that they still pack a hefty punch.

But there is also a third rather nebulous category to contend with concerning this debate. Far too often I have heard Christians, particularly those who vacillate on thorny theological matters, classify themselves as *Calminians*—a pithy title meant to suggest a person who espouses an amalgamation of Calvinistic and Arminian beliefs. These particular Christians reject the "Calvinist" or "Arminian" label outright, but instead choose to wear a mishmash of the two.

The impetus behind this third label is harmony. Calminians find merit in both Calvinism and Arminianism but regard the debate as too subjective and divisive to warrant dogmatism. Not unlike John Cassian in the fifth century (see Chapter 2), they believe that by finding a middle ground, they can bring a peaceable end to a theological war. On the surface, this seems noble because it attempts to reconcile the irreconcilable differences between Calvin (and the Reformers) and Arminius (and the Remonstrants). But in their quest for unity, Calminians defang Reformed Theology of its intended bite and declaw Arminianism of its scratch. They cannibalize both systems to such a degree that we are left with a hybrid theology that is largely innocuous.

In a nutshell, Calminians believe that it is acceptable to hold fast to both Calvinism and Arminianism, at least in part, without negating the other entirely. Such thinking affords these Christians the romantic freedom to court both theologies without ever having to wed either. It celebrates the best of both worlds, so to speak. By placing one foot in each camp Calminians sleep soundly at night, having put to rest once and for all this longstanding debate in their minds. But how they go about it is both pedestrian and problematical.

The majority of Calminians I meet, although intellectually deft and well-meaning, invariably betray their shortsightedness when pressed at length. As one evangelical explained to me, "I believe in Total Depravity, as taught in Calvinism, but I also believe in the Arminian teaching of Universal Atonement." He then proudly concluded, "I guess you could call me a Calminian." Another seasoned Christian once boasted in my ear, "I accept only three of the five points of Calvinism and two of the five points of Arminianism." She ended her harangue with the bashful admission, "I suppose I have two dogs in the fight."

By holding a syncretistic position, these individuals are representative of a growing class of evangelicals who flaunt a Frankenstein theology. They fraternize with other beliefs—keeping what they like and surgically removing what they don't—until a theological monster emerges. And in so doing, Calminians prove to be doctrinal mutts rather than pure breeds. But as both the studied Arminian and the devout Calvinist will attest, any attempt to crossbreed Arminianism with Calvinism is ineffective. It is tantamount to crossbreeding a dog and a cat; they are mutually exclusive articles with incompatible DNA.

Notwithstanding its inconsistencies, Calminianism remains an attractive prospect for those who are scandalized by God's sovereignty. It neutralizes their anxiety over predestination, placates their discomfort concerning free-will, and satisfies their uncertainty around election. In effect, these evangelicals prefer the titillating goose bumps that Arminianism offers when it says that unregenerate men are morally free and that Christ loves everyone uniformly and died for all men equally. But they also want the majesty and confidence offered by Calvinism that says God sovereignly controls all things, including the eternal security of the redeemed. Calminianism, so it seems, is the perfect opium for the theologically schizophrenic. But the reality is, when fleshed out to its logical conclusions, it is not only untenable but is intellectually, philosophically, and theologically incongruent.

Those who retreat to the safety net of a middle ground do so at the cost of their credibility, for both Calvinism and Arminianism are each built upon their sequential five points which stand in stark contrast to one another. Thus, to acquiesce on one point in either system is to crash its entire system. Stated differently, Calvinism and Arminianism are systematic theologies comprised of five interconnected links that make up their respective chains. To remove one link from either chain is to break it altogether. To compromise on one point for the sake of theological balance with the other, as Calminians do, is not only to un-systematize both but is to become discombobulated and incoherent in one's thinking. This truth cannot be overemphasized.

For instance, one cannot accept the Calvinist doctrine of Total Depravity and still believe, as Arminians do, that election is conditioned upon the foreseen faith and free-will choice of a spiritually dead sinner. How an unregenerate man whose self-will is enslaved to sin can make such an *un-enslaved* decision to accept Christ we are not told. The only alternative is to cheapen the extent of man's innate depravity and his deadness, and to discount altogether his inability to incline himself toward the things of God. And this is exactly what Calminians do. But as we have seen, morally enslaved and spiritually dead sinners do not have the freedom or cognizance to "choose election" any more than a physical slave or a literal corpse has the ability to command his own destiny. By insisting that a totally depraved sinner is "alive enough" and is "willingly able enough" to become elect, in spite of his state of reprobation, is to manifestly align with Arminianism.

On this crucial point Calminianism breaks rank with Reformed Theology. It leaves in its path a wake of destruction that, like Arminianism, glories in the autonomy of man, denies God's sovereign freedom in election, and cheapens the Bible's teaching on the depravity and reprobation of sinful man. In short, the Calvinist doctrine of Total Depravity outright negates the Arminian doctrine of Conditional Election, and vice versa. The two cannot be reconciled nor coexist in one system (unless, of course, they are redefined at the start).

Likewise, one cannot accept the Arminian doctrine of Universal Atonement—that Christ made *propitiation* (satisfaction) and *expiation* (cleansing) for the sins of *all* men by his shed blood on the cross—and still hold equally to the Calvinist position that only "a few" are elected for salvation. The two positions are contradictory. To *atone* for all mankind's sins is to invariably *save* all sinners. But how all the sins of the world can be "paid" for on the cross—to include the sin of unbelief—while still maintaining that only the Elect are saved and the majority of the world is hell-bound for their unbelief (which supposedly was atoned for) we are once again not told. Such a paradoxical view, which is a favorite of Calminians, is irreconcilable and exposes their woeful misunderstanding of the atonement.

As will be explained in greater detail in the chapters that follow, to atone for sin means to redeem someone from the consequences of sin. Therefore to have one's sins atoned for is to be fully pardoned, not partially paroled. And to be fully exonerated, to the Bible's way of thinking, is to unavoidably enter the gateway that leads to salvation. Thus, to side with Arminians, as Calminians do, and teach that Christ's atonement redeems *all men* without passion or prejudice, but still maintain allegiance to Calvinism's assertion that only an elect few are saved, is to believe in a blatant contradiction.

The redemption that Christ earned for "his people" (Matt. 1:21)—which, by necessity, secures their salvation (Luke 19:10; 2 Cor. 5:21; Gal. 1:3-4; 1 Tim. 1:15; Tit. 2:14)—includes all that is involved in bringing them into a right relationship with God. However, if Christ's atonement is universal, so then must be the salvation that accompanies it. And universal salvation is something the Bible strictly forbids (cf. John 3:18). The Arminian view of Universal Atonement, therefore, outright negates the Calvinist view of Unconditional Election, and vice versa. Again, unless these terms are redefined at the onset, they cannot be reconciled nor coexist in the same system.

I recognize that not everyone grasps the philosophical and theological intricacies behind Calminianism or the collateral damage left in its backwash. These issues are highly complex. But suffice it to say that when the veneer of the debate is pulled back there are only two labels, not three, from which a person can choose. There is no middle ground. And without failure, when Calminianism is weighed on the scale of neutrality it is ultimately found in the balance left wanting. It is anything but nonpartisan or middle-of-the-road.

When Calminians are theologically and philosophically pressed at length, they almost always prove to be full-on Arminians. Dr. R.C. Sproul notes the following:

> There are a host of folks who call themselves four-point Calvinist because they can't swallow the doctrine of limited atonement. ... When I have talked to people who call themselves four-point Calvinists and have had the opportunity to discuss it with them, I have discovered that they were no-point Calvinists. They thought they believed in total depravity, in unconditional election, in irresistible grace, and in the perseverance of the saints, but they didn't understand these points.[128]

Likewise, Dr. James White, the director of the apologetics ministry *Alpha and Omega Ministries* and a teaching elder at the Phoenix Reformed Baptist Church in Arizona, writes:

> Upon examination the vast majority of those who call themselves "four point Calvinists" [i.e. Calminians] are actually not Reformed at all, for their objections are to God's freedom in electing men to salvation and to the total inability of man in his sin.[129]

The options available to us are straightforward: Either a sinner has the freedom to choose Jesus Christ (Arminianism), or he has forfeited his freedom as a burden of Original Sin (Calvinism). Either a sinner is sick from sin and partially reprobate (Arminianism), or he is dead in sin and is depraved in totality (Calvinism). Either God elects a sinner based on what He foresees in him (Arminianism), or He elects him based solely on His sovereign decree (Calvinism). Either a sinner shares in the glory of his salvation by freely cooperating with God's grace prior to regeneration (Arminianism), or God *first* regenerates him without his cooperation in order to save him afterward (Calvinism). Either God woos or entices a sinner to Christ by outward grace on the gamble that it won't be resisted (Arminianism), or God tames the rebel will by inward grace while dragging the sinner irresistibly to Himself (Calvinism). Either a Christian's salvation is vulnerable, and can be lost by an act of the will (Arminianism), or it is eternally secure regardless of the extent of his past, present, or future rebellion (Calvinism). Lastly, either Christ made atonement *possible* for all sinners by his death on the cross (Arminianism), or Christ's atonement was *actual* and is applied only to select beneficiaries decided upon in advance (Calvinism).

Any attempt to philosophize our way out of these two sides or to suggest a third medium so as to avoid a theological headache is doubletalk. Neither Calvinism nor Arminianism allows for any hybrid between them. God is either wholly sovereign or not sovereign at all. Man is either entirely free or not free at all. Christ either made atonement or he did not. No such doctrines exist in the Bible that teach that God is "mostly sovereign" or man is "somewhat free" or Christ "potentially atoned" for all men. By definition these words—*sovereignty, freedom,* and *atonement*—are absolute. There is no middle ground. A Christian must pick one of only two sides.

I am not alone in my analysis of Calminianism, as any well-studied Arminian will also attest. In fact, a leading Arminian scholar and famed theologian, Roger Olson, Professor of Theology at George W. Truett Theological Seminary and author of *Arminian Theology: Myths And Realities* agrees. In a recent posting on his blog, entitled *My Evangelical Arminian Theological Musings*, he is rather forthright on the matter. Olson writes:

> There is no middle ground between Calvinism and Arminianism with regard to the three crucial doctrines about which they differ: election (conditional or unconditional), atonement (limited or universal) and grace (resistible or irresistible). ... I argue that, whereas Calvinists and Arminians have much in common, there is no hybrid of them or middle ground between them.[130]

In the end, all five points of Calvinism cancel out the five points of Arminianism, and vice versa. They are contradictions in terms that cannot be mutually supported, either in part or in full. This makes Calminianism not only unviable but overly simplistic in its attempt to mend fences. Owing to its intricacy, the Calvinism-Arminianism debate deserves much deeper consideration than a third-party label, and those who wear it, are willing to give.

Apart from their dignified effort to find a happy medium, we must consider why Calminians believe a middle ground is even necessary in the first place. What exactly do they demur most about Calvinism or Arminianism that prevents them from embracing either five-point system in total rather than just in part? What particular petal in T.U.L.I.P. do they find so objectionable that it warranted their defection from Reformed Theology centuries ago and launched a fringe movement? And what continues to stoke its fire today, even in spite of its well-known inconsistencies?

The answer to all of these questions is hardly surprising. If there are two words in the Reformed lexicon that makes the blood of Western evangelicals boil hot—to say nothing about the tempers of many evangelists and missionaries worldwide—it's the Calvinist doctrine called Limited Atonement. At the root of virtually every denial of Calvinism is an omnipresent loathing for this doctrine.

The visceral response that Limited Atonement evokes from Calminians goes well beyond the borders of our seminary classrooms and is found in virtually every sector of the Christian Church. Simply inquire of the layperson in the pew or the nominal skeptic on the street as to whether or not they believe the Bible teaches that Jesus died for everyone, including them, and they will generally answer in the affirmative. Suggest the contrary, however, and watch their eyebrows point in umbrage. So it is with Calminians. If for no other reason, the theology of Calminianism was brought to bear on the Christian Church primarily because of its opposition to Limited Atonement. It continues to be one of the most, if not *the* most, contested tenets of Calvinism (as well as the most underappreciated and misunderstood). Calminians exist, really, because Limited Atonement refuses to go away.

By rejecting Limited Atonement and subscribing to other points of Calvinism, such as Total Depravity or Unconditional Election, Calminian theology betrays its inconsistencies. Dr. Loraine Boettner, who was no small authority on the issue, said as much when he wrote:

> It will be seen at once that this doctrine [of Limited Atonement] necessarily follows from the doctrine of election. If from eternity God has planned to save one portion of the human race

and not another, it seems to be a contradiction to say that His work has equal reference to both portions, or that He sent His Son to die for those whom He had predetermined not to save, as truly as, and in the same sense that He was sent to die for those whom He had chosen for salvation. *These two doctrines must stand or fall together. We cannot logically accept one and reject the other. If God has elected some and not others to eternal life, then plainly the primary purpose of Christ's work was to redeem the elect* (emphasis added).[131]

Because the vast majority of Christians in America likely classify themselves as Calminians—that is, they are opponents of Limited Atonement but exponents of two or more points in T.U.L.I.P.—it is imperative that we first have a proper understanding of Christ's atonement before launching a counter-assault. As a primer, therefore, we will not only devote considerable space to the work of Christ on the cross but will dedicate the next chapter to the theological and philosophical quagmires inherent to the Arminian teaching of Universal Atonement. After laying the groundwork, we will then counter the Arminian view with an exposé on Limited Atonement.

In the meantime, it behooves us to remember that, in spite of the popularity that comes with protesting such an unpopular teaching, Limited Atonement has played an instrumental role throughout Church history. Moreover, it is far from a minority report. This particular doctrine has in fact been championed by some of the greatest minds the Church has ever received and, to that end, has been decisively endorsed by one Church council after another (see Appendix). That Christ died for his elect, and his elect *only*, is far from theological racism, as some Arminians and Calminians dare to suggest. Rather, it is a breathtaking doctrine of grace.

Reflection Questions:

1. Why do you suppose the doctrine of Limited Atonement disturbs, indeed offends, many Christians today—particularly evangelists and missionaries?

2. Thus far in your understanding of the Calvinism-Arminianism debate, do you consider *Calminianism* a viable option and an acceptable middle-ground? Or are Calvinism and Arminianism "all or nothing" propositions?

3. What do you find most agreeable or disagreeable about *Calminianism*?

Chapter 15

Payment or Possibility?

From our study on Total Depravity we learned that man, when left untouched by the Holy Spirit, is intrinsically wicked, spiritually enslaved, oppressed, and blinded; he is dead in sin and unable to choose God of his own desire. This is the natural state of fallen men everywhere, including the redeemed prior to their regeneration. Following that, we saw from our review of Unconditional Election that God has chosen, or predestined, an elect group from this vast pool of depraved sinners to comprise His Church. This He has graciously done from all eternity, irrespective of man's foreseen faith or anything meritorious in the sinner, according to His good pleasure. Thus, we arrive at the "L" in the T.U.L.I.P. acronym—and the logical continuation of Unconditional Election—Limited Atonement.

We can define Limited Atonement in abstract terms by answering the following question: What is the link between Unconditional Election and Limited Atonement? The answer is as awesome as it is poetical. In the same way that all believers were chosen by God in eternity past to be a love gift to Christ (John 6:37; 17:6, 24) so Christ was appointed as a love gift from all eternity to be their Redeemer (cf. 1 Pet. 1:20). That is to say, the Father not only chose believers for the Son but He also chose the Son to be the Savior for all believers. This is Unconditional Election as exercised among the Godhead. Those sovereignly elected by the Father are inextricably linked to the atonement of the Son.

More directly, however, the doctrine of Limited Atonement, or Particular Redemption as many Reformed theologians prefer to call it, speaks of God's design in the atonement and who it was He was intending to redeem when Christ died on the cross. Calvinists uphold that Christ died as a substitute for his people and bore the full weight of God's wrath on their behalf, paying the penalty for *their sin alone*. Christ intended to ransom *only His sheep* and actually secured everything necessary for their salvation. The gifts of faith and repentance are infallibly applied by the Spirit to all for whom Christ died, thereby guaranteeing their future salvation.

Limited Atonement is both exclusive in scope and accomplished in total. It achieved exactly *what* Christ intended and for *whom* it was intended. It not only satisfied God's wrath by paying the bloody price for sin but actually *secured* the redemption of all believers for all time (Heb. 9:12). More specifically, as "The good shepherd [who] lays down his life for the sheep" (John 10:11), Jesus Christ *delivered* (Heb. 2:15), *ransomed* (1 Pet. 1:18-19), *reconciled* (Rom. 5:10), *redeemed* (Gal. 3:13), and *justified* those same sheep "by his blood" (Rom. 5:9). It's a done deal, so to speak. Christ ratified on the cross his redemptive work with the glorious words: "It is finished" (John 19:30).

All those for whom Christ died stand forever delivered, ransomed, reconciled, redeemed, and justified before God. These benefits are not contingent upon the future actions of men (and their willingness to believe) but on the past actions of God who sovereignly predestined "those who are written in the Lamb's book of life ... before the foundation of the world" (Rev. 21:7, Eph. 1:4). In other words, Christ's atonement transcends time and space and, in an inexplicable sense, actually predates the physical event itself. To the point, the apostle John reminds us that "the Lamb ... was slain *from the creation of the world*" (Rev. 13:8, emphasis added).

The Bible teaches that all believers—past, present, and future—were redeemed by Christ's work on the cross. But does this mean, as Arminians try to argue, that Reformed Theology portends that Christians are born in a saved state of being, having been redeemed by an atonement made on their behalf long before they ever existed? The answer is no. Neither Unconditional Election nor Limited Atonement *saves* anyone. In fact, the question ignores the meaning of the word *redemption*.

The reader will search in vain for any biblical evidence that suggests that the death of Christ secured a believer's salvation. Instead, the Bible makes clear that it was our *redemption* his atonement secured. "Christ redeemed us from the curse of the law," wrote the apostle Paul (Gal. 3:13). Likewise, the writer of Hebrews reminds us that it was "by means of his own blood," that Christ succeeded in "thus securing an eternal redemption" (Heb. 9:12). While redemption leads unfailingly to salvation according to Calvinism (a point Arminians are quick to contest), the meaning and application of the two terms differ.

By definition, to be redeemed means to have the guilt of sin removed from one's account by penal transaction. To be saved, however, means that same sinner is delivered from eternal punishment *by faith* in the One who made the penal transaction. Redemption, therefore, has nothing to do with a man's personal belief system. It is something Christ already accomplished and took full responsibility for. But the salvation that comes from this redemption does indeed involve confession, faith, and repentance on the part of men.

Thus, Calvinists maintain that by removing the guilt of sin through the atoning work of Christ (thereby securing redemption), the once-enslaved sinner is free to actionably repent and actionably believe in Christ (thereby receiving salvation). But lest one is tempted to conclude, as Arminians hastily do, that this sequence places the onus for salvation on the response of man, we must not forget that the ability to repent and the act of faith are gifts *granted by God* with discretion (see Chapter 12). Both redemption and salvation, in other words, are ultimately the result of divine grace.

Limited Atonement, therefore, can be summarized as follows: Christ died specifically for, and limited to, every Christian in the New Testament age, to include all believing Jews and God-fearing Gentiles who lived in the Old Testament dispensation. And in dying for them, Christ *secured* their redemption and *guaranteed* their future salvation.

Arminians, not surprisingly, take the polar opposite position. They ascribe a target audience to the atonement that is limitless. Known as Universal (Unlimited) Atonement, this view maintains that Christ died for *everyone*—not merely the Elect. No human being falls outside its reach and no sin is too heinous to be expatiated, including the sin of unbelief. Everybody, saint and sinner alike, is a recipient of the shed blood of the Savior. However, while this doctrine maintains that Christ redeemed the whole world through his death, it guarantees the salvation of no one in particular. Redemption, while important to the Arminian mindset, is not a rubberstamp guarantee that a person will be saved. Said in reverse, the deliverance from sin's punishment does not necessarily follow the removal of sin's guilt.

By dying for all men, Arminians simply mean that Christ's death demonstrated God's moral hatred for the sins of the whole world. It pictured the *type* of retribution all sinners would have incurred and the *degree* to which God would go if He was to have punished the human race instead of His Son.[132] (This is known among theologians as the Governmental Theory of the atonement as opposed to the Reformed view of Penal-Substitution). Universal Atonement sees no penal transaction in the death of Christ (no actual deliverance was made for those for whom Christ died). It rejects forensic imputation (no actual righteousness was credited to those for whom Christ died). And it insists that no sins were expunged from man's record (no actual reconciliation was made for those whom Christ died). All of these things are simply *possibilities* in Universal Atonement; contingent upon man's applied faith. Thus, in Arminianism, the sacrifice of Christ is more or less a *theoretical* atonement.

Certainly Arminians believe that the aforementioned dividends—deliverance, righteousness, redemption, and reconciliation—are available through Christ's atonement. But they maintain that they are only applied to a sinner's account after he exercises his option of faith. In the end, it is the faith of fallen man that makes the atonement of any value.

Herein hides the fallacy behind the Arminian view. These same Christians overlook the fact that the atonement dividends described in Scripture are written in the *past-tense*. They are *completed actions* "from the creation of the world" (Rev. 13:8); not simply prospective rewards for faith. All believers, both would-be and actual, have already been *delivered* (Heb. 2:15), *reconciled* (Rom. 5:10), *ransomed* (1 Pet. 1:18-19), *redeemed* (Gal. 3:13), and *justified* through "his blood" (Rom. 5:9) long before they were born, much less exercised faith. They are contingent upon nothing that man does!

Notwithstanding this glorious truth, Arminians still insist that a sinner must *do something* to reap the whirlwind of blessings. If a sinner declines the generous offer of the gospel, we are then forced to admit that Christ's death was to no avail and the atonement dividends are retracted. In short, whatever Christ accomplished on the cross, Universal Atonement teaches that he did so homogeneously—or equally for all men—but with no guarantees. In the end, it is only a potential atonement, the benefits of which hinge upon the cooperation of reprobate man. Consistent Arminians, such as Norman Geisler, admit as much. "His death on the cross made salvation possible for all men," he affirmed, "but not actual—it is not actual until they receive it by faith."[133]

It is obvious that the atonement of Jesus Christ is no small point of disagreement between Arminians and Calvinists. On one side stands the Calvinist who argues for an atonement that is exclusive; it was intended for, and is appropriated by, an elect few. It guarantees the salvation of those for whom it was intended. On the other side stands the defiant Arminian who argues for an atonement that is inclusive; it was intended for, and is available to, everybody, though it is beneficial only to the willing. It redeems *everyone* but guarantees the salvation of *no one*.

So on which side does the Bible land—Limited Atonement (Calvinism) or Universal Atonement (Arminianism)? The answer, as I see it, is Limited Atonement. But before defending this doctrine as an essential component to the Doctrines of Grace (see Chapter 16), we shall first put Universal Atonement to the acid test of Scripture. It is a widely-assumed doctrine among the majority of Christians in America today and, for that reason, warrants the remainder of our space here.

The Falsehood, Foolishness, & Failure
of Universal Atonement

Insofar as I understand Scripture—both logically and exegetically—there are at least four arguments against Universal (Unlimited) Atonement that are worthy of our consideration. Ranked in no particular order, they are as follows: (1) Universal Atonement is *incompetent*; (2) Universal Atonement is *ineffective*; (3) Universal Atonement is *inept*; and (4) Universal Atonement is *inappropriate*. Any one of these arguments—incompetence, ineffectiveness, ineptness, and inappropriateness—whether taken in part or combined as a whole, lay waste to the notion that Christ's died *effectually* for all people.

The first argument against Universal Atonement is its *incompetence*. If ever there was a doctrine that required a better understanding of the original languages of Scripture it's the atonement of Jesus Christ. In the Old Testament the word *atonement* is translated from the Hebrew verb *kaphar* (or the plural noun *kippur* that is a derivative of the verb) and appears some 69 times.[134] By definition, and without exception, *kaphar* (atonement) means "to cover [over], purge ... make reconciliation."[135] The idea, therefore, is that whenever atonement is depicted in Scripture something or someone is "covered over" and "reconciled" to an offended other. In no way is it ever a partial covering, a potential purging, or possible reconciliation, but it is always full, fitting, and finished. Dr. J.I. Packer writes, "Atonement means making amends, blotting out the offense, and giving satisfaction for wrong done; thus reconciling to oneself the alienated other and restoring the disrupted relationship."[136]

For example, long before the inauguration of the Jewish sacrificial system (cf. Lev. 17:11), the biblical concept of atonement was put into action. God instructed Noah in Genesis 6:14 to "Make yourself an ark of gopher wood. Make rooms in the ark, and cover it (*kaphar* [atonement]) inside and out with pitch." We then read that "Noah did everything just as God commanded him" (v. 22). From the use of *kaphar* (atonement) in this passage we learn that the ark of Noah was totally atoned for—that is, it was "covered over" and "purged"—with bitumen. The ark was neither potentially nor partially covered but was fully and completely sealed. Noah "reconciled" with pitch all potential leaks in the crevices of the boat's planking. It was a sufficient and efficient atonement on Noah's part that redeemed the boat's usability.

In another context, when Jacob feared for his life just before his reunion with an angry Esau, the patriarch vowed: "I will appease him (*kaphar* [atonement]) with the present that goes before me. Then afterward I will see his face; perhaps he will accept me" (Gen. 32:20). Similar to Noah in Genesis 6:14, we learn that Jacob intended to "cover over" the wrong he had committed against Esau by providing a gift of reconciliation. It was a sufficient and efficient atonement on Jacob's part.[137]

Lastly, and most famously, atonement is associated with the Day of Atonement in the Old Testament. Celebrated as Yom Kippur today, the Day of Atonement in Scripture was "the day of covering over" (*kaphar* [atonement]). It was the most sacred convocation of all the Israelite feasts and festivals, occurring only once a year (Lev. 16:1-34; 23:27-28).

On the tenth day of Tishri, the seventh month of the Hebrew calendar, the high priest performed elaborate rituals to atone for the sins of the people. Among other things, he brought with him to the tabernacle or the Temple two goats, one to be sacrificed "because of the uncleanness and rebellion of the Israelites, whatever their sins have been" (Lev. 16:16) and the other to serve as a scapegoat. The high priest would place his hands on the scapegoat's head, confess over it the rebellion and wickedness of the Israelites, and then banish the goat from the camp of Israel. The goat carried on itself all the sins of the people, which were "covered over" and "purged" from Israel's camp for another year. On this solemn holy day, God "reconciled" Himself to His chosen people. In keeping with the definition of *kaphar* (atonement), the best modern colloquialism would be to say that each year on the Day of Atonement the sins of Israel were "swept under the rug."

To summarize briefly, the biblical concept of atonement is definitive and for which literal, practical, and figurative meanings apply. It can be true *literally* by smearing tar over a boat (i.e. Noah), *practically* by providing a gift of reconciliation (i.e. Jacob), or *figuratively* by smearing animal blood over sin (i.e. the Day of Atonement). In each case, the act of "covering over" is involved.

In terms of its Christological meaning, our Lord's atonement was literal, practical, and figurative all at the same time. It was literal since Jesus died an actual death on the altar of a cross. It was practical by virtue of the fact that his death fully satisfied God's wrath. And it was figurative in the sense that Jesus is portrayed in the New Testament as the Old Testament sacrificial lamb (and scapegoat) whose death completely "covered [over]" and "purge[d]" his people from the guilt of their iniquities. There was nothing theoretical or hypothetical about it; neither was it potentially effective or only ninety-nine percent finished (with the last one percent dependent upon man's faith). It was a work of full restitution that Christ performed alone—literally, practically, and figuratively—and to God's complete satisfaction. It did not fail to meet its reconciliatory ends for those whom it was intended.

Only when we have a proper understanding of what *atonement* actually means in Scripture do we begin to see the canard that is Universal Atonement. Its proponents, though well-meaning, diminish the propitiating—or satisfactory—work of Christ on the cross by imposing an alien definition that robs the atonement of its beauty and efficacy.

The second argument against Universal Atonement is its *ineffectiveness*. Because Arminians believe that Christ's atonement was, at best, merely the demonstration of God's wrath against the sins of the world (Governmental Theory) but was not substitutionary in nature (Penal-Substitution Theory), we can rightly conclude that Universal Atonement is *ineffectual*. By ineffectual we mean that it didn't really accomplish anything, other than serve as a cautionary tale to reprobate sinners.

That Christ is said to have offered atonement for the sins of *all* men, according to Arminianism, but afterwards the majority of these same men will be eternally punished for their sin of unbelief—for which Christ supposedly already atoned—is to accept a confusing atonement that apparently failed to do its job. This truth is seen in the fact that a vast majority of human beings (for whom Christ supposedly died) will never bend the knee to him in saving faith and therefore will not enter the light of heaven. So while Christ died for all, we are told, not all will be saved. Even more harrowing, Scripture informs us that *most* people will end up in hell. So we must ask: *What kind of a universal atonement is that?*

From the testimony of his own lips Jesus rendered the notion of Universal Atonement preposterous. In point of fact, he warned that "many, I tell you, will try to enter [heaven] and will not be able to" (Luke 13:24). He said elsewhere, "the gate is wide and the way is easy that leads to destruction and those who enter by it are many" (Matt. 7:13). The "many" that Christ has in mind in these passages refer to the *majority* of people in redemptive history who have been, or eventually will be, condemned eternally to the parapets of hell. And this "many" he speaks of is juxtaposed against "the few" who have been, or eventually will be, saved eternally in the glories of heaven. His words reveal the startling truth that the salvation of the saints is a minority report. This jives with the apostle Paul who likewise said, "... only the remnant will be saved" (Rom. 9:27). Thus, if Universal Atonement is to be accepted as true, we have no choice but to conclude that the majority for whom Christ died are forever lost to the Hound of Heaven and are rotting in hell. Universal Atonement appears to be not so universally atoning after all.

So how can an atonement that claims to be universal in scope wind up so broadly ineffective? If Jesus Christ atoned for the sins of *all* men—that is, he "covered [over], purge[d] ... made reconciliation" for every human being who has ever lived—why, then, are not *all* men reconciled and saved? Even more, why are so many condemned?

Sadly, to these familiar questions we are given unconvincing answers. I was disheartened to read one Arminian blogger who took a stab at these questions only to thoughtlessly dismiss them by towing the party line. In addition to espousing an atonement that contradicts the biblical meaning "to cover

[over], purge ... [to] make reconciliation," this blogger's online rebuttal included the predictable talking points that Calvinists have come to expect from aficionados of Universal Atonement. He blogged the following:

> Jesus did die for the sins of the world ... That free gift was paid for by Jesus suffering and dying on the cross ... [But] God is not going to force that gift [of the atonement] on someone who doesn't want it. He is not going to violate our free will. Unfortunately, those people who reject God's free gift of salvation will suffer eternal torment and separation from God ... Jesus died for the sins of all people, but only the people who accepted God's free gift will benefit from that gift. The others willingly choose not to accept the gift and therefore willingly choose to suffer the consequence.[138]

Here we see the fault lines in the Arminian foundation start to quake. Everything that is crucial to gaining eternal life, we are told, rides on the autonomy of man. In order for the atonement of Christ to be of any value whatsoever it must first be appropriated by a sinner's self-induced faith. God may decree a person's salvation, the Son may die to obtain his redemption, and the Spirit may exercise His divine prerogative in bringing conviction and enlightenment. But all of this, so says Universal Atonement, is not enough to bring about salvation unless the will of the creature cooperates.

The third argument against Universal Atonement is its *ineptness*. Universal Atonement sees that vast majority of so-called "redeemed" men (for whom Christ died) end up in hell. This forced Arminian writer Rob Bell to say, "Hell is full of forgiven people God loves, whom Jesus died for."[139] Say what one will about Rob Bell's postmodern theology, and he certainly has his critics (of which I am one), but he's refreshingly consistent in his conclusions.

Hell is full of forgiven people? Can such an awful thought really be true? It is apparently so in Arminianism. If Universal Atonement is correct, and Christ redeemed all men while at the same time most of them will end up in hell, according to Jesus' own words, we have no choice but to agree with Bell. For the vast majority for whom Christ apparently died—the delivered, the redeemed, the ransomed, the reconciled, and the justified—hell is their eternal home. This is consistent Arminianism at its base level.

But lest we discount Bell's words as less than mainstream and too controversial to be taken seriously, I would caution the reader to remember that Bell stands in good company. His compatriots include renowned men of orthodoxy who have made a big splash in Church history, not the least of which is John Wesley, the leading Arminian of the eighteenth century. Wesley's words in favor of Universal Atonement should give us pause, as they reflect the same sentiment held by many evangelicals today. To Calvinists, however, they are utterly unthinkable. Wesley admitted the following:

> What! Can the blood of Christ burn in hell? ... I answer ... If the oracles of God are true, one who was purchased by the blood of Christ may go thither. For he that was sanctified by the blood of Christ was purchased by the blood of Christ. *But one who was sanctified by the blood of Christ may nevertheless go to hell;* may fall under that fiery indignation which shall for ever devour the adversaries.[140]

For Wesley, it was entirely feasible, and in fact a theological reality, that the blood of Christ, and those sanctified by it, could "burn in hell." Universal Atonement, to which Wesley subscribed, agrees with him, since the blood of Christ is purported to have been shed for all of hell's condemned occupants. Consistent Arminians and reluctant Calminians apparently have no problem embracing an atonement that offers zero guarantees and fails miserably to accomplish its intended purpose—at least for the greater part of humanity.

Such a notion should disturb any thoughtful Christian—whether an Arminian, a Calminian, or a Calvinist. To even suggest that those who have been delivered (Heb. 2:15), reconciled (Rom. 5:10), ransomed (1 Pet. 1:18-19), redeemed (Gal. 3:13), and justified (Rom. 5:9) through the sacrificial blood of Christ can just as easily be un-delivered, un-reconciled, un-ransomed, un-redeemed, and un-justified and lost to eternity by an act of free-will is the height of theological dementia. For this reason, it bears repeating one more time: If the effectiveness of the atonement is ultimately dependent upon the responsibility of men to accept it by faith, lest they face the licking flames of eternal perdition, then the atonement of Jesus Christ, in and of itself, is largely ineffectual. It only *becomes* effective, or a reality, if sinners believe that it is so.

The Arminian view of atonement pleads with us to believe that God was able to accomplish the *meriting* aspect of salvation but the *applying* aspect is dependent upon man and his free-will. It asks us to believe that God has worked out everyone's salvation up to a point, short of actually guaranteeing it, but will go no further. The implication is that God has built the bridge of salvation between Him and us, and we have only to walk over it by accepting His terms of salvation through a free act of faith. "God does his part," Arminians generally say, "and now we must do our part." On this point Dr. R.C. Sproul has observed:

> In this view faith is not only a condition for redemption, but also one of the very grounds of redemption. If the atonement is not efficacious apart from faith, then faith must be necessary for the satisfaction of divine justice. Here faith becomes a work with a vengeance because its presence or absence in a sinner determines the efficacy of Christ's work of satisfaction for this person ...

It is one thing to agree that faith is a necessary condition for the appropriation of the benefits of Christ's atoning work, for justification and its fruits. It is quite another to say that faith is a necessary condition for the satisfaction of divine justice. *If faith is a condition for God's justice to be satisfied, then the atonement, in itself, is not sufficient to satisfy the demands of God's justice* (emphasis added).[141]

To a certain extent the Arminian view of atonement, no matter how unintentional, disavows the saving ministry of the Holy Spirit, since it claims that Christ's blood has a wider application than does the Spirit's saving work. In other words, the blood of Jesus Christ reaches all men, we are told, but apparently the convicting touch of the Holy Spirit falls short. But this is a theological fallacy. Any presentation of salvation that makes the Holy Spirit's work in salvation lag behind the Father's or the Son's contradicts the inherent unity of the Trinity. The Father, the Son, and the Holy Spirit are one, both in essence and in purpose. Therefore, Christ could not possibly have died for those whom the Father did *not* decree to save and in whom the Spirit does *not* savingly work. God cannot be at odds with Himself.

The fourth argument against Universal Atonement is its *inappropriateness*. The theological and philosophical problems posed by Universal Atonement do not end with an atonement that sees the majority of so-called redeemed people wind up in hell, as outlandish as such teaching is. But this doctrine is also stricken with ailments that baffle one's sense of justice. More specifically, at issue are some of the subjects for whom Christ is said to have shed his blood under the all-inclusive umbrella of Universal Atonement. And when we consider just some of these names, we cannot help but shutter.

Modern Arminians are generally unaware of the history of Arminianism, and the fact that the phrases "Jesus took the place of sinners" or "Jesus died for us" or "Jesus' death paid the penalty for sin" are lifted straight from the Reformed doctrine of Penal-Substitution. But to apply Penal-Substitution across the board to all men for all time in every place by way of Universal Atonement is to blunder egregiously. It is to essentially say that Christ sacrificially died as a substitute for Esau whom God hated (Rom. 9:13); for Judas, "the son of perdition" (John 17:12); for the Antichrist, the "man of sin" (2 Thess. 2:3); for the whore of Babylon, and those in the false church (Rev. 17:1-2); as well as for those who commit the unpardonable sin (Matt. 12:32), who never hear the Word (Psa. 147:19-20), and those who are already condemned in hell.

Are we really to believe that Christ spilt his blood *effectually* for these individuals, to include the likes of Emperor Nero, Pontius Pilate, Bloody Mary, Pol Pot, and Adolf Hitler, on the gamble that these so-called delivered, ransomed reconciled, redeemed, and justified people would take him up on his atoning offer and voluntarily repent? How such teaching squares with divine justice goes well beyond reason.

Those who see the atonement of Christ as limited, however, see this Arminian teaching as a gross fiction, and do so without apology. If Universal Atonement is true, then Christ's atonement is merely theoretical at best; the extent of its value is worthless unless appropriated by man through faith. Secondly, if Universal Atonement is true, and Christ died and made expiation (cleansing) for every single human being who has ever lived, then the fact that the vast majority of people throughout history are eternally condemned to hell is the greatest miscarriage of divine justice known to man. And lastly, if Universal Atonement is true, we are then forced to swallow the ugly notion that Christ died a substitionary death for every notorious God-hater who has ever scarred human history and refused to repent.

The tragedy of Universal Atonement is that it makes all men *savable* while failing to save the preponderance of them. It redeems the entire world, but does not rescue the world from hell. It makes salvation *possible* for everybody but certain for no one. The comprehensive atonement of Jesus Christ is to no avail, we're asked to believe, unless depraved, reprobate, and spiritually dead sinners embrace it by an act of so-called free-will.

In the end, Arminianism leaves us with an ineffective atonement of an impotent Savior who accomplished virtually nothing. The Arminian atonement is inconsequential on its own merits. Moreover, by contending that Christ died for the vilest of men (who never repented), to include Judas Iscariot and the Antichrist, demonstrates that it is also desperately inappropriate in its reach. The only alternative to such ghastly teaching, as we will see in the following chapter, is an atonement that is limited and particular—for Limited Atonement in Calvinism is an atonement that succeeds where Arminianism fails; it's an atonement that ultimately saves where Arminianism mostly condemns; and it is an atonement that is actual and accomplished, rather than merely partial and plausible.

Reflection Questions:

1. Of the four arguments against Universal Atonement in this chapter—incompetence, ineffectiveness, ineptness, and inappropriateness—which one, in your opinion, is the most evidentiary and persuasive?

2. Do you hold to the Governmental Theory of the atonement or the Penal-Substitution theory? Which one is conducive to Limited Atonement?

3. Why do you suppose Universal Atonement appeals to so many Christians?

4. Assuming Arminianism is correct, which teaches that an unregenerate sinner receives the benefits of Christ's atonement upon exercising *self*-induced faith and so-called free-will, can he then take *some* credit for his redemption?

Chapter 16

Particular Redemption / Limited Atonement

Christmas is my favorite holiday. It's a special time of the year when the refrain of sleigh bells can be heard jinglingly in the air, drowning out the commotion of life, and crimson poinsettias abound in full bloom. It's a time when songs of glad tidings greet storefront shoppers, and passing strangers exchange cheers of good will. It's also a time when the worst of enemies seem willing, if only for a season, to set aside their grievances in the spirit of "peace on earth." Making merry around the yuletide log, stealing romantic kisses under the mistletoe, basking in a symphony of Christmas lights and garland, and drinking homemade eggnog to the chorus of *Chestnuts Roasting on an Open Fire* are the very things that "help to make the season bright." I suppose that when it comes to the holiday season, I am a modern-day Peter Pan; I've never really grown up. I cherish the 25th of December as much now as I did when I was a sleepless child on Christmas Eve.

I am not alone in my love for Christmas. Among all the festivals and holidays that mark the Christian calendar, Christmas remains the most observed and most popular in the world. Of course, much of that popularity, especially in the West, stems from its commercialization and exploitation by our free-market society. We tend to get lost in the euphoria of gift-shopping, gift-wrapping, and gift-giving—as well as in the mythology of Santa Claus, tiny elves, and flying reindeer— rather than in the historical and theological meaning behind the season. Beyond its marketing appeal and secular trappings, however, Christmas is the celebration of the incarnation of God in Jesus Christ. It is the self-revelation of the Creator who condescended in human form to reconcile Himself to His estranged creatures.

Christmas is also a time, together with Easter, where reprobate sinners *appear* to rise above their depravation and suspend their antagonism toward Christianity. For a few weeks out of the year it seems that all is well in the world. Church attendance swells across the country, people seem more receptive to the gospel, and the name of Christ is paid homage to rather than used as a pejorative. It's not uncommon, in fact, for nonreligious people to step foot in a church for the very first time come the winter holidays. And almost always they are greeted by a reenactment of the first Christmas morning, performed by a cast of lay people costumed in togas and towels.

The hallmark of the Christmas season, of course, is the Nativity story. It recounts the travails of Joseph and his fiancé, Mary, as they come to terms with her unplanned pregnancy. The drama culminates in the birth of Jesus in a Bethlehem manger.

The degree to which the Nativity story is enshrined in Christian culture easily trumps the other holy days of Christianity, even Easter or Resurrection Sunday. There is something about human nature, as Dennis Bratcher reminds us, which would rather focus on the birth of a tender baby than on the torture and death of a wrongly-accused criminal! Especially for the young at heart, the imagery of Christmas—namely, angels and a young mother, shepherds and a stable, and wise men and royal intrigue—captivate our collective imagination like nothing else.[142]

Many Americans, especially those unsympathetic to religious plotlines, turn surprisingly sympathetic when it comes to the story behind the first Christmas morning. They view it as a harmless love charm of sorts; a tall tale of tradition that, at its very best, fosters Christmas spirit. To the faithful, however, it's much more than that. It's a divinely inspired biography of spiritual importance; a story of reconciliation rooted in recorded history with real people traveling to literal places in order to bring about the actual Messiah.

But the joy of Christmas and its theological underpinnings have a short lifespan among believers and unbelievers. Both groups develop a waning interest in the Nativity not long after the holiday decorations are taken down. This is understandable, of course, for skeptics. But it is regrettable that most sober-minded Christians are no more inclined to unpack the theology of Christ's birth than non-Christians are the merits of flying reindeer. Indeed, hardly anyone gives the Nativity story any serious thought come December 26th.

As Americans, I fear we know the Nativity story almost *too* well, if not from the Christmas carols we sing then from the Christmas cards we send. All one need do is take a gander at their surroundings during the holiday season. Figurines of Joseph and Mary are commonplace. Baby statuettes and makeshift mangers are everywhere. Replicas of the wise men and shepherds are plentiful. And flying angels are par for the course. The pageantry of the Nativity is as familiar to our society, so it seems, as the folklore of Kris Kringle.

Familiarity, they say, often breeds contempt. But in the case of Christmas, it breeds blindness. That is to say, lost in the trappings of Christmas are the rich doctrinal truths that undergird the birth of Jesus of Nazareth. We have lost sight of its theological importance, having been visually impaired by wrapping paper, stocking stuffers, and pumpkin pie.

The vast majority of people who recite the Nativity story each year as a matter of custom usually do so without being able to offer a coherent explanation as to what it actually means, theologically speaking. They cannot see beyond a cuddly baby in a manger. The link between the birth of Christ and the deep Christology inherent to it are lost on them, particularly his hypostatic union, his sinless perfection, his incarnate deity, and the inner-workings of a triune God who brought it all about. And this is to say nothing about the Calvinist doctrine of Limited Atonement.

Indeed, many evangelicals are surprisingly amiss as to how the atonement of Christ, much less a limited one, squares with the story of his birth. Although it's on the written page for all to read, it often goes overlooked for sentimental reasons; it's the elephant in the room, as it were, that nobody wants to talk about. To draw from the Christmas story such an inflammatory doctrine as Limited Atonement is to invite shouts of "humbug" in some circles, for it disparages the spirit of Christmas, we're told, and denigrates the cross-work of Easter.

Popular perception would have us believe that Christ's incarnation in Bethlehem, like his death outside Jerusalem thirty-three years later, was for the good of *all men everywhere* so that the *whole world* might be reconciled to God. Even the lovable Tiny Tim, in the timeless classic *A Christmas Carol*, hinted at this universalistic notion with his famous soliloquy: "God bless us *every one!*" But was Christ's birth (and death) really meant to bless every person, or did God instead have another target audience in mind? Is Christmas (and Easter) celebrated every year in memorial to what God has accomplished on behalf *of all men everywhere* or merely for different *types* of men everywhere? The answers are found in the first few chapters of the New Testament.

Matthew conveys the Nativity story from the perspective of Joseph and his bewilderment over how he should handle his pregnant wife-to-be. The story unfolds with reassurance from God's messenger that God is at work in this extraordinary circumstance. However, Matthew gives us no details about the actual birth itself, only a few events leading up to the delivery, and then a summary of what happened "after Jesus was born" (Matt 2:1).

Luke's account, on the other hand, fills in the blanks. Most of the Nativity storyline with which we are familiar from Christmas plays and Scripture readings come from his gospel. His account is told from the perspective of Mary, a virgin, and her struggle to deal with this astonishing occurrence. Luke actually begins his narrative with the miraculous birth of John the Baptist, the forerunner to Christ, and the disbelief of his father Zechariah. The entire narrative places two women, Elizabeth (John's mother) and Mary (Jesus' mother), at the center of the story. An angelic messenger from God named Gabriel also plays a supporting role; he announces the births of both baby boys. But it is the announcement of Jesus' birth, in particular, that is of unique significance in our study on Limited Atonement. Luke records the angel's words to Mary:

> "Greetings, you who are highly favored! The
> Lord is with you ... Do not be afraid, Mary, you

have found favor with God. You will be with child and give birth to a son, and you are to give him the name Jesus. He will be great and will be called the Son of the Most High. The Lord God will give him the throne of his father David, and he will reign over the house of Jacob forever; his kingdom will never end ... The Holy Spirit will come upon you, and the power of the Most High will overshadow you. So the holy one to be born will be called the Son of God. Even Elizabeth your relative is going to have a child in her old age, and she who was said to be barren is in her sixth month. For nothing is impossible with God" (Luke 1:28-37).

These words spoken by the angel Gabriel set in motion the greatest chain of heavenly events to ever invade human history. To Mary was promised the Christ-child who was to reinstitute the Davidic line in Israel; a ruler who, having been conceived by the Holy Spirit in the virgin's womb, would reign "over the house of Jacob" for all eternity. It was a promise unlike any other; one which gave real meaning to the prophetic adage: "How beautiful ... are the feet of those who bring good news ... who proclaim salvation" (Isa. 52:7 cf. Nah. 1:15). This maiden girl, together with her carpenter husband, were God's chosen conduits to bring about "the consolation of Israel" (Luke 2:25).

But questions remain: Other than his eternal majesty, what exactly was this coming king to accomplish on earth? How far would his kingdom reach? What would his rule entail? And for whose pleasure would he serve?

Doubtless Mary could not see beyond the politics of her day and assumed from the angel's words that only the liberation of national Israel was in view (cf. Luke 1:54-55). Like most Jews in the first century, her concentration centered mainly on a political ruler who would reign, not so much on a spiritual one who came to redeem. But as we learn from Matthew's account, the angel had more in mind than geopolitics. Matthew tells us that it was to a fearful Joseph that the angel gave astonishing answers in a dream. The messenger consoled Joseph in his sleep with the words:

> "Joseph son of David, do not be afraid to take Mary home as your wife, because what is conceived in her is from the Holy Spirit. She will give birth to a son, and you are to give him the name Jesus, *because he will save his people from their sins*" (Matt. 1:21, emphasis added).

Like it or not, the details found in Matthew's account concerning Jesus' birth revolve around the central truth of Limited Atonement. They forecast, or prefigure, the doctrine to come. The angel assured Joseph with the wonderful promise that Mary's miraculous newborn would one day "save *his people* from their sins" (Matt. 1:21). The specificity of the phrase "his people" cannot be stressed enough. It seems the angel had a definite audience in view, not a universal one.

Who, then, are these people Christ came to save? And why did the messenger not include "all people" in the equation? Or, stated in reverse, if the mission of Jesus was to atone for the sins of the world, as some argue, why then did the angel use such restrictive language in describing the recipients of so great a salvation?

If we apprehend anything from Matthew 1:21, besides the pageantry of the Nativity itself, it's that Christmas is far more than sharing presents and admiring decorated evergreens. It's the story of a God who condescended to earth to atone for the sins of a select group of people which He sovereignly set apart for Himself. Moreover, we learn from the angel's annunciation to Joseph that not only is this people group limited in scope but that he will save them unfailingly. To be sure, the angel did not suggest that Christ would *try* to save them, *offer* to save them, or simply *long* to save them. Rather, he would fully and completely "save them to the uttermost" (Heb. 7:25, KJV).

This group of beneficiaries for whom Christ came and died ("his people") is not some vague, indistinct, or generic band of people who exercise their free-will so that the Savior is then free to save them. On the contrary, they are those who "God ... destined ... to obtain salvation through our Lord Jesus Christ" (1 Thess. 5:9) and whose names were "written in the Book of Life of the Lamb slain from the foundation of the world" (Rev. 13:8 cf. 17:8). They are "his people" (Matt. 1:21), "his offspring" (Isa. 53:10), his "sons and daughters ... brothers and sisters ... [his] children" (Heb. 2:10-14), his "sheep" (John 10:11), his "church" (Eph. 5:25) and "his friends" (John 15:13).

It is for these, and only these, that Christ came to die and make reconciliation with God on their behalf. And it all started on the first Christmas morning two thousand years ago in the backwater village of Bethlehem.

"It Is Finished"

Calvinism maintains that Christ's redeeming work on Calvary was definite in design inasmuch as it was absolute in accomplishment. It was intended to render complete satisfaction for certain specified sinners and, to that end, actually secured their redemption infallibly. The atonement is not limited in its power to redeem, but merely in the extent to which it reaches and will save certain individuals.

Concerning *what* Christ's death accomplished and for *whom* its benefits apply, the Word of God has much to say on the matter. In fact, the Bible spells out two specific reasons for the Messiah's coming and dying. First, he came to do the will of his Father, and second, he came to "save his people." When we apply a critical eye to both of these reasons, having already noted the perspicuity of Unconditional Election in Scripture, we naturally arrive at an atonement that cannot be anything other than limited in scale.

That Jesus' messianic mission centered on the will of his Father is indisputable. He said as much in different ways, to different people, and at different times throughout his ministry. "For I have come down from heaven not to do my will," he told a raucous crowd in Capernaum, "but to do the will of him who sent me" (John 6:38). To his disgruntled disciples who cocked an eyebrow over his conversation with a Samaritan woman, the

Lord remarked, "My food is to do the will of Him who sent Me, and to finish His work" (John 4:34, NKJV). Still, on another occasion, in response to a group of hostile Jews who were none too happy with his Sabbath miracles, he said "... for I seek not to please myself but him who sent me" (John 5:30). And lastly, we learn from Hebrews 10:9 that, while standing on the precipice of heaven, the pre-incarnate Son submitted to the Father with the words, "Here I am, I have come to do your will." The Lord's entire earthly ministry, from his manger in Bethlehem to his cross on Calvary, centered on abiding by the will of God.

So what exactly was God's will for Jesus on earth? To this question we are given a host of answers in Scripture. It is true that Jesus came into the world to reveal the Father (Matt. 11:27), to serve (Matt. 20:28), to preach the good news of the kingdom of God (Luke 4:43), to testify to the truth of God (John 18:37), to destroy the devil's works (1 John 3:8), to bring judgment (John 9:39), to fulfill the Law and the prophets (Matt. 5:17), and to call sinners to repentance (Mark 2:17). Each one of these actions was a key component in Christ's mission-statement. But equally true is the fact that just as he came to reveal, to serve, to preach, to testify, to destroy, to judge, to fulfill, and to call, he also came "to proclaim freedom for the prisoners" (Luke 4:18), to "take away our sins" (1 John 3:5), to "give his life as a ransom for many" (Matt. 20:28), and to atone "for the sins of the people" (Heb. 2:17). In short, it was "the [Father's] will to crush [Jesus] and cause him to suffer" as "a guilt offering" in order to "justify many, and ... bear their iniquities" (Isa. 53:10-11).

As it relates to the will of God in Christ's atonement, no text is as potent as John 6:35-54. There we discover our Lord's most controversial sermon, the *Bread of Life Discourse*, where he put forth in explicit detail the Father's overarching purpose in sending His Son:

> Then Jesus declared, "I am the bread of life. He who comes to me will never go hungry, and he who believes in me will never be thirsty. But as I told you, you have seen me and still you do not believe. All that the Father gives me will come to

me, and whoever comes to me I will never drive away. For I have come down from heaven not to do my will but to do the will of him who sent me. *And this is the will of him who sent me, that I shall lose none of all that he has given me,* but raise them up at the last day. For my Father's will is that everyone who looks to the Son and believes in him shall have eternal life, and I will raise *him up at the last day* ... No one can come to me unless the Father who sent me draws him, and I will raise him up at the last day ... Whoever eats my flesh and drinks my blood has eternal life, and I will raise him up at the last day" (emphasis added).

God's will for Jesus, we learn from John 6, was that he would lose none of those whom the Father had given him to save but will raise them to eternal life at "the last day." No part of that group, regardless of how prodigal, will ever be lost to the Savior. This fourfold promise that the Son will raise them up on the last day (vv. 39, 40, 44, 54) constitutes an ironclad guarantee of eternal salvation for God's people. Jesus reiterated this truth in the strongest terms when he declared on another occasion:

"I am the good shepherd. The good shepherd lays down his life for the sheep ... My sheep listen to my voice; I know them, and they follow me. I give them eternal life, and they shall never perish; no one can snatch them out of my hand. My Father, *who has given them to me,* is greater than all; no one can snatch them out of my Father's hand. I and the Father are one" (John 10:11, 27-30, emphasis added).

Later, on the night of his arrest, Jesus once again spoke of this marvelous truth in his *High Priestly Prayer*. With words drenched in anguish, he interceded as high priest (Heb. 4:14-16) on behalf of "his people"—that is, for those whom the Father had given him—with words that echoed throughout the Garden of Gethsemane:

> I have revealed you to *those whom you gave me out of the world. They were yours; you gave them to me* ... I pray for them. I am not praying for the world, *but for those you have given me, for they are yours* ... While I was with them, I protected them and kept them safe by that name you gave me. None has been lost ..." (John 17:6, 9, 12, emphasis added).

Christ's pastoral statement "They were yours; you gave them to me" is a forceful affirmation that even *before their conversion* the Lord's disciples—and by extension all true believers—belonged to God! What a wonderfully unfathomable concept to consider! Moreover, God told the apostle Paul that He had "many people in [Corinth]" who belonged to Him even though the Corinthians had yet to hear the gospel and were *not yet saved* (Acts 18:10 cf. 13:48). Having sovereignly chosen to redeem them, the Father had set them aside in eternity past for the express purpose of giving them to the Son in time and space as a love gift. In biblical vernacular, Jesus "obtained [them] with his own blood" all those given to him from the Father (Acts 20:28 ESV cf. Rev. 5:9; 14:4).

It's worth recapping for the sake of clarity: Earlier in John's gospel, in the aforementioned *Bread of Life Discourse*, the Lord had declared "All that the Father gives me will come to me" (6:37 cf. v. 39; Heb. 2:13). He repeated this truth in his *Good Shepherd* statement: "My Father ... has given them to me" (John 10:11). And he reaffirmed it in his *High Priestly Prayer*: "They were yours; you gave them to me" (John 17:6). These three statements combined suggest a specific group of people beloved by God from all eternity and preserved by Christ for safekeeping. The disciples, to include all believers for all time, were infinitely precious to the Son, not because of anything intrinsically valuable in them, but because they were promised to Him by his Father before time began (cf. 2 Tim. 1:9; Tit. 1:1).

And as Christ's *Passion* later demonstrated, Jesus considered the Father's gift so precious that he was willing to die to receive it (them).

These passages allude to Limited Atonement. Each soul inducted into this distinct group, earmarked for Jesus Christ by God's sovereign decree, is guaranteed to be raised to life at the last day and will live forevermore. Since the Bible forbids universal salvation, we understand this group (those given to the Son) to therefore be limited in number and specific in name. They are the Elect, and it is for them only, at the exclusion of all others, that Christ laid down his life. This was God's will for sending His Son into the world.

Secondly, Jesus came into the world to "save his people" from their sins—that is, he came to die for all those whom the Father had given him. The virgin birth in and of itself was a great miracle, but the child miraculously born to Joseph and Mary would perform an even greater miracle. By his *active obedience* (perfect Law-keeping) and his *passive obedience* (perfect sin-bearing), Christ set free, delivered, redeemed, and saved all those earmarked for him by the Father. And this he fully accomplished to the "uttermost," without exception and without failure (Heb. 7:25, KJV).

If we are to assume that Jesus set free, delivered, and redeemed every single person everywhere and for all time vis-à-vis Universal Atonement, we would expect to find a myriad of verses that say as much. Instead, we find only the contrary. Throughout the New Testament the various writers use *exclusive* language, and with great repetition, to describe those for whom Christ came to die. That is to say, they avoid all-inclusive terms when speaking of Christ's atonement. For example:

- Christ atoned for the sins of "**his people**" (Matt. 1:21); he was the sin-bearer who "was sacrificed once to take away the sins of **many**" (Heb. 9:28 cf. Isa. 53:11); he gave his life "as a ransom for **many**" (Matt. 20:28), and "poured out [his blood] for **many** for the forgiveness of sins" (Matt. 26:28). It goes without saying that "his people" and the "many" referred to in these texts are one and the same but, by definition, they do not constitute "all people." They are exclusive words, not all-inclusive. By virtue of the terminology (i.e. "his people" and "many" as opposed to "all people" and "everyone"), these verses have Limited Atonement in view.

- Christ died "so that in him **we** might become the righteousness of God" (2 Cor. 5:21); that is, "**we** were reconciled to God by the death of his Son" (Rom. 5:10) whereby "**we** have redemption, the forgiveness of sins" (Col. 1:14). By using the term "we," rather than "all," it is evident that the apostle Paul used exclusive language to build a case for Limited Atonement.

- Christ said that he "[laid] down his life for **the sheep**" (John 10:11), meaning "**the church** and gave himself up for her" (Eph. 5:25-27); that is, "**the flock** ... which he obtained for himself with his own blood" (Acts 20:28). If we accept these verses at face value, we are inclined to conclude that it is the Elect—and them alone—for whom Christ died. He did not die for sheep and goats combined, nor did he die for the penitent and unrepentant alike. Rather, he died for "the sheep," "the church," and "the flock."

- Christ "gave himself for **our** sins to deliver **us** ... according to the will of our God and Father" (Gal. 1:3-4) where "the blood of Jesus ... cleanses **us** from all sin" (1 John 1:7). In doing so, "Christ redeemed **us** from the curse of the law, having become a curse for **us**" (Gal. 3:13). This "our" and "us" to whom Paul and John refer stands in clear distinction from "all" or "everyone." Again, they are exclusive words, not all-inclusive.

- Christ died "for **us** while we were yet sinners" (Rom. 5:8) and "gave himself for **us** to redeem **us**" (Tit. 2:14) in order "that he might bring **us** to God" (1 Pet. 3:18). Once again, this "us" to whom Peter and Paul refer stands in contrast to "all" or "everyone." Those who were brought near to God through the death of Christ are exclusive in number and specific in name.

These are but a handful of texts that speak to a definite or particular atonement. Christ's propitiating and expiating death was geared toward, and applied to, "his people," "his church," "his sheep," "the flock," and the "many"—that is, the collective "we," "our," and "us" who make up the Elect of God. Isaiah said it best some eight hundred years before the birth of Christ when he prophesied: "He was cut off ... for the transgression of *my people* ... For he bore the sin *of many*" (Isa. 53:8, 11-12, emphasis added). Likewise, the high priest Caiaphas, when plotting Christ's death with the Sanhedrin, prophesied "that Jesus would die ... *for the scattered children of God, to bring them together and make them one*" (John 11:51-52, emphasis added). It seems both Isaiah and Caiaphas understood Limited Atonement long before John Calvin.

Jesus came into the world to do God's will, which was to save unfailingly and definitively a particular group of people given to him by the Father. We conclude, therefore, that both reasons for his coming and dying (to do God's will and to save "his people") demand the doctrine of Limited Atonement. For it was clearly not God's will to give all people to His Son nor was it His will that all people should be saved. Christ laid down his life only for his sheep and he saves only those given to him by the Father (cf. Heb. 2:13). The *Bread of Life Discourse* in John 6, the *Good Shepherd* statement in John 10, and the Lord's *High Priestly Prayer* in John 17 tell us as much.

For whom did Christ die?	
"His people"	Matt. 1:21
"My people"	Isa. 53:8
"The many"	Heb. 9:28 cf. Isa. 53:11-12; Matt. 20:28; 26:28

"The sheep"	John 10:11
"The church"	Eph. 5:25-27
"The flock"	Acts 20:28
"The scattered children of God"	John 11:51-52
"His offspring"	Isa. 53:10
"His friends"	John 15:13
"sons and daughters ... [his] children"	Heb. 2:10-14
"We," "Us," & "Our"	2 Cor. 5:21; Rom. 5:8-10; Col. 1:14; Gal. 1:3-4; 3:13; Tit. 2:14; 1 John 1:7; 1 Pet. 3:18

If the Bible is clear on one thing about the death of Christ's it's this: He sufficiently and efficaciously *ransomed* and *reconciled* his people to God as a sacrificial *substitute*, making full *propitiation* (satisfaction) for their sins. In other words, his death actually accomplished something. It was not a theoretical atonement, such as in Universal Atonement that, at best, promises only possibilities.

Universal Atonement offers an atonement that makes all men redeemable. Limited Atonement, however, redeems certain men completely. Universal Atonement offers an atonement that makes all men savable. Limited Atonement, however, saves certain men to the uttermost. To reject the Calvinist view of Limited Atonement in exchange for the Arminian view is to end up with an atonement that leaves men less than totally free or actually redeemed, a reconciliation that leaves men still estranged from God, a propitiation that leaves men still under the wrath of God, and a substitutionary death that still makes the sinner coffer up the faith to pay the debt for his sins. Redemption and reconciliation, to say nothing about Penal-Substitution and propitiation, can never be guaranteed in Arminianism; they are dependent upon what man does with his faith rather than what Christ has already done irrespective of faith.

The Bible teaches that those for whom Christ died have been eternally redeemed; they are truly free and their debt has been fully paid. It teaches that those who are reconciled to God through Christ's atonement are *actually* reconciled and the wall of separation that existed between them and God has been torn down (cf. Col. 2:14). It teaches that Christ's death on the cross was a sacrifice that fully satisfied the wrath of God. It also teaches that Christ was indeed a substitute, a kinsmen redeemer, who acted in place of, as well as on behalf of, his Elect. When Jesus died on the cross, he said, "It is finished" (John 19:30), indicating that he had fully, finally, and fruitfully ransomed the Elect. Thankfully, he did *not* say, "It is now *possible* only if people believe!"

Jesus came to do the will of his Father. He came to save his people from their sins. He came to seek and save that which was lost. He came to bear witness to the truth. And he did it all perfectly and particularly—he accomplished exactly what he was sent to accomplish—so that none of those whom the Father had given him would be lost.

Reflection Questions:

1. From what you understand about Christ's atonement, which of the following best describes the Lord's purpose in dying?

    a. He died a soldier's death, as one who dies for an entire country (out of duty)
    b. He died a martyr's death, as one who dies for a cause (out of passion)
    c. He died a parental death, as one who dies for his own child (out of duty, passion, and love combined)

2. How does the fact that God specifically elected certain sinners for salvation, and died especially for their

redemption, affect how you understand or view the atonement of Jesus Christ?

3. Does Limited Atonement make Christ's death more personal to you?

4. Having noted both Universal (Unlimited) Atonement and Limited Atonement, which seems more consistent with the character of God, and why?

Chapter 17

The Crucifixion in Context

John 3:16 is one of the most widely quoted verses from the New Testament, and is arguably the most famous prose recorded in all of antiquity. It has been called the "gospel in a nutshell" by various theologians and a "metropolis of gospel truth."[143] It is considered to be a summary statement of some of the most central doctrines of traditional Christianity. No other single statement in the Bible so aptly sums up God's redemptive purpose in Christ for fallen humanity.

At the beginning of John 3, Nicodemus, a prominent Pharisee and a ruling member of the Jewish Sanhedrin, came to Jesus under the cloak of night as a representative of Israel's intelligentsia. He sought a private interview with the Lord, convinced that Jesus was the Messiah, but equally confused by its implications. Jesus responded to Nicodemus's confession by affirming in John 3:16 that God is loving toward men and sacrificial in nature. The verse is as powerful in spirit as it is profound in structure. Christ declared:

> "For God so loved the world that he gave his one
> and only Son, that whoever believes in him shall
> not perish but have eternal life" (John 3:16).

The Lord's response to Nicodemus, as recorded by John, speaks to the love that God has for His creation and the extent of that love—so great that He sacrificed His only Son on our behalf. It teaches that anyone who believes in Jesus Christ, God's Son, will be saved. This verse gives all believers the glorious hope of eternal life in heaven through the love of God and the death of Christ.

So ubiquitous in Scripture is the message of John 3:16 that it has invaded the farthest recesses of American culture. Watch a nationally televised sporting event, for example, and notice the number of "John 3:16" placards hoisted by camera-ready fans. Consider star athletes like quarterback Tim Tebow, the first college sophomore to win the Heisman Trophy, who, among other reasons, became famous for inscribing the verse in his eye paint. In the U.S., the *In-N-Out* Burger chain prints John 3:16 on the inside of the bottom rim of their paper cups. The clothing chain *Forever 21* prints it on the bottom of their shopping bags, and *Tornado Air Systems* prints it on the packaging of their fuel-saver products. It's not uncommon, of course, to see John 3:16 written as graffiti on highway overpasses and in back alleys. It seems that wherever we turn in America, we are reminded in one way or another that God loved the world to such a degree that He sent His only Son to die for us.

The truth behind this magnificent verse hardly seems contentious. But sometimes the passages we think we know the best are the ones we actually understand the least. And this is especially true in the case of John 3:16. In fact, there are a host of Bible passages, not unlike John 3:16, which are *interpolated* with tradition rather than *interpreted* from sound exposition. And no doctrine has been more victimized by John 3:16 and its *interpolation*, including the traditionalism, eisegesis, and assumptions imposed upon it, than Limited Atonement.

In like manner as the Bereans in Acts 17:11 who were commended by Luke for their deference to Scripture, we must remember that when it comes to the discipline of biblical interpretation "context is king." This cheeky slogan simply means that the context drives the meaning of a phrase. Interpreting a Bible verse apart from its immediate context, as Dr. Ron Rhodes reminds us, is "like trying to analyze a Rembrandt painting by looking at only a single square inch of the painting, or like trying to analyze Handel's *Messiah* by listening to only a few short notes."[144]

Reinforcing Dr. Rhodes point is a popular parable that many ministers, myself included, often use to demonstrate the dangers inherent to poor hermeneutics. A man dissatisfied with his life, so the parable goes, decided to consult the Bible for guidance. He closed his eyes, flipped the Bible open, and pointed to a spot on the page. Opening his eyes, he read the verse under his finger. It said, "Then Judas went away and hanged himself" (Matt. 27:5b). Closing his eyes again, the man randomly selected another verse. This one read, "Jesus told him, 'Go and do likewise'" (Luke 10:37b). Having interpreted both verses out of context, the man had no choice but to conclude that God was commanding him to commit suicide in like manner as Judas. Not surprisingly, the man's tragic conclusion was the result of his tragic hermeneutics.

The background of a verse is absolutely crucial in determining the meaning of the foreground. Every word in the Bible is part of a verse, every verse is part of a passage, every passage is part of a chapter, every chapter is part of a book, and every book is part of the whole of Scripture. No verse in the Bible can be disassociated from the paragraph, chapter, and book in which it is found. We must endeavor, therefore, to ascertain the author's intended meaning by (1) recognizing its place in the canon; (2) taking into account the historical considerations relevant to the passage; (3) establishing the literary genre of the paragraph (i.e. poetical, prophetic, historical, narrative, apocalyptic, etc.); (4) acknowledging the audience to whom it is addressed; and (5) apprehending the author's purpose for writing.

Exegetical study of the New Testament, I hasten to add, must always be done under the watchful eye of the Old Testament, which serves as our chaperone on the road to discovery. While the New Testament interprets the Old Testament in Christian theology, the Old Testament nevertheless provides clarification and subtext to the New Testament that is not readily apparent to non-Jewish readers. In the end, the *Analogy of Faith*—the rule which stipulates that Scripture interprets Scripture— is our clarion call. It must be heeded and applied before any interpretive conclusions are made.

Sadly, today's evangelicals aren't known for being profound, sober-minded, or consistent with their hermeneutics; instead they've developed a reputation for being superficial, trivial, doctrinally erratic, and theologically naive. The case put forth against Calvinism, in my estimation, only proves this point. The so-called proof-texts brought to bear against

Limited Atonement—John 3:16 being chief among them—are supposedly numerous, formidable, and unavoidable. In most cases, Arminians tell us, they are incontrovertible. And I grant that if we arrive at our interpretations of these texts based merely on a superficial reading and allow our traditions and presuppositions to color our take-away, they might be right. But when each text is subjected to contextual analysis, rather than to a glossary of assumptions, only the opposite proves true.

The science of biblical exegesis, unfortunately, is a discipline that goes largely untapped by a vast majority of lay people. In their haste to prove Limited Atonement false, they blunder over the academics. As is so often the case, either critical analysis of their so-called proof-texts is ignored, or the immediate context is kicked to the wayside, or various word meanings are misappropriated and misapprehended, or the *Analogy of Faith* is dismissed. It is regrettable that many well-intentioned Christians remain convinced that they are purveyors of sound hermeneutics when in fact they violate almost every cardinal rule of the science.

It has been my experience that many evangelicals, particularly Arminians with whom I occasionally dialogue, stop short of going beyond the face value of Scripture. It seems they are spooked by biblical exposition; that is, if they scratch beyond the surface of a verse, they risk waking a sleeping monster (in the form of an alternative meaning) that contradicts their traditions. In many cases, they retreat from exegesis altogether, demonstrating a dispassion for Greek lexicons, a cavalier understanding of grammatical constructions, and an utter disregard for entomological roots. John Hendryx, the creator and editor of Monergism.com—arguably the most robust online resource on Reformational thought—diagnoses the problem this way:

> The movement against Reformed Theology turns out to be a kind of an irrational moral suppression of one of the most robustly God-honoring theological traditions in existence today. Even when faced with insurmountable

biblical evidence, many out there ... grind their teeth at the biblical revelation which points to God's sovereignty in the salvation of men. *There is a desperation about this anti-Calvinist movement which clings to one or two favorite verses without taking into consideration either context or what the rest of the Scriptures say* (emphasis added).[145]

So what exactly are these supposed proof-texts that many Christians allege are incontestable, plentiful, and disprove Limited Atonement outright? In brief, Arminians lay claim to four verses primarily. They cite John 3:16 unreservedly, almost mechanically really, and compound it with others like John 1:29, 1 John 2:2, and 1 Timothy 4:10—each of which speak to the fact that Jesus died for the "world" and shed his blood on behalf of "all men."

1. **John 3:16**: "For God so loved the world that he gave his one and only Son, that whoever believes in him shall not perish but have eternal life"

2. **John 1:29**: "The next day John saw Jesus coming toward him and said, 'Look, the Lamb of God, who takes away the sin of the world!'"

3. **1 John 2:2**: "He is the atoning sacrifice for our sins, and not only for ours but also for the sins of the whole world"

4. **1 Timothy 4:10**: "... we have put our hope in the living God, who is the Savior of all men"

On the surface, these verses appear to make a cocksure case against Limited Atonement and pose a legitimate challenge to the Calvinist. But when examined thoroughly, and within their immediate contexts, we see an alternative meaning suddenly emerge. So we must ask: Do John 3:16, John 1:29, 1 John 2:2, and 1 Timothy 4:10 *really* teach that Jesus Christ spilled his blood for every single human being who has ever lived, and who is currently alive, and who will one day live?

Did Jesus Die for the Whole "World"?

We know that God is the author of all Scripture (1 Tim. 3:16) and that He is not a God of confusion (1 Cor. 14:33). We therefore can be certain that no two passages of Scripture are going to teach something contrary to one another. But if this is true, how then do we reconcile the dozens of verses in Scripture that speak to an atonement that is particular, definite, and limited in scope with those that seem to purport an unparticular, universal, and unlimited atonement? To ascertain the answer, we must defer to the science of exegetical study— the critical examination, evaluation, and interpretation of the texts in question.

Three statements recorded by the apostle John, at first glance, appear to buttress the credibility of Universal Atonement. In John 3:16 the apostle quotes the Lord himself: "God so loved the *world* that he gave his one and only Son, that *whoever* believes in him shall not perish" (emphasis added). Arminians argue famously from this verse that salvation is available to everyone ("whoever"), not merely the Elect, and that Christ's death was on behalf of every single inhabitant of the earth ("the world").

In John 1:29 the apostle also cites John the Baptist who, upon seeing Jesus pass by the Jordan riverbank, declared "Look, the Lamb of God, *who takes away the sin of the world!*" (emphasis added). Elsewhere, in his first epistle to the churches in Asia Minor, he asserts that the death of Christ "is the atoning sacrifice for our sins, *and not only for ours but also for the sins of the whole world*" (1 John 2:2, emphasis added). As with John 3:16, Arminians argue from these two verses that Christ's vicarious atonement reaches beyond the Elect ("not only for ours") and clings to every person on the planet ("the whole world").

Without digging beyond their shell, it seems that John 3:16, John 1:29, and 1 John 2:2 are *prima facie* evidence in favor of Universal Atonement; namely, that the cross-work of Jesus

Christ is applicable to all men everywhere. Arminians have rallied around these verses historically, in particular John 3:16, as the substratum for their crossology. *The Five Articles of the Remonstrance*, for example, which challenged the merits of Calvinism at the Dort Synod in 1619, said as much. Article 2 states:

> That agreeably thereto, Jesus Christ, the Savior of the world, *died for all men and for every man, so that he has obtained for them all,* by his death on the cross, redemption and the forgiveness of sins; yet that no one actually enjoys this forgiveness of sins except the believer *according to the word* ["world"] *of the Gospel of John 3:16* ... (emphasis added)

In short, because John 3:16 uses the term *world* in reference to God's love, as does John 1:29 and 1 John 2:2 in reference to Christ's propitiation, we're asked to accept as legitimate orthodoxy the tradition of Universal Atonement. Apparently no further study is necessary. But are the allegations against Limited Atonement, borne from a cursory reading of these proof-texts, an open-and-shut-case as Arminians would have us believe? Is Calvinism debunked on the grounds that our English Bibles more clearly convey that which the Greek text does not?

Hardly.

The common denominator linking John 3:16, John 1:29, and 1 John 2:2 to the atonement debate is the apostle's curious use of the term *world*. All Christians, regardless of their theological pinstripes, recognize this literary feature in John's corpus. But Arminians would have us suspend our hermeneutical rules at this juncture and accept a blanket definition for *world* (to mean all human beings everywhere and for all time and without exception) which can then be applied uniformly in Scripture wherever the word is found in relationship to the atonement. That is to say, when Jesus said "God so loved the world that he gave his one and only Son," (John 3:16), Arminians maintain that John had in mind the entire human family. When the

Baptist declared that Christ "takes away the sin of the world" (John 1:29), we are told that John had in mind every single person, both living and dead. And when John wrote that the crucifixion of Christ "is the atoning sacrifice for our sins, and not only for ours but also for the sins of the whole world" (1 John 2:2), he, again, had in mind all people everywhere and for all time and without exception.

But this type of hermeneutic, much less this lone definition for *world*, is exceedingly flawed, for the meaning of the term in John's writings is not as easily ascertained as many who are unfamiliar with Greek initially suppose. While certainly handy in advancing the Arminian agenda, to apply a universalistic definition to *world* and affixing it to every text germane to the atonement is to blunder scholastically.

Translated from the Greek word *kosmos*, from which we get the English word "cosmos" (meaning "universe"), standard Greek lexicons reveal a multifaceted meaning for the term *world*. In fact, we learn from James Strong (1822-1894) and his Greek work *par excellence* that there are at least *eight* different tenses in which the word *kosmos* or "world" is employed throughout Scripture. According to Strong, *kosmos* carries with it the following definitions, depending on the context involved:[146]

1. *Kosmos* is used generically to describe "an apt and harmonious arrangement or constitution, order, government."
2. *Kosmos* describes "an ornament, decoration, adornment, i.e. the arrangement of the stars, 'the heavenly hosts,' as the ornament of the heavens" (e.g. 1 Pet. 3:3).
3. *Kosmos* describes "the world, [or] the universe" (e.g. Acts 17:24).
4. *Kosmos* describes "the circle of the earth, the [physical] earth" (e.g. John 13:1; Eph. 1:4 cf. Job 38:4).
5. *Kosmos* describes "the inhabitants of the earth, men, the human family" (cf. Rom. 3:19).
6. *Kosmos* describes "the ungodly multitude; the whole mass of men alienated from God, and therefore hostile

to the cause of Christ" (e.g. John 15:18; Rom. 3:6 cf. John 5:24).

7. *Kosmos* describes "world affairs, the aggregate of things earthly;" namely the evil world system or culture (e.g. John 12:31 cf. Matt. 4:8; 1 John 5:19).

8. *Kosmos* describes "any aggregate or general collection of particulars of any sort [such as] the Gentiles as contrasted to the Jews" (e.g. Rom. 11:12) or believers as contrasted to unbelievers (e.g. John 1:29; 3:16-17; 6:33; 12;47; 1 Cor. 4:9; 2 Cor. 5:19).

So which of the eight tenses listed above are we to apply to *kosmos* or "world" in John 3:16, John 1:29, and 1 John 2:2? And does this definition apply across the board? As already noted, exponents of Universal Atonement assume the fifth definition for all three verses; that is, Jesus is said to have died for all "the inhabitants of the earth, men, the human family." As will be seen shortly, proponents of Limited Atonement, on the other hand, ascribe to these texts the eighth definition: namely, that Jesus died for an "aggregate or general collection of particulars of any sort [such as] the Gentiles as contrasted to the Jews" or, in this case, believers as contrasted to non-believers. Both definitions are in keeping with the Greek word *kosmos* and are therefore orthodox, but only one can be correctly applied to the texts in question.

So which side is correct? Did Jesus die for all men or did he die for an aggregate of men? In deducing our answer, each of John's letters and books come into play and prove indispensible in our analysis. This includes the Gospel of John, the Book of Revelation, and the epistles of 1, 2, and 3 John. We must search these five books carefully and evaluate the writer's usual intent behind *kosmos* and how he applied the term.[147]

On this point, A.W. Pink (1886-1952), an English evangelist, Reformed pastor, and a biblical scholar of the highest order, has done Reformed Theology a monumental favor. After taking upon himself this academic task several decades ago, he found that John used *kosmos*, or "world," eighty-six times in his

corpus. He used the term in reference to the *earth* twenty-six times.[148] Three times he used it to refer to *Jews* and *Gentiles* specifically.[149] Twelve times he used *kosmos* in reference to *believers* and *unbelievers* combined, or all of *humanity*.[150] Three times he used it to refer to the *world system*, that is, the wicked ways of society.[151] Thirty-one times he used it in reference to the *wicked*, excluding believers, which is his most common use of the term.[152] And finally, John used *kosmos*, or "world," eleven times with regards only to the Elect [153]

Noting the varied usage of the term *world*, the context of each passage is critical in our deliberation, lest the meaning become absurd. As an example of such absurdity, if we use the definition for *kosmos* that Arminians apply uniformly to John 3:16, John 1:29, and 1 John 2:2—meaning all "the inhabitants of the earth, men, the human family"—and blatantly ignore context and the *Analogy of Faith*, what, then, is to stop us from applying this same definition to *kosmos* in 1 John 2:15 and in James 4:4? Those texts should give us pause:

> Do not love the world [*kosmos*] or anything in the world [*kosmos*]. If anyone loves the world [*kosmos*], the love of the Father is not in him (1 John 2:15).

> You adulterous people, don't you know that friendship with the world [*kosmos*] is hatred toward God? Anyone who chooses to be a friend of the world [*kosmos*] becomes an enemy of God. (James 4:4)

Here, as in other texts (e.g. John 12:31; Matt. 4:8; 1 John 5:19), the *world* is depicted in a negative sense and, though not directly stated, as the object of God's *hatred*. This creates all sorts of hermeneutical problems for Universal Atonement. John tells us that "God so loved the *world*" that He made "an atoning sacrifice ... for *the whole world*." At the same time, he tells us that, as Christians, we are *not* to love the world. Moreover, James adds that to love the world is to show "hatred

toward God" and to ultimately take up arms against Him as His adversary.

The puzzle is obvious. God loves the *world*. Yet God seems to hate the *world*. So which one is it? Does God love every human being in the whole world or does He hate them as His enemies? How exactly does the *kosmos* that God seemingly hates in James 4:4 jive with the *kosmos* that God obviously loves in John 3:16? Are they one and the same by definition? Pink crystallized the argument this way:

> But the objector comes back to John 3:16 and says, *"World means world."* True, but we have shown that "the world" does not mean the whole human family. The fact is that "the world" is used in a general way.

> When the brethren of Christ said "Show thyself to the world" (John 7:4), did they mean "Show thyself to all mankind"? When the Pharisees said "Behold, the world is gone after him" (John 12:19), did they mean that "all the human family" were flocking after him? When the apostle wrote, "Your faith is spoken of throughout the whole world" (Rom. 1:8), did he mean that the faith of the saints at Rome was the subject of conversation by every man, woman, and child on earth? When Revelation 13:3 informs us that "all the world wandered after the beast," are we to understand that there will be no exceptions?

> These, and other passages which might be quoted, show that the term "the world" often has a relative rather than an absolute force.[154]

If by "world" we can only mean every single human being who has ever lived and will live and without exception, as Arminians argue and which Universal Atonement demands, then we are forced to conclude from 1 John 2:15 and James 4:4

that God hates all "the inhabitants of the earth, men, the human family" as equally as He is said to love them in John 3:16, and to have died for them in John 1:29 and 1 John 2:2. And to arrive at such a contradiction is to make the Bible paradoxically absurd and theologically incongruent.

It's no mystery, of course, that the Bible has different meanings in mind—other than every single person for all time and without exception—when it speaks of the *world* in 1 John 2:15 and James 4:4. These texts draw upon the seventh tense for *kosmos* in the Greek language, specifically "world affairs, the aggregate of things earthly" (e.g. John 12:31 cf. Matt. 4:8; 1 John 5:19). In other words, to fall in love with the ways of society and to befriend secular culture, says James and John, is to be at enmity with God and to be devoid internally of His Spirit.

The Arminian hermeneutic crumbles under careful scrutiny. It fails to recognize the intent of the apostolic writers who clearly went to embellished lengths to correct the false notion that salvation was for the Jews alone. They used such phrases as "the world," "all men," "all nations," and "every creature," to correct this mistake. These expressions are intended to show that Christ died for all men without *distinction* (i.e. he died for Jews and Gentiles alike) but they are not intended to indicate that Christ died for all men without *exception* (i.e. he did *not* die for the purpose of saving each and every lost sinner). We cannot naturally assume a universalistic meaning whenever or wherever the term *world* appears in Scripture, lest blatant contradictions abound. If we show no restraint with context, the God of order quickly morphs into the Author of confusion.

Context is king, as we have duly noted. Therefore, in getting to the bottom of whether or not John 3:16, as well as John 1:29 and 1 John 2:2, teach Universal or Limited Atonement, we must bow to critical examination. Because Calvinists and Arminians agree that the term *world* is used in the same way in all three verses, though we disagree over its meaning, we need only to look at John 3:16 as our case study. What we conclude from this verse can be rightly applied to John 1:29 and 1 John 2:2 as well; on this point both sides are in agreement. The context of John 3:16 reads as follows:

"No one has ever gone into heaven except the one who came from heaven—the Son of Man. Just as Moses lifted up the snake in the desert, so the Son of Man must be lifted up, that everyone who believes in him may have eternal life. For God so loved the world that he gave his one and only Son, that whoever believes in him shall not perish but have eternal life. For God did not send his Son into the world to condemn the world, but to save the world through him. Whoever believes in him is not condemned, but whoever does not believe stands condemned already because he has not believed in the name of God's one and only Son."

To prove the Calvinist argument from context and from the *Analogy of Faith*, it is necessary to stress verse 18 in John 3, which includes the words: "Whoever believes in him is not condemned, but whoever does not believe stands condemned already." From this clause alone we can draw the full meaning of the passage. The interpretive sequence is as follows:

John 3:16-18

*"For God so loved the **world** that he gave his one and only Son, that whoever believes in him shall not perish but have eternal life ... Whoever believes in him is not condemned, but whoever does not believe stands condemned already"*

---

1. God sent his Son to save the *kosmos* ("world")
2. God did not send his Son to judge the *kosmos* ("world")
3. Believers are saved
4. Believers are not judged
5. Unbelievers are not saved
6. Unbelievers are judged
7. Since unbelievers are not saved, but are judged, contrary to the *kosmos* ("world") which is saved and not judged in John 3:16, unbelievers are not part of the *kosmos* ("world") in this passage
8. Since believers are not judged, but are saved, just as the *kosmos* ("world") in John 3:16 is saved and not judged, the *kosmos* ("world") represents only believers in this passage

The exegesis of John 3:16-18 is clear-cut. God demonstrated His love by offering His Son as an eternal sacrifice so that an aggregate of the world—that is, a specific or particular people—would receive forgiveness of sins and eternal life through faith in Christ. This aggregate of people, we learn from Revelation 5:9-10, includes different *types* of humans, but not the human race as a whole. Since it is clear in this passage (v. 18) that those *not* included among this aggregate will endure God's judgment for their unbelief, it is utterly unwarranted to read into *kosmos* some universal view of the atonement.

In the past, God exercised his redemptive love only to and for Israel. When Christ came, however, God extended that love to include the Gentile nations. By using the word *kosmos* in this context, Jesus was saying in John 3:16 that God's love was made manifest in the Son and that same love now extended beyond the borders of the covenant people to non-covenant people worldwide. In other words, Christ came and sacrificially died as a love gift for believing Jews and believing Gentiles alike. He died for different *types* of people groups, but not all people.

John sheds additional light on this interpretation in Revelation 5:9-10. While caught up to heaven in a rapturous vision, he beheld with his own eyes this aggregate of the world for which Christ died:

> And they sang a new song: "You are worthy to take the scroll and to open its seals, because you were slain, *and with your blood you purchased men for God from every tribe and language and people and nation.* You have made them to be a kingdom and priests to serve our God, and they will reign on the earth" (emphasis added).

Drawing from John's eyewitness testimony of the apocalypse, we learn that the death of Christ secured a redemption that is universally applied to all classes, types, and peoples of the earth. His atonement redeemed *from the world* men from every tribe, tongue, race, and nation. In this way we can rightly say that Christ's atonement is both universal (it extends beyond the borders of Israel to include both Jew and Gentile alike) as well as limited (it is applicable only to Jews and Gentile who have been chosen to believe).

Because the Bible clearly and adamantly opposes universal salvation, the Calvinist understands John 3:16 to say in effect: "God so loved the world—that is, He loved an aggregate group of believing men, women, and children hailing from every tribe and nation, and not just ethnic Jews—that He sent His only begotten Son that whoever believes in him will not die spiritually, but will be saved out of the world and have everlasting life."

Similarly, we understand the words of John the Baptist in John 1:29 to say: "Look! Jesus Christ! He is God's sacrificial lamb who takes away the sins of world—that is, he redeems from their sins an aggregate group of believing men, women, and children hailing from every tribe and nation." Lastly, we understand the apostle John to be saying in 1 John 2:2: "Jesus Christ is the atoning sacrifice for our sins, and not only for the Jews alone, but also for the sins of the whole world—that is, an aggregate group of believing men, women, and children hailing from every tribe and nation. He is the sacrificial Messiah for every *type* of people group; for elect Jews and non-Jews alike who believe." This same interpretation applies also to Paul's use of the term "all men" in 1 Timothy 4:10.

The doctrine of Limited Atonement is not only beautiful, it is wondrously true. The Scriptures teach that Christ's death ransomed "his offspring" (Isa. 53:10) but not the progeny of the serpent (Gen. 3:15). He died for his "sons and daughters ... [his] children" (Heb. 2:10-14) but not for "illegitimate children and not true sons" (Heb.12:8). Through his sacrifice, he ransomed his "sheep" (John 10:11) but leaves in sin the ornery goats (Matt. 25:33); he delivered his "church" (Eph. 5:25) but condemns the "synagogue of Satan" (Rev. 3:9); he made satisfaction for "many" (Matt. 26:28) but grants that most should perish (Matt. 7:13 cf. Luke 13:24). Christ died for "his people" (Matt. 1:21) and only for "his friends" (John 15:13).

Lack of theological precision ought not to be tolerated, because ambiguity is always the friend of error. Nowhere is this more evident than in the traditional handling of important texts like John 3:16. Let us remember, therefore, that while life is promised universally to all who believe in Christ, faith is nevertheless not common to all. For Christ is made known and is exalted on high for the whole *kosmos* to see, but it is the Elect whose eyes have been opened by the monergistic work of God's Spirit so that they may seek Him unfailingly by faith. Alas, it is for them and them alone that Jesus Christ died on the cross.

Reflections Questions:

1. Have you ever assumed the meaning of a particular Bible verse or passage (based upon tradition or presupposition) only to arrive at an alternative conclusion after exegetical study of the text?

2. In light of the racial divide between Jews and Gentiles in the first century, why do you suppose the New Testament writers (particularly John) invoked phrases like "the world," "all men," and "every creature" to define the scope of the atonement?

3. What do you consider to be the most appealing aspects of Limited Atonement, and why?

Section 5:

*The Scandal of Irresistible Grace & the Perseverance
of the Saints*

*"I will make an everlasting covenant with them: I will never
stop doing good to them, and I will inspire them to fear me, so
that they will never turn away from me."*

Jeremiah 32:40

Chapter 18

The God Who Drags & Draws Effectually

There is no reasonable answer, humanly speaking, that explains why I am a Christ-follower. I was not born into a religious home nor was I educated in the ways of Christianity. My father—a hardened atheist for most of his life—made no secret of his disdain for organized religion. Likewise, my mother, although raised by nominally religious parents, showed little interest in matters of a spiritual sort. My childhood was predominately secular. I had few, if any, religious friends and I certainly had no interest in being religious myself. What little I did know about Christianity, in retrospect, was ascertained mostly from Christmas carols, Easter plays, or the occasional religious movie. Yet here I am today; a middle-aged evangelical—and a pastor no less—approaching my fourth decade in the Christian faith.

How is such a thing possible?

My story is really not that much different from every other sinner throughout history who has come to personally know Jesus Christ as their Lord and Savior. We each have testimonials which, in their own unique way, defy the odds. By all accounts, we are statistical anomalies. There is no logical basis for why any idolater of sin would ever willingly forsake his gratuitous idols for a life of righteousness. So this begs the question further: How is salvation possible? How do hardened pagans ever come to revere the God they inherently revile?

The Bible does not leave us without an answer. It tells us that the miracle of conversion is accomplished by the gracious and efficacious work of the Holy Spirit. Without His leading, no sinner would ever come to God. Without His work, no sinner could ever be born-again. Without His influence, no sinner would ever find Christ palatable. The Spirit calls and drags; He makes known and reveals; He regenerates and sanctifies;

and He quickens and convicts. And He does so irresistibly and powerfully. Even the most obstinate sinner, vile and rebellious though he may be, is powerless to thwart the inward summons of the Holy Spirit. Consider, for example, the conversion story of one of the most wicked men to ever grace the pages of Church history—John Newton.

Newton was born in London, England on July 24, 1725. The son of a religious mother and an overbearing father with a penchant for drink, Newton took to seafaring when he was only eleven years-old. But a cantankerous relationship with his father (who was also the ship's commander), the brutal living conditions aboard the vessel, and the resentment of his shipmates made life on the high seas miserable for young Newton. Before long, disillusionment and despondency were his only friends.

After Newton broke from his father a few years later and entered the Royal Navy, his despondency morphed into pessimism. A chance reading of *Characteristics of Men* by Lord Shaftesbury had a profound impact on his worldview, particularly concerning religious matters. The book—which was written by a philosophical naturalist—coursed through Newton's impressionable veins like a slow poison, killing off his religious inclinations one by one. In ode to Shaftesbury, Newton came to pride himself on his religious skepticism. But what began as honest doubts soon metastasized into militant extremism. He not only convinced himself that uncertainty about God, even rank unbelief, was a staple characteristic of intellectual integrity but viewed organized religion as something to be opposed.

Newton's newfound poison opened up new vistas of intellectual freedom. Yet such freedom was only illusory as he found himself only further enslaved by his sin. Bolstered by a sailor's vulgar tongue, he considered it trivial to degrade the name of Jesus Christ. "Instead of prayer," he later recalled, "I learned to curse and blaspheme."[155]

Newton's reputation preceded him almost everywhere he went. His heart hardened to such a degree that he was known as the vilest sailor on the North Atlantic, surpassing all others in conduct unbecoming of a gentleman. On those rare occasions when his ship was at port, he made it his ambition to carouse at night, often drinking, fighting, and womanizing until daybreak. He was careless, insubordinate, foul-mouthed and no respecter of morality. In the words of one of his biographers, John Newton "plumbed the depths of human sin and degradation."[156] Newton himself later admitted: "I saw the necessity of religion as a means of escaping hell, but I loved sin and was unwilling to forsake it."[157]

Not satisfied with his own debauchery, Newton was complicit in the moral downfall of others. He took pleasure in luring impressionable sailors into his colorful lifestyle—baiting them, as it were, with forbidden fruit—and, in a very real sense, making degenerates out of them. Years later he confessed: "... abandoned as I pleased, without any controul; and, from this time, I was exceedingly vile ... I not only sinned with a high hand myself, but made it my study to tempt and seduce others upon every occasion."[158]

Growing more belligerent with each passing month, Newton perfected his knack for sacrilege. It seems he was especially talented at writing limericks of a blasphemous nature. Beyond the usual profanity native to salty seamen, he crafted a string of vulgarities that raged against the very concept of God. He made no secret of his hobby:

> I had no business to employ my thoughts ... my whole life, when awake, was a course of most horrid impiety and profaneness. I know not that I have ever since met so daring a blasphemer. Not content with common oaths and imprecations, I daily invented new ones.[159]

Things only spiraled downhill for Newton as time went on. In 1744, at the age of nineteen, he had fallen victim to unrequited love. Mary Catlett, with whom he had been in love since childhood, rebuffed his advances. Moved to despair, he jumped ship and deserted his post. Within days he was captured and returned to the boat, not as a midshipman, but as a felon to await punishment. He was confined below deck and placed in chains. In the foul, dank basement of the ship he was left alone to contemplate his unknown fate. The reproach he felt from his shipmates—his fellow disciples of degeneracy no less!—brought him to the brink of lunacy. He burned with murderous hatred.

Two days later, the morning before his ship was to shove off to India, the entire crew assembled on deck to witness Newton's court-martial and flogging. Stripped of rank and his dignity, he was verbally accosted, publicly humiliated, and reportedly given eight dozen strokes from a cat-o'-nine-tails. Lash after lash, crack after crack, came whipping down on his naked back.

There is no doubt that the shame Newton felt during his tribunal dramatically affected his disposition. Rather than reform his ways, however, he sank deeper into dissipation. He went from morally repugnant to morally un-redeemable; from a blasphemous skeptic to a neurotic atheist. Filled with rage, he contemplated murdering the ship's captain and then committing suicide by throwing himself overboard. But sober judgment eventually prevailed, preventing him from acting on his desperate impulses.

Newton's record in the Royal Navy was permanently marred by his court-martial. Fully aware of his bleak future, he negotiated his discharge from service, insisting upon an immediate transfer. His captain was more than happy to oblige him, grateful to finally rid himself of his insubordinate menace.

Nineteen days later, Newton was exchanged into service on the *Pegasus*, a merchant ship bound for Africa. Although he had no idea as to the type of goods and services trafficked on the boat, Newton preferred the year-long voyage to Africa on the merchant ship to the navy's five-year voyage to India. He accepted his new assignment with a smile on his face. Aboard the *Pegasus*, John Newton was amongst strangers who knew nothing of his raucous past or his desertion and flogging. A new career awaited him.

It wasn't until he assumed his position as deckhand on the vessel that Newton realized that his new skipper and crew were engaged in the slave trade between Africa and the West Indies. But such a morally repugnant line of work mattered little to Newton. If there was a dollar to be had, he reasoned, then, by any means necessary, a dollar should be gained. With Sierra Leone the next stop on the voyage, the *Pegasus* set sail for Africa and, in so doing, set out a new career for Newton.

By the time he turned twenty-three, Newton had advanced up the chain of command. He eventually reached the rank of captain (although not without trial and tribulation) and was given his own slave ship to ply his trade. Before long he became a leading slave trader in the industry, pedaling captured slaves between Africa, England, and the Americas.

Newton succeeded where many budding entrepreneurs had failed. Through bribery and manipulation, he developed working relationships with African tribal chiefs who, for a pittance, did his bidding. The ingenious chiefs kidnapped rival tribesmen, bound them had and foot in chains, and brought them to Newton for bartering. Other natives were baited by the crew, lured to Newton's ship by European trinkets. They came from far and wide to behold western craftsmanship only to then be subdued and incarcerated in the orlop of the boat.

Newton was in the depths of sin. He had abandoned his belief in God. He had forsaken a life of morality. And he had grown wealthy and comfortable tyrannizing people of color. But his life of satisfaction was short-lived. At the height of his depravity, while sailing across the North Atlantic, he came across a copy of *The Imitation of Christ* by Thomas à Kempis (1380-1471). With skeptical trepidation, he decided to read it. The words of Kempis haunted him immediately, particularly the following passage:

> Since life is of short and of uncertain continuance, it highly concerns you to look about you and take good heed how you employ it. O hardness of men's hearts! O the wretched stupidity that fixes their whole thoughts and cares upon the present ... whereas in truth, every work and word, and thought, ought to be so ordered as if it were to be our last; and we instantly to die, and render an account of it.[160]

Render an account for our lives, work, and thoughts?
Newton mused: "What if these things should be true!"[161]
Alarmed by the words and his own reaction to them, he angrily
threw the book aside. He was an intellectual—a skeptic at best
and an atheist at worst—and he was determined to live with the
consequences. Nevertheless, as he later wrote, "... the Lord's
time was come, and the conviction I was so unwilling to receive
was deeply impressed upon me by an awful dispensation."[162]

The spiritual conviction Newton felt when reading *The
Imitation of Christ* soon ballooned into outright desperation.
The next night, on March 10, 1748, the crew was suddenly jolted
awake as a violent storm descended upon them. Wave after wave
pounded the vessel smashing the planking, tearing the rigging,
and filling the hold with water. The pumps could not keep up
with the rising water and Newton joined his fellow mariners in
the hopeless task of funneling seawater off the boat. Hour after
hour they battled the foaming waves and blustery gales. Some
crewmembers were washed overboard in the torrent along
with livestock and much of the cargo. All hope for survival fast
disappeared.

The rigging of the boat was badly damaged and many of the
sails were in tatters. The boat's nautical location was lost on the
map and food rations were in short supply. Newton's mind was
racing. Although he couldn't understand what was happening,
he suddenly felt that he was not alone. The presence of something
or *someone* overcame him. At the same time, convinced that his
sins were too great to be forgiven, his trained memory recalled
to mind the many terrifying Scriptures learned in childhood
that condemned him. Such recollections only amplified his fear.
Day after day, as the ship continued to negotiate through the
stormy weather, he took his turn at the helm of the battered
boat, sometimes for eleven hours at a time, steering the frail ship
through the mountainous waves. All the while he re-examined
his beliefs and, in extreme anxiety, pondered the Scriptures that
haunted him.

For almost a month the boat drifted aimlessly. Newton
recorded in his journal that when all seemed lost and the ship

was sure to sink, he made a surprising distress call: "Lord, have mercy upon us." Those words, borne from intense desperation, joggled him. *Lord, have mercy on us?* How could such a plea come from the mouth of a notorious blasphemer? Even more surprising to Newton was the eventual reality that his prayer did not go unanswered. The damaged ship miraculously reached port on the northern shores of Ireland. The boat was saved and the lives of its starving crew spared.

Afterwards, Newton reflected long and hard on all that had happened. Were the treacherous events at sea meant for a greater purpose? Was he delivered from the brink of death and a watery grave for a reason? Later in his cabin he re-read what he wrote in his journal—*"Lord, have mercy on us"*—and was convinced that God had addressed him through the storm. To him, it was no longer a question of *'Is there a God?'* but *'What is God like? How may I truly know Him?'* and *'Is there still forgiveness to be had?'* He felt grace begin to work in his heart. Convinced that God's providence was responsible for his survival, he abandoned his doubt and pride. Yet Newton was baffled as to why God counted him worthy of such mercy, especially in light of his belligerent heart, countless blasphemies, and the many perversions committed in his past. Why would God save a wretch like him?

By the end of his stay in Ireland, Newton was a beaten man. He renounced his life of debauchery and publicly professed his faith in Jesus Christ. In his own words, he became "a serious professor" of the Savior. He later wrote:

> I stood in need of an Almighty Saviour, and such a one I found described in the New Testament. The Lord had wrought a marvelous thing: I was no longer an infidel. I heartily renounced my former profaneness, I had taken up some right notions, was seriously disposed, and sincerely touched with a sense of the undeserved mercy in being brought safely through so many dangers; I was sorry for my past misspent life, and purposed

> an immediate reformation ... I cannot doubt that
> this change, so far as it prevailed, was wrought
> by the Spirit and power of God.[163]

Newton was truly and irresistibly converted to Christianity. The unlikeliest of men to ever come to saving faith, his conversion was, in his own words, "wrought by the Spirit and power of God." Like the Gentiles in Romans 9 and Saul of Tarsus in Acts 9, Newton "did not pursue righteousness" on his own yet he nevertheless "obtained it, a righteousness that is by faith" (Rom. 9:30). Safe and sound in Ireland, he underwent an internal miracle. He was transformed from a child of wrath into an heir of divine blessing; from a slave of sin to a son of God.

Newton sought diligently throughout the rest of his life to remember always what he had previously been and what God had done for him. He observed the anniversary of March 10, 1748 as the day of his conversion; a day of humiliation in which he freely and willingly subjected his will to the One he so dismissively blasphemed his entire life. In order to imprint into his memory the depths of his sin from which he had been rescued by God's grace, the born-again slave trader inscribed Deuteronomy 15:15 on his mantel: "Remember that you were slaves in Egypt and the Lord your God redeemed you."

Not long after his conversion, Newton became a pastor in England, a role in which he labored faithfully as a Calvinist for more than forty years. He was beloved by his various congregations and played a key role in encouraging fellow Calvinist William Wilberforce—a British politician and philanthropist—to fight boldly against the evils of the slave trade. The Lord had indeed changed Newton's life in radical ways.

"*Amazing grace, how sweet the sound ...*" So begins one of the most beloved hymns of all time—*Amazing Grace*; a staple in the hymnals of many churches today. The lyrics continue, "*Thro' many dangers, toils and snares, I have already come; 'tis grace has bro't me safe thus far, and grace will lead me home.*" The author of those autobiographical words was none other than John Newton, the self-proclaimed wretch and slave trader who once was lost but then was found; who once was enslaved but then was set free, rescued by God's irresistible and amazing grace.

How are we to explain the miraculous conversion of such an impudent and notorious God-hater as John Newton? How can sinners like him, who exhibit no inclination whatsoever for the things of God, suddenly and eagerly surrender to Christ? How is it that someone can be spiritually lost at one moment—shackled by the chains of sin and reputed to be the vilest of men—only to be found the next moment and set free? For Calvinists, the fourth petal in the T.U.L.I.P. acronym—Irresistible Grace—provides the answer.

"For Who Can Resist His Will?"

The gospel invitation is extended to every person without discrimination, promising eternal life to those who repent and believe. Whether through general revelation (Psa. 19:1-4 cf. Rom. 1:20) or special revelation (John 1:1, 14 cf. Heb. 1:1-3), God welcomes all men without distinction to "Come, all you who are thirsty, come to the waters; and you who have no money, come" and live forevermore (Isa. 55:1). But this *outward call*, extended to both the Elect and non-elect alike, is superficial at best; it is powerless to bring sinners to Christ. The reason being is because sinners are by nature dead in sin and do not have the spiritual ears to hear it. Like John Newton, they are in and of themselves unable and unwilling to forsake their evil ways and to turn to Christ for mercy.

No amount of external threatening, outward persuasion, or promises of blessing can cause blind, deaf, dead, and rebellious sinners to bow before Christ as Lord and to look to him alone for salvation. Such an act of submission is contrary to fallen man's nature. For this reason, Calvinism teaches that, in order for the Holy Spirit to bring the Elect to salvation, He must extend to them a special *inward call* that goes beyond the outward invitation. It is a spiritual stimulant, in a manner of speaking, that arouses a sinner to life, removes his blindness, opens his ears, and quells his rebellion. This inward call accomplishes what the outward call alone cannot. Inextricably linked to spiritual regeneration, it performs a work of grace within the sinner that inevitably brings him to faith in Christ. In a word, it is *irresistible*.

If we assume that Unconditional Election ranks in the minds of non-Calvinists as the most *misleading* of the Doctrines of Grace, and Limited Atonement the most *misguided*, then the doctrine of Irresistible Grace is easily the most *mischaracterized*. Very few Christians, at least insofar as I can tell, understand this doctrine accurately as it is stated in The Westminster Confession of Faith. The preposterous caricatures imposed upon it by anti-Calvinists are plentiful, if not grossly unfair, and are to blame for muddying an otherwise clear teaching in Scripture. Sadly, there is no shortage of examples.

David Servant, executive director of *Shepherd Serve Ministries*, frames his opposition to Irresistible Grace in customary Arminian fashion:

> I can't help but wonder how God takes pleasure in people who are, against their wills, supposedly regenerated by God's irresistible grace. They are really nothing more than robots. If they love Him, it is only because they had no choice but to love Him, because they would have preferred to continue hating Him ... Their warm feelings toward Him are pre-programmed; thus true love is impossible ...
>
> [Calvinists] make human beings into robots who are incapable of making moral choices and who have no capacity to love. They make Christians to be people whom God forced against their wills to become His children.[164]

Servant does not stand alone in his criticism. In his book *Chosen But Free*, Norman Geisler writes: "Irresistible grace on the unwilling is a violation of free choice. For God is love, and true love is persuasive but never coercive."[165] With his tongue planted sarcastically in his cheek, Geisler concluded: "[God] chooses [the Elect] with His irresistible power and forces them into His kingdom against their will."[166]

Drawing upon the same straw-man argument as Servant and Geisler, Hank Hanegraaff—the president of the *Christian Research Institute* and host of the *Bible Answer Man* radio broadcast—harkened back to Perry Miller (see Chapter 4) with his gross mischaracterization of Irresistible Grace. Hanegraaff quipped over the airwaves, "God is neither a cosmic rapist who forces His love on people, nor is He a cosmic puppeteer who forces people to love Him. Instead God grants us the freedom of choice."[167]

Lastly, but not surprisingly, Dave Hunt alleges: "Irresistible Grace is an oxymoron. Grace is the opposite of irresistible."[168] He adds elsewhere, "Indeed, just as God himself cannot force anyone to love Him (a coerced response is the opposite of love), so it would be the very opposite of [irresistible] grace to force any gift or benefit of 'grace' upon anyone who did not want to receive it."[169]

Given the reputations of these men, their criticisms are not only unfortunate but absurdly inaccurate and academically inexcusable. It behooves us, therefore, to examine the doctrine of Irresistible Grace outside the margins of tradition and presupposition, but within the purview of historical orthodoxy. Our focus must be on the doctrine itself and on what Calvinists *actually* teach concerning grace, not on what Geisler, Servant, Hunt, and Hanegraaff *say* we teach or what they infer from Arminian propaganda.

So what do Calvinists mean when we say that God's grace is irresistible? How exactly does such grace align with the other petals in T.U.L.I.P.? And why is it essential to Calvinism? To answer these questions, we must first say what Irresistible Grace is *not*.

Irresistible Grace is not robotic faith. It does not mean that God forces a mechanical response from a sinner that is independent of the sinner's will. By the term *irresistible* we simply mean that God's grace is *effectual*—that is, it always produces an intended effect. Contrary to the aforementioned assertions made by Servant, Geisler, Hanegraaff, and Hunt,

Irresistible Grace does not teach that God brings sinners to
Christ against their wills, kicking and screaming, in violation
of their personal choice. It is neither antithetical to free-will
nor is it tantamount to coercion, divine bullying, spiritual rape,
or brainwashing. Quite the opposite, it simply means that God
will unfailingly save His Elect *in cooperation* with their willful
decision, not in opposition to it, by giving them the necessary
resolve to come to Him in faith. Although the outward call of
the gospel can be, and often is, rejected by men, the inward call
of the Spirit never fails to result in the conversion of those to
whom it is made.

Calvinists maintain that God draws to Himself in time and
space those whom He decreed to save in eternity past. In the
words of the Canons of Dort, they come to Him at the appointed
time "sweetly and powerfully,"[170] acting on their own accord and
from renewed affections. The Spirit creates within them a new
heart or a new nature whereby they can understand and believe
spiritual truth. In other words, what a sinner *would not* and
could not do while in his state of reprobation—namely, "Taste
and see that the Lord is good" (Psa. 34:8 cf. 1 Pet. 2:3)—God
enables him to do through the miracle of spiritual regeneration.
The intended effect is always successful and unavoidably
certain. Those quickened by God's Spirit are set free from the
chains of depravity in order that they can *freely* and *willingly*
"Taste ... the Lord." It is only then, after God has given a
sinner regenerated taste buds, so to speak, that he finds Christ
irresistibly mouth-watering. The Westminster Confession Faith
punctuates Irresistible Grace as follows:

> All those whom God hath predestinated unto
> life, and those only, he is pleased, in His
> appointed and accepted time, effectually to call,
> by His Word and Spirit, out of that state of sin
> and death, in which they are by nature, to grace
> and salvation by Jesus Christ; enlightening their
> minds, spiritually and savingly, to understand
> the things of God; taking away their heart of
> stone, and giving unto them an heart of flesh;

renewing their wills, and by His almighty power
determining them to that which is good, and
effectually drawing them to Jesus Christ; yet so
as they come most freely, being made willing by
His grace.[171]

Because the Father, the Son, and the Holy Spirit work in
tandem in the salvation of sinners, it is *impossible* for the Holy
Spirit to fail in saving those who have been given to Christ by the
Father, drawn to Christ by the Spirit, and redeemed by Christ
on the cross. The Spirit of God inevitably wins over those whom
the Father intends to save in order that "none of them is lost"
(John 17:2 cf. 6:39; 18:9).

Irresistible Grace necessarily flows from the preceding
points in Calvinism. As it so happens, one cannot subscribe
to Total Depravity and still deny the irresistibleness of God's
grace. If a sinner is depraved in totality, dead in sin, and unable
to do any good in terms of his salvation, then it stands to reason
that he needs far more than mere *assistance* to be saved. Give a
dead man a cane, for instance, and try though he might, he still
cannot muster the functioning ability to walk on his own. He is
lifeless. Instead, a dead man must first be made alive before the
cane is of any value to him. So it is with a totally depraved sinner.
God does not merely offer dead sinners some sort of spiritual
walking stick (by way of common grace) and yet leave them
paralyzed in spiritual death. On the contrary, His grace must
regenerate the dead sinner to life and, concurrently, empower
him with the basic muscles. Without Irresistible Grace, sinners
are not able to pick up their mats and "walk in truth" (3 John
1:3). They are lifeless and paralytic.

Likewise, Irresistible Grace is the logical outgrowth of
Unconditional Election. Because God has "chosen people" from
before the foundations of the earth to be "a royal priesthood, a
holy nation, a people belonging to God" (1 Pet. 2:9), the salvation
of the Elect must therefore depend upon God's sovereign
grace—not man's free-will—to bring it to fulfillment. God leaves
nothing, especially His decrees, to random chance. He grants
a new disposition to those whom He has "transformed by the

renewing of [their] minds" (Rom. 12:2) in order that, by the willful use of their new minds, "God's purpose in election might stand" (Rom. 9:11). It is by Irresistible Grace that transformed sinners exercise their own prerogative to be saved, in keeping with God's predetermined prerogative to save them.

Moreover, because Calvinists profess that Christ died only for his elect people, redeeming them fully from their sins, Irresistible Grace is inextricably linked to Limited Atonement. It *guarantees* that Christ's death was not in vain but is efficacious in application. Were it not for Irresistible Grace, the value of the atonement is, at its very best, a theoretical gamble; it is dependent upon man's supposed free-will to appropriate it. But is it theologically feasible that God would allow the death of His Son to possibly come to naught, thereby overturning His predetermined decree, if the Elect possess the freedom of the will to frustrate His intent? God forbid! It is the power of God's grace that guarantees that the sins of those for whom Christ atoned are completely "covered over" and "redemption through his blood, the forgiveness of sins," is applied to them "in accordance with the riches of God's grace" (Eph. 1:7)! It is no wonder that the apostle Paul proclaimed: "I do not set aside the grace of God," because, if otherwise left to random chance, it's possible that "Christ died for nothing!" (Gal. 2:21).

The irresistibleness of God's grace gives chosen sinners new constitutions and renewed affections by which they freely, voluntarily, willingly, knowingly, and savingly come to Christ on their own accord. It guarantees that God's eternal decree to save a people for Himself will not fail but will come about exactly as He foreordained. Lastly, far more than a crapshoot, Irresistible Grace is an ironclad guarantee that the benefits of Christ's death will be successfully appropriated by all those for whom it was intended. Nothing is left to chance. For these reasons, and more, Irresistible Grace forever stands as an indispensable doctrine in Calvinism.

Irresistible Grace is first set forth in the teaching of Jesus. In John 6:44, before a fickle Capernaum audience, the Lord said, "No one can come to me unless the Father who sent me *draws him*, and I will raise him up at the last day" (emphasis added). This statement jives with our Lord's previous words in verse 37 where he prefaced, "All that the Father gives me *will come* to me, and whoever comes to me I will never drive away" (emphasis added). These two verses combined teach that those called by God are inevitably drawn by God to Jesus Christ. They "will come" to him definitively and decisively—not possibly or potentially. Dr. John Murray (1898-1975), a Scottish-born Calvinist theologian who taught at Princeton Seminary and helped to found Westminster Theological Seminary, put it this way:

> The Father draws men, places holy constraints upon them, calls them into the fellowship of his Son, and presents them to Christ as trophies of the redemption Christ himself has accomplished. ... So perish the thought that coming to Christ finds its explanation in the autonomous determinations of the human will. It finds its cause in the sovereign will of God the Father.[172]

The word "draw" in John 6:44 is loaded with potency. It comes from the Greek word *helkō,* meaning "to draw by inward power, lead, [and to] impel." Those who are spiritually regenerated, in other words, are impelled to come to Christ by "inward power" granted them by the Holy Spirit.

The Greek nuances behind the word "draw" do not stop with mere "leading" or "impelling." Interestingly enough, *helkō* also means "to ... drag."[173] It is used explicitly in this sense in reference to a *dragnet* cast by fishermen. They "drag [*helkō*] it along" the sea to secure a great catch (John 21:6). Similarly, the word is used in reference to a legal subpoena. It carries with it the authority to "drag [*helkō*] you into the Law courts" (James 2:6, WNT). Like fish caught in a dragnet, the idea is that litigants in court are dragged into their circumstances according to the determination of another. It cannot be resisted. In both examples, whether it is fish or litigants, they are neither enticed nor wooed but are *overcome* by a higher command. Thus, in light of John 21:6 and James 2:6, we see that those irresistibly drawn to Christ in John 6:44 come to him willingly, voluntarily, freely, and knowingly because they have been dragged [*helkō*] by the Spirit through His "inward power." They are "those who have been called, who are loved by God the Father" and who are definitively "kept by Jesus Christ" (Jude 1:1).

We witness grace in action in the conversion of Lydia of Thyatira in Acts 16. A merchant of purple dyes and fabrics (for which the city of Thyatira was known), she was the first recorded convert to Christianity in Europe. Luke records her conversion this way:

> On the Sabbath we went outside the city gate to the river, where we expected to find a place of prayer. We sat down and began to speak to the women who had gathered there. One of those listening was a woman named Lydia, a dealer in purple cloth from the city of Thyatira, who was a worshiper of God. *The Lord opened her heart to respond to Paul's message* (Acts 16:13-14, emphasis added).

Why did Lydia believe in the gospel preached by the apostle Paul? The answer is because God first "opened her heart" and enabled her to act in response to what she heard. Nowhere in this passage is there even the slightest hint that this divine work performed in Lydia's heart was open to resistance. In fact, only the opposite is true. As Paul rhetorically reminds his readers, "For who can resist His will?" (Rom. 9:19, ESV).

Salvation does not depend on clever evangelistic techniques, masterful strategies, or the skills (or lack thereof) of the preacher. It is the work of God alone. "I planted the seed, Apollos watered it, but God made it grow." Paul wrote to the Corinthians. "So neither he who plants nor he who waters is anything, but only God, who makes things grow" (1 Cor. 3:6-7). In the conversion of Lydia, we see a classic example where the Holy Spirit causes planted seed to bloom, "not because of anything [Lydia had] done but because of his own purpose and grace. This grace was given [to her] in Christ Jesus before the beginning of time" (2 Tim. 1:9).

And finally, in the parable of the *Good Shepherd*, we see yet another demonstration of the irresistibleness of God's grace. The imagery that Christ used to convey the human response to the effectual call to salvation is as striking as it is comforting. Speaking of himself as a watchman over his sheep, the Lord taught:

> "... *and the sheep listen to his voice. He calls his own sheep by name and leads them out. ... and his sheep follow him because they know his voice* ... I am the good shepherd; I know my sheep and my sheep know me—just as the Father knows me and I know the Father—and I lay down my life for the sheep. I have other sheep that are not of this sheep pen. I must bring them also. *They too will listen to my voice,* and there shall be one flock and one shepherd" (John 10:3-4; 14-16, emphasis added).

Those elected, chosen, predestined, and called (the sheep) follow the Good Shepherd (Christ) when they hear his voice. After being spiritually regenerated, they have a newfound desire to go where he leads. They do not wander off or go astray from his path. They do not shut their ears to his summons. Instead, they willingly choose to abide in him. And their decision is predicated on the fact that they are known and loved by the Good Shepherd as his prized possession. Their names were "written in the book of life belonging to the Lamb that was slain from the creation of the world" (Rev. 13:8 cf. 3:5; 17:8; 20:12, 15; 21:27; Php. 4:3). They have been given to him by the Father (John 6:37). This truth alone makes certain that the sheep will obey the summons of their shepherd.

All men are dead in trespasses and sins and are unable to comprehend divine truth (1 Cor. 2:14). Unless the Holy Spirit opens their heart, as He did with the former slave-trader John

Newton and with Lydia of Thyatira, they cannot and will not comprehend and believe the gospel. Such a divine work is reserved for the Holy Spirit alone—intended for the Elect alone—and is always effectual.

Aside from the *Bread of Life Discourse* in John 6:44, the parable of the *Good Shepherd* in John 10:3-16, or the conversion of Lydia in Acts 16:13-14, the fingerprints of Irresistible Grace are plastered throughout the New Testament. Paul tells us that "We have ... received the ... Spirit who is from God, that we may understand what God has freely given us" (1 Cor. 2:13)—that is to say, it is through the quickening of the Holy Spirit that God "has given us understanding, so that we may know him who is true" (1 John 5:20). Through the calling of the Spirit, "the eyes of [our] heart may be enlightened in order that [we] may know the hope to which he has called [us]"(Eph. 1:18). To summarize, it is only through the inward call of the Holy Spirit that we come to "understand" and "know" who God truly is. He has "enlightened" us to come to Him in faith and to comprehend our calling as Christians.

The Old Testament also weighs in on Irresistible Grace. "I will *inspire them* to fear me," God said through the prophet Jeremiah, "so that they will never turn away from me" (Jer. 32:40, emphasis added). Ezekiel adds, "And I will put my Spirit in you and *move you* to follow my decrees and be careful to keep my laws!" (Ezek. 36:25-27, emphasis added). And Isaiah wrote, "Then the eyes of those who see will no longer be closed, and the ears of those who hear will listen. The mind of the rash will know and understand ..." (Isa. 32:3-4).

Each of the aforementioned phrases—"I will inspire them," "my Spirit [will] ... move you," and "the mind ... will know and understand"—all speak to the re-creative presence of the Holy Spirit who is at work in the hearts of the Elect to bring them to salvation. It is through the miracle of spiritual regeneration (says Isaiah) that elect sinners are given new dispositions whereby they are "inspired" (says Jeremiah) and "moved" (says Ezekiel) to respond in obedience to God's summons. It is irresistible and unavoidable.

Irresistible Grace is not robotic faith. It is neither antithetical to free-will nor is it indicative of divine coercion. Rather, it teaches that God will unfailingly save His Elect in cooperation with their willful decision, not in opposition to it, by giving them renewed affections to come to Him in faith. It is monergistic in origin but synergistic in application.

We cannot sidestep Irresistible Grace, no matter how aggressive our traditions or presuppositions might war against it. It is an essential component to Calvinism, to say nothing about Christianity, because it guarantees that God's plan of redemption will unfold exactly as He foreordained. Moreover, Irresistible Grace is not only the incontrovertible testimony of both Testaments in Scripture but it is also the wonderful testimony of every single Christian who has ever lived.

Just ask John Newton.

Reflection Questions:

1. Since unregenerate man cannot truly and credibly convert to Christ under coercion (i.e. at gunpoint or by threat of the sword), how credible is the Arminian charge that Calvinism promotes robotic faith? Stated differently, if you are a Calvinist, did you come to saving faith in Christ at divine gunpoint, kicking and screaming against your will? Or was your conversion a voluntary act made from your redeemed will?

2. How is Irresistible Grace related specifically to Total Depravity, Unconditional Election, and Limited Atonement?

Chapter 19

Eternal Security & Elect Saints

Geoffrey Chaucer (1343-1400), known as the Father of English literature and perhaps the greatest English poet of the Middle Ages, famously said, "All good things must come to an end." And I suppose our adventure through the Doctrines of Grace is no different. The finish line is now upon us. What an adventure it has been.

Our time spent on the road to discovery, although picturesque at moments, has not been an easy one to travel. Finger-pointing between brothers and ad hominem attacks have clouded the landscape, and back-and-forth Bible jousting has bloodied the terrain. Not surprisingly, the trail we blazed through the maze of Calvinism has left indelible tire marks in the rearview mirror. But Reformed Theology has a tendency to do just that: it strains relationships and leaves within the family of faith the tracks of discord (cf. Matt. 10:35; Luke 12:53).

In our safari through orthodoxy, we put Calvinism and Arminianism to the litmus test of Scripture. In the end, only one lionheart was left standing. We travelled back in time through Church history, having observed the titans on whose shoulders we stand today, and watched the scandal of sovereignty unfold before our eyes. We consulted Greek and Hebrew lexicons when necessary, a daunting task if ever there was one, and did our best to properly define and honorably defend our distinctives. And when the Bible was silent on a matter, we erred on the side of common sense. Through it all, the sciences of hermeneutics, etymology, theology, epistemology, and philosophy sat ready in the passenger seat, mapping the course and lighting our path along the way.

Our first excursion as tourists, so to speak, took place in our own backyard (Chapter 1). We discovered within the brotherhood of Christ the wide disparity that exists concerning

313

God's sovereign will and its relationship to human freedom. We also saw in some of the popular writings of many evangelical luminaries the hostility that Reformed Theology imbibes today—particularly among Americans. With each mile traversed we met friend and foe alike, for the Doctrines of Grace have no shortage of either.

We then retraced Calvinism's footsteps back to its origin (Chapter 2). Our itinerary led us to the free-will debate between Augustine and Pelagius at the Council of Carthage in 418, then the Third Ecumenical Council of Ephesus in 431, followed by a brief layover at the Second Council of Orange in 529. Each legislative body declared Augustine's views to be the clearest representation of Scripture. The Synod of Dort in the Netherlands came next where, in 1619, we saw the followers of Arminius and his predecessor Cassian clash with the followers of Calvin and his predecessor Augustine. We also witnessed the birth of T.U.L.I.P. amid the growing protests of the Arminian Remonstrance. Far more than simply codifying the Doctrines of Grace, the ecclesiastical forum in Dordrecht upheld the earlier rulings of Carthage, Ephesus and Orange.

Continuing on in our journey, we made a necessary pit stop to address the matter of semantics. We checked under the hood and ran a quick diagnostics test on the greasy language barrier that exists whenever Calvinists and Arminians attempt to discuss the issues that separate them (Chapter 3). At the same time, we contended with the pesky oil leak that is God's sovereignty and how it relates to the existence of sin in the world (Chapters 4-5).

Before long, we traded in our proverbial vehicle for an operating table. We put away our sightseeing binoculars and pulled out our surgical instruments. No longer tourists on a joyride, we became forensic investigators. We went to work dissecting each doctrinal pillar that supports the framework of Reformed Theology.

First came the "T" in T.U.L.I.P. Beginning with Original Sin and its universal effects on mankind (Rom. 5:12-21; 1 Cor. 15:22), we cut into *Total Depravity* with total abandonment (Chapters 8-9). We autopsied man's fallen condition under the surgical lights of Scripture and pronounced him D.O.A. Along with his spiritual deadness (lifelessness) and moral inability (powerlessness), we discovered that mankind is also inherently wicked (by the Fall), spiritually blinded (by evil), spiritually enslaved (by sin), and spiritually subjugated (by Satan). He does not have the wherewithal to save himself any more than a cadaver has the ability to perform trigonometry. In his natural state, man is a zombie who, at his worst, is condemned to die a second death in the lake of fire (Rev. 2:11; 20:6, 14-15; 21:8). At his best, he is a spiritual invalid, doomed to a catatonic existence.

Next was the "U" in T.U.L.I.P. We performed a rather intrusive biopsy on *Unconditional Election* (Chapters 10-11). In doing so, we were astonished to learn that, despite humanity's spiritual reprobation, God has elected, predestined, and chosen a remnant of dead sinners to "make alive in Christ" (1 Cor. 15:22; Eph. 2:1-5; Col. 2:13; 1 Pet. 3:18). This He has graciously done "before the foundation of the world ... having predestined us to adoption as sons by Jesus Christ to Himself" (Eph. 1:4, 11). His choice to adopt some while leaving others in their sin was not predicated on the foreseen actions of men nor on their willingness to believe but was "according to the good pleasure of his will" (Eph. 1:5) and "according to His own purpose and grace ... from all eternity" (2 Tim. 1:9). That God chose to save some when none were worth saving is a testament to His grace, mercy, and love.

After that came the "**L**" in T.U.L.I.P. We made the logical connection between Unconditional Election and *Limited Atonement* (Chapters 15-17). With our theological scalpel in hand, we performed exploratory surgery on the crucifixion of Christ. We peeled back the layers of tradition and presuppositions imposed upon it and uncovered the marvelous truth that just as all believers were chosen by God in eternity past to be a love gift to Christ (John 6:37; 17:6, 24) so Christ was chosen by the Father to die for them as their Redeemer (cf. 1 Pet. 1:20). His atonement on the cross was both exclusive in scope and accomplished in total. It achieved exactly what God intended and for whom it was intended. Christ died specifically for, and limited to, every believer for all time. And in dying for them, and for them only, he secured their redemption and guaranteed their future salvation.

We then arrived at the "**I**" in T.U.L.I.P. We saw how *Irresistible Grace* flows naturally from the preceding petals and is indispensable to Calvinism (Chapter 18). All those predestined and chosen by the Father and redeemed by Christ on the cross are inevitably drawn (even dragged) to Christ by the Holy Spirit (John 6:37, 44). It is a supernatural precursor to spiritual regeneration. The inward call of the Holy Spirit accomplishes that which the outward call alone cannot. God unfailingly saves elect sinners in collaboration with their willful decision, not in opposition to it, by granting them the compulsory determination to come to Christ in faith. The Holy Spirit overcomes each and every soul that the Father predetermined to save—infallibly and irresistibly—in order that "none of them is lost" to Christ (John 17:2 cf. 6:39; 18:9).

Beyond addressing the obvious scandal inherent to sovereignty or the particulars around the T.U.L.I.P. acronym, we also interspersed our study with subject matter seldom discussed at length on Sunday mornings or in evangelical coffee shops. Monergistic regeneration and the *Ordo Salutis* topped the list, followed by the nature of God's foreknowledge in salvation, the inconsequence of human free-will, the error of Calminianism, and the twin gifts of faith and repentance. We offered extensive treatments on each topic, particularly when, where, and how they apply to the Doctrines of Grace.

In a nutshell, we learned that being born-again *precedes* rather than *proceeds* saving faith in the *Ordo Salutis* and, furthermore, is the work of God alone (Chapters 6-7). We also determined that, in Bible passages germane to salvation, God's foreknowledge is always *causative*, not merely predictive, and is tantamount to God "*loving* in advance" those whom He foreordained to believe in His Son (Chapter 13). We corrected the stereotype which suggests that Calvinists deny the existence of free-will and showed that not only is human autonomy proof-positive in Scripture but it's also an attribute of man that is forever contaminated by the Fall of Adam (Chapter 12). In addition, we exposed the inanity of *Calminianism* which, try as it might, fails miserably in its efforts to morph Calvinism and Arminianism into a cohesive one size-fits-all system (Chapter 14). Finally, we demonstrated from Scripture that the act of repentance and the ability to believe in Christ unto salvation, far from being universal entitlements doled out equally and uniformly to all sinners, are exclusive gifts granted only to those whom God has chosen to redeem (Chapter 12).

All in all, our journey through the Doctrines of Grace has been exhaustive and scandalous. It has been informative in some places inasmuch as it has been mind-bending in others. But our work here is not yet done. With the finish line looming just ahead, we arrive at our final destination—the "**P**" in T.U.L.I.P. — and the Perseverance of the Saints.

Once Saved, Always Saved

Contemporary Christianity is not immune to folklore. It is packed full with a number of misconceptions widely embraced as factual when, in actuality, they are blatantly false. As a veteran in ministry, I have found this to be especially true even among the most seasoned saints. Like salacious gossip or a nasty rumor, these bloopers have a tendency to run amok within the Body of Christ and to take on a life of their own. We've heard them repeated so often by reputable Christians that we remain convinced they are true.

For instance, how often have we heard well-meaning Christians refer to the Millennial Kingdom of Christ as a time when "the lion will lie down with the Lamb"? For most of us, such poetical imagery seems scriptural. However, as beautiful a picture as these words convey, the reader might be surprised to learn that nowhere in the Bible are they found—the citation doesn't exist. At the very most, it's a combination of thoughts derived from only a couple of verses (Isa. 11:6 cf. 65:25).

Likewise, if we were to ask children in Sunday school or the nominal layperson in the pew how many animals of each kind Noah took into the ark prior to the Great Flood, the popular consensus would likely be "Two!" Such an answer, however, while showing a familiarity with Scripture, reveals a certain degree of ignorance. Although it is true that God instructed Noah "to bring into the ark two of all living creatures" (Gen. 6:19), it is also true that God supplemented these instructions later by telling Noah, "Take with you *seven* of every kind of clean animal, a male and its mate" (Gen. 7:2, emphasis added). Overlooked by many readers is the fact that these additional clean animals were brought aboard the ark for sustenance and sacrifice (Gen. 8:20).

Nearly all civilized people are familiar with the saying, "Cleanliness is next to godliness." This statement implies that one of the most important things in life is hygiene or purity. Popularized in a sermon by John Wesley in 1791, many people assume that it is a scriptural proverb—but it is not so. As Warren Wiersbe points out, this expression is an archaic axiom found in Babylonian and Hebrew religious tracts and repeated in the writings of Sir Francis Bacon in 1605. But it is conspicuously missing from the Bible, and for good reason. Outward cleanliness has no connection whatsoever with godliness. Jesus was crystal-clear that men are defiled or deemed godly by what is in their hearts, not by what they eat or don't eat or by how often they wash their hands (cf. Matt. 7:18-23).

Lastly, and perhaps most notably, the maxim "God helps those who help themselves" is presumably the most oft-quoted phrase thought to be imbedded in Scripture. Yet this teaching couldn't be further from the truth. Nowhere do we find in the Holy Writings such an anti-biblical sentiment. This proverb, according to Max Lucado, likely originated with Algernon Sydney in 1698 in an article titled *Discourses Concerning Government* but it most certainly did not originate with the Holy Spirit. Despite its conventional wisdom, it is an adage that stands in direct opposition to the teaching of Scripture. God *does* in fact help the helpless (Isa. 25:4; Rom 5:6)!

These misconceptions lead us to a more serious matter currently at large within the Church—namely, the Perseverance of the Saints. This is the controversial doctrine in Reformed Theology which teaches that those who are truly saved will persevere to the end and cannot lose their salvation. Heretofore known as the *Eternal Security Debate*, error and confusion over this doctrine abound in mass. Many liturgical Catholics, for example, believe that *mortal sins,* such as murder or blasphemy, if left unpardoned, can forfeit a Christian's eternal residence in heaven. A significant number of Protestant fundamentalists share this same conviction as well, although they take great care to avoid Catholic terminology. Whatever its religious backbone and no matter its wide acceptance among the faithful, to suggest that a genuine believer can be eternally condemned after having been eternally redeemed is to succumb to an *institutional* teaching, not a biblical one.

The disconnect that exists among Christians over Eternal Security is relatively simple to diagnose. Some believe that if one holds to the "once saved, always saved" mantra, as Calvinists do, then one is instinctively promoting a license to sin with impunity. On the other hand, others believe that if one rejects Eternal Security, as Arminians do, then one must be required to keep their salvation by works of obedience. While honest Christians differ on the matter, both sides tend to misrepresent the other in an effort to save face. Inevitably a war of words ensues and fractures erupt within the family of faith.

A conversation about Eternity Security can be surprisingly convoluted. It has been my experience, in fact, that if five random Arminians were asked to explain their views we would, in all likelihood, get five conflicting responses. And in some respects, the same is true with Calvinists. Inasmuch as many Arminians are woefully inconsistent in their views on Eternal Security, some Reformed writers, including a crop of medieval Reformers, have been strangely circumspect in theirs. It seems that there is enough blame to go around for muddying the doctrine. That being said, rather than invest considerable time and space citing a plethora of Arminians who object to Eternal Security, and their reasons for why, or listing a smorgasbord of Calvinists who endorse it, and their reasons for why, I believe we are much better served if we address the doctrine straightforwardly.

The Reformed tradition has historically maintained that the doctrine of Perseverance is the natural consequence or outworking of predestination in which God has unconditionally chosen certain people for salvation and exonerated them of their guilt through the atonement of Christ. These elect individuals are irresistibly drawn to Christ through the power of the Holy Spirit, who then regenerates their hearts (monergistically) and convinces them of their need for salvation. It therefore stands to reason: Since God has made satisfaction for the sins of the Elect and has drawn them (or will eventually draw them) to His Son through the Spirit; *they can no longer be eternally condemned.* They must necessarily persevere as Christians unto eternal life through the help of the Holy Spirit "in order that God's purpose in election might stand" (Rom. 9:11). To suggest otherwise, as Arminians teach, is to imply that God's foreordained decree, or "purpose in election," can be toppled.

As with Limited Atonement, the Perseverance of the Saints is an operation within the Godhead. All those who are spiritually united to Christ through the inward baptism of the Holy Spirit are eternally kept by the Father. They have been predestined unto eternal glory and are therefore assured of heaven. Christ *redeemed* His people on the cross; the Holy Spirit *renewed* them in their lifetime; and the Father *retains* them in eternity. It is wholly Trinitarian. The Westminster Confession of Faith elucidates the doctrine of Perseverance as follows:

> They, whom God hath accepted in His Beloved, effectually called, and sanctified by His Spirit, can neither totally nor finally fall away from the state of grace, but shall certainly persevere therein to the end, and be eternally saved.

> This perseverance of the saints depends not upon their own free will, but upon the immutability of the decree of election, flowing from the free and unchangeable love of God the Father; upon the efficacy of the merit and intercession of Jesus Christ, the abiding of the Spirit, and of the seed of God within them, and the nature of the covenant of grace: from all which ariseth also the certainty and infallibility thereof.[174]

Dr. Charles Hodge (1797-1878), a Presbyterian theologian and leading exponent of historical Calvinism in America during the nineteenth century, highlighted Eternal Security in his exposition on Romans 8:1. "The proposition to be established is, that there is '*no condemnation to them which are in Christ Jesus*,'" he wrote. "That is, [true believers] can never perish; they can never be separated from Christ as to come into condemnation."[175] Unpacking Romans 8 further, Hodge went on to explain:

> Perseverance (of the saints), [the apostle Paul] teaches us, is due to the purpose of God, to the work of Christ, to the indwelling of the Holy Spirit, and to the primal source of all, the infinite, mysterious, and immutable love of God. We do not keep ourselves; we are kept by the power of God, through faith unto salvation.[176]

Dr. Anthony Hoekema (1913-1988), former Professor of Systematic Theology at Calvin Theological Seminary, agreed with Hodge when he wrote "those who have true faith can lose that faith neither totally nor finally."[177] Famed hymn-writer August Toplady (1740-1778), in his provocatively titled essay *Arminianism: The Golden Idol of Freewill*, wrote: "Whom are we to thank for perseverance ... to the end? ... A child of God can soon answer this question. And he will answer it thus: 'Having obtained help of God, I continue to this day' ... Not by my own might and power, but by the Spirit of the Lord of hosts."[178]

Biblical warrant for the Perseverance of the Saints is not in short supply. Going beyond the sound bites of the aforementioned Calvinists, the Bible itself takes a high view of Eternal Security. That a redeemed person cannot lose his salvation but will persevere to the end in accord with the promises of God is the testimony of prophet and apostle alike.

Regarding true believers, God promised through the prophet Jeremiah: "I will inspire them to fear me, *so that they will never turn away from me*" (Jer. 32:40, emphasis added). The apostle Paul taught that the "whole spirit, soul and body" of a true believer will *"be kept blameless* ... The one who calls you is faithful and he will do it" (1 Thess. 5:23-24, emphasis added). He said elsewhere that "[God] will keep you strong to the end, so that you will be blameless on the day of our Lord Jesus Christ" (1 Cor. 1:8). The writer of Hebrews was careful to note that God "has made perfect *forever* those who are being made holy ... *that cannot be shaken"* (Heb. 10:14; 12:28, emphasis added). Peter reminded his readers that true believers are "shielded by God's power until the coming of the salvation" (1 Pet. 1:5). And Jude, the Lord's half-brother, was rather direct when he said that "those who have been called, who are loved by God the Father" are unequivocally "kept by Jesus Christ ... who is able to keep you from falling" (Jude 1:1, 24).

The truth behind the Perseverance of the Saints is inescapable. Jeremiah tells us that we will "never turn away;" Paul insists that we are "kept" eternally secure "until the end;" Hebrews teaches that we are "forever" saved at conversion—a certainty that "cannot be shaken." Peter testifies that we are "shielded by God's power" until the day we die. And Jude is clear-cut: Christ will "keep [us] from falling." All of these statements point directly to the fact that, having been regenerated by the Holy Spirit, true believers "were marked in him with a seal, the promised Holy Spirit, who is a deposit guaranteeing our inheritance ... for the day of redemption" (Eph. 1:13-14; 4:30). In other words, our eternal security in Christ has been signed, sealed, and delivered.

The prophets and apostles are not without good reason in their unwavering support for Eternal Security. Jesus himself was its chief advocate. The Lord's *Bread of Life Discourse* in John 6, his *Good Shepherd* statement in John 10, and his *High Priestly Prayer* in John 17 reveal his heart concerning the preservation of his saints.

Offending everyone within earshot in his *Bread of Life Discourse*, Jesus assured his critics, "And this is the will of him who sent me, that I shall lose none of all that he has given me, but raise them up at the last day" (John 6:39). Speaking of his sheep in his *Good Shepherd* statement, the Lord said, "no one can snatch them out of my hand. My Father, who has given them to me, is greater than all; no one can snatch them out of my Father's hand" (John 10:28-29). And in his *High Priestly Prayer*, Christ prayed for the eternal preservation of his followers: "Holy Father, protect them by the power of your name ... I protected them and kept them safe by that name you gave me. None has been lost ... My prayer is ... that you protect them from the evil one" (John 17:11-12, 15).

In these passages we learn that Christ will lose none of those who have been chosen, elected, and predestined and given to him as a love-gift from the Father. He will positively resurrect each and every one of them, without exception or deficit, "at the last day." Moreover, no believer can be plucked from the protective clutch of God's embrace, no matter the extent of his rebellion or the severity of his waywardness, for true converts are preserved and kept safe from "the evil one" by the "power of [God's] name."

Perhaps the most striking blow to those who reject Eternal Security comes from the pen of the apostle Paul. To the Romans the apostle wrote in crisp terms:

> Who shall separate us from the love of Christ? Shall trouble or hardship or persecution or famine or nakedness or danger or sword? ...
>
> No, in all these things we are more than conquerors through him who loved us. For I am convinced that neither death nor life, neither angels nor demons, neither the present nor the future, nor any powers, neither height nor depth, nor anything else in all creation, will be able to separate us from the love of God that is in Christ Jesus our Lord (Rom. 8:35-39).

The "love of Christ" to which Paul refers in Romans 8:35-39 represents salvation. Paul rhetorically asked the Christians in Rome if any circumstance in life is powerful enough to cause a true believer to turn against Christ in a way that would cause Christ to turn his back on the believer. The clear implication is that there is no such circumstance because there is no such possibility! At issue in Paul's question, therefore, are the power and permanence of the love of Christ for those he purchased with his own blood (Acts 20:28) and brought into the family of faith. All true believers, Paul essentially tells us, are to have confidence as we face the Day of Judgment because we are assured that the divine and indestructible love of Christ binds us eternally to him.

It is unmistakable in Scripture that God's people, at the moment of their conversion to Christ, are awarded *eternal life* (not a temporary state of eternal life). They are *kept* by God's power through faith and *nothing can separate them* from His love. They have been *sealed* with the Holy Spirit who is the *guarantee*, or earnest payment, for their salvation, and they are thus assured an *eternal inheritance*. It is for these very reasons that Calvinists champion Eternal Security and the Perseverance of the Saints.

But Calvinists must stand tall and give thoughtful answers to honest questions posed by their critics. If the Elect are eternally secure with no possibility of ever losing their salvation, then how do we explain the heap of biblical passages that speak to so-called believers backsliding irreparably (e.g. Heb. 6:4-6)? How are we to handle the dozens of passages that caution believers to remain in Christ until the end lest we fall away and are amputated from "the tree of life" for all eternity (Rev. 22:14)?

The answers to these questions, as Calvinists see it, boil down to one's definition of a Christian. Certainly there are countless people who have professed saving faith in Christ, lived morally upstanding lives before God and man, and even displayed a tremendous zeal for advancing Christ's kingdom only to later repudiate their faith altogether and to abandon Christianity once and for all. One could argue, in fact, that such a scenario is an all-too-common occurrence in the Body of Christ. If this is the case, then, doesn't it stand to reason that such tragedy debunks the credibility of Eternal Security and the Perseverance of the Saints? Is not the very existence of an apostate *prima facie* evidence that a redeemed sinner can lose his salvation?

On this point Arminians and Calvinists diverge radically in their answers. Whereas Arminians are convinced that a genuinely born-again Christian can fall from grace irreparably, the Calvinist maintains that those who do, *and do so lastingly*, were never truly saved in the first place—that is, regeneration was never truly experienced by them, righteousness was never actually imputed to their account, and eternal life never granted. Like Judas Iscariot (John 12:6), Demas (2 Tim. 4:10), and Diotrephes (3 John 1:9), they were only a shell of a believer, the inside of which was hallowed and void of the Spirit. Salvation, in other words, was never theirs to lose. It is these shell-like imposters who John has in mind when he wrote: "They went out from us, but they did not really belong to us. For if they had belonged to us, they would have remained with us; but their going showed that none of them belonged to us" (1 John 2:19).

Our Lord's beloved disciple warns us that some *professing* believers will openly defect from the faith. They are rank apostates. Yet John explains that the very fact that such apostates desert the company of believers, having renounced their faith and renewed their vows to the world, manifests their true spiritual state. To these imposters, apostates, and shell-like believers our Lord will one day say, "I never knew you" (Matt. 7:23). Again, because "none of them belonged to us," they had no salvation to lose.

This is not to say that true Christians, who are sealed by the Holy Spirit and have God's Word abiding in them, are immune to momentary lapses into apostasy. On the contrary, they can, and often do, fall into heinous sin whereby they deny the Lord with their "prodigal living" (Luke 15:13, NKJV). But the point is that, unlike legitimate apostates, genuine believers will not flounder in a state of sin permanently. As with David and Peter, each of whom fell dreadfully and drastically, prodigal sons and daughters inevitably find their way home to their Father (cf. Luke 15:11ff).

Insofar as I see it, the crux of the issue between those who oppose Eternal Security and those who champion it comes down to what one truly believes about soteriology—the doctrine of salvation. In a very real sense, to deny the doctrine of Perseverance is to come dangerously close to denying the doctrine of justification by faith. And to deny justification by faith is to deny the doctrine of salvation. And to deny the doctrine of salvation is to excommunicate oneself from the brotherhood of evangelicalism.

Protestants of all stripes confess that salvation is by grace *alone* through faith *alone* in Jesus Christ *alone*. On this point the New Testament could not be more emphatic. Ephesians 2:8-9, the seminal passage on the topic, reads as follows: "For it is by grace you have been saved, through faith—and this not from yourselves, it is the gift of God—not by works, so that no one can boast." Likewise, Romans 10:9-10 tells us "if you confess with your mouth, 'Jesus is Lord,' and believe in your heart that God raised him from the dead, you will be saved. For it is with your heart that you believe and are justified, and it is with your mouth that you confess and are saved."

The truth that salvation is attained *through* faith and *by* faith and *only* faith is amplified elsewhere in Scripture, such as Romans 4:5: "However, to the man who does not work [for salvation] but trusts God who justifies the wicked, his faith is credited as righteousness." Again, in Romans 3:22 and Romans 5:1 we read: "This righteousness from God comes through faith in Jesus Christ to all who believe ... Therefore, since we have been justified through faith, we have peace with God through our Lord Jesus Christ."

Fallen man does not contribute one iota to his salvation. He is saved by faith alone. Even the repentance he offers and the faith he exercises are *gifts* granted to him from above (see Chapter 12). And while Arminians and Calvinists may disagree on this latter point, they are nevertheless in lockstep on the former, at least on paper. Man cannot save himself nor is he capable of producing the necessary good that God demands of him. When judged by the holy standards of God, even "our righteous acts are like filthy rags," as Isaiah 64:6 reminds us. In short, we do not have what it takes to save ourselves.

I take the time to remind the reader of the basis for salvation because it is crucial to the debate before us. Arminianism teaches that the assurance of final salvation is only for those who abide and continually trust in Jesus Christ. Or as one Arminian pastor in El Paso, Texas put it: "Although God definitely promises to do his part to keep us saved to the end, this does not mean that we do not have a part to play."[179] In other words, those who do not "play their part" and fail to bear fruit—because they cease to abide in Christ—the Father inevitably "cuts off" from being *in* Christ (John 15:2). Thus, according to Arminianism, one's perseverance (and final salvation) is conditioned upon man's continued obedience to Christ. But the reader should be cautioned: Whenever the word "obedience" is used *in relationship to salvation* it is often a code-word for *works-based* salvation.

It is at this juncture that we see the danger that Arminianism poses. By denying the doctrine of Eternal Security, among other things, Arminianism confuses Law and Gospel. This is no small error. Theodore Beza (1519-1605), Calvin's successor in Geneva, wrote, "Ignorance of this distinction between Law and Gospel is one of the principal sources of the abuses which corrupted and still corrupt Christianity."[180] And this is precisely the error that Arminianism makes—it mingles Law with Grace.

Writing for *Modern Reformation Magazine*, Dr. Rod Rosenbladt, Professor of Theology at Concordia University, Irvine in Irvine, California defined the issue as follows:

> When God gives orders and tells us what will happen if we fail to obey those orders perfectly, it is in the category of what the Reformers, following the biblical text, called "Law." When God promises freely, providing for us because of Christ's righteousness the status He demands of us, this is in the category of "Gospel." It is good news from start to finish. The Bible includes both, and the Reformers were agreed that the Scriptures clearly taught ... that the Law (whether Old or New Testament commands) was not set aside for the believer. Nevertheless, they insisted that nothing in this category of "Law" could be

a means of justification or acceptance before a
holy God.[181]

So how does the denial of Eternal Security by Arminians
pervert the gospel into Law-keeping? The answer is found in
the form of a follow-up question that Calvinists have historically
put to their Arminian brethren: *If mankind is saved by faith
alone and can contribute nothing whatsoever to his salvation,*
as Calvinists teach and as Arminians say they believe, *then why
do Arminians imply that God requires faithful obedience to
maintain it?* Stated differently, *If a believer cannot do good
works to earn salvation, then why do Arminians suggest he
must do the necessary good works to keep it? Conversely, how
can he do bad works to lose it?*

To these crucial questions the Reformed church has been
awaiting substantive answers, not conjecture, for the better
part of five hundred years. And the clock continues to tick. Yet
the standard responses from the Arminian camp, when not
conspicuously silent on the matter, continue to be woefully
unconvincing.

Sometimes life-long Christians—even Calvinists—question
their final salvation. There are times when we seem completely
separated from God's favor; when we lament that we are sinners
unworthy of His blessing; and when the fruit of the Spirit is
sorely lacking in our lives. But God has vowed in His Word that,
no matter how spectacular our shortcomings, we belong forever
to Him. Nothing—not even ourselves—can separate us from
His enduring love. Even in our worst spiritual winters when
our temperature toward Him is most frigid, He whispers to our
spirit and reminds us that He will never grow cold toward us.
Thus, when the night is far spent and the day is at hand, we can
take refuge in His everlasting guarantee "that he who began a
good work in you will carry it on to completion until the day of
Christ Jesus" (Php. 1:6).

Reflection Questions:

1. How do the following sentences differ?

   a. I obey Christ's commands BECAUSE I AM SAVED
   b. I obey Christ's commands TO GET SAVED
   c. I obey Christ's commands to KEEP MY SALVATION

2. It can be argued that out of all the doctrines of
   Christianity, the Perseverance of the Saints brings the
   most joy to the Christian. Why do you suppose this is?

3. Regarding the notion that a true Christian can lose their
   salvation, a famous preacher once admitted, "If I had
   the ability to lose my salvation, I most definitely would."
   What do you suppose he meant?

Part 3:
Post Review

Scandalized by Sovereignty

"... there is no doctrine more hated by worldlings ... as the great, stupendous but yet most certain doctrine of the sovereignty of the infinite Jehovah. Men will allow God to be everywhere except upon His throne. They will allow Him to be in His workshop to fashion worlds and make stars ... but when God ascends His throne, His creatures then gnash their teeth ... for God on His throne is not the God they love. They love Him anywhere better than they do when He sits with His scepter in His hand and His crown upon His head."

Charles Haddon Spurgeon
1834-1892

Epilogue

My Confrontation with John Calvin

The debate between Calvinism and Arminianism took center stage in my life during my senior year in Bible college. Due largely to the influence of a certain professor who dared to challenge my presuppositions, I came face-to-face with my haphazard approach to theology. The more I studied the Bible under Dr. Anderson's tutelage the more it unmasked my ignorance.

I must confess that up to that point in my collegiate career I bought into much of the hype that came with academic success. My meteoric rise on the Dean's List and the routine backslapping I received from classmates bamboozled me into thinking that I was in a league of my own! Comfortable with the applause, I pursued a biblical education with relative ease and a high opinion of myself. Moreover, I was a proud libertarian, theologically speaking. I prided myself on my Arminian belief in free-will and synergistic interpretation of Scripture.

On the first day of my final semester, Dr. Anderson introduced himself to his students in an uncustomary manner. He didn't offer his lofty résumé to us as other professors tended to do; neither did he bask in the fact that he was a highly sought-after university lecturer and ordained pastor. Without wasting words, he walked into the classroom, lifted up his weathered, leather-bounded Bible for all us Arminian students to take notice, and simply said: "I am Dr. Anderson. I am a five-point Calvinist. And the epistle to the Romans, which we will be studying in the weeks to come, is a book that is going to turn your personal theology upside down. It's nice to meet you all. Shall we begin?"

And with that brusque introduction, my life changed forever. The stage was set. In the front of the classroom stood the seasoned Calvinist lecturer—a champion of predetermined election—poised with open Bible and prepared for a battle of wits. And sitting opposite him was his cocky Arminian student—an advocate of libertarian will—ready to take his master to task. My ego was ill-prepared for what lay ahead.

My esteemed professor had remarkable credentials. A former adjunct Professor of Theological Studies at Regent University and Professor of New Testament and Theology at Northwest University, Dr. Anderson flaunted advanced degrees. That he was a Reformed theologian and working pastor teaching in an Arminian college mattered little to me. A Calvinist of the highest order, he was gracious, avant-garde, and amusing yet surprisingly tenacious when it came to defending the Doctrines of Grace.

My first thoughts about Dr. Anderson were less than flattering. He seemed quirky, yet strangely doctrinaire. In hindsight, I suppose I was somewhat threatened by his obvious command of Scripture—an achievement, I learned later, that most Reformed academics wear as a badge of honor. A tall, slender man with cropped hair and a booming voice, he took to the podium in casual attire suggesting that he didn't care much for formality. At the same time, he exuded an air of supreme professionalism. But I refused to be intimidated. *Did this professor really think he was going 'turn my world upside down' from a book in the Bible that I had already read too many times to count?* I thought to myself. *What on earth could a five-point Calvinist teach me that I hadn't already gleaned from my own personal studies in Romans?*

I responded to the professor's challenge in my mind with Arminian flair and semi-Pelagian bravado: "Bring it on," I remember thinking, "Let's rumble."

And rumble we did.

It quickly became evident that the gulf between the professor's Calvinism and the classroom's collective Arminian view was colossal. I was well aware of T.U.L.I.P. and knew that Calvinism was a theological system associated with the Reformer John Calvin which emphasized the rule of God over all things, including a person's salvation. But I was convinced that such teaching belonged only to fringe elements in the Church and was in no way indicative of the majority. Never one to walk away from a good debate, I challenged my instructor to a contest of orthodoxy over the Doctrines of Grace.

Dr. Anderson and I clashed almost immediately. He came at me incessantly with the Five Points of Calvinism but I stood my ground unyieldingly on the Five Points of Arminianism. Week after week, as we swam through the Book of Romans, he hammered home T.U.L.I.P. like a pit-bull gnawing on a bone. He was relentless and ferocious. But I was equally determined. I did my best to counter his arguments whenever I could.

Some days were less animated than others, to be sure. But on those occasions where T.U.L.I.P. was front and center in Romans, Dr. Anderson and I sparred with each other seemingly to no end (much to the entertainment of my classmates). Especially unsettling to me were the Reformed doctrines of Unconditional Election and Irresistible Grace, to say nothing about the Calvinist take on free-will. Towing the standard Arminian line, I upheld that man is the final arbiter of his election, insisting that God has decreed to save through Jesus Christ, out of fallen and sinful mankind, those He *foresaw* would believe in Christ voluntarily of their own will. To suggest otherwise, as Dr. Anderson did, was to make God out to be capricious, I argued, and to rob man of his dignity. I refused to capitulate on this point.

On one occasion, after hearing my tireless argument on free-will and divine foreknowledge one too many times, Dr. Anderson rolled his eyes and blurted, "Prove it," and flopped his gnarled Bible on my desk. The sound it made crashing on the metal desktop still haunts me. "Show me from Scripture, Mr. Gann, where it teaches that God determines the Elect based on His foreknowledge of our faith."

"First Peter," I quickly responded, flexing my muscles for all to see. "In chapter one, verse two, Peter tells us that we *'have been chosen according to the foreknowledge of God the Father.'*"

Dr. Anderson grinned. "Ah, I see you've done your homework on this issue."

I sat smugly. "I have," I answered.

"Well then it should come as no surprise to you that the word *foreknowledge* in the passage you just cited does not necessarily mean what you think it means. You simply *assume* its meaning; that God 'observed before' or 'knew in advance' who would believe in Him and, on that basis, made His decision. However, when we properly understand the context of the passage, Mr. Gann, we soon realize that God's foreknowledge actually refers to His having *'fore-loved.'*"

Dr. Anderson continued: "The Greek word for 'foreknown'— *proegno*—is used some seven times in the New Testament. Only twice does it mean what you say it means, Mr. Gann. In fact, five times it refers to an intimate knowledge within a personal relationship, not unlike Adam *'knowing'* Eve and begetting Cain and Abel. In other words, God's foreknowledge isn't confined to God 'knowing in advance' but rather pertains to His 'loving in advance.' To the point, Peter uses *proegno* eighteen verses later, where he speaks of Jesus Christ being *'foreknown before the foundation of the world.'* Peter clearly implies a predetermined relationship in the knowledge of the Lord that goes well beyond mere foresight. More than just knowing about him, God intimately loved His Son from all eternity. This is the picture that's painted for us in the Greek with *proegno.*"

All eyes in the classroom darted toward me as I ogled the professor's Bible sitting on my desk. I didn't understand a word he had just said. As far as I was concerned his appeal to the Greek language was gibberish. With my face flushed with blood, I feigned disagreement in order to maintain my façade of self-confidence and quickly handed his Bible back to him. I didn't know where or to whom to turn in response.

But my professor didn't move. He waited for my answer. Unable to bear the awkwardness any longer, I offered a couple of analogies by way of deflection. First, I suggested that the salvation process is much like a person drowning: God throws a life preserver of salvation to those who are capsized in sin, and each person has the free-will to either take hold of it or to swim on their own. God will not do the swimming for us. As a follow-up, I also equated salvation to that of a sick person in need of a remedy: God offers His medicine of salvation to spiritually sick people and they, in turn, have the free-will to ingest it or not. God will not force-feed the spiritually ailing through an intravenous tube. My illustrations seemed reasonable enough, but were lost on my professor.

Dr. Anderson responded, "The strength of your view, Mr. Gann, is that it recognizes that fallen man's spiritual condition is severe enough that it requires God's grace to save him. The weakness of your position, however, is that it fails in the same manner that each of your analogies fail. What good is medicine to a man who is already pronounced dead? What good is a life preserver for a victim who has already drowned? I ask you Mr. Gann, what good is grace if it is only offered outwardly to inwardly dead creatures incapable of responding to it?"

He continued with his cross-examination: "You rest under the misguided notion that mankind is simply injured spiritually. You wrongfully assume that he still possesses some semblance of spiritual awareness to make a distress call. What you fail to comprehend, or are unwilling to come to terms with, is the biblical fact that mankind comes into this world spiritually stillborn. He is beyond injured or sick. He is born spiritually dead. And all the help that is offered him cannot cure him. No medicine in the world, no matter how advanced, can heal a man who's already dead. Like Lazarus in John 11, the spiritually dead first require the miracle of spiritual revivification."

My confused silence pleaded no contest. I decided to save face and let the matter drop for the time being. But Dr. Anderson had no intention of letting me off the hook. He continued on with his diatribe, insisting that the result of Unconditional Election is the *guaranteed* positive response by the Elect to the inward call of the Holy Spirit. He suggested that all those whom God has elected in eternity past will certainly come to knowledge of him in their lifetime through the miracle of spiritual regeneration.

"What a comfort it is to know," he exclaimed, "that the gospel of Christ will penetrate and rejuvenate our hard, sinful hearts and effectually save us through the inward call of the Holy Spirit! It is irresistible and unavoidable!"

Irresistible and unavoidable? I was offended that such an educated man could so flippantly discount man's free-will in the conversion process. That God would draw men to Himself against their will was unthinkable to me! My rebuttal was straightforward, if not familiar to him. The entire gamble of salvation, I protested, relied solely on the fact that mankind has the choice to either acquiesce or to resist the wooing of the Holy Spirit. To think otherwise was to demote man to an automaton and to promote God to an autocrat.

At long last, there was one point of contention in which my professor and I surprisingly agreed—the eternal security of the Elect. Dr. Anderson was clear: those called and justified will certainly be glorified. The work of sanctification, which God has brought about in the Elect, will continue without failure until it reaches its fulfillment in eternal life. Christ assures the Elect that he will not lose any of those given to him but will raise each and every one of them at the end of time. "The Calvinist stands upon the Word of God," my professor said, "and trusts in Christ's promise that he will perfectly fulfill the will of the Father in saving all those whom the Father has given to him in eternity past as a love gift."

Although I was an Arminian, I deviated from my fellow free-will Christians on this point and sided with my professor. I believed in the credo *"once saved always saved"* whereas classical Arminianism teaches that an authentic believer can fall from grace just as easily as he received grace by a free act of the will. Despite my capitulation on this point, Dr. Anderson was quick to highlight the glaring inconsistency in my theology.

"Mr. Gann, I stand here befuddled."

"How is that, Professor Anderson?" I asked.

"Enlighten me if you will," he began. "You argue vociferously for man's ability and moral right to make a free-will decision to accept Jesus Christ as Lord and Savior—on condition that they respond affirmatively to outward grace—is that so?"

"That is so," I answered. "That's what I believe."

"Even though sinners are dead in sin, according to Colossians 2:13 and Ephesians 2:1, and are incapable of responding to such grace because, according to 1 Corinthians 2:14, they are *'spiritually discerned?'*"

I choked on my response. Dr. Anderson then surveyed the students in the classroom like a prosecuting attorney making his closing argument before a jury. "To be clear, Mr. Gann: you believe that fallen man is 'alive enough' and possesses the free-will to accept or reject salvation and that any divine violation of human agency is a cardinal no-no?"

My heart started to beat rapidly and I could feel my face warm over. It was obvious that my professor was priming the pump, so to speak, in order to paint my theology as buffoonery. I continued cautiously. "Yes," I said. "God's grace cooperates with my faith synergistically wherein the final decision to submit to Christ is at my discretion. That's the whole drift of New Testament teaching."

"And to be clear," he said, "you stand in opposition to your Arminian brethren on the point of eternal security when you state that it is your belief that once a person makes the free-will decision to follow Christ he is eternally secure? And you agree with the Calvinist that believers can neither lose their salvation nor deny their Savior afterward?"

"Absolutely, Dr. Anderson, and I am not alone in that view. On this point I divorce myself from historic Arminianism, I admit. Those who leave the faith demonstrate that they never were truly believers to begin with. Genuine believers will never deny the faith, and I cite as my proof-text 1 John 2:19."

"I concur," he said. "But how is it that you believe, Mr. Gann, that once a person is saved, his free-will just mysteriously disappears? If the truly saved cannot deny the gospel but are eternally kept by God's decree what does that do to free agency that you're so passionate about protecting? It seems in your systematic deduction of soteriology, human beings have the free-will to make a decision for Christ—which God would never violate—yet, once saved, God removes man's free-will so that they won't reverse their decision and fall from grace."

I answered quickly, "Well, I wouldn't say God removes man's free-will—that would be a dishonest interpretation of my views. I would simply agree with the Calvinist on this point and say that, after genuine regeneration takes place, God *transforms* a person's free-will."

"By transforming a saved man's free-will what you actually mean is that God *overcomes* man's free-will in order to align it with His own, correct?"

I knew I was in trouble. I couldn't turn the proverbial car around.

Seeing that I was jumbled, he continued his cross-examination without pause: "I find it ironic that it's unconscionable to you that Calvinism would even suggest that God overcomes a man's supposed free-will in order to save him, nevertheless you seem okay with it once a person is saved, so long as it serves your greater purpose for eternal security. It seems acceptable in your view to insist upon man's free-will *before* salvation yet permissible to rob him of it *afterward*."

I fought hard to make a cogent response but found myself at a loss for words. Finally I blurted, "Dr. Anderson, I don't think that is a fair assessment of my position. A true Christian will not deny the gospel after salvation. The apostle John tells us that true believers, those who have been authentically regenerated, will do no such thing."

"So, in effect, Mr. Gann, true Christians—those authentically regenerated—not only *will not* deny the gospel of Jesus Christ and lose their salvation, but *cannot* do so if John's words are to be accepted as true? The phrase '*will not*' connotes volition and the word '*cannot*' denotes ability. In other words, true Christians will neither desire, nor have the ability to desire, to ever be unsaved once genuinely regenerated, isn't that so?"

"Yes, that's correct," I attested. "Paul says in 1 Corinthians 6:19 that '*you are not your own; you were bought at a price.*' God therefore owns us and keeps us and has given us renewed minds and a new way of thinking. We are His property and He protects us eternally as our rightful Owner. And Paul and John both tell us that true Christians cannot deny their Savior because the Lord purchased us with his own blood and promises that no one—including ourselves—can snatch us out of his hands."

His arms waving in agitation, Dr. Anderson put me in my place. "Mr. Gann, as a Calvinist I wholeheartedly agree with you. But being the four-point Arminian and the one-point Calvinist that you are—or a Calminian—puts your theology at an irreconcilable disadvantage. It seems you want your cake, and you want to eat it too. You reject Calvinism and its teaching about God's absolute and exhaustive sovereignty in salvation on the grounds that it violates man's supposed free-will. Yet on the other hand you seem to imply that a saved man cannot lose his salvation by an act of free-will because God's sovereign will trumps all. So my question for you is simple: If God has decreed man's salvation to be secure as the rightful Owner over that man, to which we both agree, and that saved man is therefore incapable of recanting his profession of faith, why do you so nonchalantly accept that God infringes upon man's free-will *after* salvation to keep that man saved, but protest the Calvinist assertion that God infringes upon it *beforehand* in order to save him?"

Again, I sat dumbfounded, pondering his remarks. Finally, Dr. Anderson returned to his original point: "As I said, I find it ironic, if not hypocritical, Mr. Gann that you believe—whether you choose to admit it or not—that once a person is saved that person no longer apparently possesses the free-will to leave the faith that he once exercised to believe the gospel. The Calvinist understanding of eternal security, Mr. Gann, to which you subscribe, is incompatible with the other points of Arminianism that you so vehemently defend. You must pick which side you're on, and you must do so thoughtfully."

The only defense I could muster was a weak suggestion that I get back to him later with a more coherent response. "I'll be waiting," he said smiling, patting me on the shoulder.

My Great Awakening

As I sat in my college classroom week after week balking at Dr. Anderson's views and protesting his Calvinistic coloring of the Bible, it was evident to everyone in the class that our traditional and comfortable beliefs were on trial by the T.U.L.I.P. acrostic. The more I opened my mouth on behalf of my classmates to rebut my professor and to argue in favor of man's free agency the more he called attention to the theological quagmires that ensnared me (and from which I could not easily escape). But I refused to back down. My soteriological views, as mainstream as they were at the time, were under assault by the guns of criticism and I was too pigheaded to acknowledge my bleeding. I refused to go down without a fight.

Things finally came to a head about five weeks into the class. On one particular evening, much to the enjoyment of others, Dr. Anderson and I volleyed back and forth for nearly four painstaking hours over the heated doctrine of election. He took his customary Calvinist position—holding tenaciously to the view that salvation is solely dependent upon the sovereign choice of God and applicable only to those whom He sovereignly chose to call and regenerate. Not to be undone, I held tightly to the school of soteriological thought which taught that election and calling were available to all mankind and dependent upon man's choice.

For weeks I had put forth every argument I could possibly muster to debunk my professor's command of Scripture, to include radically twisting various Bible verses to help my dying cause. At one point during a lively exchange, I even *falsified* Scripture in utter desperation to prove my point. When he politely challenged me to cite the phantom chapter and verse which I had invented, I deflected his attention and changed the subject.

I fired the last round I had in my chamber. I obstinately, and rather boldly, insisted that mankind indeed possesses a libertine will that determines one's election and any view to the contrary stood outside the pale of orthodoxy. In not so many words I accused my professor of being unorthodox, almost sacrilegious really. In polite return, Dr. Anderson systematically and meticulously undressed my halfcocked allegations with sacred Scripture. He held me accountable to the contexts of the biblical texts I had distorted (to say nothing about those I had invented), escorted me through Church history and the ecclesiastical confessions of the Church which contradicted me (see Appendix), forced me to come to terms with the etymology of certain Greek words, and then left me wallowing in self-righteous slobber. At last, after nearly a month-and-a-half, I waved the white flag of surrender.

Like a long humdrum movie with an unexpected twist ending, my confidence was suddenly upended without warning. Everything I was taught to believe about interpreting the Bible through my Arminian lens, particularly around soteriology, had been invalidated by Dr. Anderson. Equally embarrassing to me was the fact that—owing to my vocal protests against his anti-Arminian bent—I had inadvertently become his classroom case study. Insisting that we leave our presuppositions at the door, our class was undone by Dr. Anderson's Calvinistic approach to biblical interpretation. Over the course of a semester, and despite my many objections, he methodically dismantled our convenient views on free-will and, in turn, my sense of self. The self-assured Arminian that I was had been brought to ruin.

My conversion to Calvinism was not immediate, however. I went on to dedicate the next year to investigating the merits of Reformed Theology. (I was surprised to learn that many of my favorite authors and Bible teachers were Calvinists). I piqued my professor's brain as best as I could before class, during class, and after class. I put him to the test with as many philosophical or biblical grenades I could possibly throw that could blow up his theology and bring into disrepute the tenets of Calvinism. I then compared his answers with inspired Scripture. Seeing that I was now sincere and no longer adversarial, Dr. Anderson graciously entertained every question I posed, countered every objection I raised, and walked me through the biblical depiction of God until, at long last, my concerns were satisfied.

While in my final year of college, I had come to realize that everything I had been taught to believe about my personal salvation in Christ had been built upon faulty *presuppositions*. Unknowingly, I had *imposed* these presuppositions upon Scripture rather than allow Scripture to stand on its own and inform my presuppositions. Although college had deepened my appreciation for the Bible, it also called my attention to how undisciplined my Bible study habits actually were. Oddly enough, the sense of personal-awakening that usually accompanies the start of a student's collegiate career occurred at the tail end of mine.

I had allowed my presuppositions, assumptions, and traditions to steer me off course. Having been a Christian since my youth, I had *supposed* that it was my own intellect that was the driving force behind my free-will choice to be a Christ-follower; that I had been at least *smart enough* to comprehend the glorious truth that going to heaven was a lot better than going to hell. I had also *supposed* that I was merely one of the fortunate sinners in the world *lucky enough* to be born in the West and to have been exposed to the gospel at an early age. Lastly, I had *supposed* that I had been *humble enough* to recognize my own need for a Savior.

It was not until I came under the full weight of Scripture that I realized that these quiet assumptions marked me as someone who had done *something* in which he could boast. In short, I had either been smarter, luckier, or more humble than the poor chap who wanted nothing to do with God, or who had never heard the gospel. Yet the Bible makes no allowance for such confidence (cf. Eph. 2:8-9). Never before had I ever stopped to consider that my role in salvation was passive; I owed everything to a proactive God who—for reasons lost on me to this very day—elected me for salvation unconditionally in eternity past.

My faulty presuppositions—which were not mine alone but are shared by the vast majority of evangelicals today—were shattered when I was introduced to Dr. Anderson and reintroduced to the Book of Romans. Undeniably, if asked back then what the basis of my salvation was I could rip off the most orthodox answer without batting an eye: *"I am saved by grace alone through faith alone."* Yet when my personal theology was fleshed out and juxtaposed against Scripture, I realized that what I truly believed was antithetical to the salvific prescription found in Holy Writ.

Absent in my beliefs was any real acknowledgement that it was the sovereign act of God who elected me in eternity past, predestined me, drew me to Himself, liberated my enslaved will, transformed my heart, renewed my thinking, and compelled my conversion "in order that God's purpose in election might stand" (Rom. 9:11). As difficult as it was for my ego to digest, I came to understand that I brought nothing of value to the banquet of salvation, not even rudimentary table scraps. Even the faith I exercised and the repentance I practiced were granted to me in advance by the grace of God.

No Christian is born a Calvinist. Reformed Theology is a system of belief that only begins to unfold after honest evaluation, painstaking prayer, scrupulous study, and arduous hermeneutical wrestling. That you hold this book in your hands is, in some way, a testament to the fact that you are a student of Scripture. Moreover, it further indicates that, unlike my early days in college, you are willing (or have been made willing) to step outside your presuppositions to hear the voice of our sovereign God.

Our Lord's sovereignty may be scandalous to our natural Pelagian way of thinking, but it's my prayer that this book has informed your opinion in such a way that the majesty of Calvinism shines through to your heart as the beacon of light that it is. To that end, may you join the ranks of Calvinists everywhere and sing with us the exquisite refrain first sung by the prophet Jonah nearly three thousand years ago: "Salvation comes from the Lord" (Jnh 2:9).

It is only fitting that we bring our journey to an end with the poignant words of arguably the greatest Calvinist that the Church has ever received, save for Calvin himself. He is quoted more than any other man in Calvinistic circles, including in this book, and his impact on the Doctrines of Grace will last into eternity. I bid the reader *adieu* with the words of the venerable Charles Haddon Spurgeon:

> It is no novelty, then, that I am preaching; no new doctrine. I love to proclaim these strong old doctrines, that are called by nickname *Calvinism*, but which are surely and verily the revealed truth of God as it is in Christ Jesus. By this truth I make a pilgrimage into [the] past, and as I go, I see father after father, confessor after confessor, martyr after martyr, standing up to shake hands with me ... taking these things to be the standard

of my faith, I see the land of the ancients peopled with my brethren; I behold multitudes who confess the same as I do, and acknowledge that this is the religion of God's own church ...[182]

There is no soul living who holds more firmly to the doctrines of grace than I do, and if any man asks me whether I am ashamed to be called a Calvinist, I answer—I wish to be called nothing but a Christian; but if you ask me, do I hold the doctrinal views which were held by John Calvin, I reply, I do in the main hold them, and rejoice to avow it.[183]

Appendix

Councils, Creeds, Confessions, & Calvinism

"Men treat God's sovereignty as a theme for controversy, but in Scripture it is a matter for worship."

J.I. Packer

Appendix

Councils, Creeds, Confessions, & Calvinism

To what extent has Calvinism influenced the Christian Church and guided her interpretation of Scripture? The answer is not very comforting to free-will proponents. A brief survey of the various creeds, confessions, catechisms, and statements of faith, produced from an assortment of denominations and ecclesiastical bodies throughout Church history reveals a markedly Calvinistic bent. I therefore conclude our study with this rather lengthy Appendix if for no other reason than to convey to the reader that Reformed Theology, by and large, is no minority report. In fact, too pronounced to be ignored, Calvinism (and its predecessor Augustinianism) has been the majority view for well over a millennium. Formalized in the early councils of the Church and brought to bear during the Protestant Reformation, the preponderance of these creeds, confessions, and catechisms sing the exquisite refrain of the Doctrines of Grace.

But we must also consider the skepticism of some who are inclined to dismiss man-made creeds as nonbinding and overrated. It is true that the historical confessions of the Church are exempt from inspiration and do not vie for our allegiance in the same manner as Scripture. But, as David Bennett notes, we embrace our creeds because they define the boundaries within which we operate. While a creed is a "rule" in one sense of the word, it is more accurately a metaphorical boundary-line or fence, dividing the safe (or correct) areas from the unsafe (or incorrect). For this reason, many creeds summarize only the basic points of belief, because as boundaries their purpose is to define the lines one should not cross.[184] And the Church has gone to great lengths historically to formally flesh out these truths and to safeguard these lines. William Hetherington states the case for creeds and confessions this way:

The Christian Church, as a divine institution, *takes the Word of God alone, and the whole Word of God, as her only rule of faith;* but she must also frame and promulgate a statement of what she understands the Word of God to teach.

This she does, not as arrogating any authority to suppress, change, or amend anything that God's Word teaches; but in discharge of the various duties which she owes to God, to the world, and to those of her own communion. *Thus a Confession of Faith is not the very voice of divine truth, but the echo of that voice from souls that have heard its utterance, felt its power, and are answering to its call* (emphasis added).[185]

While no creed or confession is spiritually binding on a Christian, per se, we nevertheless uphold these traditional documents as beneficial for having guided and illuminated the Church for centuries. These formal declarations preserve the advancements we have made in the knowledge of Christian truth. They discriminate the truth from false teaching. They serve as the basis of fellowship for likeminded believers, and they exist for our instruction by summarizing the totality of the Bible's teachings. And in virtually every ecclesiastical endeavor in history that set out in search of truth, the Doctrines of Grace have risen to the fore and have won the day.

Dr. Kenneth Talbot once remarked, "The doctrine of Calvinism has never been defeated because you can't defeat the Scripture. Calvin's teaching is the true teaching of Christ [and] Paul, as they are presented in the Scripture. Thus it is impossible to defeat this teaching."[186] And Talbot does not stand alone. The creeds, confessions, and catechisms of the Christian Church, which span two thousand years of history, bear his comments out.

The Third Council of Ephesus (431)

By the beginning of the fifth century the idea that Christ was both God and man, or "'wholly God and wholly man," began to spark a myriad of theological questions. Did Christ have a split-personality? Did he possess two distinct natures or only one? Was Jesus mostly God and only partially man, or was he mostly a man who merely possessed a spark of divinity? These questions became the seed of a bitter quarrel between the bishops in Alexandria and Antioch. Although neither theological school opposed Christ's oneness, they were indispensably compelled to downplay one nature in exchange for the other. Understanding the true identity of Christ was therefore the foremost reason the Third Ecumenical Council of Ephesus was convened in 431.

But in crafting the Church's formal stance on Christology, the Third Ecumenical Council of Ephesus also took to task Celestius, a disciple of Pelagius, who denied man's moral inability in salvation. Like his tutor before him, Celestius opposed Augustine of Hippo and his doctrine of Total Depravity and taught that all humanity is born without ancestral sin. He was convinced that a sinner's low morality could be reformed by self-generated effort, and upheld that free-will trumped the need for divine grace in sanctification and salvation.

The Council of Ephesus submitted its final ruling based on the findings of the Synod of Carthage (418) which stated in part: "It has pleased the Council to decree that whosoever denies the little ones ... have inherited no original sin from Adam ... let him be anathema: for no other meaning ought to be attached to what the Apostle has said: 'Sin entered the world through one human being' (Rom. 5:12)."

Germane to Augustinianism was the council's position on Total Depravity. The Council of Ephesus issued an edict ratifying a letter from Pope Celestine condemning and deposing Pelagius by inference—and his disciple Celestius directly—for preaching false doctrine. The essential point which is material to Calvinism is that Pelagius' pupil, Celestius, was condemned by the Third Ecumenical Council of Ephesus for his denial of

Total Depravity and his belief in man's moral ability. The ruling was as follows:

> **Canon IV.** If any of the clergy should fall away, and publicly or privately presume to maintain the doctrines of Nestorius or Celestius, it is declared just by the holy Synod that these also should be deposed.

The Canons of the Council of Orange (529)

The Council of Orange was an outgrowth of the controversy between Augustine and Pelagius. This controversy had to do with the degree to which human beings are responsible for their own salvation and the role God's grace plays in bringing about salvation. The Pelagians held that human beings are born in a state of innocence and that the idea of a sinful nature, or Original Sin, as argued by Augustine, was a theological fabrication. The teachings of Pelagius, and his follower Celestius, were eventually denounced at the Third Council of Ephesus in 431.

Only a few years later a more palatable version of Pelagianism was introduced by John Cassian called semi-Pelagianism (which ultimately resurfaced as Arminianism a thousand years later during the Reformation). Although more orthodox in detail, the Council of Orange objected to the semi-Pelagian doctrine that the human race, though fallen and adversely affected by Original Sin, is still essentially "good" enough to lay hold of the grace of God through an act of unredeemed human will. The Council of Orange upheld the ruling of the Third Council of Ephesus and renewed the Church's allegiance to Augustine's view that repudiated any notion that man cooperates with God's grace in the salvation process. The following canons of 529 by the Latin Church in Orange, France, greatly influenced Reformed doctrine. The specific points ratified at the Council of Orange that sustain Calvinism are as follows:

> **Canon 6.** If anyone says that God has mercy upon us when, apart from his grace, we believe, will, desire, strive, labor, pray, watch, study, seek, ask, or knock, but does not confess

that it is by the infusion and inspiration of the Holy Spirit within us that we have the faith, the will, or the strength to do all these things as we ought; or if anyone makes the assistance of grace depend on the humility or obedience of man and does not agree that it is a gift of grace itself that we are obedient and humble, he contradicts the Apostle who says, "What have you that you did not receive?" (1 Cor. 4:7), and, "But by the grace of God I am what I am" (1 Cor. 15:10).

Canon 7. If anyone affirms that we can form any right opinion or make any right choice which relates to the salvation of eternal life, as is expedient for us, or that we can be saved, that is, assent to the preaching of the gospel through our natural powers without the illumination and inspiration of the Holy Spirit, who makes all men gladly assent to and believe in the truth, he is led astray by a heretical spirit, and does not understand the voice of God who says in the Gospel, "For apart from me you can do nothing" (John 15:5), and the word of the Apostle, "Not that we are competent of ourselves to claim anything as coming from us; our competence is from God" (2 Cor. 3:5).

Canon 8. If anyone maintains that some are able to come to the grace of baptism by mercy but others through free will, which has manifestly been corrupted in all those who have been born after the transgression of the first man, it is proof that he has no place in the true faith. For he denies that the free will of all men has been weakened through the sin of the first man, or at least holds that it has been affected in such a way that they have still the ability to seek the mystery of eternal salvation by themselves without the revelation of God. The Lord himself shows how contradictory this is by declaring that no one is able to come to him "unless the Father who sent me draws him" (John 6:44), as he also says to Peter, "Blessed are you, Simon Bar-Jona! For flesh and blood has not revealed this to you, but my Father who is in heaven" (Matt. 16:17), and as the Apostle says, "No one can say 'Jesus is Lord' except by the Holy Spirit" (1 Cor. 12:3).

Canon 13. Concerning the restoration of free will. The freedom of will that was destroyed in the first man can be restored only by the grace of baptism, for what is lost can be returned only by the one who was able to give it. Hence the Truth itself declares: "So if the Son makes you free, you will be free indeed" (John 8:36).

Canon 19. That a man can be saved only when God shows mercy. Human nature, even though it remained in that sound state in which it was created, could by no means save itself, without the assistance of the Creator; hence since man cannot safeguard his salvation without the grace of God, which is a gift, how will he be able to restore what he has lost without the grace of God?

Canon 20. That a man can do no good without God. God does much that is good in a man that the man does not do; but a man does nothing good for which God is not responsible, so as to let him do it.

Conclusion. And thus according to the passages of Holy Scripture quoted above or the interpretations of the ancient Fathers we must, under the blessing of God, preach and believe as follows. The sin of the first man has so impaired and weakened free will that no one thereafter can either love God as he ought or believe in God or do good for God's sake, unless the grace of divine mercy has preceded him. We therefore believe that the glorious faith which was given to Abel the righteous, and Noah, and Abraham, and Isaac, and Jacob, and to all the saints of old, and which the Apostle Paul commends in extolling them (Heb. 11), was not given through natural goodness as it was before to Adam, but was bestowed by the grace of God.

And we know and also believe that even after the coming of our Lord this grace is not to be found in the free will of all who desire to be baptized, but is bestowed by the kindness of Christ, as has already been frequently stated and as the

Apostle Paul declares, "For it has been granted to you that for the sake of Christ you should not only believe in him but also suffer for his sake" (Phil. 1:29). And again, "He who began a good work in you will bring it to completion at the day of Jesus Christ" (Phil. 1:6). And again, "For by grace you have been saved through faith; and it is not your own doing, it is the gift of God" (Eph. 2:8). And as the Apostle says of himself, "I have obtained mercy to be faithful" (1 Cor. 7:25, cf. 1 Tim. 1:13). He did not say, "because I was faithful," but "to be faithful." And again, "What have you that you did not receive?" (1 Cor. 4:7). And again, "Every good endowment and every perfect gift is from above, coming down from the Father of lights" (Jas. 1:17). And again, "No one can receive anything except what is given him from heaven" (John 3:27). There are innumerable passages of Holy Scripture which can be quoted to prove the case for grace, but they have been omitted for the sake of brevity, because further examples will not really be of use where few are deemed sufficient.

According to the catholic faith we also believe that after grace has been received through baptism, all baptized persons have the ability and responsibility, if they desire to labor faithfully, to perform with the aid and cooperation of Christ what is of essential importance in regard to the salvation of their soul. We not only do not believe that any are foreordained to evil by the power of God, but even state with utter abhorrence that if there are those who want to believe so evil a thing, they are anathema. We also believe and confess to our benefit that in every good work it is not we who take the initiative and are then assisted through the mercy of God, but God himself first inspires in us both faith in him and love for him without any previous good works of our own that deserve reward, so that we may both faithfully seek the sacrament of baptism, and after baptism be able by his help to do what is pleasing to him. We must therefore most evidently believe that the praiseworthy faith of the thief whom the Lord called to his home in paradise, and of

Cornelius the centurion, to whom the angel of the Lord was sent, and of Zacchaeus, who was worthy to receive the Lord himself, was not a natural endowment but a gift of God's kindness.

The Augsburg Confession (1530)

In 1530, Emperor Charles V convened a parliament of princes in Augsburg, Germany with the aim of putting an end to ecclesiastic dissension. Each leader was asked to state in writing his religious opinions and the ecclesiastical abuses that needed correction. The prince elector of Saxony set Philipp Melanchton to the task of crafting the theological consensus. Upon completion, it was then submitted to Martin Luther for approval. "I like it very much and would not wish to correct or modify it," Luther said of The Augsburg Confession. "Moreover it would not be appropriate as I cannot tread so swiftly."

Throughout his life, Melanchton never stopped working on the confession or its defense. The 1540 edition was signed by John Calvin. As soon as 1555, the 1530 version of The Augsburg Confession became the official Confession of Faith of the Lutheran Church.[187] The specific points of The Augsburg Confession which address and sustain Calvinism either directly or indirectly are as follows:

Article II: Of Original Sin.
Also [our churches] teach that since the fall of Adam all men begotten in the natural way are born with sin, that is, without the fear of God, without trust in God, and with concupiscence; and that this disease, or vice of origin, is truly sin, even now condemning and bringing eternal death upon those not born again through Baptism and the Holy Ghost.

[Our churches] condemn the Pelagians and others who deny that original depravity is sin, and who, to obscure the glory of Christ's merit and benefits, argue that man can be justified before God by his own strength and reason.

Article XVIII: Of Free Will.

Of Free Will [our churches] teach that man's will has some liberty to choose civil righteousness, and to work things subject to reason. But it has no power, without the Holy Ghost, to work the righteousness of God, that is, spiritual righteousness; since the natural man receiveth not the things of the Spirit of God (1 Cor. 2,14); but this righteousness is wrought in the heart when the Holy Ghost is received through the Word.

These things are said in as many words by Augustine in his *Hypognosticon, Book III*: We grant that all men have a free will, free, inasmuch as it has the judgment of reason; not that it is thereby capable, without God, either to begin, or, at least, to complete aught in things pertaining to God, but only in works of this life, whether good or evil. "Good" I call those works which spring from the good in nature, such as, willing to labor in the field, to eat and drink, to have a friend, to clothe oneself, to build a house, to marry a wife, to raise cattle, to learn ... useful arts, or whatsoever good pertains to this life. For all of these things are not without dependence on the providence of God; yea, of Him and through Him they are and have their being. "Evil" I call such works as willing to worship an idol, to commit murder, etc.

[Our churches] condemn the Pelagians and others, who teach that without the Holy Ghost, by the power of nature alone, we are able to love God above all things; also to do the commandments of God as touching "the substance of the act." For, although nature is able in a manner to do the outward work, (for it is able to keep the hands from theft and murder,) yet it cannot produce the inward motions, such as the fear of God, trust in God, chastity, patience, etc.

The Belgic Confession (1561)

During the sixteenth century the churches in the Netherlands were exposed to terrible persecution by the Roman Catholic

Church. To protest Rome's cruel oppression, and to prove to their persecutors that adherents of the Reformed faith were law-abiding citizens who professed true Christian doctrine, Guido de Brás prepared The Belgic Confession. In the following year a copy was sent to King Philip II, together with an address that declared that its petitioners were willing to obey the government concerning secular matters, but that they would "offer their backs to stripes, their tongues to knives, their mouths to gags, and their whole bodies to the fire," rather than deny the truth expressed in this confession.

In composing The Belgic Confession the author drew from a particular confession of the Reformed churches in France published two years earlier and written chiefly by John Calvin.[188] Regrettably, the immediate purpose of securing freedom from persecution was unsuccessful and de Brás himself suffered martyrdom. The specific points of The Belgic Confession which address and sustain Calvinism either directly or indirectly are as follows:

Article 15: The Doctrine of Original Sin
We believe that by the disobedience of Adam original sin has been spread through the whole human race.

It is a corruption of all nature—an inherited depravity which even infects small infants in their mother's womb, and the root which produces in man every sort of sin. It is therefore so vile and enormous in God's sight that it is enough to condemn the human race, and it is not abolished or wholly uprooted even by baptism, seeing that sin constantly boils forth as though from a contaminated spring.

Nevertheless, it is not imputed to God's children for their condemnation but is forgiven by his grace and mercy—not to put them to sleep but so that the awareness of this corruption might often make believers groan as they long to be set free from the "body of this death" (Rom. 7:24). Therefore we reject the error of the Pelagians who say that this sin is nothing else than a matter of imitation.

Article 16: The Doctrine of Election
We believe that—all Adam's descendants having thus fallen into perdition and ruin by the sin of the first man—God showed himself to be as he is: merciful and just.

He is merciful in withdrawing and saving from this perdition those whom he, in his eternal and unchangeable counsel, has elected and chosen in Jesus Christ our Lord by his pure goodness, without any consideration of their works. He is just in leaving the others in their ruin and fall into which they plunged themselves.

Article 17: The Recovery of Fallen Man
We believe that our good God, by his marvelous wisdom and goodness, seeing that man had plunged himself in this manner into both physical and spiritual death and made himself completely miserable, set out to find him, though man, trembling all over, was fleeing from him. And he comforted him, promising to give him his Son, "born of a woman" (Gal. 4:4) to crush the head of the serpent (Gen. 3:15) and to make him blessed.

The Thirty-Nine Articles of the Church of England (1563)

The Thirty-nine Articles of the Church of England, commonly called the Thirty-Nine Articles, are the historic defining statements of Anglican doctrine that emerged in sixteenth-century England. The articles developed out of an attempt to establish a national Church of England that would maintain its Catholicism but incorporate the insights of Protestantism. In this sense, the Articles offer a "middle path" between the beliefs and practices of Rome and its Protestant counterparts in Germany and Geneva.

Established by Convocation of the Church in 1563, under the direction of the Archbishop of Canterbury, who used the Forty-Two Articles of Thomas Cranmer as inspiration, the Thirty-nine Articles were made a legal requirement by the English Parliament in 1571. They are printed in the *Book of Common Prayer* and other Anglican prayer books. Most of the substance of the articles can be labeled as Reformed Catholicism.[189] The specific points of the Thirty-Nine Articles which address and sustain Calvinism either directly or indirectly are as follows:

Article IX: Of Original or Birth Sin

Original sin standeth not in the following of Adam (as the Pelagians do vainly talk), but it is the fault and corruption of the nature of every man that naturally is engendered of the offspring of Adam, whereby man is very far gone from original righteousness, and is of his own nature inclined to evil, so that the flesh lusteth always contrary to the spirit; and therefore in every person born into this world, it deserveth God's wrath and damnation. And this infection of nature doth remain, yea, in them that are regenerated, whereby the lust of the flesh, called in Greek *phronema sarkos* (which some do expound the wisdom, some sensuality, some the affection, some the desire of the flesh), is not subject to the law of God. And although there is no condemnation for them that believe and are baptized, yet the Apostle doth confess that concupiscence and lust hath itself the nature of sin.

Article X: Of Free Will

The condition of man after the fall of Adam is such that he cannot turn and prepare himself, by his own natural strength and good works, to faith and calling upon God. Wherefore we have no power to do good works pleasant and acceptable to God, without the grace of God by Christ preventing us that we may have a good will, and working with us when we have that good will.

Article XVII: Of Predestination and Election

Predestination to life is the everlasting purpose of God, whereby, before the foundations of the world were laid, He hath constantly decreed by His counsel secret to us, to deliver from curse and damnation those whom He hath chosen in Christ out of mankind, and to bring them by Christ to everlasting salvation as vessels made to honour. Wherefore they which be endued with so excellent a benefit of God be called according to God's purpose by His Spirit working in due season; they through grace obey the calling; they be justified freely; they be made sons of God by adoption; they be made like the image of His only-begotten Son Jesus Christ; they walk religiously in good works; and at length by God's mercy they attain to everlasting felicity.

As the godly consideration of Predestination and our Election in Christ is full of sweet, pleasant, and unspeakable comfort to godly persons and such as feel in themselves the working of the Spirit of Christ, mortifying the works of the flesh and their earthly members and drawing up their mind to high and heavenly things, as well because it doth greatly establish and confirm their faith of eternal salvation to be enjoyed through Christ, as because it doth fervently kindle their love towards God: so for curious and carnal persons, lacking the Spirit of Christ, to have continually before their eyes the sentence of God's Predestination is a most dangerous downfall, whereby the devil doth thrust them either into desperation or into wretchedness of most unclean living no less perilous than desperation.

Furthermore, we must receive God's promises in such wise as they be generally set forth in Holy Scripture; and in our doings that will of God is to be followed which we have expressly declared unto us in the word of God.

The Heidelberg Catechism (1576)

The Heidelberg Catechism was composed in Heidelberg, Germany at the request of Elector Frederick III, who ruled the *Palatinate*, an influential German province, from 1559 to 1576. This catechism is thought to be written by Zacharias Ursinus and Caspar Olevianus.

The catechism was approved by a synod in Heidelberg in January 1563. The Synod of Dort approved The Heidelberg Catechism some fifty years later, and it soon became the most ecumenical of the Reformed catechisms and confessions. The catechism has been translated into many European, Asian, and African languages and is the most widely used and most warmly praised catechism of the Reformation period. The specific points of The Heidelberg Catechism which address and sustain Calvinism either directly or indirectly are as follows:

1. Q. *What is your only comfort in life and death?*

    A. That I am not my own, but belong with body and soul, both in life and in death, to my faithful Saviour Jesus Christ. He has fully paid for all my sins with His precious blood, and has set me free from all the power of the devil. He also preserves me in such a way that without the will of my heavenly Father not a hair can fall from my head; indeed, all things must work together for my salvation. Therefore, by His Holy Spirit He also assures me of eternal life and makes me heartily willing and ready from now on to live for Him (Matt. 10:29-31; Luke 21:16-18; 1 Cor. 3:23; 6:19, 20; 2 Cor. 1:21-22; 5:5; Rom. 8:14-16, 28; 14:7-9; Tit. 2:14; 1 Pet. 1:5, 18-19; John 6:39-40; 8:34-36; 10:27-30; 2 Thess. 3:3; Eph. 1:13-14; Heb. 2:14, 15; 1 John 1:7; 2:2; 3:8).

5. Q. *Can you keep all [of God's Law] perfectly?*

    A. No, I am inclined by nature to hate God and my neighbor (Gen. 6:5; 8:21; Jer. 17:9; Rom. 3:10, 23; 7:23; 8:7; Eph. 2:3; Tit. 3:3; 1 John 1:8, 10).

6. Q. *Did God, then, create man so wicked and perverse?*

    A. No, on the contrary, God created man good and in His image, that is, in true righteousness and holiness, so that he might rightly know God His Creator, heartily love Him, and live with Him in eternal blessedness to praise and glorify Him (Gen. 1:26-27, 31; Eph. 4:24; Col. 3:10; Psa. 8).

7. Q. *From where, then, did man's depraved nature come?*

A. From the fall and disobedience of our first parents, Adam and Eve, in Paradise, for there our nature became so corrupt that we are all conceived and born in sin (Gen. 3; Rom. 5:12, 18-19; Psa. 51:5).

8. Q. *But are we so corrupt that we are totally unable to do any good and inclined to all evil?*

A. Yes, unless we are regenerated by the Spirit of God.

9. Q. *Is God, then, not unjust by requiring in His law what man cannot do?*

A. No, for God so created man that he was able to do it. But man, at the instigation of the devil, in deliberate disobedience robbed himself and all his descendants of these gifts (Gen. 1:31; 3:6, 13; John 8:44; 1 Tim. 2:13-14; Rom. 5:12, 18-19).

27. Q. *What do you understand by the providence of God?*

A. God's providence is His almighty and ever present power, whereby, as with His hand, He still upholds heaven and earth and all creatures, and so governs them that leaf and blade, rain and drought, fruitful and barren years, food and drink, health and sickness, riches and poverty, indeed, all things, come not by chance but by His fatherly hand (Prov. 16:33; 22:2; Jer. 5:24; 23:23-24; Matt. 10:29; John 9:3; Acts 14:15-17; 17:24-28; Heb. 1:3).

28. Q. *What does it benefit us to know that God has created all things and still upholds them by His providence?*

   A. We can be patient in adversity, thankful in prosperity, and with a view to the future we can have a firm confidence in our faithful God and Father that no creature shall separate us from His love; for all creatures are so completely in His hand that without His will they cannot so much as move (Deut. 8:10; Job. 1: 12, 21-22; 2:6; Psa. 39:10; 55:22; Prov. 21:1; Acts 17:24-28; James 1:3; 1 Thess. 5:18; Rom. 5:3-5; 8:38-39).

The Canons of Dort (1619)

The decision of the Synod of Dort on the five main points of doctrine in dispute in the Netherlands is popularly known as The Canons of Dort. It consists of statements of doctrine adopted by the synod which met in the city of Dordrecht in 1618-19. Although this was a national synod of the Reformed churches of the Netherlands, it had an international character, since it was composed not only of Dutch delegates but also of twenty-six delegates from eight foreign countries.

The Synod of Dort was held in order to settle a serious controversy in the Dutch churches initiated by the rise of Arminianism. Jacob Arminius, a theological professor at Leiden University, questioned the teaching of Calvin and his followers on a number of important points. After Arminius's death, his own followers—the Remonstrants—presented their views on five of these points in 1610. The Arminians taught election based on foreseen faith, universal atonement, partial depravity, resistible grace, and the possibility of a lapse from grace. In their response, The Synod of Dort rejected these views and set forth the Reformed doctrine, namely, Unconditional Election, Limited Atonement, Total Depravity, Irresistible Grace, and the Perseverance of the Saints. The articles are as follows:

Article 1: God's Right to Condemn All People

Since all people have sinned in Adam and have come under the sentence of the curse and eternal death, God would have done no one an injustice if it had been his will to leave the entire human race in sin and under the curse, and to condemn them on account of their sin. As the apostle says: The whole world is liable to the condemnation of God (Rom. 3:19), All have sinned and are deprived of the glory of God (Rom. 3:23), and the wages of sin is death (Rom. 6:23).

Article 2: The Manifestation of God's Love

But this is how God showed his love: he sent his only begotten Son into the world, so that whoever believes in him should not perish but have eternal life.

Article 3: The Preaching of the Gospel

In order that people may be brought to faith, God mercifully sends proclaimers of this very joyful message to the people he wishes and at the time he wishes. By this ministry people are called to repentance and faith in Christ crucified. For how shall they believe in him of whom they have not heard? And how shall they hear without someone preaching? And how shall they preach unless they have been sent? (Rom. 10:14-15).

Article 4: A Twofold Response to the Gospel

God's anger remains on those who do not believe this gospel. But those who do accept it and embrace Jesus the Savior with a true and living faith are delivered through him from God's anger and from destruction, and receive the gift of eternal life.

Article 5: The Sources of Unbelief and of Faith

The cause or blame for this unbelief, as well as for all other sins, is not at all in God, but in man. Faith in Jesus Christ, however, and salvation through him is a free gift of God. As Scripture says, It is by grace you have been saved, through faith, and this not from yourselves; it is a gift of God (Eph.

2:8). Likewise: It has been freely given to you to believe in Christ (Phil. 1:29).

Article 6: God's Eternal Decision

The fact that some receive from God the gift of faith within time, and that others do not, stems from his eternal decision. For all his works are known to God from eternity (Acts 15:18; Eph. 1:11). In accordance with this decision he graciously softens the hearts, however hard, of his chosen ones and inclines them to believe, but by his just judgment he leaves in their wickedness and hardness of heart those who have not been chosen. And in this especially is disclosed to us his act—unfathomable and as merciful as it is just— of distinguishing between people equally lost. This is the well-known decision of election and reprobation revealed in God's Word. This decision the wicked, impure, and unstable distort to their own ruin, but it provides holy and godly souls with comfort beyond words.

Article 7: Election

Election [or choosing] is God's unchangeable purpose by which he did the following: Before the foundation of the world, by sheer grace, according to the free good pleasure of his will, he chose in Christ to salvation a definite number of particular people out of the entire human race, which had fallen by its own fault from its original innocence into sin and ruin. Those chosen were neither better nor more deserving than the others, but lay with them in the common misery. He did this in Christ, whom he also appointed from eternity to be the mediator, the head of all those chosen, and the foundation of their salvation. And so he decided to give the chosen ones to Christ to be saved, and to call and draw them effectively into Christ's fellowship through his Word and Spirit. In other words, he decided to grant them true faith in Christ, to justify them, to sanctify them, and finally, after powerfully preserving them in the fellowship of his Son, to glorify them.

God did all this in order to demonstrate his mercy, to the praise of the riches of his glorious grace.

As Scripture says, God chose us in Christ, before the foundation of the world, so that we should be holy and blameless before him with love; he predestined us whom he adopted as his children through Jesus Christ, in himself, according to the good pleasure of his will, to the praise of his glorious grace, by which he freely made us pleasing to himself in his beloved (Eph. 1:4-6). And elsewhere, those whom he predestined, he also called; and those whom he called, he also justified; and those whom he justified, he also glorified (Rom. 8:30).

Article 8: A Single Decision of Election
This election is not of many kinds; it is one and the same election for all who were to be saved in the Old and the New Testament. For Scripture declares that there is a single good pleasure, purpose, and plan of God's will, by which he chose us from eternity both to grace and to glory, both to salvation and to the way of salvation, which he prepared in advance for us to walk in.

Article 9: Election Not Based on Foreseen Faith
This same election took place, not on the basis of foreseen faith, of the obedience of faith, of holiness, or of any other good quality and disposition, as though it were based on a prerequisite cause or condition in the person to be chosen, but rather for the purpose of faith, of the obedience of faith, of holiness, and so on. Accordingly, election is the source of each of the benefits of salvation. Faith, holiness, and the other saving gifts, and at last eternal life itself, flow forth from election as its fruits and effects. As the apostle says, He chose us (not because we were, but) so that we should be holy and blameless before him in love (Eph. 1:4).

Article 10: Election Based on God's Good Pleasure

But the cause of this undeserved election is exclusively the good pleasure of God. This does not involve his choosing certain human qualities or actions from among all those possible as a condition of salvation, but rather involves his adopting certain particular persons from among the common mass of sinners as his own possession. As Scripture says, when the children were not yet born, and had done nothing either good or bad ..., she (Rebecca) was told, "The older will serve the younger." As it is written, "Jacob I loved, but Esau I hated" (Rom. 9:11-13). Also, All who were appointed for eternal life believed (Acts 13:48).

Article 11: Election Unchangeable

Just as God himself is most wise, unchangeable, all-knowing, and almighty, so the election made by him can neither be suspended nor altered, revoked, or annulled; neither can his chosen ones be cast off, nor their number reduced.

Article 12: The Assurance of Election

Assurance of this their eternal and unchangeable election to salvation is given to the chosen in due time, though by various stages and in differing measure. Such assurance comes not by inquisitive searching into the hidden and deep things of God, but by noticing within themselves, with spiritual joy and holy delight, the unmistakable fruits of election pointed out in God's Word—such as a true faith in Christ, a childlike fear of God, a godly sorrow for their sins, a hunger and thirst for righteousness, and so on.

Article 13: The Fruit of This Assurance

In their awareness and assurance of this election God's children daily find greater cause to humble themselves before God, to adore the fathomless depth of his mercies, to cleanse themselves, and to give fervent love in return to him who first so greatly loved them. This is far from saying that this teaching concerning election, and reflection upon it, make God's children lax in observing his commandments or carnally self-assured. By God's just judgment this does usually happen to those who casually take for granted the grace of election or engage in idle and brazen talk about it but are unwilling to walk in the ways of the chosen.

Article 14: Teaching Election Properly
Just as, by God's wise plan, this teaching concerning divine election has been proclaimed through the prophets, Christ himself, and the apostles, in Old and New Testament times, and has subsequently been committed to writing in the Holy Scriptures, so also today in God's church, for which it was specifically intended, this teaching must be set forth--with a spirit of discretion, in a godly and holy manner, at the appropriate time and place, without inquisitive searching into the ways of the Most High. This must be done for the glory of God's most holy name, and for the lively comfort of his people.

Article 15: Reprobation
Moreover, Holy Scripture most especially highlights this eternal and undeserved grace of our election and brings it out more clearly for us, in that it further bears witness that not all people have been chosen but that some have not been chosen or have been passed by in God's eternal election—those, that is, concerning whom God, on the basis of his entirely free, most just, irreproachable, and unchangeable good pleasure, made the following decision: to leave them in the common misery into which, by their own fault, they have plunged themselves; not to grant them saving faith and the grace of conversion; but finally to condemn and eternally punish them (having been left in their own ways and under his just judgment), not only for their unbelief but also for all their other sins, in order to display his justice. And this is the decision of reprobation, which does not at all make God the author of sin (a blasphemous thought!) but rather its fearful, irreproachable, just judge and avenger.

Article 16: Responses to the Teaching of Reprobation
Those who do not yet actively experience within themselves
a living faith in Christ or an assured confidence of heart,
peace of conscience, a zeal for childlike obedience, and
a glorying in God through Christ, but who nevertheless
use the means by which God has promised to work these
things in us—such people ought not to be alarmed at the
mention of reprobation, nor to count themselves among the
reprobate; rather they ought to continue diligently in the use
of the means, to desire fervently a time of more abundant
grace, and to wait for it in reverence and humility. On the
other hand, those who seriously desire to turn to God, to be
pleasing to him alone, and to be delivered from the body of
death, but are not yet able to make such progress along the
way of godliness and faith as they would like—such people
ought much less to stand in fear of the teaching concerning
reprobation, since our merciful God has promised that he
will not snuff out a smoldering wick and that he will not
break a bruised reed. However, those who have forgotten
God and their Savior Jesus Christ and have abandoned
themselves wholly to the cares of the world and the pleasures
of the flesh—such people have every reason to stand in fear
of this teaching, as long as they do not seriously turn to God.

Article 17: The Salvation of the Infants of Believers
Since we must make judgments about God's will from his
Word, which testifies that the children of believers are holy,
not by nature but by virtue of the gracious covenant in
which they together with their parents are included, godly
parents ought not to doubt the election and salvation of
their children whom God calls out of this life in infancy.

**Article 18: The Proper Attitude Toward Election
and Reprobation**
To those who complain about this grace of an undeserved
election and about the severity of a just reprobation, we
reply with the words of the apostle, Who are you, O man,
to talk back to God? (Rom. 9:20), and with the words of

our Savior, Have I no right to do what I want with my own? (Matt. 20:15). We, however, with reverent adoration of these secret things, cry out with the apostle: Oh, the depths of the riches both of the wisdom and the knowledge of God! How unsearchable are his judgments, and his ways beyond tracing out! For who has known the mind of the Lord? Or who has been his counselor? Or who has first given to God, that God should repay him? For from him and through him and to him are all things. To him be the glory forever! Amen (Rom. 11:33-36).

The Westminster Confession of Faith (1646)

The Westminster Confession of Faith is a Reformed confession of faith, in the Calvinist theological tradition. Although drawn up by the 1646 Westminster Assembly, largely of the Church of England, it became and remains the "subordinate standard" of doctrine in the Church of Scotland, second only to the Bible, and has been influential within Presbyterian churches worldwide.

In 1643, the English Parliament called upon "learned, godly and judicious Divines" to meet at Westminster Abbey in order to provide advice on issues of worship, doctrine, governance, and discipline of the Church of England. Their meetings, over a period of five years, produced the confession of faith, as well as a Larger Catechism and a Shorter Catechism. For more than three centuries, various churches around the world have adopted the confession and the catechisms as their standards of doctrine.

The Westminster Confession of Faith was modified and adopted by Congregationalists in England in the form of the Savoy Declaration (1658). Likewise, the Baptists of England modified the Savoy Declaration to produce the Second London Baptist Confession (1689). English Presbyterians, Congregationalists, and Baptists would together (with others) come to be known as Nonconformists, because they did not conform to the Act of Uniformity (1662) establishing the Church of England as the only legally-approved church, though they were in many ways united by their common confessions, built on the back of the

Westminster Confession.[190] The significant articles in view here are as follows:

Chapter III. Of God's Eternal Decree

I. God from all eternity, did, by the most wise and holy counsel of His own will, freely, and unchangeably ordain whatsoever comes to pass; yet so, as thereby neither is God the author of sin, nor is violence offered to the will of the creatures; nor is the liberty or contingency of second causes taken away, but rather established.

II. Although God knows whatsoever may or can come to pass upon all supposed conditions; yet has He not decreed anything because He foresaw it as future, or as that which would come to pass upon such conditions.

III. By the decree of God, for the manifestation of His glory, some men and angels are predestinated unto everlasting life; and others foreordained to everlasting death.

IV. These angels and men, thus predestinated, and foreordained, are particularly and unchangeably designed, and their number so certain and definite, that it cannot be either increased or diminished.

V. Those of mankind that are predestinated unto life, God, before the foundation of the world was laid, according to His eternal and immutable purpose, and the secret counsel and good pleasure of His will, has chosen, in Christ, unto everlasting glory, out of His mere free grace and love, without any foresight of faith, or good works, or perseverance in either of them, or any other thing in the creature, as conditions, or causes moving Him thereunto; and all to the praise of His glorious grace.

VI. As God has appointed the elect unto glory, so has He, by the eternal and most free purpose of His will, foreordained all the means thereunto. Wherefore, they who are elected, being fallen in Adam, are redeemed by Christ, are effectually called unto faith in Christ by His Spirit working in due season, are justified, adopted, sanctified, and kept by His power, through faith, unto salvation. Neither are any other redeemed by Christ, effectually

Chapter V. Of Providence

I. God the great Creator of all things does uphold, direct, dispose, and govern all creatures, actions, and things, from the greatest even to the least, by His most wise and holy providence, according to His infallible foreknowledge, and the free and immutable counsel of His own will, to the praise of the glory of His wisdom, power, justice, goodness, and mercy.

II. Although, in relation to the foreknowledge and decree of God, the first Cause, all things come to pass immutably, and infallibly; yet, by the same providence, He orders them to fall out, according to the nature of second causes, either necessarily, freely, or contingently.

III. God, in His ordinary providence, makes use of means, yet is free to work without, above, and against them, at His pleasure.

IV. The almighty power, unsearchable wisdom, and infinite goodness of God so far manifest themselves in His providence, that it extends itself even to the first fall, and all other sins of angels and men; and that not by a bare permission, but such as has joined with it a most wise and powerful bounding, and otherwise ordering, and governing of them, in a manifold dispensation, to His own holy ends; yet so, as the sinfulness thereof proceeds only from the creature, and not from God, who, being most holy and righteous, neither is nor can be the author or approver of sin.

V. The most wise, righteous, and gracious God does oftentimes leave, for a season, His own children to manifold temptations, and the corruption of their own hearts, to chastise them for their former sins, or to discover unto them the hidden strength of corruption and deceitfulness of their hearts, that they may be humbled; and, to raise them to a more close and constant dependence for their support upon Himself, and to make them more watchful against all future occasions of sin, and for sundry other just and holy ends.

VI. As for those wicked and ungodly men whom God, as a righteous Judge, for former sins, does blind and harden, from them He not only withholds His grace whereby they might have been enlightened in their understandings, and wrought upon in their hearts; but sometimes also withdraws the gifts which they had, and exposes them to such objects as their corruption makes occasion of sin; and, withal, gives them over to their own lusts, the temptations of the world, and the power of Satan, whereby it comes to pass that they harden themselves, even under those means which God uses for the softening of others.

VII. As the providence of God does, in general, reach to all creatures; so, after a most special manner, it takes care of His Church, and disposes all things to the good thereof.

Chapter VI. Of the Fall of Man, of Sin, and the Punishment thereof

I. Our first parents, being seduced by the subtilty and temptations of Satan, sinned, in eating the forbidden fruit. This their sin, God was pleased, according to His wise and holy counsel, to permit, having purposed to order it to His own glory.

II. By this sin they fell from their original righteousness and communion, with God, and so became dead in sin, and wholly defiled in all the parts and faculties of soul and body.

III. They being the root of all mankind, the guilt of this sin was imputed; and the same death in sin, and corrupted nature, conveyed to all their posterity descending from them by ordinary generation.

IV. From this original corruption, whereby we are utterly indisposed, disabled, and made opposite to all good, and wholly inclined to all evil, do proceed all actual transgressions.

V. This corruption of nature, during this life, does remain in those that are regenerated; and although it be, through Christ, pardoned, and mortified; yet both itself, and all the motions thereof, are truly and properly sin.

VI. Every sin, both original and actual, being a transgression of the righteous law of God, and contrary thereunto, does in its own nature, bring guilt upon the sinner, whereby he is bound over to the wrath of God, and curse of the law, and so made subject to death, with all miseries spiritual, temporal, and eternal.

The Waldensian Confession (1655)

Rome's persecution of certain Protestant groups in the decades that followed the Reformation is a scarlet stain in the history of the Christian Church. In January 1655, the Duke of Savoy gave the Waldensians—a group of Reformed evangelicals—two impossible options: Attend the Catholic Mass, or abandon their homes and land in the lower valleys and move to the upper valleys. Rather than abandon their faith, men, women, children and the sick waded into icy lakes and rivers and ascended frozen peaks to reach the homes of their destitute brethren in the upper valleys. But the Catholics were not satisfied.

The Italian army enlisted the help of five thousand French soldiers. Early on Easter week, the French Catholics, just as they had done in their massacre of French Protestant Huguenots on Saint Bartholomew's Day in 1572, began their attack but had little success against the small Waldensian army. With the help of treachery, they persuaded the Waldensians that they were coming in peace, so that the villagers even housed and fed them. At dawn on Easter Sunday, the Catholic forces began their campaign of murder, torture, rape and looting; over 1,700 Waldensians perished in what is known today as the Piedmont Easter Massacre. In response, the Waldensians published a manifesto—The Waldensian Confession—that rallied their brethren around their core beliefs. The specific points of The Waldensian Confession which address and sustain Calvinism either directly or indirectly are as follows:

VIII. That man, who was created pure and holy, after the image of God, deprived himself through his own fault of that happy condition by giving credit to the deceitful words of the devil.

IX. That man by his transgression lost that righteousness and holiness which he had received, and thus incurring the wrath of God, became subject to death and bondage, under the dominion of him who has the power of death, that is, the devil; insomuch that our free will has become a servant and a slave to sin: and thus all men, both Jews and Gentiles, are by nature children of wrath, being all dead in their trespasses and sins, and consequently incapable of the least good motion to any thing which concerns their salvation: yea, incapable of one good thought without God's grace, all their imaginations being wholly evil, and that continually.

X. That all the posterity of Adam is guilty in him of his disobedience, infected by his corruption, and fallen into the same calamity with him, even the very infants from their mother's womb, whence is derived the name of original sin.

XI. That God saves from this corruption and condemnation those whom he has chosen {from the foundation of the world, not for any foreseen disposition, faith, or holiness in them, but} of his mercy in Jesus Christ his Son; passing by all the rest, according to the irreprehensible reason of his freedom and justice.

XII. That this faith is the gracious and efficacious work of the Holy Spirit, who enlightens our souls, and persuades them to lean and rest upon the mercy of God, and so to apply the merits of Jesus Christ.

The Midland Confession of Faith (1655)
(Various Churches of the Midlands in England)

In the Midlands in 1655, General Baptists far outnumbered their Calvinistic brethren. The General Baptist Confession of 1651 had been signed by members of thirty congregations of the area, but when the Particular Baptists (those who believed in Limited Atonement) met in 1655 to constitute their Midland Association, there were but fourteen of their churches in the eight counties, and only seven of them were as yet willing to associate.

Two principal factors led to the formation of the Midland Association in 1655. One was the general trend among Baptists at that time toward associating. In promoting this trend the London churches took the lead, and they evidently were concerned with the beginnings of the organization in the Midlands. The other factor promoting the organization of the Association was the great activity of the Quakers in the Midlands in 1654 and 1655.

The confession was probably modeled after the London Confession of 1644 but its statements are original. In spite of its brevity, the theological portion is a careful and praiseworthy summary of Calvinistic Baptist doctrine of the seventeenth century. The primary purpose of the confession was instructional rather than apologetic.[191] The specific points of The Midland Confession of Faith which address and sustain Calvinism either directly or indirectly are as follows:

4th. That though Adam was created righteous, yet he fell through the temptations of Satan; and his fall overthrew, not only himself, but his posterity, making them sinners by his disobedience; so that we are by nature children of wrath, and defiled from the womb, being shapen in iniquity and conceived in sin (Psa. 51:5; Rom. 5:12-15).

5th. That God elected and chose, in His Eternal counsel, some persons to life and salvation, before the foundation of the world, whom accordingly He doth and will effectually call, and whom He doth so call, He will certainly keep by His power, through faith to salvation (Acts 13:48; Eph 1:2-4; 2 Thess. 2:13; 1 Pet. 1:2, etc.).

6th. That election was free in God, of His own pleasure, and not at all for, or with reference to, any foreseen works of faith in the creature, as the motive thereunto (Eph 1:4; Rom. 11:5-6).

7th. That Jesus Christ was, in the fullness of time, manifested in the flesh; being born of a woman; being perfectly righteous, gave himself for the elect to redeem them to God by his blood (John 10:15; Eph. 5:25-27; Rev. 5:9).

The London Baptist Confession of Faith (1689)

The Baptist Confession of Faith of 1689 has its roots firmly in The Westminster Confession of Faith of 1646. In most instances the two confessions are identical. It differs from the Westminster Confession in its understanding of the Church and Baptism. It is representative of the Reformation spirit of *sola scriptura* (Scripture Alone) as being "the only sufficient, certain, and infallible rule of all saving Knowledge, Faith and Obedience." The specific points of The London Baptist Confession of Faith which address and sustain Calvinism either directly or indirectly are as follows:

Chapter 9: Of Free Will

1. God hath endued the will of man with that natural liberty and power of acting upon choice, that it is neither forced, nor by any necessity of nature determined to do good or evil (Matt. 17:12; James 1:14; Deut. 30:19).

2. Man, in his state of innocency, had freedom and power to will and to do that which was good and well-pleasing to God, but yet was unstable, so that he might fall from it (Eccl. 7:29; Gen. 3:6).

3. Man, by his fall into a state of sin, hath wholly lost all ability of will to any spiritual good accompanying salvation; so as a natural man, being altogether averse from that good, and dead in sin, is not able by his own strength to convert himself, or to prepare himself thereunto (Rom. 5:6; 8:7; Eph. 2:1, 5; Tit. 3:3-5; John 6:44).

4. When God converts a sinner, and translates him into the state of grace, he freeth him from his natural bondage under sin, and by his grace alone enables him freely to will and to do that which is spiritually good; yet so as that by reason of his remaining corruptions, he doth not perfectly, nor only will, that which is good, but doth also will that which is evil (Col. 1:13; John 8:36; Php. 2:13; Rom. 7:15, 18-19, 21, 23).

5. This will of man is made perfectly and immutably free to good alone in the state of glory only.

Chapter 10: Of Effectual Calling

1. Those whom God hath predestinated unto life, he is pleased in his appointed, and accepted time, effectually to call, by his Word and Spirit, out of that state of sin and death in which they are by nature, to grace and salvation

by Jesus Christ; enlightening their minds spiritually and savingly to understand the things of God; taking away their heart of stone, and giving unto them a heart of flesh; renewing their wills, and by his almighty power determining them to that which is good, and effectually drawing them to Jesus Christ; yet so as they come most freely, being made willing by his grace (Rom. 8:30; 11:7; Eph. 1:10-11, 17-19; 2:1-6; 2 Thess. 2:13-14; Acts 26:18; Eze. 36:26-27; Deut. 30:6; Psa. 110:3; Songs 1:4).

2. This effectual call is of God's free and special grace alone, not from anything at all foreseen in man, nor from any power or agency in the creature, being wholly passive therein, being dead in sins and trespasses, until being quickened and renewed by the Holy Spirit; he is thereby enabled to answer this call, and to embrace the grace offered and conveyed in it, and that by no less power than that which raised up Christ from the dead (2 Tim. 1:9; Eph. 1:19, 20; 2:5, 8; 1 Cor. 2:14; John 5:25).

3. Elect infants dying in infancy are regenerated and saved by Christ through the Spirit; who worketh when, and where, and how he pleases; so also are all elect persons, who are incapable of being outwardly called by the ministry of the Word. (John 3:3, 5-6, 8).

4. Others not elected, although they may be called by the ministry of the Word, and may have some common operations of the Spirit, yet not being effectually drawn by the Father, they neither will nor can truly come to Christ, and therefore cannot be saved: much less can men that receive not the Christian religion be saved; be they never so diligent to frame their lives according to the light of nature and the law of that religion they do profess.

Chapter 17: Of the Perseverance of the Saints

1. Those whom God hath accepted in the beloved, effectually called and sanctified by his Spirit, and given the precious faith of his elect unto, can neither totally nor finally fall from the state of grace, but shall certainly persevere therein to the end, and be eternally saved, seeing the gifts and callings of God are without repentance, whence he still begets and nourisheth in them faith, repentance, love, joy, hope, and all the graces of the Spirit unto immortality; and though many storms and floods arise and beat against them, yet they shall never be able to take them off that foundation and rock which by faith they are fastened upon; notwithstanding, through unbelief and the temptations of Satan, the sensible sight of the light and love of God may for a time be clouded and obscured from them, yet he is still the same, and they shall be sure to be kept by the power of God unto salvation, where they shall enjoy their purchased possession, they being engraven upon the palm of his hands, and their names having been written in the book of life from all eternity (Psa. 89:31-32; Mal. 3:6; John 10:28, 29; Php. 1:6; 2 Tim. 2:19; 1 John 2:19; 1 Cor. 11:32).

2. This perseverance of the saints depends not upon their own free will, but upon the immutability of the decree of election, flowing from the free and unchangeable love of God the Father, upon the efficacy of the merit and intercession of Jesus Christ and union with him, the oath of God, the abiding of his Spirit, and the seed of God within them, and the nature of the covenant of grace; from all which ariseth also the certainty and infallibility thereof (Jer. 32:40; Rom. 5:9-10; 8:30; 9:11, 16; John 14:19; Heb. 6:17-18; 1 John 3:9).

3. And though they may, through the temptation of Satan and of the world, the prevalency of corruption remaining

in them, and the neglect of means of their preservation, fall into grievous sins, and for a time continue therein, whereby they incur God's displeasure and grieve his Holy Spirit, come to have their graces and comforts impaired, have their hearts hardened, and their consciences wounded, hurt and scandalize others, and bring temporal judgments upon themselves, yet shall they renew their repentance and be preserved through faith in Christ Jesus to the end (Psa. 32:3-4; 51:10, 12; 2 Sam. 12:14; Isa. 64:5, 9; Matt. 26:70, 72, 74; Eph. 4:30; Luke 22:32, 61, 62).

The New Hampshire Confession (1833)

The New Hampshire Baptist Convention appointed a committee on June 24, 1830, to prepare a statement of faith, which was published by the Board of the Convention in 1833. The confession reflects the *moderate* Calvinism of the time.

The New Hampshire Confession was widely accepted by Baptists, especially in the Northern and Western States, as a clear and concise statement of their faith. They considered it in harmony with, but in a milder form than, the doctrines of older confessions which expressed the Calvinistic Baptist beliefs that existed. The specific points of The New Hampshire Confession which address and sustain Calvinism either directly or indirectly are as follows:

Article 3: Of the Fall of Man

We believe that man was created in holiness, under the law of his Maker; but by voluntary transgression fell from that holy and happy state; in consequence of which all mankind are now sinners, not by constraint, but choice; being by nature utterly void of that holiness required by the law of God, positively inclined to evil; and therefore under just condemnation to eternal ruin, without defense or excuse.

Article 7: Of Grace in Regeneration

We believe that, in order to be saved, sinners must be regenerated, or born again; that regeneration consists in giving a holy disposition to the mind; that it is effected in a manner above our comprehension by the power of the Holy Spirit, in connection with divine truth, so as to secure our voluntary obedience to the gospel; and that its proper evidence appears in the holy fruits of repentance, and faith, and newness of life.

Article 11. Of the Perseverance of Saints

We believe that such only are real believers as endure unto the end; that their persevering attachment to Christ is the grand mark which distinguishes them from superficial professors; that a special Providence watches over their welfare; and they are kept by the power of God through faith unto salvation.

Southern Baptist Theological Seminary: The Abstract of Principles (1858)

After the idea to found a seminary caught on among Southern Baptists in the late 1850s, James Petigru Boyce called on his fellow Princeton alum, Basil Manly, Jr. to draw up the "Abstract of Principles" in 1857 for what would eventually become charter document for The Southern Baptist Seminary.

Manly, Jr. took up the task with vested diligence, working for much of the spring of 1858 on the document. Once completed, Manly, Boyce, John Broadus, E.T. Winkler, and William Williams hammered out the final draft after five intensive days of study, working from the 1689 London Baptist Confession of Faith, the Westminster Confession, the Philadelphia Confession, and the 1833 New Hampshire Confession. The specific points of The Abstract Principles which address and sustain Calvinism either directly or indirectly are as follows:

IV. Providence
God from eternity, decrees or permits all things that come to pass, and perpetually upholds, directs and governs all creatures and all events; yet so as not to destroy the free will and responsibility of intelligent creatures.

V. Election
Election is God's eternal choice of some persons unto everlasting life—not because of foreseen merit in them, but of his mere mercy in Christ—in consequence of which choice they are called, justified and glorified.

VI. The Fall of Man.
God originally created man in His own image, and free from sin; but, through the temptation of Satan, he transgressed the command of God, and fell from his original holiness and righteousness; whereby his posterity inherit a nature corrupt and wholly opposed to God and His law, are under condemnation, and as soon as they are capable of moral action, become actual transgressors.

The Missouri Synod (1932)

The Lutheran Church—Missouri Synod (LCMS) is a traditional, Confessional Lutheran Christian denomination in the United States. With 2.4 million members, it is both the eighth largest Protestant denomination and the second-largest Lutheran body in the U.S. after the Evangelical Lutheran Church in America. The Synod was founded at Chicago, Illinois, in 1847 by German immigrants. The LCMS is headquartered in St. Louis, Missouri. The Missouri Synod, while rejecting the traditional "double-predestination" of Calvinism, reads in part:

Of Man and Sin
6. We teach that the first man was not brutelike nor merely capable of intellectual development, but that God created man in His own image (Gen. 1:26, 27; Eph. 4:24; Col. 3:10), that is, in true knowledge of God and in true

righteousness and holiness and endowed with a truly scientific knowledge of nature (Gen. 2:19-23).

7. We furthermore teach that sin came into the world by the fall of the first man, as described [sic] Gen. 3. By this Fall not only he himself, but also his natural offspring have lost the original knowledge, righteousness, and holiness, and thus all men are sinners already by birth, dead in sins, inclined to all evil, and subject to the wrath of God (Rom. 5:12, 18; Eph. 2:1-3). We teach also that men are unable, through any efforts of their own or by the aid of "culture and science," to reconcile themselves to God and thus conquer death and damnation.

Of the Election of Grace

35. By the election of grace we mean this truth, that all those who by the grace of God alone, for Christ's sake, through the means of grace, are brought to faith, are justified, sanctified, and preserved in faith here in time, that all these have already from eternity been endowed by God with faith, justification, sanctification, and preservation in faith, and this for the same reason, namely, by grace alone, for Christ's sake, and by way of the means of grace. That this is the doctrine of the Holy Scripture is evident from Eph. 1:3-7; 2 Thess. 2:13, 14; Acts 13:48; Rom. 8:28-30; 2 Tim. 1:9; Matt. 24:22-24.

36. Accordingly we reject as an anti-Scriptural error the doctrine that not alone the grace of God and the merit of Christ are the cause of the election of grace, but that God has, in addition, found or regarded something good in us which prompted or caused Him to elect us, this being variously designated as "good works," "right conduct," "proper self-determination," "refraining from willful resistance," etc. Nor does Holy Scripture know of an election "by foreseen faith," "in view of faith," as though the faith of the elect were to be placed before their election; but according to Scripture the faith which the

elect have in time belongs to the spiritual blessings with
which God has endowed them by His eternal election.
For Scripture teaches [in] Acts 13:48: "And as many as
were ordained unto eternal life believed." Our Lutheran
Confession also testifies (Triglot, p. 1065, Paragraph 8;
M. p. 705): "The eternal election of God however, not
only foresees and foreknows the salvation of the elect,
but is also, from the gracious will and pleasure of God in
Christ Jesus, a cause which procures, works, helps, and
promotes our salvation and what pertains thereto; and
upon this our salvation is so founded that the gates of
hell cannot prevail against it (Matt. 16:18), as is written
[in] John 10:28: "Neither shall any man pluck My sheep
out of My hand"; and again [in] Acts 13:48: "And as
many as were ordained to eternal life believed ..."

37. But as earnestly as we maintain that there is an election
of grace, or a predestination to salvation, so decidedly do
we teach, on the other hand, that there is no election of
wrath, or predestination to damnation. Scripture plainly
reveals the truth that the love of God for the world of
lost sinners is universal, that is, that it embraces all men
without exception, that Christ has fully reconciled all
men unto God, and that God earnestly desires to bring
all men to faith, to preserve them therein, and thus to
save them, as Scripture testifies (1 Tim. 2:4): "God will
have all men to be saved and to come to the knowledge of
the truth." No man is lost because God has predestined
him to eternal damnation. Eternal election is a cause
why the elect are brought to faith in time (Acts 13:48);
but election is not a cause why men remain unbelievers
when they hear the Word of God. The reason assigned
by Scripture for this sad fact is that these men judge
themselves unworthy of everlasting life, putting the
Word of God from them and obstinately resisting the
Holy Ghost, whose earnest will it is to bring also them
to repentance and faith by means of the Word (Act 7:51;
13:46; Matt. 23:37).

38. To be sure, it is necessary to observe the Scriptural distinction between the election of grace and the universal will of grace. This universal gracious will of God embraces all men; the election of grace, however, does not embrace all, but only a definite number, whom "God hath from the beginning chosen to salvation" (2 Thess. 2:13), the "remnant," the "seed" which "the Lord left" (Rom. 9:27-29), the "election" (Rom. 11:7); and while the universal will of grace is frustrated in the case of most men (Matt. 22:14; Luke 7:30), the election of grace attains its end with all whom it embraces (Rom. 8:28-30). Scripture, however, while distinguishing between the universal will of grace and the election of grace, does not place the two in opposition to each other. On the contrary, it teaches that the grace dealing with those who are lost is altogether earnest and fully efficacious for conversion. Blind reason indeed declares these two truths to be contradictory; but we impose silence on our reason. The seeming disharmony will disappear in the light of heaven (1 Cor. 13:12).

39. Furthermore, by election of grace, Scripture does not mean that one part of God's counsel of salvation according to which He will receive into heaven those who persevere in faith unto the end, but, on the contrary, Scripture means this, that God, before the foundation of the world, from pure grace, because of the redemption of Christ, has chosen for His own a definite number of persons out of the corrupt mass and has determined to bring them through Word and Sacrament, to faith and salvation.

40. Christians can and should be assured of their eternal election. This is evident from the fact that Scripture addresses them as the chosen ones and comforts them with their election (Eph. 1:4; 2 Thess. 2:13). ... To sum up, just as God in time draws the Christian unto Himself through the Gospel, so He has already in His eternal election endowed them with "sanctification of the Spirit and belief of the truth" (2 Thess. 2:13). Therefore: If, by the grace of God, you believe in the Gospel of the forgiveness of your sins for Christ's sake, you are to be certain that you also belong to the number of God's elect, even as Scripture (2 Thess. 2:13), addresses the believing Thessalonians as the chosen of God and gives thanks to God for their election.

Endnotes

Preface

1 Notwithstanding the Christological debate at the Council of Nicaea in 325, which addressed the relationship of Jesus to God the Father, I contend throughout this book that the Calvinism-Arminian debate is without equal in terms of its degree of controversy, impact, longevity, and scope.

2 Michael S. Horton; *For Calvinism*; (Zondervan, 2011); p. 15

3 Mark Ross, *Essentials Unity, In Non-Essentials Liberty, In All Things Charity*, as cited at pietist.blogspot.com/2009/10/who-said-essentials-unity-in-non.html#!/2009/10/who-said-essentials-unity-in-non.html

Introduction: *Debating the Debatable*

4 Martin Luther, *The Bondage of the Will*; (Sovereign Grace Publishers, 2001); p. 11

5 Mark Ross, *Essentials Unity, In Non-Essentials Liberty, In All Things Charity*, as cited at pietist.blogspot.com/2009/10/who-said-essentials-unity-in-non.html#!/2009/10/who-said-essentials-unity-in-non.html

6 C.S. Lewis, *Mere Christianity*; (Simon & Schuster/Touchstone, 1996); pp. 136-37

7 J.I. Packer, *Knowing God*; (InterVarsity Press, 1993); p. 19

8 James R. White, *The Potter's Freedom*; (Calvary Press Publishing, 2009); pp. 40-41

Chapter 1: *The Controversy of Calvinism in Contemporary Times*

9 *Scholasticism* is a medieval theological and philosophical system of learning based on the authority of St. Augustine and other leaders of the early Christian Church, and on the works of Aristotle. It sought to bridge the gap between religion and reason.

10 Audio Recording published at http://voiceofthesheep. wordpress.com/2010/02/10/calvinism-is-christianity-without-jesus

11 Roger Olson, *Essay: My Biggest Problem with Calvin/ Calvinism*, cited at evangelicalarminians.org/Roger-Olson-My-Biggest-Problem-with-Calvin-Calvinism

12 John H. Boyd, *Christianity Versus the God of Calvin*, (Xulon Press, 2006); p. 79

13 Adrian Rogers; Sermon: *"Why I Am Not A Five Point Calvinist;"* delivered on November 10, 1997

14 John Phillips, *Exploring the Gospel of John: An Expository Commentary*; (Kregal Publications, 1989); p. 129

15www.erguncaner.com/2006/10/11/questions-on-neo-calvinism-part-1

16 Charles H. Spurgeon, *Autobiography: Volume I, The Early Years*, (Banner of Truth; Revised edition; 1962); p. 173

17 Dave Hunt, *What Love Is This? Calvinism's Misrepresentation of God*; (Multnomah Books, 2002); p. 27

18 As cited as www.spurgeon.org/calvinis.htm

19 As cited at www.the-highway.com/caltoday_Warfield.html

20 Eric Holmberg, *Amazing Grace: The History & Theology of Calvinism*; Study Guide and Workbook, (The Apologetics Group; 2009); p. 111

21 John MacArthur, *Why I Am a Calvinist, Part 5*; www.gty. org/Resources/Articles/10194

22 As cited at www.the-highway.com/caltoday_Warfield.html

23 Deuteronomy 2:20 reads, "But Sihon king of Heshbon refused to let us pass through. *For the Lord your God had made his spirit stubborn and his heart obstinate in order to give him into your*

hands" (emphasis added). Here God hardened the king's heart, as with Pharaoh, so as to prevent his capitulation to Israel. Why? The answer is because God wanted him dead! And this line of reasoning is in keeping with Jesus' own words in John 12:39-40 concerning the Jews. John writes, "For this reason they could not believe, because, as Isaiah says elsewhere: 'He has blinded their eyes and hardened their hearts, *so they can neither see with their eyes, nor understand with their hearts, nor turn—* and I would heal them'" (emphasis added). Like with Pharaoh and Sihon, the apostle John does not say the Jews "would not" believe—although this is inferred in the parallel passage and in other Scriptures—but goes a step further and says that the Jews *could not* believe—denoting inability. And this was due precisely to the fact that God hardened their hearts, as He had with Pharaoh and Sihon, thereby preventing their repentance. In the end, to write as I have that God hardened people's hearts so as to prevent their repentance is not only accurate but is the logical conclusion of God's deliberate hardening. We see this again in the genocide of the Canaanites. Did God prevent the Canaanites from entering into a treaty with the Israelites so that He could condemn them rather than make peace with them? The answer is yes! God prevented their positive response to Israel. Joshua 11:19-20 spells it out for us: "... not one city made a treaty of peace with the Israelites, who took them all in battle. *For it was the Lord himself who hardened their hearts to wage war against Israel, so that he might destroy them totally, exterminating them without mercy"* (emphasis added).

24 Charles H. Spurgeon, *Sermons, Vol. 2;* (Baker Book; 1987); p. 124

25 R.C. Sproul, *What Is Reformed Theology?;* (Baker Books; 1997); p. 137

Chapter 2: *The Birth of Calvinism & Arminianism*

26 Eric Holmberg, *Amazing Grace: The History & Theology of Calvinism*; Study Guide and Workbook, (The Apologetics Group; 2009); p. 18

27 This inward call to the Elect is not to be misconstrued with the outward, or general, call that goes out to all men indiscriminately when the gospel is preached.

28 Jacobus Arminius, *The Works of James Arminius, Vol. 3*; trans. James and William Nichols (Baker Book House, 1986), p. 455

29 Ibid. Vol. 2, p. 725

30 Eric Holmberg, *Amazing Grace: The History & Theology of Calvinism*; Study Guide and Workbook, (The Apologetics Group; 2009); p. 68

31 Canons of Dort, Second Head of Doctrine; The Rejection of Errors, Article III

Chapter 3: *Scaling the Language Barrier*

32 Walter R. Martin, *The Kingdom of the Cults*; (Bethany House Publishers, 1985); p. 18

33 Ibid. p. 21

34 Journal of Discourses 1:50-1; 8:115

Chapter 4: *How Sovereign is Sovereign?*

35 Jacobus Arminius, *Works of James Arminius, Vol. 2*; (Wesleyan Heritage Collection), p. 460

36 Charles H. Spurgeon; *Divine Sovereignty; A Sermon (No. 77)*; Delivered on 5/4/1856

37 A Grace Bridge Panel Discussion; September 26, 2001

38 James R. White, *The Potter's Freedom*; (Calvary Press Publishing, 2009); p. 41

39 Strong's Number: 1413; www.studylight.org/isb/view.cgi?number=1413

40 John Phillips, *Exploring the Gospel of John: An Expository Commentary*; (Kregal Publications, 1989); p. 100

41 John Phillips, *Exploring the Gospel of Mark: An Expository Commentary*; (Kregal Publications, 2004); p. 74

42 John Phillips, *Exploring the Gospel of John: An Expository Commentary*; (Kregal Publications, 1989); p. 129

43 Greg Laurie, *A New Beginning: The Reality of Hell—I; Luke 16*; broadcast date: 1/10/2010

44 James R. White, *The Potter's Freedom*; (Calvary Press Publishing, 2009); p. 54

45 Rob Bell, *Love Wins: A Book About Heaven, Hell, and the Fate of Every Person Who Ever Lived*; (HarpeOne Publishers, 2011); pp. 103-04

46 The Westminster Confession of Faith (1646); 3:1

47 Andrew Womack; *The Sovereignty of God*; cited at www.awmi.net/extra/article/sovereignty_god

48 Ibid. Andrew Womack; *The Sovereignty of God*

49 A.W. Tozer, *The Attributes of God*; (Christian Publications, Inc., 1997); pp. 48-49

50 Dave Hunt & James White, *Debating Calvinism*; (Multnomah Publishers, 2004); p. 48

51 Audio Recording published at voiceofthesheep.wordpress.com/2010/02/10/calvinism-is-christianity-without-jesus.

Chapter 5: *Sovereignty & Sin: The Blame Game*

52 The Byzantine manuscripts of Acts 15:18 read, "Known unto God are all his works from the age [i.e., from the beginning]"; but, the critical text of Nestle/Aland (27th edition), following codex *Sinaiticus* and others, reads simply, "the Lord who makes these things known from the age [i.e. the beginning]". However, in either variant, the point remains that the plan of redemption was designed long before its actual accomplishment in history; it was not a series of responses to mere happenstance created by human rebellion, but unfolded in time according to a previously existing master plan. This is the same point that is made in Isaiah 45:21, from which Acts 15:18 is taken (for additional study, see: www.reformationtheology.com/2009/07/the_sovereignty_of_god_and_the.php).

53 Jonathan Edwards, *Freedom of the Will, Vol. 1 of The Works of Jonathan Edwards*, edited by Paul Ramsey; (Yale University Press; 2009)

54 John Calvin, *Concerning the Eternal Predestination of God* (James Clarke and Co., 1961), pp. 121-22

55 J. Ligon Duncan III, *Sound Doctrine; Proclaiming A Cross-Centered Theology*; (Crossway; 2009); p. 53

56 When asked how he reconciled the tension between God's sovereignty and man's self-will, Charles Surgeon concluded, "You do not have to reconcile friends."

Chapter 6: *The Order of Salvation (Ordo Salutis)*

57 The resurrected body, unlike the physical body, will not deteriorate or pass away. We should be careful not minimize what Jesus accomplished in the first resurrection by confusing it with other resuscitated bodies that died a second time. Jesus is the first and only resurrection and His body is what we as believers in Him have to look forward to at his second coming. Therefore those individuals raised from the dead in the Bible, apart from Jesus Christ, are better qualified as resuscitations rather than resurrections if for no other reason that they all eventually died natural deaths again.

58 Charles H. Surgeon, *Unbinding Lazarus*, Sermon no. 1776, Metropolitan Tabernacle Pulpit (Pasadena, TX: Pilgrim Press, 1985), 30:219

59 As cited at www.reformedonline.com/view/reformedonline/Total%20Depravity%20revised.htm

60 Interestingly enough, while the concept of regeneration permeates both the Old and New Testaments, the word itself appears only twice in the Greek concordance; once in reference to renewal (Matt. 19:38) and once in the context of rebirth (Tit. 3:5).

61 Blue Letter Bible. "Dictionary and Word Search for *paliggenesia* (Strong's 3824)." Blue Letter Bible. 1996-2011

62 Charles H. Spurgeon; *Light, Natural and Spiritual*; Sermon no. 660, Metropolitan Tabernacle Pulpit (Pasadena, TX: Pilgrim Press, 1985)

63 It should be noted at this point that Calvinism does not teach that God saves men robotically. Rather, it contends that monergistic regeneration is an act of preparatory grace that frees a sinner from his chains of oppression so that he can willingly and freely believe in Christ without coercion.

64 Billy Graham, *How To Be Born Again*; (Word Publishers, 1989); pp. 150, 162

65 Lewis Sperry Chafer, *The Ephesian Letter: Doctrinally Considered*; (The Bible Institute Colportage Association, 1935); pp. 64-64

Chapter 7: *Monergistic Regeneration*

66arminianperspectives.wordpress.com/2008/05/15/what-can-the-dead-in-sin-do

67dtbrents.wordpress.com/category/what-it-means-to-be-spiritually-dead

68 www.studylight.org/isb/view.cgi?number=3498

69 *Vine's Expository Dictionary*; (Baker Books; 1981); p. 273

70 Ibid. www.studylight.org/isb/view.cgi?number=3498

71 Dave Hunt and James White, *Debating Calvinism*; (Multnomah Publishers, 2004); p. 79

72 Norman Geisler, *Chosen But Free* (Bethany House; 2001); pp. 233-234. as cited in James R. White, *The Potter's Freedom* (Calvary Press Publishing; 2009); p. 91

73 As cited as www.arminianchronicles.com/2010/01/arminius-on-regeneration.html

74 www.reformedonline.com/view/reformedonline/newbirth.htm

75 Common Grace is a theological concept in Protestant Christianity, primarily in Reformed and Calvinistic circles, referring to the grace of God that is common to all humankind. It is distinguished from Special grace which, in Reformed theology, is the grace by which God redeems, sanctifies, and glorifies his people. Unlike common grace, which is universally given, special grace is bestowed only on those whom God elects to eternal life through faith in Jesus Christ.

Chapter 8: *The Walking Dead*

76 R.C. Sproul, *What is Reformed Theology?*; (Baker Books, 1997); p. 129

77 John MacArthur, *Slave*; (Thomas Nelson, 2010); p. 201

78 Charles H. Spurgeon, Metropolitan Tabernacle Pulpit (Pasadena, TX: Pilgrim Press, 1985), 21:365 as cited in James R.

White, *The Potter's Freedom* (Calvary Press Publishing, 2009); p. 75

Chapter 9: *The Moral Inability of the Reprobate Will*

79 John F. Kennedy; speech delivered in person before a joint session of Congress on May 25, 1961.
80 NASA was already embroiled in a legal battle with Madelyn Murray O'Hare, the celebrated opponent of religion, over the Apollo 8 crew reading from Genesis while orbiting the moon at Christmas. NASA kept the Communion of Apollo 11 secret for two decades. The memoirs of Buzz Aldrin and the Tom Hanks' Emmy-winning HBO mini-series, *From the Earth to the Moon* (1998), brought awareness to this act of Christian worship.
81 As cited at www.liturgy.co.nz/blog/first-communion-moon/1203
82 John MacArthur, *Slave*; (Thomas Nelson, 2010); pp. 120-21
83 R.C. Sproul, *Willing to Believe*; (Baker Books, 1997); p. 64
84 Ibid. p. 47
85 J.I. Packer, *Evangelism & The Sovereignty of God*; (Inter-varsity Press; 1991)
86 Loraine Boettner, *The Reformed Doctrine of Predestination*; (Phillipsburg: Presbyterian and Reformed Publishing Company, 1932); pp. 61-62
87 www.studylight.org/isb/view.cgi?number=1410
88 The Westminster Confession of Faith (1646); 9:3
89 atheism.about.com/library/FAQs/christian/blfaq_hist_pelagius.htm
90 As cited at www.spurgeon.org/sermons/0111.htm

Chapter 10: *Unconditional Election in the Old Testament*

91As cited at doctor.claudemariottini.com/2010/02/election-of-israel.html
92 Eric Holmberg; *Amazing Grace: The History & Theology of Calvinism*; Study Guide and Workbook; (The Apologetics Group; 2009); p. 49

Chapter 11: *The Chosen of God*

93 Rooted in the sufficiency of Scripture, Nouthetic counseling is form of Christian counseling developed by Jay E. Adams, and published in his 1970 book, *Competent to Counsel.*
94 Ron Block, *Doorway*: "Things Aren't Always as They Seem"; Rounder Music, 2007
95 Alexander M. Jordan; as cited at jordansview.blogspot. com/2007/02/arminian-vs-reformed-theology.html
96 Eric Holmberg, *Amazing Grace: The History & Theology of Calvinism*; Study Guide and Workbook; (The Apologetics Group, 2009); p. 51
97 Arthur Wallis, *God's Chosen Fast*; (Christian Literature Crusade, 1968); pp. 11-12
98 Dave Hunt & James White, *Debating Calvinism*; (Multnomah Publishers, 2004); p. 96
99 Lewis' position on Calvinism and Arminianism is somewhat muddled. While some Reformed theologians, like J.I. Packer refer to Lewis as a Calvinist, others insist that the Christian thinker was a proponent of Classical Arminianism.
100 Michael Horton, *Christless Christianity*; (Baker Books; 2008); p. 98

Chapter 12: *Faith & Repentance*

101 The apostle Thomas, also called "Didymus" was likely a twin: Thomas was not a proper name, but meant *twin* in Aramaic, as does "Didymus" in Greek.
102 Tom Carter, *2,200 Quotations from the Writings of Charles H. Spurgeon*; (Family Christian Press, 1988); p. 175. Also see Charles Spurgeon, *"The Marvelous Magnet"*—Sermon No. 1717—Metropolitan Tabernacle Pulpit.
103 April 4, 2009 - Craig vs. Hitchens Debate from Biola University
104 Loraine Boettner, *The Reformed Doctrine of Predestination*; (P & R Publishing, 1991)
105 R.C. Sproul, *The I AM Statements*, audio lecture; Legionnaire Ministries

106 Dave Hunt & James White, *Debating Calvinism*; (Multnomah Publishers, 2004); pp. 212-13

107 Blue Letter Bible. "Dictionary and Word Search for metanoia (Strong's 3341)". Blue Letter Bible. 1996-2012

108 Blue Letter Bible. "Dictionary and Word Search for *lagchanō* (Strong's 2975)". Blue Letter Bible. 1996-2011

109 Dave Hunt & James White, *Debating Calvinism*; (Multnomah Publishers, 2004); p. 213

110 Kay Arthur, *FamilyLife Today with Dennis Rainey, Healing for Marriage*: broadcast date: 3/16/2011

Chapter 13: *Fore-love or Foresight*

111 Dave Hunt & James White, *Debating Calvinism*; (Multnomah Publishers, 2004); pp. 98-99

112 The Westminster Confession of Faith (1646); 3:5-6

113 It should be noted that some Arminians suggest that predestination is corporate—that it is the Church as a whole who has been predestined—not individuals.

114 Dave Hunt & James White, *Debating Calvinism*; (Multnomah Publishers, 2004); p. 103

115 www.merriam-webster.com/dictionary/foreknowledge

116 James Arminius, *The Works of James Arminius*, (London: Longman, Hurst, Rees, Orme, Brown, and Green, 1825-1828); pp. 247-48

117 Andy Heer, *"Does God Know the Future?"* *The Arminian Magazine*. Issue 1. Spring 2010. Volume 28

118 John Wesley, *On Predestination*, Sermon 58; (cited from the 1872 edition—Thomas Jackson, editor).

119 R.C. Sproul, *What is Reformed Theology?* (Baker Books, 1997); p. 145

120 Dave Hunt & James White, *Debating Calvinism*; (Multnomah Publishers, 2004); pp. 101, 103

121 2 Cor. 1:12; Gal 1:13; Eph 2:3; 4:22; Phil 1:27; 1 Tim 4:12; Heb 13:5, 7; James 3:13; 1 Pet. 1:8; 2:12; 3:1, 2, 16; 2 Pet. 2:7; 3:11

122 Gen. 43:30; 1 Kings 3:26; Psa. 109:18; Isa. 16:11; 63:15; Jer. 31:20; Lam. 1:20; 2:11; Phlm. 7, 12, 20

123 Josh. 6:17, 18; 7:1, 11–13, 15; 22:20; 1 Chron. 2:7

124 strongsnumbers.com/greek/4268.htm cf. Bauer, Arndt, Gingrich, A Greek - English Lexicon of the New Testament and Other Early Christian Literature.

125 Louis Berkhof, *Systematic Theology*; (Eerdmans, 1976); p. 112

126 Edgar C. James, *"Is Foreknowledge Equivalent to Foreordination?"* Bibliotheca Sacra 122, No. 487 (July 1965): p. 218

Chapter 14: *The Rise of Frankenstein Theology*

127 See Collin Hansen, *Young, Restless, Reformed: A Journalist's Journey with the New Calvinists*; (Crossway Books, 2008).

128 R.C. Sproul, *The Truth of the Cross* (Reformation Trust Publishing, 2007); pp. 140-142

129 Dave Hunt & James White, *Debating Calvinism*; (Multnomah Publishers, 2004); p. 178

130 www.patheos.com/community/rogereolson/2011/06/04/ is-there-a-middle-ground-between-calvinism-and-arminianism

131 Loraine Boettner, *Limited Atonement*, as cited at http:// www.the-highway.com/atonement_Boettner.html

Chapter 15: *Payment or Possibility?*

132 Although many Arminians object to the accusation, such as Roger E. Olson, and insist they believe in the Reformed doctrine of penal substitution in Christ's atonement, the truth is that most Arminians ignorantly hold to the moral government theory instead.

133 Norman Geisler, *Chosen But Free*; (Bethany House Publishers; 1999); p. 80

134 Brown, Driver and Briggs, *Brown-Driver-Briggs' Hebrew Definitions;* (Hendrickson Publishers, 1996)

135 Blue Letter Bible. "Dictionary and Word Search for *kaphar* (Strong's 3722)". Blue Letter Bible. 1996-2011

136 J.I. Packer, *Concise Theology: A Guide to Historic Christian Belief*; (Tyndale House Publishers, Inc., 1993); p. 134

137 What is more, the resulting ceasefire between the two brothers foreshadowed Christ's atoning reunion with his own spiritual brothers. Christ laid claim to this reconciliation in Hebrews 2 where he is said to have atoned for "my brothers ... the children God has given me" by making "their salvation perfect through suffering" (2:10-11, 13).

138   jesusandfaith.com/2010/02/10/did-christ-jesus-die-for-the-sins-of-everyone

139 Rob Bell, *Velvet Elvis: Repainting the Christian Faith*; (Zondervan, 2006); p. 146

140 *The Works of John Wesley, Vol. 10*; (Baker Books, 1996); p. 297

141 R.C. Sproul, *What is Reformed Theology?*; (Baker Books; 1997); pp. 165-66

Chapter 16: *Particular Redemption / Limited Atonement*

142 Dennis Bratcher, *The Christmas Season*; (CRI / Voice, Institute, 2011); January 03, 2011

Chapter 17: *The Crucifixion in Context*

143 John Philips, *The Gospel of John: An Expository Commentary*; (Kregal Publications, 1989); p. 71

144 Ron Rhodes, *Rightly Interpreting the Bible: Methodology*; as cited at http://home.earthlink.net/~ronrhodes/Interpretation.html

145 John Hendryx, Arminian *Suicidal Tendencies (Part II): How Does Reformation Theology Interpret John 3:16? (Exposing the Straw Man)*, as cited at www.monergism.com

146 Blue Letter Bible. "Dictionary and Word Search for *kosmos* (Strong's 2889)". Blue Letter Bible. 1996-2011

147 Each instance in the writings of John for the word "world" are as follows: John 1:9, 1:10, 1:29, 3:16, 3:17, 3:19, 4:42, 6:14, 6:33, 6:51, 7:4, 7:7, 8:12, 8:23, 8:26, 9:5, 9:32, 9:39, 10:36, 11:9, 11:27, 12:19, 12:25, 12:31, 12:46, 12:47, 13:1, 14:17, 14:19, 14:22, 14:27, 14:30, 14:31, 15:18, 15:19, 16:8, 16:11, 16:20, 16:21, 16:28,

16:33, 17:5, 17:6, 17:9, 17:11, 17:12, 17:13, 17:14, 17:15, 17:16, 17:18, 17:21, 17:23, 17:24, 17:25, 18:20, 18:36, 18:37, 21:25, 1 John 2:2, 2:15, 2:16, 2:17, 3:1, 3:13, 4:1, 4:3, 4:4, 4:5, 4:9, 4:14, 4:17, 5:4, 5:5, 5:19, 2 John 1:7, Rev. 3:10, 11:15, 12:9, 13:3, 13:8, 16:14, 17:8

148 The earth: John 13:1; 6:14; 9:5a; 9:32; 9:39; 10:36; 11:27; 16:21; 16:28; 17:5; 17:11a; 17:12; 17:23; 17:24; 18:36; 18:37; 21:25; 1John 4:1; 4:9; 2 John 1:7; Rev. 11:15; 13:8; 17:8

149 Jews and Gentiles: John 4:39; 18:20; Rev. 16:14

150Believers, unbelievers and humanity: John 1:9-10; 3:17; 3:19; 7:4; 8:26; 9:5b; 12:19; 12:25; 14:30; 14:19; 16:11; Rev. 3:10

151 World system: John 12:31; 1 John 5:19; 4:3-4

152 The wicked: John 5:24; 7:7; 8:23; 12:31; 13:1; 14:17; 14:22; 14:31; 15:18-19; 16:8; 16:20; 17:6; 17:9; 17:11b; 17:15-16; 17:17; 17:21; 17:23; 17:25; 1 John 2:15-17; 3:1; 3:13; 4:5; 4:17; 5:4-5; Rev. 12:9; 13:3

153 The Elect: John 1:29; 3:16; 3:17c; 6:33; 12:46-47; 6:51; 8:12; 11:9; 1 John 2:2; 4:14

154 A. W. Pink, *Objections to God's Sovereignty Answered by Arthur W. Pink*, internet sermon

Chapter 18: The God Who Drags & Draws Effectually

155 John Newton, *Out of the Depths*; (Kregel Publications; Revised edition, 2003); p. 18

156 John R.W. Stott, *The Message of Galatians*; (Inter-Varsity Press, 1968); p. 110

157 Dick Bohrer, *John Newton: Letters of a Slave Trader Freed by God's Grace*; (Moody Press, 1983); p. 10

158 *The Works of John Newton, Vol. 1*; (Banner of Truth Trust, 1985); p. 13

159 Ibid. p. 23

160 Bernard Martin, *An Ancient Mariner* (Wyvern Books, 1960); p. 51

161 *The Works of John Newton, Vol. 1*; (Banner of Truth Trust, 1985); p. 25

162 Ibid. p. 25

163 John Newton, *Out of the Depths*; (Moody Press, 2003); pp. 82–83

164 David Servant, *The Five Points of Calvinism Considered*; (www.ShepherdServe.org; 2007) pp. 5, 20

165 Norman Geisler, *Chosen But Free*; (Bethany House Publishers; 1999); p.35

166 Ibid. p. 47

167 Hank Hanegraaff, *Bible Answer Man*, broadcast date: 2/4/2000; as cited at testallthings.com/2007/03/19/hank-hanagraaff

168 Dave Hunt & James White, *Debating Calvinism*; (Multnomah Publishers, 2004); p. 209

169 Dave Hunt, *What Love Is This? Calvinism's Misrepresentation of God*; (Multnomah Books, 2002); p. 291

170 The Canons of Dort, Article 16

171 The Westminster Confession (1646); 10:1

172 John Murray, *Soli Deo Gloria: Essays in Reformed Theology*, ed. R.C. Sproul; (Presbyterian and Reformed Publishing, 1976)

173 Blue Letter Bible. "Dictionary and Word Search for *helkō* (Strong's 1670)." Blue Letter Bible. 1996-2012

Chapter 19: *Eternal Security & Elect Saints*

174 The Westminster Confession of Faith (1646); 17:1-2

175 Charles Hodge, *A Commentary on Romans: Vol. 3*; (The Banner of Truth Trust, 1975); p. 110

176 Ibid. p. 113

177 Anthony A. Hoekema, *Saved by Grace*; (William B. Eerdmans Publishing Company, 1994); p. 234

178 As cited at www.ondoctrine.com/2top0101.htm

179 Tom Brown, *Tom Brown Ministries*, as cited at www.tbm.org/losesalvation.htm

180 Theodore Beza, *The Christian Faith*, trans. by James Clark; (Focus Press, 1992); p. 41

181 Rod Rosenbladt, *Modern Reformation: Reclaiming the Doctrine of Justification* (May/June 2003)

Epilogue: *Scandalized by Sovereignty*

182 Charles H. Spurgeon, September 2, 1855, at New Park Street Chapel, Southwark
183 Charles H. Spurgeon, *Autobiography: Volume I, The Early Years*; (Edinburgh, 1985); p. 173

Appendix: *Councils, Creeds, Confessions & Calvinism*

184 David Bennett; www.ancient-future.net/creeds.html
185 William Hetherington; *The History of the Westminster Assembly of Divines*; (Nabu Press, 2011); p. 343
186 Eric Holmberg; *Amazing Grace: The History & Theology of Calvinism*; Study Guide and Workbook; (The Apologetics Group, 2009); p. 134
187 *La confession d'Augsbourg*, Beauchesne, Paris, 1983 as cited at www.museeprotestant.org
188 As cited at www.reformed.org
189 Extracted from www.newworldencyclopedia.org/entry/Thirty-nine_Articles
190 Extracted from en.wikipedia.org/wiki/Westminster_Confession_of_Faith
191 Extracted from www.reformedreader.org/ccc/eebac.htm